European Impact and Pacific Influence

# LIBRARY OF INTERNATIONAL RELATIONS

Series ISBN 1 86064 080 X

1 The Business of Death: Britain's Arms Trade at Home and Abroad
   *Neil Cooper*
   ISBN 1 85043 953 2

2 The Age of Terrorism and the International System
   *Adrian Guelke*
   ISBN 1 85043 952 4

3 Fin de Siècle: The Meaning of the Twentieth Century
   *Alex Danchev*
   ISBN 1 85043 967 2

4 On Liberal Peace: Democracy, War and the International Order
   *John MacMillan*
   ISBN 1 86064 010 9

5 Organized Anarchy in Europe: The Role of States and
   Intergovernmental Organizations
   *Håkan Wiberg and Jaap de Wilde*
   ISBN 1 86064 062 1

6 Tanker Wars: The Assault on Merchant Shipping during the
   Iraq–Iran Crisis, 1980–88
   *Martin S. Navias and E.R. Hooton*
   ISBN 1 86064 032 X

7 The United Nations and International Peacekeeping
   *Agostinho Zacarias*
   ISBN 1 86064 065 6

8 The Politics of International Crisis Escalation
   *P. Stuart Robinson*
   ISBN 1 86064 064 8

9 After the Cold War: Security and Democracy in Africa and Asia
   *William Hale and Eberhard Kienle*
   ISBN 1 86064 136 9

10 America and the British Labour Party: The Special Relationship
   at Work
   *Peter Jones*
   ISBN 1 86064 106 7

11 Hollow Victory: The Cold War and Its Aftermath
   *Robert H. Baker*
   ISBN 1 86064 124 5

12 The Nuclear Free and Independent Pacific Movement: After Mororua
   *Roy Smith*
   ISBN 1 86064 101 6

# European Impact and Pacific Influence

*British and German Colonial Policy in the Pacific Islands and the Indigenous Response*

EDITED BY

Hermann J. Hiery

AND

John M. MacKenzie

Tauris Academic Studies
I.B. Tauris Publishers
LONDON • NEW YORK
The German Historical Institute

Published in 1997 by Tauris Academic Studies
an imprint of I.B.Tauris & Co. Ltd
45 Bloomsbury Square, London WC1A 2HY
175 Fifth Avenue, New York, NY 10010

In association with the German Historical Institute London

In the United States of America and Canada distributed by
St Martin's Press, 175 Fifth Avenue, New York, NY 10010

A full CIP record for this book is available
from the British Library

A full CIP record for this book is available
from the Library of Congress

ISBN 1 86064 059 1

Set in Monotype Ehrhardt by Lucy Morton, London SE12
Printed and bound in Great Britain by WBC Ltd,
Bridgend, Mid Glamorgan

Dedicated to the memory of Sione Lātūkefu,
Tongan and Pacific Historian

A PUBLICATION OF THE GERMAN
HISTORICAL INSTITUTE LONDON
GENERAL EDITOR: Adolf M. Birke

# Contents

# Glossary

| | |
|---|---|
| *Bezirksamtmann* | District officer; the leading German colonial official for a specified area. In 1914 the German Pacific was divided into five *Bezirke* headed by one *Bezirksamtmann* each: Rabaul, Friedrich-Wilhelmshafen, Käwieng, Yap and Ponape. Samoa, which was too small, had no *Bezirksamtmann*, but *Stationsleiter* (local administrative officials). |
| *fa'aSamoa* | The way in which Samoans think, feel and act. |
| *Kaiser* | The German Emperor. |
| *Landeshauptmann* | A title used for the German colonial officials who were in charge of New Guinea (Georg Freiherr von Schleinitz, 1886–88; Reinhold Kraetke, 1888–89; Georg Schmiele, 1892–95) or the Marshall Islands (Dr Georg Irmer, 1893–98; Eugen Brandeis, 1898–06) under company rule. |
| *laplap* | Loin cloth. |
| *Luluai* | Government-appointed chief in German New Guinea. |
| *malira* | Love magic. |
| *mana* | A Polynesian term denoting authority, power and influence, inherent to some people, but not to others. |
| *matai* | The head of a Samoan family. |

| | |
|---|---|
| *mau* | Two opposition movements by Samoans against colonial regimes. The first was a traditionalist attempt by the orator Lauati to conspire against German colonial overrule. The other was much more a mass democratic movement against New Zealand authority. Its leaders were of the indigenous oligarchy, but its policies and aims were strenuously supported by grassroots Samoans. |
| *pakeha* | Maori term for the European population. |
| *Pater* | A Roman Catholic priest belonging to a religious order. |
| *Reichskolonialamt* | The German Colonial Office; it was founded in 1907 (before that, all colonial affairs were handled by the *Auswärtiges Amt*, the German Foreign Office). There were three colonial secretaries (Bernhard Dernburg, 1907–10; Friedrich von Lindequist, 1910–11; Wilhelm Solf, 1911–18) and one *Kolonialminister* of the Republic (Johannes Bell, 1919–20), before the office was closed down. |
| *Reichstag* | The German parliament. |
| *Schutzgebiet* | Literally the German word for 'protectorate', its legal meaning is more like that of a colony. Officially all German colonies (except Kiaochow/Tsingtao, which was a 'Pachtgebiet' or leasehold territory) were termed 'Schutzgebiete'. |
| *tulafale* | Samoan orator. |

## ABBREVIATIONS

| | |
|---|---|
| AAC | Australian Archives Canberra |
| ABCFM | American Board of Commissioners for Foreign Missions |
| BAP | Bundesarchiv Potsdam |
| CPP | Commonwealth (of Australia) Parliamentary Papers |
| DKB | Deutsches Kolonialblatt |
| DKGG | Die deutsche Kolonial-Gesetzgebung |
| JPS | Journal of the Polynesian Society |
| LMS | London Missionary Society |
| MH | The Missionary Herald |
| RKolA | Reichskolonialamt |

# Foreword

*European Impact and Pacific Influence* was the title of a conference held at Kloster Andechs, near Munich, in the European summer of 1994. In the past, the German Historical Institute in London has organized a number of conferences on colonialism. The decades of often emotionally led debate about a theory of imperialism have resulted more or less in deadlock. Gone are the days when it was fashionable to blame Europeans and European colonizers for all the negative developments that took place after the colonial empires had crumbled and new and independent states had come into being.

This is not to say that the history of colonialism must be completely rewritten. Nor has the glory of the lost empires become a new focus for historians now that dreadful conditions haunt many postcolonial societies, and despondency seems to have replaced dependency almost everywhere. But there can be no doubt that, for far too long, Marxist thinking has dominated historical research in the field of colonialism and imperialism.

In the past, European historians have claimed that Europeanized versions of European colonialism took little account of the indigenous side. But they themselves, albeit with a better conscience, have neglected the part played by the local population. In their view, the actions and reactions of non-Europeans were always determined by the European aggressor. If colonials had turned the colonized into victims, now colonial historians subjected them to their theories and dogmas. The boundaries of 'true' indigenous behaviour were thus clearly defined: non-Europeans could suffer from or rebel against Europeans. Other patterns of behaviour were assumed not to have existed, and were not investigated. It comes as no surprise that those who did not fit into these European concepts of non-European behaviour were generally ostracized and branded as colonial Quislings.

Pacific historians have been in the forefront in showing that culture contact and European contact meant more than domination and subjugation. They have concentrated on the process of culture contact as such. The history of contact is *per se* never a one-sided story. While it is true that a real symbiosis is hardly ever the result of such an event, many exchanges certainly did take place. But our book goes one step further. We are looking not only at how indigenous actions influenced the intellectual baggage that Europeans brought with them, but also at how Europeans themselves were changed by Pacific patterns of behaviour. Many questions were of central concern in our debate. Did the British and Germans differ in this respect? Where was the European impact stronger, and where was it weaker? Did Pacific mores, life-styles and viewpoints have more influence in one place than another? And why?

Those who participated in the conference, colonial and Pacific historians, anthropologists and legal experts, came from all over the globe. It was only natural for our approach to be interdisciplinary. The finest contributions are presented in this volume and will, we hope, stimulate further debate and research.

Kloster Andechs was a perfect choice for this conference, the last to be held under my directorship of the German Historical Institute in London. I should like to thank Abbot Odilo Lechner and his Cellarer, Frater Lambert Stangl, for their hospitality. I should also like to thank my successor, Professor Peter Wende, for his commitment to seeing this book reach production stage. Angela Davies and Karina Urbach helped to put the manuscript into its final form. My final thanks go to I.B.Tauris Publishers, and in particular Lester Crook, for their effort in publishing this book.

The participants in this conference included Dr Sione Lātūkefu and his wife, Dr Ruth Fink-Lātūkefu. Sadly, it turned out to be Sione's final conference. This book is dedicated to his memory — a great Tongan and Pacific Island historian.

*Adolf M. Birke*

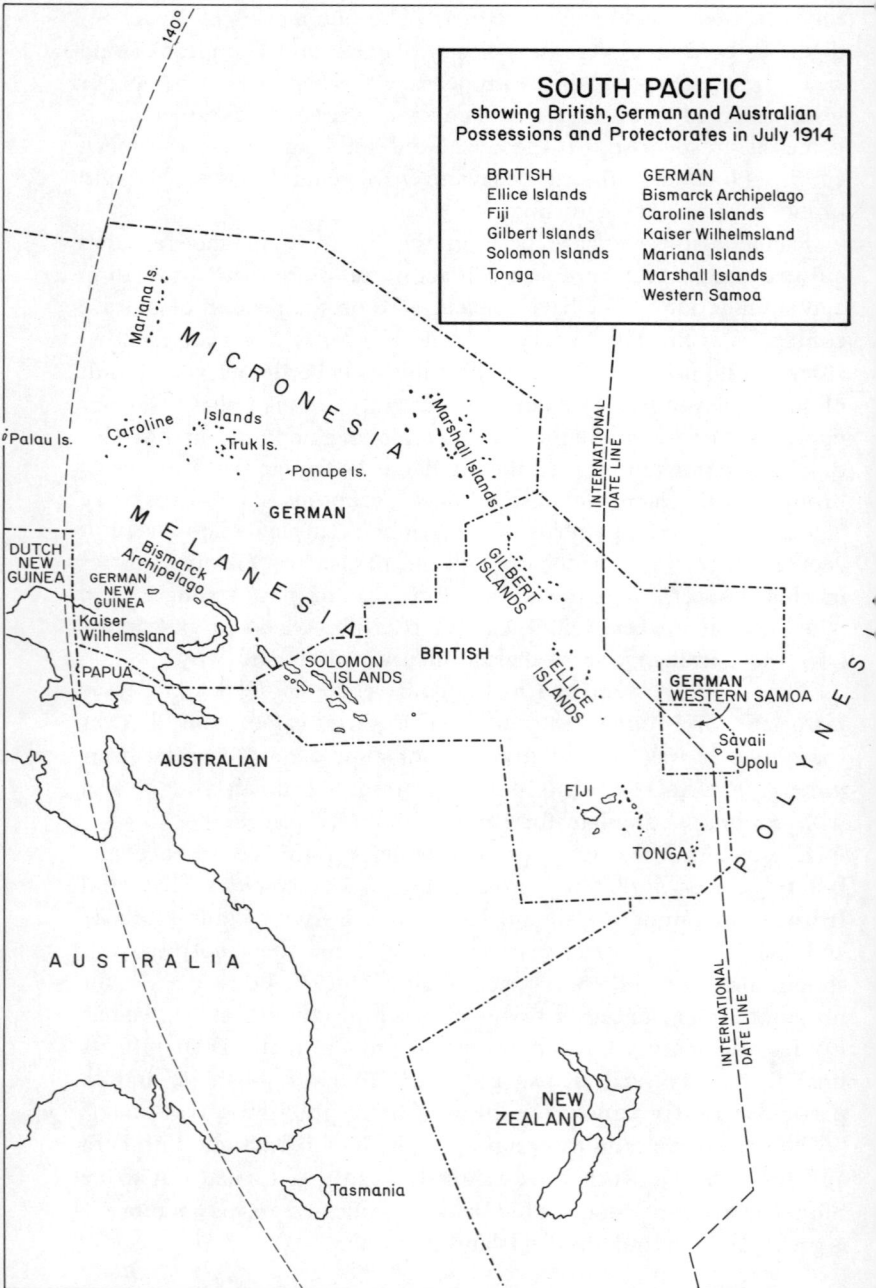

SOUTH PACIFIC
showing British, German and Australian
Possessions and Protectorates in July 1914

| BRITISH | GERMAN |
|---|---|
| Ellice Islands | Bismarck Archipelago |
| Fiji | Caroline Islands |
| Gilbert Islands | Kaiser Wilhelmsland |
| Solomon Islands | Mariana Islands |
| Tonga | Marshall Islands |
| | Western Samoa |

# Introduction

## HERMANN J. HIERY
## AND JOHN M. MACKENZIE

The Pacific is a vast ocean that contains a myriad islands. Australia, almost the size of a continent, and New Zealand are the paramount geographical units and stand apart; the others have been classified under the labels Melanesia, Micronesia and Polynesia. As with all nomenclature, this has its shortcomings and is far from satisfactory. However, the various cultures of Melanesia have so much in common that distinguishes them from Polynesians and Micronesians (and vice versa) that attempts to replace the traditional, established designations are even further from being convincing. Such self-congratulatory proposals may have more to do with the damaged ego of academics who have run out of innovative steam and try to make up for it by marking out new signposts and watchwords.

The islands' distance from the centres of European expansionism, and their geographical isolation from other continents, meant that contact with non-Pacific cultures was limited. Such contact was not completely unknown before Europeans set out to search for bounds to their curiosity, but as far as we know it did not have much impact on indigenous, Pacific developments. Continuous contact really began when the Ibero-Europeans crossed the ocean on their way to circumnavigate the globe. From the sixteenth century on, the Spanish regularly visited the northern South Pacific from America en route to the Philippines. European impact in its Spanish variation certainly had dramatic consequences for the Marianas and their people.[1] How much of the rest of Micronesia was also opened to European views and concepts of life is still unclear; there is much speculation about stranded ships and the possible influence of Spanish or Portuguese genes even outside Micronesia,[2] but so far decisive archaeological evidence has not turned up, and what has come to us in oral reports from New Guinea, Australia and elsewhere is too vague to be considered conclusive.

There can be no doubt, however, that the effects of the European arrival in the Americas also started to have an impact in the Pacific region from the sixteenth century on, that is, long before formal contact between Europeans and most Pacific Islanders was established. Historians now commonly agree that the staple food of Pacific Islanders received at least one important supplement as a consequence of American-European contact. The arrival of the sweet potato gave the daily diet of the Pacific peoples more variety, and its impact on their lives and social structures can hardly be overestimated. The change of indigenous flora and fauna as a result of later European impact is an important issue in this book.

Still, the sixteenth and seventeenth centuries are the Pacific's dark ages, as far as our knowledge of possible Pacific–European contact is concerned. As we all know, this drastically changed with the arrival of James Cook on the scene. It was really the beginning of a shared, if coincidental, Anglo-German interest in the region. While the British called the tune and from now on worked towards some type of formal military and/or political control, the Germans, coming from an altogether different form of state background, were more interested in collecting scientific data. Without a unified state there was no organized German effort, but the reports and activities of the two Forsters were widely read and discussed[3] and provided a stimulus to other Germans who only too eagerly followed in their footsteps, if not with British support, then with that of other interested European powers.[4]

In the past, the common view has been that Europeans came with economic purposes in mind. While it would be fatuous to dismiss such motives, it is necessary to point out that in comparison to (almost all) other regions outside Europe, the Pacific was a relatively poor target for commercial exploitation. Much more than their products, it was the people that fascinated the Europeans. To be sure, images of the 'noble savage' had also emerged in the Americas and even in Africa, but nowhere did this view become more commonplace than in the South Pacific.[5] The fact that cannibalism, that worst of all nightmares to Europeans, was most widespread here (and not in America or Africa) could not, apparently, diminish the prevailing view. If cannibalism was noticed, it was a feature that somehow contributed to the image of the wild, free man. But the 'noble savage' had at least as much to do with the European perception of indigenous women as with that of men. A female cannibal simply does not exist in the annals of European (male) discoverers. Without any doubt, the conception of the 'noble savage' also had sexual connotations. It is striking that, except for a comparatively short period at the very beginning, the noble savage image was never applied to the Australian Aborigines.

Polynesian women, with their long black hair and almond-shaped eyes, appeared to be the living models of what European men longed for. Deprived of normal sexual behaviour for a much longer time than those travelling to Africa, Asia or the Americas, European sailors to the Pacific discovered a very different female attitude towards sexuality. To their astonishment, they found women who would take the initiative without facing punishment, physical abuse or moral disgrace. Furthermore, the fact that Pacific island women appeared to be able to separate emotions and sexuality seemed to be almost beyond belief, and contributed to their legendary status in the eyes of European men.

For far too long historians have eschewed the obvious, namely that probably not the very first, but the first lasting impact was made between European men and indigenous women. And while this book concentrates on contact in colonial times, there can be no question that the interaction between Europeans and Pacific islanders, Pacific islanders and Europeans, in all phases of contact history, was predominantly the contact between the two sexes. The questions of how images of the 'other' originated, were shaped and perpetuated, need to be examined in this context. Such an enquiry might also shed more light on lingering problems such as how (or how much) the colonial population was able or unable to influence the colonialists, or to resist, co-operate, or manipulate them. Only very recently has sexuality been accepted as an important factor in reconstructing colonial history.[6] For us it was clear from the beginning that it had to be included in such an undertaking, even if research in this area is only just emerging.

With Cook, the main area of contact shifted from the north to the south, or rather south-east, from Micronesia to Polynesia. That region became the first real bone of contention among European powers that coveted political influence in the Pacific. The French,[7] the British, and later the Americans and Germans all contested the islands. Tiny Samoa, in particular, aroused European jingoism. With a land-mass smaller than Rhode Island, and only about 18 per cent of the size of Hawai'i, and beyond that no real economic or strategic importance, it is indeed astonishing to see the fascination it held for the European great powers. It was the centre of the first German bid for colonies, in 1880, and in 1889 the craving for its possession almost provoked a world war between Britain, the United States and Germany.[8] Unable to extend its colonial profile in the Pacific because of a continuing struggle with the Boers in South Africa, Great Britain eventually had to renounce its claims to Samoa in favour of the United States and Germany.

The treaty of 14 November 1899, which settled British and German disputes over Polynesian islands until the outbreak of the First World War, meant that Tonga, the other group of Polynesian islands coveted by both Great Britain and Germany, finally came into the British sphere of influence. Legally speaking, the islands were never a colony but only a British protectorate. In fact, however, the British 'advisors' to the indigenous monarch pulled the real political strings. In 1914, King George Tupou II tried unsuccessfully to remain neutral between Great Britain and Germany.

In Melanesia, the British and German sides had come to an understanding as early as April 1886. This was amended in February 1900, when the major northern parts of the Solomon Islands (Shortland, Choiseul, Isabel) were handed over to the British as a result of the Anglo-German agreement over Samoa. From then on, only the northernmost Solomon islands of Buka and Bougainville remained part of the German colony of New Guinea. But the political decision over the atolls of Nukumanu, a Polynesian enclave in a predominantly Melanesian area, provides another striking example of the significance that European colonialism gave to the assumed character of a people. When the German commander raised the flag there in 1889, he noted that it was 'the most miserable part of the whole Pacific'. There were only 200 people, and its economic value was almost non-existent. But after a visit and report by the German governor – 'It is a surprisingly tall and handsome race. And they live a happy life' – the German Foreign Office insisted on having the islands back. Finally, London announced on 8 January 1902 that it had revoked a proclamation of October 1900 declaring the group to be British.

It could be argued that Anglo-German relations concerning their respective Pacific colonies were quite good. There was even a combined Anglo-German company to facilitate exploiting common economic interests in the region.[9] Without doubt, the British colonial model, as Woodruff Smith convincingly demonstrates in this book, had a profound impact upon German colonial policy. The example of imperial rule in British India influenced the German Pacific. Solf's policies in Samoa are a case in point. The other side of this coin was an apparent British admiration for German colonial activities in the region.[10]

It is also useful to point, as Smith does, to the overall German colonial experience in Africa. Giving greater weight to non-economic sources than has been given in the past, Smith points to a specific civil-service mentality. Primarily shaped by the British model, it saw economic development embedded in a comprehensive programme of socio-economic change. This was thought to be a gradual but (as Smith makes clear) not necessarily slow process,[11] building on indigenous mentalities and existing structures. At times, it could offer a governmental shield of protection against capitalist exploitation. Conflicts between administrators and European companies and individuals, lobbying for more 'rights' and concessions, were therefore anything but rare. African interests became a key factor in colonial policy-making. Decisions such as that to make the indigenous lingua franca the official language of instruction in German schools in Africa applied in the Pacific as well.[12] Generally it could be argued that the 'civil-service mentality' was even more marked in the Pacific, where the different social and mental background of the administrators,[13] and a longer term in office, was likely to produce stronger resistance to the bullying tactics of capitalist enterprises and entrepreneurs. Also, the influence of the central colonial authorities was much more limited, owing to the remoteness of some regions and islands from Berlin.

Still, the Pacific was not Africa. The history of the colonial Pacific resists what might be a typically European inclination to subsume it under a kind of wider African colonial experience. Apart from the very (but for some not so) obvious difference with regard to population,[14] Anglo-German relations in the Pacific were influenced, if not marred, by the presence of two large British settler colonies, Australia and New Zealand. Both had their own imperialist dreams,[15] which increasingly collided with the German colonial presence in the Pacific. By 1912 they had come to a secret agreement to divide the German colonies in the event of a European war.[16] While Australia itself is outside the scope of this collection, its imperialism in the region does merit attention. The essays about the different British and German approaches toward justice, arguably one of the strongest and most lasting legacies of the European impact, have been supplemented by an article on the Australians in New Guinea. As Allan Healy's contribution to this volume shows, the assumption that suggests itself, namely that Australia followed the British example, is altogether wrong.

The book is divided into four parts. As can be seen from the individual contributions, much research has been done in the fields of mutual perceptions, and the impact of European laws and justice. Less is known about the ecological impact and the influence of the different Pacific and European attitudes toward sexuality on shaping images and policies. Geographically, the essays range from New Guinea, the anthropologists' paradise, in the west, to Tonga and Samoa in the east; from the former British and German parts of Micronesia in the north, to New Zealand in the south.

This volume does not claim to provide a synopsis of British and German attitudes in the colonial Pacific and the varied responses of islanders. But we hope that the essays presented here can show that such a work would indeed be a necessary and worthwhile enterprise.

## Notes

1. Felipe de la Corte y Ruano Calderon, *Memoria descriptiva e histórica de las Islas Marianas*, Madrid, 1876; Luis de Ibanez y Garcia, *Historia de las Islas Marianas con su derretero, y de las Carolinas y Palaos*, Granada, 1886.

2. Robert Langdon, *The Lost Caravel*, Sydney, 1975; *The Lost Caravel Re-explored*, Canberra, 1988.

3. From the wealth of information that is available on Reinhold and, in particular, Georg Forster, Eberhard Berg's *Zwischen den Welten*. *Anthropologie der Aufklärung und das Werk Georg Forsters* (Berlin, 1982) gives the best insight into Forster's influence on shaping German (and, indeed, British) perceptions of the Pacific.

4. Noteworthy are the Russian Pacific expeditions. Cf. Otto von Kotzebue, *A Voyage of Discovery into the South Sea and Bering's Straits, for the purpose of exploring a North-East Passage in 1815–1818*, 3 vols., London, 1821; and Louis Charles Adélaide de Chamisso de Boncourt, 'Remarks and Opinions of the Naturalist of the Expedition', ibid., vol. 2. Before the foundation of the German nation state it was, curiously enough, the Austrians who started the only 'German' expedition to the Pacific. Cf. Karl von Scherzer, *Narrative of the Circumnavigation of the Globe by the Austrian Frigate Novara, undertaken by order of the Imperial Government in the years 1857, 1858, and 1859*, 3 vols., London, 1861–63. For the influence German scientists on board the *Novara* (among them several zoologists, botanists, geologists and ethnologists) had on New Zealand society, cf. Gertraut Maria Stoffel, 'The Austrian Connection with New Zealand in the Nineteenth Century', in James N. Bade (ed.), *The German Connection. New Zealand and German-Speaking Europe in the Nineteenth Century*, Auckland, 1993, pp. 21–34.

5. A typical example of such a view is Alan Moorehead, *The Fatal Impact. An Account of the Invasion of the South Pacific 1767–1840*, Harmondsworth, 1968. The classic study is by H.N. Fairchild, *The Noble Savage. A Study in Romantic Naturalism*, New York, 1928.

6. The main credit for this contribution to historiography must go to Ronald Hyam, *Empire and Sexuality. The British Experience*, Manchester, 2nd edn 1991.

7. For the French, see Robert Aldrich, *The French Presence in the South Pacific 1842–1940*, Honolulu, 1990.

8. Paul M. Kennedy, *The Samoan Tangle. A Study in Anglo-German-American Relations 1878–1900*, Dublin and New York, 1974. Cf. also his 'Bismarck's Imperialism: The Case of Samoa 1880–1890', *The Historical Journal* 15 (1972), pp. 261–83.

9. For the Pacific Phosphate Company and the production of phosphate on Nauru during colonial times, see Maslyn Williams and Barrie Macdonald, *The Phosphateers. A History of the British Phosphate Commissioners and the Christmas Island Phosphate Commission*, Carlton, 1985; also Christopher Weeramantry, *Nauru. Environmental Damage under International Trusteeship*, Melbourne, 1992. For the German colonial period, Stewart Firth, 'German Labour Policy in Nauru and Angaur, 1906–1914', *Journal of Pacific History* 13 (1978), pp. 36–52, needs emendation.

10. See, for instance, B. Pullen Burry, *In a German Colony; or Four Weeks in New Britain*, London, 1909. For Anglo-German relations in Africa, see Michael Fröhlich, *Von Konfrontation zur Koexistenz. Die*

*deutsch–englischen Kolonialbeziehungen in Afrika zwischen 1884 und 1914*, Bochum, 1990.

11. This is a view shared by many of Germany's former colonial subjects in Africa. Cf. the comment by A. E. Afigbo, 'it would appear that in retrospect the former German colonial subjects ... think that the takeover by the French and the British slowed down their development'. *The Making of Modern Africa*, vol. 2, New York 1971, 2nd edn 1986, pp. 2–3.

12. Hermann Joseph Hiery, *Das Deutsche Reich in der Südsee. Eine Annäherung an die Erfahrungen verschiedener Kulturen*, Göttingen, 1995, p. 151.

13. Cf. ibid., p. 321.

14. Cf. the remarks by an anthropologist who worked in Africa and in the Pacific: 'African models were positively misleading when applied to New Guinea; ... one can only understand many aspects of New Guinea societies ... by a total and systematic reversal of the principles which govern ... African societies.' C. R. Hallpike, *Bloodshed and Vengeance in the Papuan Mountains. The Generation of Conflict in Tauade Society*, Oxford, 1977, p. v.

15. For Australia, see the standard work by Roger C. Thompson, *Australian Imperialism in the Pacific. The Expansionist Era 1820–1920*, Carlton, 1980; for New Zealand, Angus Ross, *New Zealand Aspirations in the Pacific in the Nineteenth Century*, Oxford, 1964. Forthcoming is Roger C. Thompson, 'Australische und neuseeländische Reaktionen auf den deutschen Kolonialismus im Pazifik', in Hermann Hiery (ed.), *Handbuch der 'deutschen' Südsee*, Paderborn, Schoeningh, 1997.

16. Ian McGibbon, *The Path to Gallipoli. Defending New Zealand 1840–1915*, Wellington, 1991, pp. 208–9 and 239–43. For their actions in the First World War, see now also Hermann Joseph Hiery, *The Neglected War. The German South Pacific and the Influence of World War I*, Honolulu, 1995.

# 2

# Contexts of German Colonialism in Africa: British Imperialism, German Politics, and the German Administrative Tradition

WOODRUFF D. SMITH

The purpose of this chapter is to discuss ways in which the history of European colonization in Africa might shed light on aspects of German colonial activity in the Pacific. This purpose could be achieved to some extent by focusing on the direct transfer of administrative and commercial practices from one area to the other. Clearly, within the public consciousness of German colonialism, German East Africa, German South West Africa, Togo, and Cameroon carried far more weight than did Germany's Pacific holdings. Colonial policy was generally formulated and debated with regard to the African empire, and policies initiated by the central colonial authorities were usually implemented in Africa first.[1] But it seems to me that this is not a very interesting way of looking at the subject and contributes little toward constructing a framework for discussion of British and German colonization in the Pacific.

What I propose to do instead is to focus on some of the many socio-cultural contexts which made up German colonialism in Africa and suggest ways in which they might illuminate aspects of colonialism in the Pacific. Traditionally, historians have approached the interaction of cultures under colonial circumstances within an intellectual framework that treats each side in the interaction as though it were culturally homogeneous – in essence, as an ideal type. In recent years, we have become aware that this approach to non-European cultures reflects a colonialist perception of such cultures as the 'other', an inverted mirror of European culture. We have been less conscious of the fact that we tend to treat the European side as equally uniform. In reality, of course, neither the Europeans nor the 'other' were in fact culturally homogeneous. Real cultures encompass variety, tensions, ambiguities and contradictions. If we want to understand the dynamics of colonialism in particular cases, we need to be able, in a relatively coherent way, to understand the complexities, the contradictions, the variations in aim and attitude that characterized each side. We are accustomed to considering only a few aspects of heterogeneity among European colonialists: differences between nationalities in their approaches to indigenous peoples, and differences between interest groups (missionaries, for example, as against planters) within an individual colony. We need to be able systematically to take account of the fact that the very culture of European colonialism – even the colonialism of a single nation such as Germany – was heterogeneous and complex. This we can attempt through analysing the sociocultural contexts of colonialism; this has the added benefit of allowing us to give greater weight than we have traditionally given to non-economic sources of European colonial behaviour, and to integrate some of the new critical cultural and linguistic analysis of colonialism into discussions of policy.

The 'contexts' discussed here are an attempt to deconstruct the phenomenon of German colonialism in Africa and to regroup the resulting elements into a number of clusters useful for purposes of explanation. It is assumed that people, both individually and as members of groups or institutions, think, discuss and act within the framework of a number of contexts that exist simultaneously in the cultures to which they belong. These contexts overlap because they share elements, and thinking and acting within one or more contexts often creates tensions, ambiguities and contradictions – sometimes in individuals, and frequently within groups. A context usually includes a characteristic array of ideas and attitudes, and often social structures, institutions, behaviour patterns and material objects that the people whom the historian is studying consciously regarded as fitting together in some natural, coherent way.[2] A context also frequently incorporates a characteristic mode of discourse employed by an identifiable discourse community. The discourse community usually constructs on an ongoing basis a narrative (often closely linked to political ideologies) that explains why, in relation to the context as a whole, things are as they are and how they ought to change. Contexts often encompass disagreements on specific issues, in which case they reflect consensus not on the resolution of the issues, but rather on the terms in which the issues are disputed.

In the limited space available here, I can discuss only three of the contexts within which Germans in Africa thought, spoke and acted during the era of the *Kaiserreich*. For the same reason, I shall concentrate primarily on the socio-cultural world of colonial officials.

## The Context of International (British) Imperialism

Germans, as latecomers to the imperial game, tended to think about their overseas possessions within a context of ideas, images, words and behaviour derived from their perceptions of the colonial experiences of other nations – pre-eminently, Great Britain. During the Wilhelmian era, this imperial context was actually part of a large socio-cultural framework (analysed by Paul Kennedy in his study of pre-1914 Anglo-German antagonism) in which educated Germans constructed meanings for many different aspects of public life and culture around comparisons with Britain and the British.[3]

The context of British imperialism (as constructed in Germany) included a distinctive narrative: the history of the British Empire and its growth through a process of national grasping for power, wealth and prestige. According to the narrative, Britain's mid-nineteenth-century status as the world's wealthiest and most powerful state had been due largely to her overseas empire, and also to the possession by her people of traits that both contributed to and arose from her colonial success. To a certain extent, the German notion of *Weltpolitik* in German political discourse was constructed around the desire to write a parallel German narrative. Colonial officials like Wilhelm Solf and writers like Paul Rohrbach were quite explicit about this desire.[4] The discourse of German imperialism (especially in official circles and in the press) tended to be adapted from the vocabulary and the perspectives of British imperialism.

The context of British imperialism was also constructed around several sets of linked images, ideas and attitudes. These sets were not necessarily consistent with each other. For educated Germans, Britain served as a political model – both positively and negatively, depending on one's orientation to the issues of German politics. Liberals looked to Britain as a model of parliamentarism, and so did anti-liberals. In the former case, the point about the British model that most appealed was the (apparent) fact that the British had not allowed parliamentarism (or more recently, democracy) to interfere with the process by which Britain became and maintained herself as a great imperial power.[5] Anti-liberals professed to believe that it was precisely the parliamentary and democratic elements of the British constitution that made Britain vulnerable to replacement by Germany as the world-dominating state.[6] In either case, the general issue of whether or not Britain was a fit political model for Germany was tied to a specific version of the narrative of how Britain acquired an empire.

Colonial officials and others concerned with Germany's African colonies also tended to think in terms of specific models of imperial rule derived from the British Empire. It was common for discourse about administrative procedure, law, development policy, and 'native policy' to be couched in terms of examples drawn from British practice.[7] The British imperial model came in several major forms, which made it convenient for German officials and other colonialists to choose British examples that were appropriate to their interests and intentions. Like most models, the British imperial example influenced, but did not wholly determine, the outlooks of the people who made use of it.

The example of imperial rule to which German officials in Africa most frequently looked was British India. Not only did India provide a wealth of well-documented instances in practically every area of colonial administration, but the enormous prestige that accrued to the British as the successors of the Moguls gave India a special place in the minds of German colonialists who saw Germany as Britain's eventual equal or successor as an imperial power.[8] One of the major ideas adapted from British practice in India was indirect rule through native princes. Such an example could not, of course, be followed everywhere in German Africa – in some areas because of the absence of indigenous political structures sufficiently similar to the Indian princely states, and in some areas because the nature of German economic intentions required that indigenous elites be bypassed. But in several places, it was employed even when it was not entirely consistent with other aspects of policy.

The most significant case was German East Africa – the coastal region of which possessed a well-established political structure and a Swahili-speaking Muslim elite. In the 1890s, after the elite's initial resistance had been crushed, German officials attempted to build an Indian-style native governmental system.[9] The decision to use Swahili rather than German in East African schools was related to this aim. The *askaris* (Muslim infantry) of the East African 'protective force' were organized on the model of the Indian Army. During the administration of Governor Freiherr von Rechenberg in 1906–12, political reliance on the Swahili-speaking elite became even more pronounced, through deliberate imitation of the Indian model.[10] Richard Kandt, the German administrator in Ruanda-Urundi (adjacent to German East Africa), established with the rulers of those kingdoms a relationship modelled on that of British residents at Indian princely courts.[11] When the finances of East Africa were reformed just after 1900, the financial system of British India was used as a model.[12]

The British Empire provided other examples to German colonialists. In areas where a substantial European population existed or was projected, such as South West Africa, parallels to British white settlement colonies were much discussed. Settlers, and those who wanted to identify themselves with settlers, pointed out the prosperity of Australia and New Zealand and the prospects of South Africa and Canada as validation of their argument that policy should primarily advance settler interests. They also pointed to the American Revolution to show what happened when colonial authorities took a different course. Officials (with some exceptions, such as Friedrich Lindequist, Colonial Secretary 1910–11) tended to reject the British settlement colonies as a model, in part because Germany had no colonies that really corresponded to them geographically, and in part because of the anti-administrative political construction of the history of British settlement colonies.[13]

British imperialism also influenced the behaviour of German officials in Africa. The image of the British colonial official as the phlegmatic, paternalistic white ruler of 'child-like' native peoples, expressing the power and virtues of Europe governance through personal example, was an important pattern for German officials. Some presumably adopted it as a result of the fashionableness of the English gentleman as a type, while others may have been attracted by the way it legitimated them as gentry, which their degrees and civil offices did not.[14] Another image, that of the Anglo-Saxon settler in North America, Australasia or South Africa as a rugged individualist, able to formulate opinions by himself and critical of bureaucratic authority, also had an important place in German colonialist thinking. Some argued that an important reason to have colonies was to produce such people. Admittedly, because they were rulers and exploiters of indigenous peoples, settlers would display racist attitudes and behaviour patterns associated with the inhabitants of British white colonies.[15] Colonial officials, in part because they saw themselves, not the settlers, as the rulers of indigenous peoples, tended to think that the British settlement colonies reinforced their apprehensions about the application of the settlement model.[16]

## The Political and Ideological Context

The context of international imperialism intersected with a second major socio-cultural context defined by the place of colonies in domestic German politics and ideology. This second context was extremely complicated, but some of its aspects can be summarized in terms of a general narrative about Germany's colonial mission that was accepted by most Germans who favoured an overseas empire, and two conflicting ideological traditions of German colonialism, which produced different constructions of the narrative.

The general narrative was rehearsed frequently in speeches by politicians and officials, in the pages of pro-colonial newspapers, and in the Reichstag.[17] According to the narrative, the possession and expansion of a colonial empire was a natural consequence of political unification and an essential concomitant of nationhood. An overseas empire staked Germany's claim to great-power status and helped to secure the country's world interests. Overseas colonies, if properly located and developed, would support the German economy and attract German emigrants, keeping the latter within the German economic and cultural sphere. The experience of seizing, expanding and ruling an overseas empire helped to encourage a sense of unity among all Germans and to develop a truly national character. The German colonial narrative had great political significance because it appeared to offer political parties, interest groups, and even the national government a means of increasing public support for their positions through identifying those positions with the correct unfolding of the narrative. Hans-Ulrich Wehler focused on one aspect of this in arguing that Bismarck became a supporter of colonial expansion in the early 1880s because he believed that colonialism could be used to promote social unity, or at least to undercut support for the left liberals among the bourgeoisie and for the social democrats among the workers.[18] The Pan-German League heavily emphasized colonial issues, in part because its leaders believed that aggressive overseas imperialism would help to define German nationality.[19]

These expectations were, however, largely disappointed. The actual German colonial empire differed substantially from the mythical empire around which the colonial narrative centred. Moreover, German colonialist thinking was in fact split into two ideological traditions that proved difficult to reconcile. Colonialists could try to avoid the first problem intellectually by arguing that the colonies would eventually live up to expectations, if they could be increased in size or governed more effectively. But this made demands which the state could not easily meet. The second problem was serious both because the two ideologies had incompatible implications for policy and behaviour and because they tended to be adopted by competing political groups. German colonial officials in Africa found that whenever they attempted to do something of significance, their actions were interpreted in Germany as outgrowths of one of the two ideologies, and were therefore open to attack by adherents of the other ideology.

One of the colonial ideologies focused on the role of colonies as supports for the growth of German industry and commerce. This ideology came to be closely tied to the outlook on German foreign and imperial policy most often described as *Weltpolitik* at the turn of the century.[20] Many policy initiatives in the African colonies were conceived and interpreted within the scope of economic colonialism and *Weltpolitik*. On the whole, German officials found this ideological framework most useful for conceptualizing development and native policy and the role of the colonies in international politics. The attempt to use colonial concession companies as vehicles for development in the 1890s and just after 1900 was clearly framed within the structure of economic colonialism. So also were the policies followed after 1900 in Togo, German East

Africa, and parts of Cameroon, according to which the local German government was charged with modernizing the economic and social infrastructure of the colony and encouraging European investment. A classic (and well-publicized) example of economic colonialism in practice was Togo, where Governor Count Zech put into place a modernization programme built around what he hoped would emerge as an educated, aggressive, capitalist peasantry.[21]

The other German colonialist ideology was originally derived, like the first, from liberal politics. It focused not on the economic role of colonies, but on emigration and the effect of colonial settlement on German culture. Settlement colonies were initially seen as places where emigrants could go in preference to America and set up mostly as farmers, thereby retaining their connection to Germany. This idea was still propounded well after the last great wave of German emigration in the 1890s, but the supposed cultural effects of colonial settlement were increasingly emphasized. Colonies were represented as places where the values and virtues of the German peasantry could be protected against the threat of continuing industrialization in Germany itself, on the grounds that peasant culture was more genuinely German and more important than were the cultural characteristics of industrial society.[22]

In the contentious post-Bismarckian political scene, settlement colonialism came to be closely linked to the new anti-democratic organizations of the radical right and to political agrarianism, while economic colonialism was identified with proponents of economic modernization. The linkage was not invariable, but around 1900 the alignment of the colonial ideologies with conflicting sides in domestic political disputes became more direct and predictable. Although there was nothing inherently progressive about the political implications of economic colonialism and although there *were* vaguely populist aspects of the settlement view, it was the former that came to be connected to a new colonial reform movement after about 1906.[23]

These tendencies gave colonial interest groups significant access to the political stage in Germany. Proposed colonial policies came to be debated not so much in their own terms as in terms of the ideological split between settlement and economic colonialism and the sides of the issues to which the colonialist ideologies were linked. Even in colonies where there were few settlers on the peasant model, it was not uncommon for European plantation owners to call for support for their interests on the basis of the settlement ideology – often in opposition to the policies of colonial administration. In German East Africa, a fairly small group of plantation owners in the north managed in 1903 to redirect to their region an official scheme for railway-building in the central region that was supposed to encourage economic development based on indigenous African peasant farming. The northern, or Usambara, railway was built against the original intentions of the authorities (and at enormous expense) because the settlement ideology allowed the planters to attract substantial support in the Reichstag. In 1907, after the appointment of Bernhard Dernburg as Colonial Secretary, a reform programme based on the economic colonialist ideology included the building of the previously rejected central railway.[24] In East Africa as elsewhere, development policy (and therefore native policy) was framed in part by the political and ideological context of colonialism in Germany.

## The Administrative and Legal Context

Yet another context of German colonialism was one defined by a discourse and theoretical framework derived from the German bureaucratic tradition of administration and law. Within the colonial empire, this tradition was the property of a limited group: officials who possessed the standard qualifications of German civil servants and who shared the discourse and common intellectual framework of the Prussian-German bureaucratic elite. The colonial bureaucracy's strong adherence to the tradition was perhaps due to its tenuous formal connection to the metropolitan bureaucracies. Bismarck had originally planned to rule some of the new colonies through German merchants under a consular apparatus, while other possessions would be governed by chartered monopoly companies such as the German East Africa Company and the New Guinea Company. No colonial civil service would be necessary. But Bismarck's scheme was rendered inoperable by the complexity and the rapid expansion of the overseas empire.[25] In the 1890s, the imperial government had to take over the direct administration of most colonies. Initially, a motley collection of army officers, adventurers and businesspeople filled administrative positions, but the new Colonial Department of the Foreign Office moved steadily to establish a colonial administration along standard civil service lines. Gradually, the department recruited junior officials with the proper credentials (university training in law, state examination, bureaucratic internship) to serve as *Bezirksamtmann*s and staff administrators. By the time an independent Colonial Office was formed in 1907 and an era of colonial reform begun under Bernhard Dernburg, some of these men had reached high positions, including colonial governorships (Wilhelm Solf, for example, in Samoa). But until 1910, colonial administrators were officially contract employees, not civil servants with transferable tenure.[26] The colonial civil service enjoyed little prestige among *Reich* departments. Nevertheless, it managed to recruit a corps of ambitious, well-educated young bourgeois men – some (like Solf) of considerable ability – who increasingly shaped the direction of official colonialism. The reform of the overseas empire that began in 1907 under Dernburg was essentially directed by trained and dedicated bureaucrats.[27]

Although the German civil service was not intellectually homogeneous, it certainly possessed a narrative mythic history and a theory that explained its role in German society.[28] The civil service was supposed to be the embodiment of rationality in government. In a changing world, a highly educated, impartial bureaucracy was the best agency for finding the appropriate mean among the conflicting forces that disturbed society. Early in its existence, the Prussian civil service had accepted a leading role in promoting material progress and industrialization – for the good of the state and society as a whole, not necessarily for the immediate best interests of businesspeople. This role remained a major part of the self-conceived mission of German civil servants in the nineteenth century. Specific intellectual images varied over time, according to philosophical fashions: at first Platonic guardians, then managers of the *Rechtstaat*, officials had developed a hint of scientific empiricism by the turn of the century. This was probably strongest in the colonial service. The better colonial officials, mostly trained in law, tended to develop semi-academic specialities in ethnography, linguistics, or the study of indigenous and colonial law, in part as a way of enhancing their standing as members of an educated elite and improving their career prospects. Heinrich Schnee, the last German governor of East Africa, did linguistic research. Zech, governor of Togo, was an amateur ethnographer. The Oriental Seminar of the University of Berlin encouraged this sort of activity, as did the Colonial Institute of Hamburg and the central colonial administration itself.[29]

Much that was distinctive about German colonial governments can be understood as manifestations of the civil service mentality. This mentality was partly at the root of the post-1900 tendency of German colonial administrations (except in Southwest Africa) to conceive of economic development as necessarily embedded in a comprehensive programme of socio-economic change focusing on indigenous peoples and building on their existing cultures. These peoples would be protected by the state against the more egregious forms of capitalist exploitation, and through a gradual (but not slow) process be turned into peasants, workers, voluntary subjects, and taxpayers of a German world empire.[30] That, at any rate, was the theory, fully in keeping with the self-conception of conscientious civil servants. Solf and Rechenberg, who were certainly practical and competent administrators, clearly believed that the theory was realizable, and they managed to convince Dernburg. Civil servants of this type aggressively rejected the view that they were agents of particular German interests. There was bound to be conflict between their aims and those of the interest groups. Planters in East Africa wanting railways that would support their own operations, concession companies in Cameroon seeking forced labour for rubber production, settlers in Southwest Africa planning to expropriate African land and cattle – all thought that the local authorities were duty bound to give highest priority to their demands. Officials, although they might agree to do so under pressure from Germany or (occasionally) out of conviction, generally did not accept this view. At the very least, organized African interests, especially when represented by hereditary chiefs (for example, in coastal East Africa) who fitted the model of native elites according to theories of indirect rule, were supposed to be factored into policy priorities. The history of Germany in Africa is marked by conflicts between European interests and the official administration, conflicts that can be explained partly on the basis of the peculiar outlook of the German colonial service.

## Notes

1. Woodruff D. Smith, *The German Colonial Empire*, Chapel Hill: University of North Carolina Press, 1978, p. 108.

2. For a more complete discussion of socio-cultural contexts in historical analysis, see Woodruff D. Smith, 'Complications of the Commonplace: Tea, Sugar, and Imperialism', *Journal of Interdisciplinary History*, vol., 23, no. 2 (1992), pp. 259–78.

3. Paul M. Kennedy, *The Rise of the Anglo-German Antagonism 1860–1914*, London: Allen & Unwin, 1980, pp. 103–23.

4. Entries in Solf's diary of his visit to South West Africa as Colonial Secretary in 1912, *Nachlaß* Wilhelm Solf, Bundesarchiv, Koblenz, 36/4, fol. 32–40; Paul Rohrbach, *Der deutsche Gedanke in der Welt*, Düsseldorf and Leipzig: Langewiesche, 1912, pp. 5–10.

5. Rohrbach, *Deutsche Gedanke*, pp. 45, 76–7.

6. Ernst Hasse, *Deutsche Politik: Das Deutsche Reich als Nationalstaat*, Munich: J.F. Lehmann, 1905, pp. 79–145.

7. For an example of this discourse, see attachment to *Deutsche Kolonialzeitung*, 26 April 1900, pp. 181–3.

8. See Emil Zimmermann, *Das deutsche Kaiserreich Mittelafrikas als Grundlage einer neuen deutschen Weltpolitik*, Berlin: Verlag der Europäischen Staats- und Wirtschaftszeitung, 1917.

9. T. Gunzert, *Native Communities and Native Participation in the Government of German East Africa*, mimeograph, Deutsche Gesellschaft für Eingeborenenkunde, n.d. – probably 1920s.

10. John Iliffe, *Tanganyika under German Rule, 1905–1912*, Cambridge: Cambridge University Press, 1969, pp. 119–23.

11. Gunzert, *Native Communities*, pp. 17–18.

12. Ernst Ludwig Radlauer, *Die lokale Selbstverwaltung der kolonialen Finanzen*, Breslau: Marcus, 1909, pp. 27–44.

13. Woodruff D. Smith, *The Ideological Origins of Nazi Imperialism*, New York: Oxford University Press, 1986, pp. 113–29; Rohrbach, *Deutsche Gedanke*, pp. 133–60.

14. See 1905 by Solf in *Nachlaß* Solf, 26/7, fol. 19–33.

15. Rohrbach, *Deutsche Gedanke*, pp. 133–60.

16. See *Nachlaß* Solf, 28/9, fol. 1–11 (correspondence on native and settlement policy), 1906.

17. See, for example, the debate on the 1914 colonial estimates in *Stenographische Berichte über die Verhandlungen des Reichstages*, vol. 294, pp. 7897–7953 (7–9 March 1914).

18. Hans-Ulrich Wehler, *Bismarck und der Imperialismus*, Cologne: Kiepenheuer & Witsch, 1969.

19. Roger Chickering, *We Men Who Feel Most German: A Cultural Study of the Pan-German League, 1886–1914*, Boston: Allen & Unwin, 1984, pp. 108–18, 213–52.

20. Smith, *Ideological Origins*, pp. 52–82.

21. Woodruff D. Smith, 'Julius Graf Zech auf Neuhofen (1868–1914)', in L.H. Gann and P. Duignan (eds.), *African Proconsuls. European Governors in Africa*, New York: Free Press, 1978, pp. 473–91.

22. Smith, *The German Colonial Empire*, pp. 9–12.

23. Smith, *Ideological Origins*, pp. 142–4.

24. Ibid., pp. 122–4, 127; *Deutsche Kolonialzeitung*, 15 January 1903, pp. 21–2.

25. Smith, *The German Colonial Empire*, pp. 45–7.

26. *Kolonialzeitung*, 30 April 1910, pp. 285–6.

27. Smith, *Ideological Origins*, pp. 124–9.

28. George Steinmetz, *Regulating the Social. The Welfare State and Local Politics in Imperial Germany*, Princeton: Princeton University Press, 1993, pp. 49–50, 104–6.

29. Woodruff D. Smith, *Politics and the Sciences of Culture in Germany, 1840–1920*, New York: Oxford University Press, 1991, pp. 168–71.

30. See W.H. Solf, *Kolonialpolitik. Mein politisches Vermächtnis*, Berlin: Hobbing, 1919.

# PART I

---

# Perceptions of Each Other

## HERMANN J. HIERY

Contact between the Melanesians of what is today Papua New Guinea and Europeans came relatively late, in most cases not before the late nineteenth or early twentieth century. This meant that anthropologists and ethnologists were among the first to be present when cultural contact actually took place. Thus these scientists were not only in a unique position to study 'traditional' societies at the beginning of contact with Europeans, but were themselves primarily responsible for the European image of indigenous societies. They also greatly shaped the perceptions that indigenous peoples had of Europeans. And finally, those considered to be experts on non-European behaviour had a considerable impact on the subsequent behaviour and development of those they came to study – a fact that has been widely neglected in the past. While they were initiating contact, they influenced its direction as well. They were not just witnesses of what happened, as most of them liked to see themselves; they were also actors. Sometimes their actions had dramatic and uncontrollable consequences.[1]

Markus Schindlbeck (Chapter 3) demonstrates the impact of ethnological collecting on the people living in the vicinity of the Sepik, New Guinea's largest river. The ethnologists' activities were so strong an element in the interaction with Europeans that by December 1912 the indigenous population had come to the conclusion that every white was a collector. Market mechanisms could be observed: not only did European demand raise the price of 'traditional' commodities, it also influenced what was produced. European perceptions increasingly defined what was 'traditional' Melanesian art. Both what Europeans desired and Melanesians could provide, and the things that Melanesians wanted and Europeans gave to them, stimulated change and thus profoundly transformed 'traditional' societies.

Cultural exchange was not limited to trade alone. Europeans and Melanesians alike had other objectives in mind as well. While Europeans meant to use their goods in attracting a Melanesian workforce to their plantations, Melanesians hoped to manipulate the indigenous perception of Europeans to their own advantage: the image of the European and his goods was intended to lure traditional enemies into a trap where they would finally be overpowered by their Melanesian foes with advanced European technology at their disposal.

Schindlbeck shows that indigenous behaviour in offering artefacts to foreigners as trade followed established patterns. Relationships were based on and evolved around exchange. The fact that Europeans obviously followed similar lines of behaviour reinforced the view that, despite their external differences, they were related beings. One of the mysteries for Europeans has been the local readiness to part with human skulls. While in most cases it is not clear whether they were ancestor or enemy skulls, Schindlbeck believes that ancestor skulls were certainly among those offered for 'trade'. The evidence he gives might throw some light on this riddle. A widespread belief among Melanesians that the white man was connected with the afterlife made ethnologists local addressees for questions concerning the destiny of dead relatives. To many indigenous people, it must have looked as if the remains of the dead were only being taken to their proper place – and by people who were closely associated with such places. The eagerness of Europeans to acquire skulls might even have strengthened common perceptions that associated them with the Melanesian afterlife.

Collecting was an important element in the interaction between Pacific Islanders and Europeans elsewhere in the Pacific. One of the earliest and most widespread trade items was tattooed Maori heads. Fierce tattooed Maori became a standard feature of early European images of the Pacific. In his fascinating study, James Belich (Chapter 4) shows how quickly these earlier perceptions were supplanted by more idealized perceptions. While Europeans in New Zealand continued to differentiate strongly between the largely Anglo-Saxon European settler community and the Maori, new stereotypes emerged that made earlier negative connotations fade. Maori came to be seen as still savages, but 'white' savages; natives that were as close to Europeans as natives could ever become. Maori were considered to be superior to all other non-European natives. This special view included the notion of the 'Aryan' Maori, a belief which centred around the idea that Maori and European had the same 'Aryan' ancestors.

The heroization of the Maori contributed to the greatness of the British Empire, and the special place New Zealand held in this empire. It is a curious coincidence that Germans harboured similar views about 'their' Polynesians.[2] Belich points out that this attempt to include the Maori in a colonial ideology was not a one-sided affair. While a common feeling of being 'Maori' only developed as an antithesis to a colonial Anglo-Saxon identity, Maori participated and added to this perception. They saw their new image as giving them a chance to gain a foothold in hitherto exclusively European circles, to cushion the effects of European impact, and thus to have more influence on their own future. And indeed, colonial New Zealand was early in acknowledging the right of the indigenous people to have a say in politics: Maori had access to legislation and politics from 1867 (a century before Australian Aborigines were accepted as citizens), and were able to hold executive powers a decade or so later.

Similar rights and influence were long denied to the Samoans by New Zealand as a mandatory power. Yet in the eyes of the occasional European visitor, the effects of European colonial impact seem to have been smallest on Samoa. From the outside it looks as if the local traditions of all the Polynesian cultures survived most strongly here, where so many 'great' nations competed for influence; and *fa'aSamoa* – the way in which Samoans think, feel and behave – has become something of a trademark in the Pacific. Generally respected as a special Samoan claim to be different, the implied demand that all others – whether Islanders or Europeans – should honour and respect this precept has acquired strong political connotations. And though it is now frequently seen as a specific form of Samoan political correctness that attempts to sweep Samoan inadequacies under the carpet and keep potential non-

Samoan competitors away, there can be no doubt that every Samoan who pleads this cause has immediately gained an edge in any argument with a foreigner.

Samoan pride survives to much the same extent as Samoan customs, so that for many it forms an essential part of *fa'aSamoa*. Seemingly untarnished by a colonial past and a variety of colonial rulers, it has been denounced by less amiable observers as downright arrogance.[3] But in the past, legions of non-Samoans have arrogated to themselves the right to speak for Samoa. Many reduced the Samoans to mere witnesses to the author's allegations.[4] It is therefore commendable that Peter Hempenstall here (Chapter 5) retrieves Samoan sources as 'an attempt to overcome the colonialist imagination'. As far as historians have been aware, few Pacific Islanders have left written statements about the colonial past. One famous exception is the Micronesian Luelen Bernart.[5] His view of Ponapean history gave rise to a prolific debate among historians.[6]

Hempenstall may be right in suggesting that more indigenous testimonies and papers exist than most historians have assumed. But the mere existence of records is not sufficient; they have to be made available. Hempenstall does this by presenting two authors and two texts. Both Te'o Tuvale and I'iga Pisa were witnesses of the German and New Zealand colonial administration. Te'o Tuvale's 'Notes on Samoan History' was written on the instructions of the New Zealand Military Administrator, Colonel Robert Logan. This does not necessarily mean that his history is merely a Samoan rubber-stamp on that colonial past. Yet Hempenstall is right to point out that these indigenous texts reflect the perceptions of particular groups whose views must be taken into account, first *ipso facto* and second because they shed additional light on a past that can never be seen as monochromatic. But they certainly do not represent the exclusive Samoan view in contrast to a European one. Hence it would be inappropriate to argue that as 'indigenous' sources they are somehow closer to historical 'truth'. Hempenstall's careful attempt to unveil two unknown Samoan histories should not be seen as a green light to those who act as if indigenous perceptions were the only histories in the world. To play indigenous historiography off against European historiography would be academic dishonesty. It was therefore already opposed some time ago.[7]

Indigenous sources and European sources each portray an important side of a history that has many faces and values. I'iga Pisa is a case in point. As Hempenstall shows, he was involved in Lauati's[8] attempt to conspire against Solf's policies to undermine the role of the traditional speakers. The conspirators were exiled to Saipan and the Samoan chiefs there were regarded as political prisoners – this is not only Samoan perception but was the German 'official' view as well.[9] Three members of the group, I'iga Pisa among them, were officially pardoned by Solf, at that time the Colonial Secretary, in mid-March 1914. But because of the outbreak of the European War, the decision could not be implemented.[10] When the flood of war reached the Pacific, and the Japanese occupied German Micronesia, I'iga Pisa distanced himself from the others who rushed to return to Samoa. It seems that he deliberately wanted to await the outcome of the war, before making crucial decisions that would have not only personal but also political implications.[11] Having returned to Samoa after the war, I'iga Pisa was the only surviving *matai* of those originally exiled to Saipan. All the other chiefs had perished in the great *faama'i*, the influenza epidemic of 1918. Lauati himself had not even been able to turn back to his island, dying of dysentery *en route* in Tarawa. Was this the hand of God, as some Samoans were quick to claim? Be that as it may, there certainly was a hint of magic about I'iga Pisa.

To a European it looks as if I'iga Pisa had learnt one lesson from his previous experience: never to question the authority of the colonial government in power. It was thus only natural that he became an employee of the New Zealand administration and a steadfast supporter of this government in its deepest crisis during the *mau* in the 1920s. I'iga Pisa's history, therefore, was influenced not only by his adherence to a special social class and lineage; it was deeply shaped by his own personal experiences and, above all, by his desire to justify his own past behaviour and defend the social status he had acquired. This is not to depreciate his story, but to put it into a perspective that includes his own behaviour and experience.

There can be no doubt that the way in which different peoples view their genesis, existence and physical end is greatly influenced by contact with other peoples who have different conceptions of these questions. How much impact European forms of Christianity had on Pacific Islanders is as much a matter of dispute as the influence Pacific Islanders exercised while adopting Christianity.[12] The religious behaviour of the Samoans in particular has perplexed many observers. While some argue that traditional Samoa was corrupted under the impact of Christianity, and that Samoa's social and political structures crumbled as it suffered from ideological confusion (and in consequence easily fell prey to European powers), others have noted that Christianity was so closely entangled in *fa'aSamoa* that there was little left that a European would recognize as Christian.

In a fascinating study, Thomas Bargatzky (Chapter 6) identifies the *matai* performing the kava ceremony as the real, original priesthood of traditional Samoa. The obvious resemblance of this traditional ceremony to the Christian Eucharist prepared the way for a synthesis between Christianity and *fa'aSamoa*, whereby the ancient political and social structures could be retained and in principle allowed to function as they had done before. Similarly, in Micronesia, the strange fact which Arthur Knoll reports, namely that some islander converts outdid the American congregationalists in their attempts to impose Puritan behaviour, might be explained in terms of one traditional set of strict behavioural rules replacing another.

Europeans at the time simply did not perceive this. While they saw a predominantly libertinarian attitude towards all matters of daily life, especially sexuality, they failed to recognize the significance of taboos in these societies. Food taboos, for instance, could readily be given up because new taboos were already waiting to become incorporated into the new old life. And, as it had been in the past, the observation of these taboos quite naturally became necessary to receive the advantages of the new order. The difficulties of observing the rituals of, for example, a Puritan Sunday, were a *conditio sine qua non* for the new religion to thrive, and the exclusivity this observance could confer upon certain followers who wielded power and authority further guaranteed its acceptance.

That this new order was indeed never really a new order of things was grasped by most Europeans. Yet they failed to see what was really the *Pudel's Kern* of the matter. What Pacific Islanders perceived of Christianity was not necessarily congruent with traditional Western European perceptions. Pacific Islanders had become Christians, not Europeans.

# Notes

1. On the Micronesian island of Tobi an epidemic broke out in October 1911 which eventually killed almost 40 per cent of the total population. The cold from which a member of the Hamburger Südsee Expedition was suffering was directly responsible for these deaths. The ethnologists had earlier visited the island to study the 'traditional' behaviour of its people. Hermann Joseph Hiery, *Das Deutsche Reich in der Südsee (1900–1921). Eine Annäherung an die Erfahrungen verschiedener Kulturen*, Göttingen: Vandenhoeck & Ruprecht, 1995, p. 170.

2. See ibid., pp. 28–9 and 32. Samoans were considered to be the 'Germans' of the South Seas.

3. But the disparaging remarks by Paul Theroux (*The Happy Isles of Oceania: Paddling the Pacific*, London: Hamish Hamilton, 1992, pp. 322–62) are disqualified by the attitude of an author who vividly displays his own arrogance.

4. Typical for this attitude is the Mead–Freeman debate.

5. *The Book of Luelen*, edited by John L. Fischer, Saul H. Riesenberg and Marjorie G. Whiting, Canberra: Australian National University Press, 1977.

6. See David Hanlon, 'The Path Back to Pohnsakar: Luelen Bernart, his Book and the Practice of History on Pohnpei', *Isla* 1 (1992), pp. 13–36; and Rufino Mauricio, 'A History of Pohnpei History or *Poadoapoad*: Description and Explanation of Recorded Oral Traditions', in Donald H. Rubinstein (ed.), *Pacific History. Papers from the 8th Pacific History Association Conference*, Guam, 1992, pp. 351–80. See also my comments in *Das Deutsche Reich in der Südsee*, pp. 317–18.

7. 'I am not an adherent of the view, commonly expressed nowadays by some expatriates and by some of my fellow Pacific islanders, that outsiders can never fully understand our cultures. I believe it is possible for an outsider with ability, inclination, and time to gain a very full understanding of how islanders think and feel. It does, however, require a very real effort to rid oneself of preconceptions and prejudice. The islander faces a different problem: he must detach himself sufficiently from his own culture to see it objectively.' Sione Lātūkefu, 'Conclusion: Retrospect and Prospect', in James A. Boutilier, Daniel T. Hughes and Sharon W. Tiffany (eds.), *Mission, Church, and Sect in Oceania*, New York, 1978, p. 463.

8. While 'Lauaki' is currently the prevalent form of pronunciation among most Samoans, and has been made 'historically correct' since Davidson, I prefer the original spelling. At the time, the pronunciation 'Lauaki' (and even more so, the spelling) was considered anathema by linguists and anthropologists alike. Moreover, the sound change from the *t* into the *k* is quite recent. The Reverend George Brown, a Pacific missionary of standing, considered it to be of European influence as the traders

were the first heard using it. Even in June 1915 no tulafale speaking at a fono would use the *k* pronunciation. Whether it had been already in use ten years earlier is even more doubtful. As Lauati is generally seen as the best tulafale Samoa had in colonial times, it seems quite clear that he himself would have preferred the accepted pronunciation of old. A convinced traditionalist, he most probably would have abhorred the spelling of his name the Davidson school inaugurated. At the time, using the *k* instead of the *t* was derogatorily called *O le nanu faa-Tutuila* (Tutuila jabber, or wrong speech). See Rev. George Brown, 'Remarks on Samoan Sound Changes', *MAN* 16 (1916), pp. 181–3. See also A.M. Hocart, 'A Samoan Sound Change', ibid., pp. 42–3.

9. *Das Deutsche Reich in der Südsee*, p. 296.

10. The relevant file is in BAP: RKolA Nr. 3067.

11. Hermann Hiery, 'West Samoans between Germany and New Zealand 1914–1921', *War & Society* 10 (1992), pp. 53–80, esp. 58–9.

12. See Boutilier, Hughes and Tiffany (eds.), *Mission, Church, and Sect in Oceania*, and in particular the contribution by Dorothy Ayers in that volume.

# 3

# The Art of the Head-Hunters: Collecting Activity and Recruitment in New Guinea at the Beginning of the Twentieth Century

## MARKUS SCHINDLBECK

At the beginning of this century artists such as Picasso, Nolde and Ernst discovered art in ethnographic pieces from Africa and Oceania. The resulting reorientation led to important changes in our own contemporary art. This was made possible by the extensive collecting activity of the end of the nineteenth and the beginning of the twentieth centuries. More and more exotic carvings, paintings and other pieces entered European and North American museums and private collections. There they served as sources of inspiration for modern artists.

One of the sources of these pieces of art was north-east New Guinea and the Bismarck Archipelago. The travelling collectors were looking for anthropological material and plant and animal specimens, but also for decorated pieces of art. Thus Pacific islanders were soon engaged in an episodic exchange relationship with Europeans. From the written evidence and the collections we can reconstruct what the Pacific Islanders offered to foreigners and what they hid from them. Through this selective process, people from the Sepik River and from other regions influenced what went into collections, and thus the image of themselves that Europeans, and later on North Americans, projected in their museums and publications.[1]

During the first years of contact, collecting activity was an important element in the interaction between Pacific islanders and

Europeans. It was largely dictated by the recruiting of labourers in certain areas of New Guinea. Sometimes the collectors themselves became recruiters. The objects offered in exchange for masks and other artefacts attracted men to plantation labour. As collecting formed a characteristic part of the activities of the first Europeans entering New Guinea, it also influenced the way in which Pacific islanders perceived these white foreigners.

Unfortunately, we have almost no contemporary statements by people from New Guinea about the collecting activities of Europeans. During my stays in Papua New Guinea from 1972 to 1974 and from 1979 to 1981, people asked me several times about the whereabouts of all the collected artefacts. We can only imagine how mysterious it must have been for them in 1910.

In an article in the journal of the Museum für Völkerkunde, Berlin, Felix von Luschan, at that time director of its African and Pacific Department, compares the discovery of artefacts from the Sepik area with that of antiquities from Benin in 1897.[2] Sepik artefacts were first appreciated and studied in 1908 and 1909. Curiously enough, the Sepik River had been discovered much earlier, in 1885, by Otto Finsch. The first European expedition up the river took place on 5–6 April on the ship *Samoa*.[3] They travelled only the lower part of the river, up to the village which was later known as Singrin. As far as interaction with natives of that area is concerned, we are informed that people came on board to sell weapons and ornaments, but mainly eels. They were persuaded to come near the ship by the offer of red cloth, glass beads and similar things. Schellong, who participated in that trip, mentions that they were able to buy the widely disseminated necklaces of dogs' teeth, and spear-throwers.

The first scientific expedition took place on the ship *Ottilie* under the direction of Landeshauptmann Freiherr von Schleinitz.[4] Schrader and Hollrung were the scientists on board. They travelled on the river from 20 July to 10 August 1886. Schrader mentions that the natives offered them spears decorated with a human vertebra, clay vessels, tobacco and other objects in exchange for clothes, bottles, beads and shells. They were even able to barter for human skulls.[5] In one village the natives killed a dog on their arrival as a sign of peace, and specially decorated spears were stuck point down into the ground.

The following year the Neu-Guinea-Compagnie organized

another expedition, which was in the Sepik region from 28 June to November 1887.[6] They built a station at Zenap and later another near the village of Malu. The first station was staffed by four Europeans, twelve Malays and four men from the Bismarck Archipelago. They also visited the village of Malu but relations with the natives turned out to be difficult.[7] On 7 November they left their camp and went downstream. They acquired a number of artefacts, some of which are today kept in the museum in Brunswick. As mentioned above, collectors did not return to the field until 1908. It is not quite clear why the Neu-Guinea-Compagnie did not send further expeditions into the Sepik area. They were probably disappointed by the results of the earlier expeditions.

One of the main reasons for the further exploration of the interior of New Guinea was the need for labour: 'After Hahl's ascent of the Sepik River in 1908, a naval commander commented: "For the Governor the first consideration in the further opening of the river basin is whether natives from there can be recruited as manpower".'[8]

One of these recruiting ships also carried George Dorsey from the Museum in Chicago. He went with Heine, the administrator of the Neu-Guinea-Compagnie. They stayed on the lower Sepik River for only a few days in 1908. While the captain and Heine tried to recruit labourers, Dorsey collected from seven different villages. In an article for the *Chicago Tribune* he wrote that they

> anchored in the middle of the river in front of the village of Olim, where the captain and Mr Heine went ashore to get boys. They returned in a half hour empty handed. In the meantime I had a busy half hour on the *Siar*, trading with the men who had come out in their long, fine canoes. They were keen for knives and small axes, and I got some wonderfully beautiful feathered spears.[9]

The next stop was near the village of Magem:[10]

> Evidently they were prepared for us, for within ten minutes after we anchored, our boat was fairly surrounded by canoes with men eager to trade feathered spears, carvings, pottery etc. for knives. But I was not allowed to trade for fear it would interfere with recruiting. Mr Heine and I at once went ashore to see if we could buy a boy [...  and] were at once presented with a leaf of tobacco and a beautifully feathered spear and were besought to trade for all sorts of things which we declined. Finally the excited crowd grew quiet and we sat down on a

large upturned canoe and in pidgin English talked to a lad from the coast who put our words into the language of our 'pilot' who in turn told the people why a boat had ascended the river for the first time in twenty years. [...] While Mr Heine spread his wares and eloquency for a boy, I looked about the village. [...] Everybody stared at us, for to the majority of these people [...] we were the first whites they had ever seen [...] our visit was not understood and they were afraid of us.

Dorsey was permitted to enter Tambaran houses.[11] But the recruiting drive was unsuccessful, and Dorsey could not buy anything: 'Heine objected, fearing I would spoil the chance to get boys, that if they got iron they would be satisfied.' During the afternoon they went again to the village, but no boys could be taken and Dorsey was finally allowed to barter: 'the busiest thirty minutes I ever spent in my life, though I have done some strenuous collecting in the last seven weeks. During this time I made eighty-six individual purchases, my most prized possessions being several wonderfully decorated and carved skulls.'

Dorsey mentions three grades of acculturation in the areas of mainland New Guinea known at that time: (1) In Potsdamhafen the people were well supplied with beads, knives and axes. They had to pay taxes, so they asked for money. (2) Down the Sepik River they had a few knives and axes, so that they were ready for beads and calico. (3) The Magem people were different: 'they have had just enough experience of steel knives and axes to know the superiority of such tools [...] they wanted steel and wanted it badly, especially small axes. Their contempt for beads, fish hooks, fish lines, looking glasses, and especially calico was simply superb.' Downriver Dorsey had another chance: 'in ten minutes I got over forty interesting specimens, including two carved drums and many beautiful head-dresses of birds of paradise.' Then they put ashore their two pilots, who were now dressed in white cotton suits, with several blue bead necklaces and an axe each.

What is astonishing is the readiness of the indigenous people to give things away, including skulls. In a letter that Heine wrote to the director of the museum in Berlin, he mentions that Dorsey collected more than one thousand pieces. The following year Heine went upstream again on the *Siar*, with the German collector Richard Neuhauss. During this trip Heine himself collected some pieces. Neuhauss collected about 150 pieces.

By this time several ships had gone upriver, but I do not have access to records for all of them.[12] From 18 to 22 November 1909, the German warship *Cormoran* carrying Albert Hahl, the Governor, travelled 183 nautical miles upriver. They were able to barter with five large villages. The trade goods most commonly asked for were axes and unworked iron, but not beads and the like.[13]

When the Hamburger Südsee Expedition[14] travelled along the Sepik River in 1909, they found that people were asking high prices on the Lower Sepik, and this was explained by Dorsey's trading. Even in the village of Muangem (Magem), people were by now well equipped with iron. The expedition travelled further upstream. In Kambrinum there was a great welcome for them: they were greeted with loud shouting, the sounds of the wooden trumpets and slit gongs. People freely offered skulls. A special ceremony was held when one of the whites first set foot on land. A man spat coconut milk over him. In Mandanam the most popular goods were mirrors, fish hooks, cotton, beads, arm rings and knives, followed by axes and large knives. In contrast to later practice, during these first encounters women and children were present among the crowds offering artefacts. Along the middle Sepik, in Timbunke, iron was already known. People asked for unworked iron. Many artefacts including clay pots and stone axes were exchanged for mirrors, nails and bottles. But the situation could also change suddenly. The next day the Europeans were no longer welcome. Attempts were made to prevent them from landing and bridges were pulled down. Only by showing off their military power by shooting at a coconut palm were the Europeans able to clear a path to enable them to enter a ceremonial house. But even then the men from Timbunke tried to take away some masks into the nearby bush. This expedition spent only fourteen days on the river. During this time nine hundred ethnographic artefacts were collected.

In 1910, A.B. Lewis from the Chicago museum travelled on the Sepik for seven days, again on the same ship as Dorsey, the *Siar*. Lewis had similar problems to Dorsey when it came to collecting, because the German captain feared that it might disrupt the recruiting. In a letter he wrote:

> The captain was trying to get native labourers, and on the way up would not allow me to buy anything, but on the way down he concluded to buy himself, and gave me permission to do likewise. I got

nearly 300 specimens on the river altogether many of them very interesting. The captain got about 2,000 but he made the whole crew work
for him, and I had only my two native boys.[15]

The captain had little success with recruiting while they
anchored off Bin at the mouth of the river. Lewis had to wait

while they (the first and the second mates) tried to get men through a
young man who had been taken to Friedrich Wilhelmshafen the year
before. He was not a labourer, and had been treated as a guest, and
many things were given to him including a suit of white duck and cap.
He had a chest, and bag of old beer bottles. No labourers volunteered,
however. The boy was to go with us up the river and translate, but
after returning to ship, he slipped away back to village in a native
canoe.

In the next village (Pagim), however, people brought him new
carvings. When they returned to the village on the way back, they
offered him 'great numbers of freshly modelled heads and faces in
clay (nearly black). Some were well done.'[16]
The connection between collector and recruiter was even more
apparent during the next large-scale expedition in this area,
mounted by the Museum für Völkerkunde of Berlin. This expedition was also financed by the German Government, the Reichskolonialamt and the Deutsche Kolonialgesellschaft. One of its aims
was to open up new territory for the recruitment of labourers.[17]
The main part of the expedition stayed on the river from February
1912 to September 1913. It consisted of six scientists, the crew of
the ship, fifty native soldiers and 120 carriers as part of the group.
Among the anthropologists was Adolf Roesicke, who did most of
the collecting work, although other members of the expedition,
such as the geographer Behrmann and the well-known anthropologist Thurnwald, also collected.[18] During this expedition, 5,800
ethnographic pieces were assembled. Roesicke gives a great deal of
detail about how he acquired the specimens in the collection.[19]
As soon as the ship *Komet* entered the Sepik on 28 February
1912, natives clothed in white European suits paddled towards the
ship in a canoe. In Kopar, the first village Roesicke visited, some
people spoke Pidgin, a sign that contact with Europeans had already been established. Mommsen, who was in command of the
ship *Condor*, visited the village of Timbunke with Roesicke in
December 1912. In a report he mentioned that the natives had

gained the impression that every white was a collector. As soon as members of the expedition went ashore, people were waiting to exchange artefacts. An axe or iron was given for many pieces. They assembled in the men's house and offered masks, weapons, cassowary daggers, clay pots and stone axes.

Roesicke had most contact with native people in the village of Malu near the expedition's main camp. At first they came to the main camp with their canoes. Even on the day when the expedition landed to build the camp, the *Komet* was surrounded by boats carrying about 70 people. They all offered carvings. On 10 March a boat arrived with 32 men and boys. They brought fish arranged on rattan, coconuts, betel and some artefacts. They were very shy and landed with the stern of the canoe towards the *Komet* so that Roesicke could exchange only with the first man in the boat. At the end of the transaction, the Malu people threw some smaller pieces towards the whites. Roesicke thought they were intended as gifts. The people also made a strange gesture, which he did not understand, touching their navels and noses with their hands. This gesture may have indicated friendship and common descent. Along the middle Sepik the navel is a symbol of unity and friendship. When the Malu people left, they wiggled their knees while standing in the front and the back of the boat. I would interpret this as a kind of Naven ceremony. Exchange between Malu men and whites had happened for the first time, and so had to be marked by ceremonial behaviour.[20]

From the first weeks, there was bartering between the camp and people from Malu. On 1 April, Roesicke visited the village of Malu for the first time. But the Malu people disliked the Melanesian policemen accompanying Roesicke, and finally these had to remain on the boats. Exchange took place in a special house. Roesicke gave fish hooks for stone axes, and iron blades in exchange for hand drums. But the whites could not move around the village and they were not allowed to enter the dwelling houses. Malu people blocked the path with spears, saying 'mai', which means 'go!'

After spending a year in the area, Roesicke made one of the few comments to throw some light on the Sepik people's perception of the Europeans. In the village of Yensemangwa, which is a Iatmul village of the Middle Sepik, he noted on 29 May 1913:

There was an interesting conversation. They asked for the name of my father, my children and my mother and were astonished to hear that all have the same name. Then they asked whether I had seen their dead. They brought me some skulls and explained to me that this is what always remains, but where do the people go? Do they go into the ground or up to heaven? They asked whether I had seen them in Madang, or at my place. The Malu people had told (the Yenshemangwa) that I am a child of the sun. And they asked me if the sun is where I come from.[21]

The people of the Middle Sepik area have a dualistic social system. Their clans are grouped into two moieties, the mother moiety and the sun moiety. In the mythology, the sun moiety is often associated with cultural achievements, whereas the mother moiety is the origin of basic substances like earth and human beings. According to Middle Sepik mythology the white people separated from New Guineans just as the younger brother separated from the older brother or the sun from the earth. Even today, therefore, white people are often classified as members of the sun moiety. The conversation recorded by Roesicke shows us how people tried to understand his social position. The knowledge about the land of the dead attributed to Roesicke is also part of the indigenous explanation of the European social order.

In 1912 and 1913, a number of recruiting ships arrived. Roesicke tried to persuade some people from the village of Malu to go to Madang. Finally, on 22 January 1913, he was successful, and left Malu with nine men. They told him about a plan of their own. Roesicke was to use trade goods to attract some canoes from Bandai (an Iatmul village), which the Malu people would then shoot with their spears standing on the German ship. When they reached the open sea they asked Roesicke whether the same water would inundate the villages of Malu and Ambunti. On 25 January they arrived at Friedrich-Wilhelmshafen. The Malu people stayed in the barracks. On 27 January there was a big sing-sing (celebration) in the city. Roesicke bought a pig for the Malu people and they also received some big knives. They were shown the room with weapons and were very impressed. In this room they saw a picture of the Kaiser, which one of the Malu men recognized. The sing-sing was to celebrate the Kaiser's birthday. Over the following days, Roesicke introduced the Malu people to the plantations. On 1 February Roesicke noted that the Malu people were homesick and that they were weeping. They crawled under his legs and promised him that they would send their children from Malu to the plantations if only they could get home. Two days later they left.

When they reached Iatmul area in Timbunke, the Malu people started trading the exchange goods that they had acquired in Madang for necklaces and armlets. In the village of Kararau they exchanged again. This time they bought flat clay pots and rain capes for their women. In Yensemangwa they traded again for clay pots as the ones from Kararau had got broken. Before they left, Roesicke had given them gifts: one axe, one mirror, one little knife, and one *laplap* or loin cloth each. Before presenting these things he had given them a talk: he encouraged them to send their children to work, as they had seen that they were treated well. When they reached Malu they were greeted with cries of 'Kubujaai'.[22] People in the canoes started dancing and moving the canoes; bow and stern splashed on the water. They brought the goods on land: a pig, pots, rain capes, sago and yam, and many trade goods. In the meeting house young boys imitated adults and danced, striking the slit gongs and wooden trumpets. Women talked about how they had wept over their sons and brothers. The Malu people were telling stories about what they had seen.

This episode makes clear that the members of the expedition were involved in preparations for future recruiting. Thurnwald, who stayed in the area longer than Roesicke, wrote that the *Bezirksamtmann* of Friedrich Wilhelmshafen, having obtained the ship *Kolonialgesellschaft* from the expedition, travelled up the river to recruit people by force.[23]

Collecting was one of the economic transactions between the natives and the Europeans. This exchange relation between collector and natives must be seen in the context of the economy of the culture. It was therefore highly variable. Claims that collecting was impossible because people did not offer anything reveal the economic background of this relationship. Roesicke mentions that in such cases people did not want the things that Europeans offered them.

The importance of this interaction between collector and the group visited is also clearly demonstrated by Michael O'Hanlon's comments about his recent work in the Highlands: 'I did not find myself a free agent; assembling a collection according to my own whim. I discovered that my collecting was constrained by local processes and rules, with the upshot that the collection I made partly mirrored in its own structure local social organisation.'[24] During my own collecting activity in the Sepik area I observed similar phenomena. The structure of clan organization and of age-groups was reflected in the availability of objects given away to foreigners. The weakening or disappearance of certain social phenomena such as age-groups made it difficult to obtain specific objects. Local rules were also extended to the collector. When I assembled material of the male initiation I had to build a special house to store it, as otherwise the 'power' of these objects would have harmed my house guests and informants.

If we consider the activities of people offering artefacts to Europeans, we must recognize that they were trying to establish a relationship with the white people. Their behaviour followed traditional patterns. Village people always had a specific relationship with their neighbours, who were either enemies or trading partners. To offer artefacts was part of that traditional behaviour. During my own fieldwork in the Sepik area in 1972, I recorded a myth about the establishment of a market exchange relation between two groups of villages. When the ancestors met they exchanged certain objects which are today kept in the villages, and are regarded as symbols marking the foundation of this exchange relationship.

As soon as the ethnographic objects were given away, they were 'historically refigured'.[25] The objects became commodities. They were given new meanings by the Europeans, who used them for their own projections. 'To a large extent, the movement of all these articles from indigenous to European exchange circuits was a movement of commoditization.'[26] The process of commoditization further underlined the fact that artefacts were collected in the same way as plantation labourers. The statements reported above make it clear that at this time the same people did the collecting and the recruiting. Beads and iron were given away for masks and for men.

Analysing these instances of interaction between Europeans and New Guinea people from the period of first contact, we recognize that on the one hand Europeans were integrated into a trade system which was already known. People of the Sepik River always traded with other groups. This trade also included artefacts such as pottery or paddles. Thus the trade with pots, masks or other items was nothing new. As we have seen, this trade was also accompanied by ritual behaviour. On the other hand, another aspect seems to have been involved because of the readiness to give away human skulls. Though we do not know if they were ancestor or enemy skulls, it is clear that in a number of cases ancestor skulls were given. Today people explain cases of illness or death in their villages in terms of these actions by their grandfathers who did not look after the bones of their ancestors.

I assume that the fact that Europeans accumulated such large quantities of artefacts reinforced the impression of some people in New Guinea that these whites were actually related to their own group, and that they had come back to their grandchildren to ask for necklaces, shells, flutes and masks. Certainly other factors supported this perception. In the Sepik area the Europeans came from the east. For people living in the Middle Sepik area the land of the dead is located in the east.

In traditional societies, imported material is given a special place and special treatment. Some of the New Guinea people certainly thought that Europeans used these masks and carvings in a ritual way comparable to their own. Looking at museum exhibitions with all the restrictions imposed on the visitors, people of the Sepik River might think in a similar way even today.

## Notes

1. See also my summary on the history of collecting activity in 'The Art of Collecting – Interactions between Collectors and the People they Visit', *Zeitschrift für Ethnologie* 118 (1993), pp. 57–68.

2. Felix von Luschan, 'Zur Ethnographie des Kaiserin-Augusta-Flusses', *Baessler-Archiv* 1 (1911), pp. 103–17.

3. See Otto Schellong, *Alte Dokumente aus der Südsee*, Königsberg, 1934, pp. 57–60.

4. *Nachrichten über Kaiser Wilhelms-Land und den Bismarck-Archipel*, vol. 2, no. 4 (1886), pp. 123–8.

5. Schleinitz and the scientists give no explanation for this readiness to give away human skulls. In other places collectors found it difficult to collect human bones. Finsch writes of the people of Blanche Bay in New Britain that if one villager gave away a skull, others would follow. They were secretly given to him packed in leaves. During his eight-month stay he sent 167 skulls to Virchow in Berlin (Otto Finsch, *Ethnologische Erfahrungen und Belegstücke aus der Südsee*, Vienna, 1893, p. 114). The readiness to part with human remains was certainly stimulated by the great

demand for skulls and bones among European anthropologists during that time.

6.  *Nachrichten über Kaiser Wilhelms-Land und den Bismarck-Archipel*, vol. 3, no. 5 (1887), pp. 189–92; vol. 4, no. 1 (1888), pp. 23–32.

7.  The report mentions obstruction and thieving by the people of Malu, which led to hostilities when the Malayans on the expedition were attacked with arrows. The Germans then used their firearms.

8.  Stewart Firth, 'The Transformation of the Labour Trade in German New Guinea, 1899–1914', *Journal of Pacific History* 11 (1976), p. 56. On the further development of the Sepik area Hahl writes: 'As the growing demand for plantation labour ruled out the possibility of abandoning the recruiting route up the river which had already been opened up, we were faced with the new and important task of winning over these magnificent stone age people as well as the vast river valley and its tributaries, working our way forward steadily without bloodshed.' Albert Hahl, *Governor in New Guinea*, edited and translated by Peter G. Sack and Dymphna Clark, Australian National University Press: Canberra, 1980, p. 127.

9.  George A. Dorsey, 'People of Guinea Marvel at Whites'/'Rich in Specimens Dorsey Returns', *Chicago Tribune*, 1909 (with kind permission of the Department of Anthropology Archives, Field Museum of Natural History, Chicago).

10.  Magem and all the other villages Dorsey visited are situated on the lower part of the Sepik River.

11.  Generally it was easier to enter the Tambaran or men's houses than the dwelling-houses.

12.  During November 1908 *Bezirksamtmann* Full travelled upstream on the ship *Roland*; see Hahl 1980, p. 126.

13.  There are different reports on this voyage: Freiherr v. Spiegel, *Meere, Inseln, Menschen* Berlin 1934, pp. 88–102; Pfarrius, S.M.S. Cormoran im Kaiserin-Augusta-Fluß, *Deutsches Kolonialblatt* (1910), pp. 236–8.

14.  F.E. Hellwig, 'Tagebuch der Expedition', in *Allgemeines. Ergebnisse der Südsee-Expedition 1908–1910*, Hamburg, 1927, pp. 160–75.

15.  Letter to Simms, Chicago, 7 September 1910. Archives of the Department of Anthropology, Field Museum of Natural History, Chicago.

16.  From the diary of A.B. Lewis, Joseph N. Field South Pacific Expedition 1909–13, Archives of the Department of Anthropology, Field Museum of Natural History, Chicago.

17.  The major aim of the expedition was to open up new territory in the colony, mainly along the hitherto unknown tributaries of the Sepik River.

18.  Little is known about Roesicke, as he died soon after the war in 1919. His notes and photographs were partly published by Behrmann. Roesicke was born in 1881 in Berlin. His father was director of a brewery in Berlin and a member of the German Reichstag from 1890 until 1903.

After finishing his studies in chemistry Roesicke went on a world trip, visiting Egypt, Sudan, Japan, China and Southeast Asia. Before he travelled to New Guinea he worked as a volunteer in the Museum für Völkerkunde in Berlin.

19. For the following see his diary, Archives of the Museum für Völkerkunde, Berlin.

20. See Gregory Bateson, *Naven*, London, 1936.

21. Roesicke diary, Archives of the Museum für Völkerkunde, Berlin.

22. *kubu* means rattan; I interpret this as an expression of common descent or common line (rattan).

23. Letter of 20 December 1913 to Hilde Schubert, who later became his wife; Archives of the Museum für Völkerkunde Berlin. Thurnwald writes: 'Der Bezirksamtmann von Friedrich-Wilhelmshafen, der jetzt die 'Kolonialgesellschaft' bekommen hat, hatte nichts eiligeres zu tun, als nun den Strom – glücklicherweise nur bis Malu – heraufzufahren und an allen Orten, wo er nicht gerade Fieber hatte oder morphiumkrank war (er ist nämlich starker Morphinist) anzuwerben und zwar, da er, den die Leute nicht kannten, keine Leute gutwillig bekam, gewaltsam, d.h. er holte die Leute durch Polizeisoldaten aus den Dörfern weg, ob sie sich sträubten oder nicht.'

24. Michael O'Hanlon, *Paradise. Portraying the New Guinea Highlands*, London, 1993, p. 55.

25. Nicholas Thomas, *Entangled Objects. Exchange, Material Culture, and Colonialism in the Pacific*, Cambridge, Mass., 1991, p. 125.

26. Ibid., p. 150.

# 4

# Myth, Race and Identity in New Zealand

## JAMES BELICH

I

This chapter is about aspects of the collective identity of two
peoples, Maori and Pakeha, the neo-Polynesians and neo-British of
New Zealand. It deals in the interactions of myth and history, of
race, tribe and nation, of Europe and the Pacific, and of Us and
Them. It does so in the conviction that New Zealand, an intersection between two cultures exceptionally prone to spawning re-
productions of themselves, is a good place to study such matters.
It is an exercise in the *social* history of ideas, rather than their
intellectual history. The latter can lapse into a kind of intellectual
granny-hunting, debating which ancestor to make eponymous: was
it Social Lamarckianism, Biological Spencerism, or Social Darwin-
ism? The former pursues the lower and wider role of ideas as lenses
on, and determinants of, history. This is a field in which testing is
difficult; the essay is speculative, and caution is invoked if not
delivered herein.

   A key assumption is that socialized (widely disseminated and
culturally valued) ideas can congeal into discernable knots or
currents, without deliberate artifice or conspiracy. 'Myth' is a
convenient label, though we should note that these are not merely
falsehoods to be debunked, nor texts to be deconstructed, but
important historical refractors and determinants. Modern myths
can be seen as fluid cultural motifs, shifting according to time and

context and layered so that acceptance of one element encourages, but does not absolutely require, acceptance of another. Each may derive cohesion through dissemination from a common source, but also from atheoretical thinkers with similar backgrounds making similar choices from sets of options limited by a shared conceptual language. There is an element of convergent evolution as well as of shared descent. Occupying a space between theories and attitudes, myths can draw on the former, but sometimes do so eclectically and inconsistently, knotting strategically contradictory theories together to provide tactical legitimation. So we find several works of mid-nineteenth-century New Zealand ethnography simultaneously using monogenist, polygenist and evolutionist racial theories.[1] Myths interact with theories 'above' and attitudes 'below', but can lead as well as be led by them.

I look first at Pakeha constructions of Us and Them in the nineteenth century; then at their Maori equivalents; and finally at the new ideology, which resolved tensions within and between the two, in the period 1880s–1920s, the hinge of modern New Zealand history. For brevity I use some problematic terms: Polynesian, native, race, Pakeha; collaborator, savage and tribe. Collaborator is not intended pejoratively; savage refers to European stereotypes not real people; and tribe is used to mean all large Maori kin-groups: tribes, sub-tribes, and closely related groups of both.

Europeans saw Pacific peoples through various lenses of pre-conception, and understanding racial optics is important for the study of contact. Between the benign yet distortive Noble Savage at one extreme, and folk ethnocentrism at the other, were three knots of race-related thought, centred around stereotypes of Black (permanently inferior), White (convertible), and Grey (dying) Savages. The Black Savage, linked to polygenist theory, asserted the fixity of racial characteristics; some upward movement for tribal peoples might be possible, but there was an irreducible core of difference and, usually, inferiority. This stereotype had more influence and persistence in New Zealand than some writers allow. The polygenist doctrine of the infertility of half-castes was often applied to Maori to the end of the nineteenth century; popular literature long alleged a Maori propensity to slough off the trappings of civilization and revert to barbarism at 'the call of the pah'. The contemporary myth of the 'Frozen Maori', whose traditions cannot change while remaining Maori, arguably has homologies with the Black Savage. But the other two stereotypes are more central to this story.

The Grey or Dying Savage originated with perceptions of Amerindian depopulation in the sixteenth century, and was applied by early European observers to the peoples of the Pacific from the late eighteenth. Softer variants saw native decline as reversible and regrettable, a consequence of imbibing the vices rather than the virtues of Europe.[2] Harder variants strengthened from the 1820s, and received apparent scientific legitimation from 1859. Organicist variants, in which peoples naturally flourished, aged and died like individuals, with or without European contact, were sometimes applied to Maori. 'By a law, the aboriginal Maori fades away before the white man, and was fading away, as if to make room for the new denizens, before even they appeared.'[3] But Dying Maori died mainly through the Fatal Impact of Europe. The kernel of truth in the myth of Fatal Impact was that Europeans, scarred veterans of pox and pestilence, survived their own diseases much better than did the epidemiological virgins of the Pacific. The kernel of myth in the truth was that, with differential immunity a mystery to them, Europeans sought metaphysical explanations of it, inexorable Laws of Nature or Providence. In New Zealand at least, this led to an exaggeration of native decline; empty villages were automatically attributed to the ravages of disease rather than a summer at the beach.[4]

The White, or Whitening, Savage stereotype, a product of monogenism, evangelism, humanitarianism and ethnocentric measurement, ranked peoples according to their perceived similarities to Europeans, and assumed that some were eager and able to ascend this ladder with suitable help, though in practice seldom to the topmost rungs. Peoples like the Australian aboriginals were never forgiven for their lack of interest in Europe; peoples like the Maori were congratulated for their interest. It was automatically taken to indicate that becoming as European-like as possible, as quickly as possible, was their heart's desire. Adaption was regularly mistaken for adoption, and in some European eyes Maori developed a reputation for being the most convertible of all savages, despite such peccadilloes as cannibalism.[5]

These stereotypes of natives implied obvious roles for the associated Europeans – heirs to the Dying, bleaching agents to the Whitening. But the interaction of conceptions of Us and Them went

further, through *archetyping* and *anti-typing*. Maori were sometimes
archetyped or idealized, as with the Noble Savage and some Whitening Savages. Unable to bear the notion of his Whitening Maori
eating rats, New Zealand historian and humanitarian Frederick
Moss described the Polynesian rat or *kiore* as 'a kind of small
rabbit'.[6] Natives were also anti-typed into living lessons on what
not to be, to act as polar opposite to a European archetype, often
very highly idealized. The European of contact literature is often
archetyped, not real. Archetyping was sometimes used deliberately,
to maintain what Europeans believed was a mystique of their own
superiority in native minds. The New Zealand Censor, commenting
on films suitable for Western Samoa in 1929, felt that: 'Even a
picture with the famous dog Rin Tin Tin would be questionable as
the dog frequently fights and overcomes the villain – a white man.'[7]
Maintenance of the European archetype was generally less deliberate. Definitions of European crime and madness may have tightened
in contact situations; levels of eccentricity or public debauchery
acceptable before whites were not acceptable before blacks. Racial
and social archetypes and anti-types interacted. Missionaries, for
example, divided natives into convertible or unconvertible; and
Europeans into agents of vice or virtue, Fatal Impact or Whitening.
Savages and salvages, savagers and salvagers, was the missionary
Us-ing and Them-ing matrix. Conceptions of Us and Them served
each other, and shifted in response to each other.

European conceptions of Maori from 1820 to 1920 can be seen
as a contest between White and Dying Savage myths, with the
Black Savage making sporadic forays from the background. Both
main stereotypes offered subordinating colonialism as their practical paradigm of ethnic relations, with and without long-term
futures for Maori. Between 1840 and 1860, the Whitening Savage
gained some ascendancy, helped by perceived Maori enthusiasm
for Christianity, commerce and civilization. Embryonic New
Zealand British collective identity incorporated the notion that
Pakeha were prime exponents of the alleged English genius for
native-handling. From the outset, European New Zealand-ness
consisted partly in having the best blacks and in treating them
best. Even in this period, however, the Dying Maori still acted to
cushion the ideologically subversive reality of Maori parity with
the settlers in war, economics and politics – Maori successes could
be dismissed as transitory. In the 1860s, large-scale conflict,

perceived Maori rejection of the things and thoughts of Europe, and evidence of population decline encouraged a resurgence of the Dying Maori, which dominated to the mid-1880s, and remained strong to the 1900s.

Maori no doubt stereotyped and misread Europeans too. The explorers' ships, floating villages populated solely by men, may have been taken for nomadic communities of homosexuals. Several early European visitors had their chests groped to establish if they were male or female, and were offered sexual hospitality in the form of boys.[8] Maori also conceptually lumped Europeans together and attached generic labels to them, notably the term *Pakeha* from 1814, and this mirrored back into the Pakeha self-image.[9] Despite the heavy Pakeha emphasis on Englishness and Britishness, 'European' was often their local self-designation, and still is, and this may also reflect Maori influence. Europe, *Uropi*, was easier to transliterate than England, *Ingarangi*. Confrontation with a Maori Them increased the Pakeha sense of Us, and combined with other factors to reduce the sense of regional and ethnic difference among Pakeha, especially in the North Island where Maori were numerous. The wars of the 1860s stimulated Us-ing and Them-ing, as wars often do, and weakened provincial governments in relation to the colonial one. Martial mythology distinguished old British from New Zealand British in ways flattering to the latter, foreshadowing the Anzac Legend.[10]

From the late 1830s to the early 1880s, propaganda designed to attract streams of British migrants and money portrayed New Zealand as a latent paradise, peculiarly destined to be brought to fruition by select British stock. New Zealand was to deliver progress without the price, paradise without the serpent, and Britain without the Irish, and prophecies of a great future abounded. Other neo-Britains, of course, used the same rhetoric, but the New Zealand addiction was extreme. 'The Britain of the South' and its variants was New Zealand's most common by-name in the nineteenth century, penetrating British as well as New Zealand conceptual language and mirroring back. Some propagandists believed, or pretended to, that New Zealand's future would exceed Britain's, playing Carthage when Britain Tyred. 'It is not enough to call New Zealand the Britain of the South ... New Zealand is much superior to Britain ... in predicting for it the most brilliant future we know ... that we are far, very far, below the inevitable truth.'[11]

The Pakeha population did explode from 500 to 500,000 in about forty years, and the economy grew to match, partly through sheep and gold, partly through its own growth. From the 1860s, conflict and confidence in the future reduced the desire and the need for the Whitening Savage; both nature and natives were inevitably to be swept aside in the inevitable march to a Greater British manifest destiny.

Nemesis struck between about 1885 and 1901. Stagnation eroded growth rates; it was the act of federation that shrank New Zealand to a quarter of its former size in local relativities; and economic, technological and cultural shifts tightened links with Britain against the grain of expectations about the progressive development of colonial nationalism. New Zealand was more subordinate to Britain in the first quarter of the twentieth century than in the third quarter of the nineteenth. My label for this many-faceted phenomenon is 'recolonization'. The subordination was largely voluntary; it was by no means supine; and it had important benefits for New Zealand. The shift can be seen as from an American model of the future, in which Britain is reproduced, even exceeded, with an expectation of ultimate independence; to a Scots model of permanently close but junior partnership, retaining some room for qualitative superiority in certain spheres. Greater Britain, emphasizing both quality and quantity, gave way to Better Britain, emphasizing quality alone.[12]

This transformation of Pakeha collective identity, 1880s-1920s, was effected through the refurbishing of older axioms and the addition of new ones, and many of both were race-related. They included renewed emphasis on a 'myth of better stock' – the notion that the first settlers were the cream of the British population; and a cult of climatic determinism, inverting modern attitudes to sun and wind, whereby New Zealand's temperate and bracing climate conduced to racial improvement.[13] Climatic determinism was a knot of thought where theories converged, and it was strengthened by the intersection. For environmentalist monogenists, cold could turn Adam white, and heat turn Australian settlers black, in a century or two. For polygenists and Anglo-Saxonists, temperate latitudes were the only proper home for the Anglo-Saxon racial type; either they or their testicles died in the tropics.

Newer racial reinforcements for Better British collective identity included a powerful ruralism, which insured against racial degeneracy; progressive social legislation and developments such as the Plunket Society, which ensured that more children would be Made Fit if not Born Fit; and substantial though sometimes ambiguous engagement with the international social purity and feminist movements, using at least the rhetoric of racial purity, racial improvement and racial destiny. Recolonization also demanded racial homogeneity, for the security of sameness, and so that Britain could constantly be told that blood was thicker than water, or at least thicker than French lamb or Danish butter. That New Zealand was '98 per cent British' was a common slogan of recolonization. The New Zealand government was careful to ensure that its military contribution in the First World War was proportionally greater than that of other dominions.[14] War, like sport, was alleged to demonstrate New Zealanders' sub-racial superiority, as well as racial loyalty, to old Britain. There were intriguing shifts in the usage of terms 'New Zealander', 'Briton', 'English', and 'Anglo-Saxon'. The game was to demonstrate New Zealand's indissoluble links with Britain, while at the same time giving New Zealand distinctiveness, even qualitative though not quantitative superiority. Racial myths were key cards. The game was not easy; it took forty years to win, and at the beginning of it, in the 1880s, Pakeha collective identity was in crisis. It is in this context that Pakeha intellectuals looked up, and saw the Maori passing by.

## II

Kinship was the conceptual language of Maori social organization, not necessarily the thing itself. Scholars in New Zealand and elsewhere warn of the dangers in assuming that lineage was inflexible, and of static and reductionist conceptions of the tribe.[15] It is useful to adapt Benedict Anderson[16] and distinguish between actual groups, which regularly lived or operated together, imagined groups, which might link several actual ones through a shared collective identity, and zones in which community could or could not be imagined. Traditional and post-contact evidence suggests that the conventional taxonomy of extended family, sub-tribe and tribe – *whanau*, *hapu* and *iwi* – does not accommodate the most common form of large actual group, which fell between, or even outside, tribe and sub-tribe. I have found it helpful to think in terms of three zones, looking out from the Maori village: a kin zone (one large heterogenous 'tribe' or a few closely related ones) in which grouping was relatively easy; a neighbour zone, to which your kin zone was connected by regular interaction or distant but active kin links, in which grouping was possible; and a stranger zone, with whom links were irregular, defunct or non-existent, and in which grouping was not conceivable.

This schema facilitates an attempt to explain the apparent capacity of Maori society rapidly to disseminate innovation, both before and after contact. Briefly, the process was driven by rivalry for mana or prestige between leaders and groups, encouraged by the fluidity of definitions of both. A crucial qualification is that this rivalry could be co-operative as well as competitive. It proceeded through successive *currencies* of rivalry: greenstone tools, large canoes, vast fishing nets, and pa fortifications before contact; iron tools, muskets, chapels and mills after it, as well as local partnerships with European individuals, stations and settlements. Rivalry mattered most, but was pursued least ruthlessly, within the kin zone; it mattered least, but was pursued most ruthlessly, in the stranger zone. Triumphs against strangers were mere means to the end of rivalry with kin and neighbours. This can explain such things as the failure of the great musket-wars general Hongi Hika to turn his conquests into empire, which mystified Europeans. His conquests in the stranger and even the neighbour zones mattered to him only in so far as they facilitated his ascendance in his kin zone. His onslaughts were merciless abroad, limited and almost ritualized at home.

Actual and imagined grouping was affected by rivalry, and was itself a currency of it. It made for fission as well as fusion, but it is the latter that interests me here. Regular sharing of a large resource – greenstone ground, *pa* (fort), or European settlement – by a group of groups encouraged them to institutionalize their co-operation, to imagine it as well as act it. This was especially so when the output of the resource – security in the case of a pa – was not easily divisible. Groups made pa; pa also made groups. Groups and chiefs who did best in the competition for successive currencies attracted more members and adherents. Group aggregation accelerated after contact. Fresh currencies of rivalry came thicker and faster; a more reliable economic surplus, derived from pigs and potatoes, funded an intensification of long-range interaction; and cheaper transport and participation in European interactive networks and communications infrastructures facilitated it. Some groups split up, loosened or disappeared; others tightened, merged or succeeded in imposing their names on whole kin zones, even neighbour zones. By the mid-nineteenth century, the whole of Maoridom was arguably a single neighbour zone; heterogenous, diverse and conflictual, but with most of its parts interacting positively or negatively, and perhaps with a vague sense of shared identity, even if only negative – a shared non-Europeanness.

New Zealand in 1769 was a monolingual world. To Maori, Europeans must instantly have constituted an order of strangeness greater than was the case with peoples who had experience of linguistic strangers, analogous to the arrival of aliens who communicated by sign language or telepathy. Collective names for the new Them came into use, as we have seen, as did Maori names for Us. The first known use of the term 'Maori' in its modern sense was in 1801, within ten years of the beginning of regular contact, and by the 1830s it was common in Maori mouths.[17] It was also quite common in European mouths, but here it competed with 'New Zealanders' for the next fifty years. Maori names for the whole country, which may not have existed at all before contact, also came into use.

Let me now oversimplify Maori strategies of grouping among themselves, and of managing interaction with Pakeha, into three pairs. All Maori both resisted and collaborated with Europe in various ways, but some emphasized one strategy more than the other in the shared aim of maintaining autonomy. Resisistance or collaboration could use two organizational shapes: tribal or pan-tribal. Pan-tribalism split in turn into two variants: *inter*-tribal movements (alliances or federations based on tribal building blocks); and *supra*-tribal movements, usually prophetic, which were to some extent subversive of tribalism, and sometimes of such things as traditional chieftainship as well. Resisters took the early lead in pan-tribalism with such inter-tribal organizations as the landholding and King Movements of the 1850s, and supra-tribal prophetic movements such as Kai Ngarara, Pai Marire and Ringatu in the 1850s and 1860s. Collaborators made the pan-tribal running subsequently, with the inter-tribal Kotahitanga and Young Maori movements of the 1880s and 1890s, and with the supra-tribal Ratana Church from 1918.

None of these organizations was pan-Maori in the sense that

they embraced the whole of Maoridom, but they were trans-Maori
– they knew no zonal boundaries – and for this even a vague sense
of pan-Maori identity was useful. Us-ing was encouraged by the
rise of Them. Pakeha first became a serious threat to Maori independence in 1845, and from the 1880s the balance of military,
political and economic power shifted decisively in their favour,
even in main Maoridom – the northern two-thirds of the North
Island. While the tribe remained the bedrock of Maori cultural
resilience, there was a definite, though by no means universal,
emergence of a sense of Maoriness from 1850. It was a response to
the European Them, but it was not European-led. Te Ua
Haumene, prophet of Pai Marire, instructed his lieutenants: 'Do
not be concerned for your own village. No, be concerned for the
whole land.'[18] Wiremu Tamehana, the 'Kingmaker', sought 'some
plan by which the Maori tribes should become united; that they
should assemble together and become one, like the Pakehas'.[19] The
adherents of Kai Ngarara in the 1850s saw it as a movement that
would 'combine all the race together, and become strong to have
their own way with the white people'.[20]

To the 1880s, resistance, actual or threatened, violent or non-
violent, was important in protecting autonomy, and it often took
pan-tribal shapes. Collaboration in this period usually took tribal
shapes. From the 1880s, armed resistance ceased to be viable.
Collaboration therefore held less value for Pakeha, and both strategies sought to protect autonomy and identity with greatly reduced
hands of cards. Groups from the resistance tradition tried disen-
gagement: negatively controlling, though by no means eliminating,
interaction with Pakeha. Collaborators now turned to pan-
tribalism, and used engagement, positively controlling interaction
by seeking a foothold in Pakeha political and ideological systems
and using it to lever up Maori status and material conditions.
They looked for something which would renew the value of
collaboration in Pakeha eyes. This strategy converged with an older
Maori policy of ethnic relations that had always competed with
the European paradigm of subordinating colonialism: marriage
alliance. When two unrelated Maori groups lived in long-term
proximity, they often attempted to institutionalize close and peaceful relations through intermarriage: first a few chiefly pairings;
then many lower-ranking ones. Shared offspring might be joined
by shared ancestors – a new emphasis on shared descent. Collective

identities were not necessarily fused by this process, but rendered linked yet distinct, twinning rather than merging. This strategy had outmatched the European paradigm until the late 1830s, and competed with it with some success until the 1860s, but was in urgent need of refurbishing by the late nineteenth century.

## III

From the mid-nineteenth century, with momentum increasing from the 1880s, Pakeha scholars moved into the field of Maori history. The key group was led by S. Percy Smith, and the whole process might be called Smithing – forging a picture of the Maori past for Pakeha ideological purposes. Components of the picture included the notion of the Moriori or Maruiwi: a blacker, inferior, more Melanesian, pre-Maori people, who were exterminated or absorbed by the superior Maori in ancient times. This alleged genocide, though later used for different purposes, was originally intended as a compliment. For the Social Darwinist Smithians, the Maori had triumphed in a struggle for existence and were the better for it. A second component was Io, a Jehovah-like supreme god whose alleged worship helped whiten Maori religion. A third was the Great Fleet, 'The Great New Zealand Myth', and its precursors, which gave Maori a heroic and European-like history of exploration and settlement. From the more recent past came a laundered legend of the New Zealand Wars, which emphasized the courage and Christian chivalry of Maori resisters over and above their effectiveness. The wars were portrayed as 'gentlemanly bouts of fisticuffs', with gloves on, after which the combatants kissed and made up.[21] But the key motif of the Smith version was the notion of The Aryan Maori.

In 1885, the Smithian Edward Tregear published a little book of this name. From crude philological and mythological comparisons, Tregear deduced that the Maori, like all Polynesians, were tanned Europeans, the forgotten wing of an ancient Indo-Aryan diaspora. Tregear's thesis met instant ridicule; he tried to withdraw the book; and recent posterity has tended to treat it as a joke, or at best an intellectual curiosity.[22] It was a joke, but the joke was on us, because it prevents us from seeing that *The Aryan Maori* became the symbolic bible of Maori–Pakeha relations. Ideas of a shared Indo-European Aryan origin date back to the mid-eighteenth century, and were proselytized by Max Müller in the mid-nineteenth, as Tregear acknowledged. He did not acknowledge that Polynesian Aryanism, or something close to it, had been postulated by a dozen earlier writers.[23] But the social history of ideas has its own Darwinian tendencies: the fittest ideas flourish, and fitness is defined by the social utility of the moment, not intellectual merit or originality.

For Pakeha, the Aryan Maori legitimated European colonialism in New Zealand as family reunion. Maori populated a runeless and ruinless land with a respectably lengthy, romantic and distinguishing, yet European-like, history. It overcame the Maori as an obstacle to the recolonial demand for racial homogeneity. 'Owing to his exceptional characteristics', announced a leading newspaper in 1901, 'the Maori interferes in no way with our national homogeneity. His position is... unique.'[24] Like the Great Fleet, it provided a shared or at least funnelled origin for Maori. At least in the abstract, it levered up Maori status in European eyes.

Acceptance of an Aryan origin for the Maori was never universal, and it was sometimes expressed cautiously or indirectly, but it was very widely and deeply spread. While Tregear's methods were criticized, writes his recent biographer, Kerry Howe, 'there was widespread acceptance of the notion of Aryan origins for Maoridom'.[25] Keith Sinclair confirmed that 'it was widely believed that the Maoris were a "branch of the Caucasian race".'[26] By the 1900s, there was 'a general consensus of opinion that the Maori ... are a Polynesian, that is originally an Aryan race'.[27] A 'revised edition' of A.H. Reed's immensely popular *Story of New Zealand* informed young readers as late as 1974 that Maori were descended from 'a people called Aryans', as was 'our own Anglo-Saxon race'.[28] Even Sherlock Holmes was on the job. On an 1890s visit, his creator, Conan Doyle, was delighted to find that New Zealand scholars had 'worked out the very fact that I had surmised, that the Maoris are practically of the same stock as Europeans'.[29]

Indirect acceptance of Maori Aryanism took the form of 'best blacks' if not 'white blacks'. In Egypt in 1915, New Zealand troops were offically warned that Egyptians were 'lower on the human scale' than the Maori, who were 'very different to the ordinary coloured race'.[30] In the 1920s, the populist tabloid *Truth* pulled no punches over 'noisome and noxious niggers' and almost choked on its own Sinophobia, yet was sympathetic towards some Maori grievances, and was seldom anti-Maori.[31] Better blacks were associated with New Zealand by the world – rather more, ironically, than Better Britons. Young British readers were informed that 'no finer coloured race exists in the world'.[32] Australians discovered in school textbooks that Maori were 'a far superior race to the Australian blacks', and in novels that they were 'the finest race of darkies in the world'.[33]

The Aryan Maori was the apotheosis of the Whitening Maori myth complex; yet it synthesized with its antithesis, the Dying Maori. The Smithian drive to collect and re-invent Maori tradition was hastened by the belief that Maori would soon die out, which Tregear himself accepted.[34] That Maori Aryanism was to be posthumous reduced its conceptual risks for Pakeha, and so facilitated its initial acceptance. The Aryan Maori was born and bred during the high tide of Fatal Impact thought, the last fifteen years of the nineteenth century. Now residual legatees of the Dying Maori by kinship as well as geographic succession, Pakeha groomed and Smithed their prospective estate with care. Following a bar or two behind the scholars, popular culture freely co-opted Maori symbols, initially with little sense of their having living owners. Pakeha hockey teams and children were given Maori names; Maori motifs featured large in public competitions to design national emblems – which had not been the case in the 1880s; 'kia ora' was advocated as a national greeting, even by Pakeha who disliked Maori; and 'Maorilanders' became a populist nickname for European New Zealanders. Pakeha musicians and artists in the decades around 1900 were fascinated by Maori subjects, as was the country's leading woman photographer. 'Her fascination with Maoridom led to her most disturbing image; a self-portrait with a moko painted on her chin.'[35] In the midst of this premature popular taking up of the inheritance, and the equally premature scholarly embalming process, the Maori Mummy woke up.

From about 1900, evidence that the Maori were not dying out after all strengthened, and from the 1910s it became difficult to deny. Pakeha had now to cope with an Aryan Maori present as well as a past. This did not sweep away denigratory racialism by any means. The indelibly different Black Savage still held some sway; a noble Maori past and an ignoble present could be reconciled through the mechanism of racial decline, with modern Maori seen as degenerate vestiges of noble forebears. Above all, full assimilation and cultural extinction could replace physical extinction. Many commentators looked forward to a time when Maori would exist only as a 'golden tinge' on the skins of their Pakeha cousins. But such assimilation required intermarriage, and implied at least in theory that the Maori were 'worthy' of it. While assimilation was formal policy to the 1960s, in practice Aryanism also generated potential levers for the maintenance of Maori identity. When superior natives, and the superior treatment of natives, were key ways in which you portrayed New Zealand to the world, and told the difference between Australian Britons and New Zealand ones, living proof was useful. Despite persistent racial prejudice and discrimination that varied regionally and according to other factors, New Zealand did deliver this proof. Maori had been guaranteed four seats in the colonial parliament in 1867, exactly a century before Australian aboriginals achieved full citizenship. There were Maori members of the Executive from the 1870s, and acting Prime Ministers from 1909. Conservative governments of the 1920s and 1930s, even in the midst of economic depression, were persuaded to pump hundreds of thousands of pounds into Maori rural development, and to make at least nominal reparation for unjust land dealings in the previous century.

Like its relative, Better Britonism, Maori Aryanism was symbolized in the Pakeha popular mind by war and sport. Pakeha celebrated the achievements of Maori battalions in both world wars. When a visiting South African rugby team complained in 1921 about having to play blacks, with 'spectacle of thousands of Europeans frantically cheering on band of coloured men to defeat own race' adding insult to injury, they received an indignant response from New Zealand Rugby officialdom – not a sub-culture noted for its enlightenment. The Maori 'should not be looked upon as nothing better than a kaffir'.[36] Maori battalions and Maori rugby, like Maori schools and Maori seats in Paliament, clearly contradicted the formal policy of assimilation, yet became accepted and even applauded by Pakeha. Rates of intermarriage require further research, but it can be shown that one category of mixed-bloods suddenly rocketed in the decade 1911–21, out of all proportion to increases in either Maori or Pakeha populations, and at a time when the surplus of Pakeha males was diminishing towards normalcy.[37] The social taboo against white man/black woman marriages, weak to the 1860s, weakened again from about 1900.

The taboo against white woman–black man matches, an inner sanctum of racial prejudice, remained quite strong, but seems to have been less strong than in comparable societies at this time.[38] New Zealand Aryanism did have benign effects. The superiority of New Zealand settler-native relations was real as well as mythical. I suggest that this was partly due to the strength of racial ideas, not their weakness.

New Zealand Aryanism played roles outside Maori origins. Trademarks of New Zealand consumer goods used swastika motifs from the 1910s to the 1930s, including a line of agricultural tools which superimposed the swastika over 'Kia Ora', until it was replaced in 1939 with the profile of a goat.[39] More significant is the possible role of Aryanism in New Zealand Sinophobia, which strengthened greatly in the 1880s – well after the gold rushes with which it is usually associated – and remained very strong to the 1930s.[40] New Zealand may have emphasized its few Chinese as antitypes to replace natives who could not be used as negative referents. Immigration policy in general was arguably more Aryanist than white. Aryanism had a flexible embrace, but median definitions included most northern and western Europeans, and excluded most southern and eastern ones. This definition very accurately describes New Zealand's preferred immigrants to the 1970s.[41] Aryanism also facilitated New Zealand's special need to accommodate its numerous Scots, and to Britonize its Irish. Celts were not Anglo-Saxons, but they were Aryans. Tregear's narrowest definition consisted of the Maori and 'his Norse and Celtic brothers'.[42] Indeed, the inventions of New Zealand and Scotland have intriguing analogies: Lowlander/Pakeha firmly linked to, yet clearly distinct from, England, using the cultural co-option of romantic and martial Highlander/Maori to facilitate the distinction without damaging the link.

But perhaps the most intriguing feature of New Zealand Aryanism is Maori participation in it. There had always been some Maori agency in the formation of European images of Them. The young, far-travelled Northland chief Ruatara, Samuel Marsden's co-adjutor in bringing Christianity and European agriculture to New Zealand, was the first personification of the Whitening Maori, a hero of missionary literature. A poem on his premature, noble, and semi-Christian death in 1816 won an undergraduate poetry prize at Cambridge in 1823.[43] There was an element of deliberation in Ruatara's contribution to the image of his people in the European mind, such as the implication that Maori worshipped a supreme god, and repeated assertions that they were prime prospects for conversion.[44] The legacy of Ruatara persisted. New Zealand's first professional historian, the Arawa scholar Te Rangikaheke, was paid by Governor Grey in the late 1840s to record Maori tradition. Apart from giving his own tribe precedence, Rangikaheke deliberately neatened legend into a form he rightly considered to be digestible for a Pakeha audience. Grey subsumed and further laundered the work under his own name in his *Polynesian Mythology*, but this magnified its effect.[45] Official sponsorship of Whitening representations of the Maori extended to Maori artists, scholars, and cultural groups, as well as to Pakeha image-makers.[46]

Key Maori contributors to the Aryan Maori myth and its allies were leaders of the Young Maori movement: James Carroll, Maui Pomare, Apirana Ngata and Peter Buck, all of whom became knights and cabinet ministers between the 1890s and the 1940s. In 1899, Carroll suggested that the teachings of the 1860s Maori scholar Te Matorohanga be edited and copied for preservation. They were eventually transmuted into the *Lore of the Whare-wananga* by Percy Smith, a core text of Smithianism. But before this they passed from pre-contact tradition through mediating Maori minds including those of Te Matorohanga, Te Whatahoro Jury, and a 1907 committee of Maori elders, also instigated by Carroll.[47] Ngata and Buck, the leading Maori intellectuals of their day, had scholarly doubts about aspects of the Smith and Carroll version. But at least in practice they accepted its main lines, and helped legitimate and proselytize them. Both explicitly endorsed the idea of an Aryan Polynesian origin, which also lurks behind the title of the renowned anthropologist Buck's popular book, *The Vikings of the Sunrise*.[48]

Aryanism, the Great Fleet and Io merged or at least funnelled Maori history and could be useful to pan-tribalism. Io may have been a retrospective invention, but he was not solely a Pakeha one. He was invoked by the King Movement in 1858, and in the 1860s.[49] The Young Maori were enthusiasts for what they repeatedly called 'racial consciousness' and unity among Maori, while sometimes acknowledging that it needed to be built from refurbished tribal bricks. They organized the Maori Battalions and the unification of Maori rugby, delicately negotiating their way past assimilationist Pakeha hesitations about seperatism. Ngata sought to avoid 'any cry of colour or separatism' in setting up the Prince of Wales Rugby Cup for competition between the four quarters of Maoridom in 1928, in accordance with the wishes of the late James Carroll. He hoped it would be 'a strong cementing influence', bonding tribes, as well as improving Maori rugby.[50] When the Maori battalion was dispersed among Pakeha units in 1916, its Maori backers threatened to stop recruitment, and set up such an outcry that the decision was reversed.[51] Sport and war, like shared myths of origin, bonded Maori as they did Pakeha. Tribalism remained stubborn, as did inter-tribal and supra-tribal entities from the resistance tradition. But in various campaigns stretching from the 1900s, Ngata in particular sought to reconcile differences and reduce antagonisms. Many foundered on the rock of tribalism, but some succeeded, and they culminated in 1950 in the celebration of the sixth centenary of the arrival of the Great Fleet.

All these measures were also explicitly intended to augment Maori status in the Pakeha mind – not for its own sake, but as a point of leverage, renewing the value of Maori collaboration for Pakeha. The aim was, in Ngata's words, 'influencing Pakeha opinion to a more kinly attitude and respect towards the Maori'.[52] As Pomare wrote of 1914: 'Just as New Zealand, as a country, used the war to prove its loyalty and worth to Britain, many Maori New Zealanders wished to use it to prove their loyalty and worth to Pakehas'.[53] Buck felt that Pakeha 'have not given due credit to the part played by the Maori himself in bringing about the post he now occupies'.[54] He was quite right. Stubborn tribal resilience in both nineteenth and twentieth centuries, pan-tribal military resistance in the nineteenth, and pan-tribal ideological collaboration in the twentieth were keys to the suvival of Maori identity and cultural autonomy. Their success was imperfect but substantial. Aryanism and its associated myths bonded Maori and linked, distinguished, and enhanced them in relation to Pakeha, just as Better Britonism and Aryanism served Pakeha in relation to Britain. There were Maori precedents too. After all, sharing ancestors as well as descendants was a feature of the ancient diplomacy of marriage alliance.

Brief summary over-neatens this story and gives too great an impression of ideological conspiracy. I am also aware of the dangers of inverting the traditional exaggeration of the native as victim into an exaggeration of the native as agent, and I am not claiming that New Zealand was typical. But I am claiming that it is suggestive. Unconscious or semi-conscious systems do congeal in the social history of ideas; and their concourse can sometimes be more important than their discourse. Racial mythology could archetype as well as anti-type, include as well as exclude, and persist without its labels once they became unfashionable. Contact was not a single encounter, in which European and non-European conceptions of Us and Them remained static, but an continuing ricochet – as much in the dimension of thoughts as in the dimensions of things and acts.

## Notes

1. Ferdinand von Hochstetter, *New Zealand*, London, 1867 (German original, 1863); A.S. Thomson, *The Story of New Zealand – Past and Present – Savage and Civilized*, 2 vols, London, 1859; Thomas Chomondeley, *Ultima Thule, or Thoughts Suggested by a Residence in New Zealand*, London, 1854.

2. E.g. *The Resolution Journals of Johann Reinhold Forster, 1772–5*, (4 vols), ed. Michael E. Hoare, London, 1982, vol. 2, p. 308; John Savage, *An Account of New Zealand in 1805*, ed. A.D. Mackinlay, Wellington, 1939, pp. 88–9.

3. *Southern Cross* (Auckland), 6 August 1863. Also see A.K. Newman, 'A Study of the Causes Leading to the Extinction of the Maori', *Transactions and Proceedings of the New Zealand Institute* (hereafter *TPNZI*), 14 (1882), pp. 459–77.

4. A key element of this exaggeration was the overestimation of populations at contact. See Ian Pool, *Te Iwi Maori: A New Zealand Population, Past, Present, and Projected*, AUP, 1991, ch. 3. It has recently been argued that Maori birth rates were increasing from the mid-nineteenth century. D.G. Sutton, 'Maori Demographic Change, 1769–1840: The Inner Workings of "a picturesque but illogical simile"', *Journal of the Polynesian Society* (hereafter *JPS*), 95 (1986), pp. 291–339.

5. M.P.K. Sorrenson, 'How to Civilize Savages. Some "Answers" from Nineteenth-century New Zealand', *New Zealand Journal of History* 9 (1975) pp. 97–110.

6. Frederick J. Moss, *School History of New Zealand*, Auckland, 1889, p. 5.

7. Quoted in M.J. Field, *Mau: Samoa's Struggle for Freedom*, Auckland, 1991 (orig. 1984), p. 69.

8. J.L. Nicholas, *Narrative of a Voyage to New Zealand*, 2 vols, London, 1817, vol. 2, p. 101; Diary of M. De Sainson, in Dumont D'Urville, *New Zealand 1826–7*, ed. Olive Wright, Wellington, 1950, p. 207; Joseph Banks, quoted in Ann Salmond, *Two Worlds. First Meetings between Maori and Europeans, 1642–1772*, Auckland, 1991, p. 251.

9. Ormond Wilson, *Hongi Hika to Hone Heke: A Quarter-Century of Upheaval*, Dunedin, 1985, pp. 86–8.

10. James Belich, 'War', in Colin Davis and Peter Lineham, eds., *The Future of the Past: Themes in New Zealand History*, Palmerston North, 1991, pp. 130–31.

11. *New Zealand Examiner*, 19 March 1861.

12. The recolonization thesis, and the case for shifts of this kind in Pakeha collective identity, is presented and documented in Vol. 2 of my general history of New Zealand, *The Bridge of History* (Penguin, forthcoming).

13. E.g. Thomson, *The Story of New Zealand*, vol. 1, pp. 37, 45; vol. 2, p. 230. Sinclair, *A Destiny Apart: New Zealand's Search for National Identity*, Wellington, 1986, pp. 81–3.

14. Paul Baker, *King and Country Call: New Zealanders, Conscription, and the Great War*, Auckland, 1988, p. 138.

15. E.g. Kwen Fee Lian, 'Settler Colonialism and Tribal Society: Maori–Pakeha Relations in the 19th Century', Ph.D. thesis, Victoria University of Wellington, 1986; and 'Interpreting Maori History: A Case for A Historical Sociology', *JPS* 96 (1987) pp. 445–71; Patricia Crone, 'The Tribe and the State', in John H. Hall, ed., *States in History*, Oxford, 1986; Stephen Cornell, 'The Transformation of the Tribe: Organization and Self-concept in American Ethnicities', *Ethnic and Racial Studies* 11 (1988) pp. 27–47.

16. *Imagined Communities: Reflections on the Origin and Spread of Nationalism*, London, 1983.

17. Wilson, *Hongi Hika to Hone Heke*, pp. 89–90.

18. 'Te Ua Gospel', trans. in L.F. Head, 'Te Ua and the Hauhau Faith in the Light of the Ua Gospel Notebook', MA thesis, Canterbury University, 1983, p. 63.

19. Tamehana to Gore Browne, 7 June 1861, *Appendices to the Journals of the House of Representatives*, 1861, E-1B, p. 19.

20. Bronwyn Elsmore, *Mana From Heaven: A Century of Maori Prophets in New Zealand*, Tauranga, 1989, p. 135; see also p. 129.

21. James Belich, *The New Zealand Wars and the Victorian Interpretation of Racial Conflict*, Harmondsworth, 1988, p. 15 and *passim*. On other components of the Smithed version see M.P.K. Sorrenson, *Maori Origins and Migrations. The Genesis of Some Pakeha Myths and Legends*, Auckland, 1979; D.R. Simmons, *The Great New Zealand Myth*, London, 1976; Michael Belgrave, 'Archipelago of Exiles. A study of the Imperialism of ideas. Edward Tregear and John Macmillan Brown', MA thesis, University of Auckland, 1979; Giselle Byrnes, 'Savages and Scholars: Some Pakeha Perspectives on the Maori, 1890s-1920s', MA thesis, Waikato University, 1990.

22. Edward Tregear, *The Aryan Maori*, Wellington, 1885. A stinging contemporary critique was A.S. Atkinson, 'The Aryo-Semitic Maori', *TPNZI* 19 (1886), pp. 552–76.

23. Kerry Howe, *Singer in a Songless Land: A Life of Edward Tregear, 1846–1901*, Auckland, 1991, pp. 49–51. J.L. Nicholas (*Narrative of a Voyage to New Zealand*, vol. 2, p. 288) and A.S. Thomson (*The Story of New Zealand*, vol. 1, p. 227) should be added to the list of Tregear's precursors. On international Aryanism, see Leon Poliakov, *The Aryan Myth: A History of Racist and Nationalist Ideas in Europe*, Falmer, 1974 (orig. 1971).

24. Quoted in Angela Ballara, *Proud to be White? A Survey of Pakeha Prejudice in New Zealand*, Auckland, 1986, p. 55.

25. Howe, *Singer in a Songless Land*, p. 64.

26. Sinclair, *A Destiny Apart*, pp. 197–9.

27. Max Herz, *New Zealand: The Country and its People*, London (trans. from German), n.d. [1900s].

28. Wellington, 1974 (orig.1945), pp. 25–6.

29. Sir Arthur Conan Doyle, reprinted in J. Eisen and K.J. Smith, *Strangers in Paradise*, Auckland, 1991, p. 173.

30. Quoted in C. Pugsley, *On the Fringe of Hell/New Zealanders and Military Discipline in World War One*, Wellington, 1991, pp. 20, 30.

31. Richard S. Joblin, 'The Breath of Scandal: *New Zealand Truth* and Interwar Society, 1918–39', MA thesis, University of Auckland, 1990, pp. 135, 143–9.

32. E.C. Buley, *A Child's History of Anzac*, London, 1916, p. 164.

33. Stewart Firth and Robert Darlington, 'Racial Stereotypes in the Australian Curriculum', in J.A. Mangan (ed.), *The Imperial Curriculum: Racial Images and Education in the British Colonial Experience*, London and New York, 1993, p. 83; Daniel Pulseley, quoted in Lawrence Jones, 'The Novel', in Terry Sturm (ed.), *The Oxford History of New Zealand Literature*, Auckland, 1991, p. 122.

34. Howe, *Singer in a Songless Land*, p. 65.

35. Sandra Coney et al., *Standing in the Sunshine: A History of New Zealand Women Since they Won the Vote*, Auckland, 1993, p. 281; also see p. 248; Sinclair, *A Destiny Apart*, pp. 190–94; *The Kia Ora Coo-ee*, March–December 1918, reprinted by Cornstalk, n.p., 1981; Charles A. Wilson, *Around New Zealand*, Auckland, 1925; J.M. Thomson, *The Oxford History of New Zealand Music*, e.g. p. 212; Leonard Bell, *Colonial Constructs: European Images of Maori, 1840–1914*, Auckland, 1992.

36. Quoted in Warwick Roger, *Old Heroes: The 1956 Springbok Tour and the Lives Beyond*, Auckland, 1991, p. 36.

37. Calculated from G.M. Bloomfield, *New Zealand: A Handbook of Historical Statistics*, Boston, 1984, esp. p. 81. Also see Te Rangi Hiroa (Peter Buck), 'The Passing of the Maori', *TPNZI* 55 (1924), pp. 362–75; Graham Butterworth, *Maori/Pakeha Intermarriage*, Five Talks on the Concert Programme, 1988; Atholl Anderson, *Race Against Time: The Early Maori–Pakeha Families and the Development of the Mixed Race Population in Southern NZ*, 1991.

38. Keith Sinclair, *Kinds of Peace: Maori People after the Wars 1870–85*,

Auckland, 1991, p. 26.

39. Richard Wolfe, *Well Made New Zealand. A Century of Trademarks*, Auckland, 1987, pp. 8, 18–23.

40. Peter O'Connor, 'Keeping New Zealand White', *New Zealand Journal of History* 2 (1968), pp. 41–65; Robert A. Huttenback, *Racism and Empire: White Settlers and Colored Immigrants in British Self-Governing Colonies, 1830–1910*, Ithaca, N.Y., 1976; David Pearson, *A Dream Deferred: The Origins of Ethnic Conflict in New Zealand*, Wellington, 1990.

41. R.A. Lochore, *From Europe to New Zealand. An account of our Contintental Settlers*, Wellington, 1951; K.W. Thomson and A.D. Trlin (eds.), *Immigrants in New Zealand*, Palmerston North, 1970, e.g. p. 74.

42. Tregear, *The Aryan Maori*, p. 90.

43. T.M. Hocken, *A Bibliography of the Literature Relating to New Zealand*, Wellington, 1909, p. 40.

44. See Samuel Marsden, 'Memoir of Ruatara', in Robert McNab, *Historical Records of New Zealand*, 2 vols, Wellington, 1908, vol. 1, pp. 338–46, and Nicholas, *Narrative of a Voyage to New Zealand*, vol. 1, *passim*.

45. Jennifer Curnow, 'Wiremu Maihi Te Rangikaheke: His Life and work', *JPS* 94 (1985), pp. 97–147; George Grey, *Polynesian Mythology and Ancient Traditional History of the Maori*, ed. W.W. Bird, Christchurch, 1956 (Maori orig. 1854).

46. For example, the carver Jacob Heberley. See Roger Neich, 'Heberley, Jacob William', in *The Dictionary of New Zealand Biography*, vol. 2, ed. C. Orange, Wellington, 1993.

47. Smith, *The Lore of the Whare-Wananga*, 2 vols, Polynesian Society Memoirs 3 and 4, 1913–15; D.R. Simmons, 'Te Matorohanga, Moihi', in *The Dictionary of New Zealand Biography*, vol. 2.

48. Philadelphia, 1938. Also see M.P.K. Sorrenson (ed.), *Na To Hoa Aroha/ From Your Dear Friend. The Correspondence between Sir Apirana Ngata and Sir Peter Buck, 1925–50*, 3 vols, Auckland, 1986–87, vol. 1, p. 104; vol. 3, p. 262.

49. Judith Binney, 'Maori Prophet Leaders', in Keith Sinclair (ed.), *The Oxford Illustrated History of New Zealand*, Auckland, 1990, p. 173; Elsmore, *Mana From Heaven*, pp. 170–71, 210.

50. *Buck–Ngata Correspondence*, vol. 1, pp. 114, 120.

51. Wira Gardiner, *Te Mura o Te Ahi. The Story of the Maori Battalion*, Auckland, 1992, p. 20.

52. *Buck–Ngata Correspondence*, vol. 1, pp. 178–80.

53. Quoted in Baker, *King and Country Call*, p. 211.

54. *Buck–Ngata Correspondence*, vol. 1, pp. 133.

# 5

# The Colonial Imagination
# and the Making and Remaking
# of the Samoan People

PETER HEMPENSTALL

Samoa has been the object of a long history of European conversation since the first Europeans contacted the area in 1787.[1] Over and
over again images of the Samoan people have been cannibalized to
construct a people of legendary proportions, a template for the
fashioning of a wide range of European views about cultural differences, colonial history and the nature of the indigene. Linnekin has
shown how the tale of the Samoan attack on La Perouse at Fagasa
in Tutuila in 1787 acquired 'folkloric stature in Europe',[2] representing the Samoans as the ultimate savages of the South Seas,
whose islands were avoided for years because of their evil reputation. New tellings of the tale through the nineteenth century, based
on gradually accumulating evidence and increased contact, redeemed
the Samoans and gave them a pivotal role in the development of
European discussions around the theme of the noble savage, by
turns socially at peace and warmly hospitable, or dangerously tem-
peramental with a tendency to become violent. Their image followed
them into the twentieth century, even after Western Samoa had
become a sovereign nation-state. A teacher living among the Samoans
in the 1960s described them as the ancient Greeks of the Pacific, an
ornament to Odysseus's native Ithaca:

> The fighting, the shameless boasting, the explosions of anger, the
> quenchless laughter, the weeping, feasting, trickery and speech-making

that took place on the beach at Troy would have made Samoan eyes sparkle. It was all according to Samoan custom....[3]

Samoa was also a major laboratory for the development of social science theory during the twentieth century. Margaret Mead's research into the social and emotional dynamics of Samoan adolescence demonstrated, to the satisfaction of cultural determinists in the United States, that Samoa was a homogeneous society where girls experienced a far less stressful adolescence than was assumed to be the case for American youth. Whole worlds of theory in cultural anthropology were erected upon this research. In the late twentieth century the Samoan islands were thrown into prominence yet again with Derek Freeman's attack on Mead's research methods and her positive portrayal of Samoan life. Freeman's contentions – that Mead was virtually duped by her local informants and that Samoan social and emotional life contained a profoundly dark side of sexual violence and inter-generational tension – sent shock waves across the landscape of American social science and were aired extensively in the mass media.[4]

Samoans have also been appropriated by historians of colonialism, as the exemplary indigenous community caught up in the history of western imperialism. The orthodox narrative histories of the Samoan islands establish several themes as the core of the Samoan experience. The Samoans fight among themselves while their islands are being fought over by the Great Powers; they are eventually partitioned between Germany and the United States at the end of the nineteenth century. American Samoa then diverges onto its own, separate track under US naval tutelage (and history), while the islands of Western Samoa are ruled by a succession of colonial regimes. The Samoan people and their leaders never surrender their homeland, instead sustaining campaigns of political and physical resistance against colonial domination until independence is achieved in 1962 as the Pacific's first modern nation-state.[5]

The central space in this nationalist mythic tale is occupied by the story of the *mau* movement of the 1920s and 1930s, the campaign of non-cooperation and attrition waged by Samoans against the New Zealand colonial regime. The transforming event is Black Saturday, when Tupua Tamesese Lealofi, one of the 'royal' title-holders and a leader of the *mau*, was gunned down by police with ten other Samoans while appealing for peace among a crowd of marchers protecting a *mau* official from arrest. The movement received its anthem on that day, and in Tamasese's dying words the rallying cry of an independence movement that sustained Samoans through to the 1960s: 'My blood has been spilt for Samoa. I am proud to give it. Do not dream of avenging it, for it was spilt in keeping peace. If I die peace must be maintained at any price.'[6]

A continuing tendency to colonize the Samoans via the western imagination is present in the central events and the strong characters of these stories. Samoan history has the colour of, in Marshall Sahlins's words, 'a Manichean showdown',[7] a simple confrontation of black and white opposites, which reflects the liberal, historicizing priorities of anti-colonial historians in the west. Since the 1960s, Pacific historians have been constructing histories which reverse the consideration of the Pacific islands as fragments of empire, their peoples objects of conquest and of imperial policy. They have attempted to restore agency to Islanders, put choices into their hands, portray them as clearly intentioned actors in their own histories.[8] Samoans have been caught up in these (anti-) colonial morality tales. On one side are a set of arrogant, bullying imperialists; on the other a traditionalist community of freedom-loving, proto-nationalist indigenes. But often these narratives have spoken *for* Samoans, through European archival texts. Even while reading these against the grain, historians have fitted Samoans within historiographical traditions to do with colonial resistance, which simplify the pattern of their initiatives and responses.

How do we overcome the colonialist imagination implicit in these practices? Despite their anti-colonial motivations, they still codify and normalize images of a whole people in ways that distance them, the margins, from us, the centre. This imaging of Samoans keeps them as an undifferentiated ethnic group, fixed as a uniform historical agent, or it raises up isolated individuals who, in their historical actions, have the look about them of Carlylean Enlightenment heroes. Part of the answer lies in letting Samoan-created texts into the discourse in order to complicate the story, texts with varying trajectories of explanation, which prohibit the easy acceptance of reductionist formulas about colonial history because they are dense with ambiguities.

The texts of imperialism are not 'the only game in town'.[9] Entwined with them are a variety of Samoan documents which have remained largely invisible, or underutilized in the historiographical development of colonial and anti-colonial history. Much of Samoans' history, as they conceptualize it, is quite literally hidden – locked away in family papers under mattresses, or in notebooks in the briefcases of lineage titleholders (the *matai*). This history includes the genealogical record of families' claims to eminence, their rights to land and titles and connections to ancestral events long before Europeans, the *palagi* (the cloud bursters), appeared.[10] It remains in the control of Samoans and will continue to perform its cultural functions. But some Samoan histories are in the form of written narratives, constructed by their authors around their personal histories under colonial rule. These deserve drawing in from the margins of visibility for their power to remake the images of the Samoans as a colonized people.

Two such texts are the 'Notes on Samoan history' by Te'o Tuvale, and Tofa I'iga Pisa's '*Mau e Pule*', the history of a Samoan resistance movement during the German period. The first is a written history of Samoa to 1918. Te'o Tuvale was a member of the remarkable Petaia lineage, the son of a pastor of the London Missionary Society, Va'aelua Petaia, who was a student in the foundation year of the Malua seminary, 1845, and one of a group of Samoans who assisted in translating the Bible into the Samoan language.[11] The family was also involved in collecting and writing down for publication by the mission the book of *fa'alupega*, the ceremonial namings of the principal titles and the genealogical connections of lineages recited by villagers on important occasions. Its publication helped to shore up traditional Samoan life during the disruptive years of the nineteenth century. Te'o Tuvale was appointed in 1878 as assistant secretary to the official indigenous Samoan government seated in Mulinu'u. He remained there or nearby through the rise and fall of successive Samoan regimes as they struggled to impose Samoan shape on European political activities of the high imperialist age. By the time Germany, in 1900, became the official colonial power in the western Samoan islands, Te'o had held positions as secretary of A'ana district, clerk to the Land and Titles Commission set up by the Berlin Conference, and chief judge at Mulinu'u. Like other church and political elites in his lineage he had travelled abroad, spending some years in Fiji during the wars of the late 1880s. In 1900 he led a troupe of traditional dancers to Germany, where he met the Kaiser and was presented with a gold watch, which is still in the possession of the family.

Te'o served Governor Wilhelm Solf as translator, though his duties ranged more widely, as tutor on village affairs and protocol, adviser and mediator in disputes, and an active participant in the contests for power between the German colonial regime and traditionalist chiefs. According to Davidson, many of the Petaia family were essentially conservative functionaries in a paternalistic system of colonial rule, and 'in so far as they were content with merely filling this role, they cut themselves off from the more progressive circles in which the Samoa of the future was being planned'.[12] But bureaucrats like Te'o were shrewd in factional intriguing, and they kept Sa Petaia in the front rank of government and church service (for these were complementary not opposite dimensions in Samoan life), so that the lineage Sa Petaia secured power and prestige at crucial junctures. The present-day Prime Minister of Western Samoa and former President of the Samoan Congregational Church, Tofilau Eti Alesana, is a Petaia, great-grandson of that first Christian, Va'aelua Petaia.

Te'o Tuvale's history of Samoa was written at the behest of the New Zealand military administration, which took over the colony of Samoa from the Germans in 1914. It was completed shortly before his death in 1919, after a lifetime of service to his people and to his people's colonial governments. It was, as Te'o himself says in his preface, the product of stories gathered over many years for his own use and interest, and is divided into two clear sections – 'Different versions of the ancestors and of the beginning of Samoa together with a record of events in past times down to the present day' [Preface]. The first section draws on a body of informed knowledge about ancestral themes – the origins of titles, proverbs, place names and particular events – which, with hindsight, seem organized around the establishment and continual legitimization of the Malietoa title and the lineage upon which it was bestowed; much of this history is corroborated by subsequent collections and reconstructions.[13] Chapter V (p. 15) begins the recounting of events in Samoa since 1822 and here Te'o establishes – as far as we can tell, independently – a line of events from which subsequent western-style histories of the islands have not substantially departed. His narrative is never purely event-centred history for, though arranged chronologically, it establishes the boundaries of the significant cultural structures and their workings that mattered most to Samoans of the day, particularly the rich tradition of title competition and the oratorical contests that are the central art form of Samoan society. Te'o wrestles with an explanation of the most dramatic changes in Samoan life – the redefining of Samoanness as Christianity took hold, and the intervention of Europe in district conflicts. It is no accident that the story of the opening of the first European store (1849) and the first Bible printed in Samoan (1855) belong together on the same page (17).

Te'o Tuvale's own life is intertwined with these events: his birth, education, appointments to government service, along with those of his brothers and cousins, affirm the Petaia line's place in the Christian redemptive history of Samoa, and incorporate the family at the centre of a story of patriotic political evolution. Te'o figures most prominently in a series of encounters which define a complex history of disagreement and negotiation among the political elite. One such was a dispute in 1883 over the term of the reign of the King as proclaimed in the constitution, which led to another district and factional fight in a long series. Te'o as secretary to the government, in a creative amalgam of traditional virtue and modernizing practice, appeals to both a native patriotism *and* the stabilizing effect of European constitution-making in his plea for peace:

> I beseech you orators to think of your country and not again advise the spilling of blood, because if you do so the control of our country will be taken over by the Three Powers. You Namulauulu, say that the reckoning of Malietoa's term is incorrect and that murderers have not been punished. I wish to show you that the Constitution of a Government is not founded on the punishing of murderers alone. All Governments are founded on laws and those who transgress these laws are punished. The Constitution of this Government has not been made known to everyone. The King is not a murderer nor is our Government. The day the King was appointed is recorded and recognized but not in the way Namalauulu suggests. Let it be known that although there are disputes at present they are disputes under the *Pule* [one of the confederations of district power] of Malietoa the King. Incorrect opinions and words are not wanted nor is favouritism. These things are useless and if they end in the spilling of blood the Three Powers will take over the control of our country. The usefulness of our chiefs and orators will be gone. (p. 36)

Similarly, during the European-provoked turmoil of 1899, which led finally to the partition of the islands, Te'o takes part in the battles around Apia on the side of Malietoa Tanumafili against Mataafa Josefo. He acts at the centre of affairs in saving Tanumafili from roving bands of Mataafa supporters (pp. 64–5) and organizes a letter to the European consuls which helps to stop the fighting between the factions. During the German period, except when he is absent in the Kaiserreich, Te'o is at the side of the Governor, Wilhelm Solf, as he tries to disband the traditional cartels of chiefly power (*Tumua* and *Pule*). Solf gambles with civil war in his contest for power with resisting chiefs, but is eventually triumphant thanks to the assistance of Samoan intermediaries like Te'o. In 1910 Solf strides off to Berlin to capture new political heights at the centre of empire, leaving the Samoans – and Te'o – to see out the German period and to come to terms with the next colonial regime under the New Zealanders.

Te'o's 'Notes' construct a patriotic history for Samoa which affirms its place among the nations and sends a message to the new *palagi* that 'Samoa', the nation, is worthy of respect. 'Samoa' had fought for control of her destiny through the years of bitterness and battle; she had national aspirations, symbolized in Te'o's emphasis on the flag of the indigenous government, the centre of a continual contest with the flags of the European powers. A strong note of already-existing Samoan sovereignty underlies the description of Samoan arguments about paramount authority, which Europeans saw (and have since continually characterized) as premodern chaos and disturbance. And the history makes clear, in its record of continuing disputation with the Germans, that what Samoan chiefs believed they were accepting with partition in 1900 was protection by a European state, not unlimited power over them.

Samoa was already in the process of transformation from warring lineages organized across districts into a state with natural boundaries and a fixed cultural profile. As Linnekin points out, a discourse revolving around Samoa's special identity had already developed since the years of struggle against Tonga, which ruled over the Samoan islands some time in the sixteenth century; the expulsion of the Tongans is counted one of the great events in Samoan history.[14] Europeans had added to that process in the nineteenth century. They defined Samoan conflicts over the paramount titles as a kingship dispute in the European manner, and actively intervened to bring about a unified kingdom under one monarch, at a time when Samoans were suffering from ideological confusion as Christianity weakened the beliefs surrounding the authority of their chiefs.[15] As a functionary of various Samoan governments and their European allies, Te'o was himself a part of the discourse. His history is testament to his immersion in the politics shaping an embryonic state.

Te'o Tuvale's 'Notes on Samoan History' have not achieved a prominent place in the library of texts about Samoa's history. His granddaughter, Peggy Fairbairn-Dunlop, herself an academic and critic of Samoan writings, has categorized Te'o's work as a replica of the European word, a kind of alien textualization which uses written language as a bid to access the *palagi*'s secrets of power and authority.[16] The historical anthropologist Jocelyn Linnekin treats it as part of what she calls the 'centering project' or the 'nationalist project' — the historically constructed western vision of Samoa as a unified nation, which is replicated again and again in all the written genres of Samoan history.[17]

Western critics have a tendency to cry 'inauthentic' at the blending of pre-western, colonial and post-colonial forms of storytelling, either because they do not measure up to our self-defined, modern categories of historical analysis or because they seem to assimilate a bastardized form of western values which leaves 'traditional' historical forms unrecognizable.[18] Literary critics of post-colonial writings condemn the so-called 'mimic men' whose creations are a derivative collaboration with the imperial centre, mimicking the politics and the historicizing/literary categories of the west, and denying their own origins in the culture of the periphery.[19] Te'o's history can be read as the first kind of mimicry — a colonized, historical narrative in western chronological form. The politics of its creation have a great deal to do with that. The 'Notes' were written on instruction for the New Zealand Military Administrator, Colonel Logan. Their terms of reference are the political events that establish the framework for relations of power between Samoans and Europeans. Their aim, at least personally for Te'o, is to affirm the author's role in the events of the moment that Te'o reads as constituting a sympathetic history of Samoa for Logan: Te'o as servant and adviser of indigenous and foreign governments, as peacemaker where possible but warrior where necessary, in the cause of right order and stability.

But the text's signals are also more complicated than those of a mere piece of imperial collaboration. Mimicry can be an ambiguous act, a situational counterpart of resistance, a form of 'defensive warfare'.[20] In his mimicry of the western word and its categories of event. Te'o does not deny his Samoanness for a handful of New Zealand silver. Though with hindsight he recognized that multiple claimants to authority in a divided Samoa increased the likelihood of a European takeover, his history does not convey any sense that the Samoan polity lacks civility and power, or that it is one step from chaos. Nor is his history a heroic charting of progress towards unified nationhood. Te'o acknowledges divisions among Samoan parties over choices and tactics at crucial moments; indeed he gives voice to those who opposed him and his conceptions. Ultimately, the 'Notes' present a historical vision of Samoa's colonial days that accepts dissension and compromise by Samoans in the making of Samoa: the anti-colonial motif is muted; the colonized speak with discordant voices; traditionalists are vanquished by the colonial state, but at the end of the story tradition is still powerful, for the leading Malietoa and Tupua lineages survive with their prestige intact among the body of Samoans, and they are in formal positions of colonial recognition, as 'advisers' to the Governor; fine mats are still given ceremonially to embody that prestige and titles are still conferred according to *fa'aSamoa*.

The second Samoan text comes out of the euphoria of independence in January 1962. It is an unpublished manuscript history of the *mau e pule* of 1909, the movement of opposition to Solf's native policies, characterized by historians as colonial rebellion. Organized by the talking chief Lauaki Namulauulu Mamoe, the *mau e pule* ended for Lauaki and seventy other Samoans in banishment to the Mariana Islands for the rest of the German period. The manuscript was dictated in Samoan by Tofa I'iga Pisa to his daughter and translated into a rough English by a colleague, Gatoloai Peseta; the original Samoan version has so far eluded discovery. There is an English translation in Samoa, and another among the papers of the late J.W. Davidson, Professor of Pacific History at the Australian National University, who was constitutional adviser to the Samoans in the years leading up to independence.[21]

Tofa I'iga Pisa's own history is central to the threads of the tale and to the enterprise of constructing this text. Born in 1882, I'iga Pisa grew to fame as a composer of poetic songs. He was 'prone to enthusiasm and volatile at times',[22] and in 1909, as a young *matai* of twenty-seven, he acted as Lauaki's lieutenant in the affair with Solf, at one point taking a central role as 'Secretary to the Reconciliation' between Lauaki and the Governor. Exiled along with Lauaki, he settled down on Saipan to learn German in order to secure a government job on his return to his homeland. But with the outbreak of war and the arrival of the Japanese in Saipan, I'iga Pisa decided that English was a language more likely to profit him now that New Zealand had taken over in Samoa. Unlike the other exiles who were returned to Samoa in 1915, I'iga Pisa did not see his homeland again until 1919. He made a dramatic, lone canoe voyage to Guam and acquired his English by working for the United States Navy in Guam and Hawaii. Once back in Samoa, he served under a series of New Zealand Secretaries of Native Affairs as a translator and bureaucrat; he became a particular friend of C.G.A. McKay, who was later New Zealand's Secretary of Island Affairs in Wellington. I'iga Pisa served on the Constitutional Convention of 1954 and was later a Faipule in the parliament. At independence he was a ramrod straight chief of eighty years, the last of the exiled *matai* of 1909 left alive. As one of the last of the few remaining colonial elites from the German period, I'iga Pisa was part of the politics which brought the Western Samoan nation to fruition, with a Christian constitution dedicated to the customs of traditional Samoa (*aganu'u a Samoa*), and a national parliament in which only *matai* could be electors and elected.[23] I'iga Pisa represents a crucial link with the nationalist story of who the Samoans as a people imagined themselves to be at the point of independence in 1962.[24]

I'iga Pisa's history is in two sections. The first, intended as an introduction to the 1908 movement is, at fifty-six pages of type, in fact longer than the section on the *mau e pule* itself (thirty-six pages). There is a message here, for the history is really about ancient district ties and historical alliances stretching back to Samoa's 'time of darkness' before the coming of Christianity. Lauaki's father, Namalauulu Atamu, was presented with the title Lauaki by the Tongan king Tuitonga Gigigigi in 1828 and it was handed on to his son Mamoe. Lauaki Namulauulu Atamu was alive and nearby when Malietoa Vai'inupo accepted the Christian gift from John Williams in 1830. From that point of transformation in Samoa's story onwards, his son Lauaki Namulauulu Mamoe figures prominently as perhaps the islands' greatest talking chief during the nineteenth and twentieth centuries. I'iga Pisa says of him: 'If he were to speak in harmonious expression which broke the hearts of the people, an audience listening to, would shed tears; or if speaking with words of encouraging attitude, an army wherein Lauaki took the lead, would all arise with bravery to fight.' (pp. 4–5).[25] A man who took what he wanted from the benefits of western contact, including adherence to the London Missionary Society and a masterly exploitation of the Bible as a tool for his great oratory, Lauaki was none the less in politics an absolute traditionalist. His political faith and loyalty were pre-eminently with the Malietoa title and the holders of that title, and I'iga Pisa's history documents Lauaki's jealousy for their dignity down through the latter decades of the nineteenth century.

At a point in the early 1880s, Lauaki begins to see himself as the defender, not just of the Malietoas but of Samoa-wide unity and tradition. The story begins to turn on the struggle to unify Samoa against the increasing invasiveness of the European powers: after Malietoa Laupepa is exiled by the Germans in 1887, Lauaki works to make Mata'afa Josefo from the Tupua lineage the new Malietoa To'oa in order to give Samoans a focus of loyalty against the German-supported regime of Tupua Tamasese Titimaea. He returns to the side of Malietoa Laupepa after the latter is brought back from exile by the European powers and made King. In 1898 Lauaki insists on carrying out the last will of the dying Laupepa and conferring titular supremacy once again on Mata'afa Josefo, as the best way to unify Samoa. When the European powers refuse to endorse this Samoan solution and civil war follows, Lauaki proposes reconciliation of all parties and a joint Samoan government to rule under the German flag. But when the German Governor, Solf, also evades the recognition of Samoan authority and tries to break up the alliances of chiefs, which traditionally control the paramount titles, Lauaki becomes the sometimes secret, sometimes open, centre of resistance to Solf.

And so he plans every detail of the movement that becomes known as *mau e pule*, the mass descent on Mulinu'u peninsula, the seat of government, when Solf returns from leave in Germany in 1908, to press for the restoration of traditional Samoan political organization.

I'iga Pisa's history chronicles all the developments of the movement, including its collapse in a celebrated confrontation with Solf in 1909. Samoans were by then enjoying a new era of peace and moderate prosperity and could not be persuaded to choose the imperatives of their older history.[26] Emotionally, I'iga Pisa recounts his own capture (though he proclaims his innocence of working against the Germans) and the rituals of colonial deportation. Solf treats Lauaki and the party of exiles with high honour, thanking them for their thoughtfulness and capability in ending the 'trouble' in peace, and sending them forth according to a resolution of the Kaiser, 'not on punishment but on a "dignified tour"' (p. 28). They were being sent to the Mariana Islands, where they might visit all lands under Germany but must stay away from the American-held island of Guam. I'iga Pisa was originally to be punished in Samoa, but Lauaki asks him to accompany the exiles to Saipan in order to record the traditional histories stored in their heads and hearts. The departure is emotional, resonant with allegories proclaimed by Lauaki. Solf and his lieutenants are there to see them off, together with countless *fautasi* (long boats) filled with relatives and friends; a naval band farewells them with a Samoan hymn and the German national anthem. I'iga Pisa muses: 'This recognized that our party was of a high respected one according to the statement by the Governor, but it was not a rebellion...' (p. 32).

I'iga Pisa's history is a distinctive variation on the resistance mythology that connects Samoa's story to the *mau* movement of the 1920s and 1930s. Perhaps it has remained largely invisible in the west because of that – the centre defines the stories that tell the history of the periphery. I'iga Pisa, writing in 1962, was making sense of his present life and experience as Samoa assumed nation-statehood, creating a story of affirmation and pride in a national political genealogy, through remaking the past.[27] But his is the conservative voice of customary politics, whose reordering of memory replaces the modern story of state formation (the evolution of nationalist movements; the liberation struggle of the *mau*) with an older 'natural history', shaped by a much more traditionalist vision of who Samoans were. It constructs the Samoans as agents in their own history and pushes that agency back to first contact, indeed beyond. Nation-statehood was not a new creation but a *recovery* of independence, a return to Samoans defining the track they always wanted to travel, which was self-government grounded in *aganu'u a Samoa*. I'iga Pisa's '*Mau e pule*' is, like Te'o's history, rich in the cultural dynamics that underlay community politics in colonial times.[28] It is a history embroidered with poetry and powerful oratory, the elegies proclaimed at the death of great ones, the bravery of warriors in war, the family and district alliances that were the life-blood of Samoan political connections.

Lauaki, the quintessential traditionalist who embodies all that is customary in the modern Samoan state of the 1960s, is the model for this conservative recovery of the nation. He, not the *mau*, is the link between past and present. According to I'iga Pisa, his chosen voice, Lauaki recognizes this in the allegory he spoke to Solf on their departure from Samoa in 1909: the little band of exiles was a sacrificial offering for the youth of Samoa, against a time in the future 'when Samoa will govern its own government according to its own traditions and customs, when younger generations will attain modern training in running European governments similar to your important efforts' (p. 30, second section). 'The words of prophecy which Lauaki usually spoke', wrote I'iga Pisa in 1962, meshing Samoan and Christian tradition in a new-old salvation tale, 'became reality at present as we think of the present conditions in Samoa today. Now Samoa has already gained its own independence which is founded in God. Past generations who lay in graves did not see this great event' (p. 31, second section).

We must be careful not to claim too much for these texts. They were after all created by elite, male voices using the West's written word to produce western-style historical imaginings.[29] No text produced in the colonial environment by the colonized is free of the constraining politics of that condition. Nor do their visions of the Samoan past by any means constitute the whole of Samoan identity. The Samoans' sense of themselves as a historical community is not exhausted by one homogeneous image. The core traditions constructed to express identity contain seams of varying density and consistency. Self-government may have been the consistent aspiration of Samoans through one hundred years of colonialism but, as Meleisea makes clear, it was not based on any codified sense of Samoan tradition.[30] A discourse revolving around *fa'aSamoa* had evolved over a century of European contact, embodied in a variety of movements for tradition and modernization, each with its own politics and rhetoric, and its internal cleavages.[31] Te'o and I'iga Pisa represent elements of that continuing conversation – two Samoan writers canvassing the past in both colonial and *fa'aSamoa* terms, pressing into personal and cultural service both western history forms and their own sense of time and event.

Their histories are, however, capable of disturbing the familiar formulas by which Samoan history is measured and its people imagined. To the extent that they bring back to the centre stories of traditional communities acting according to *fa'aSamoa* symbols and practices, they undermine the 'nationalist project' which tells Samoa's story in terms of the evolution of the western nation-state. Like the transactions of colonialism upon which they reflect, these writings are ambiguous in their meanings, sometimes complicit with colonial interests, sometimes resistant to them, expressing what E.P. Thompson calls 'the crucial ambivalence of our human presence in our own histories'.[32] They attest to a multitude of experiences under colonial regimes, including those of privileged elites and those of the 'subaltern' class.[33] There is no generic experience of the West and its colonialisms, no representative text which fixes its meanings for Samoans. Te'o and I'iga Pisa affirm the importance of particular events, which have multiple meanings for different groups of people.[34] In so doing, they contribute to building a more complex imagined past of the Samoans and unsettle the mythology that has made the Samoan people central to our western reading of the Polynesian 'savage/other'.

That they have not been central to mainstream historical reconstructions of Samoa up to now does not mean that they have not been part of the historical literature that created that past for Samoans. There has always been a tension between western and island forms of representing colonial history. According to some commentators, Samoans have been traditionally suspicious of the written narrative form of history, preferring their greatest art – oratory – or forms of social realist fiction *à la* Albert Wendt.[35] But the record demonstrates that since the translation of the Christian scriptures in the middle of the nineteenth century, Samoan cultural production has supported the written word in disparate forms down through the years, serving an assortment of traditional and modern functions. Samoans have been imagining themselves in spoken word and written language, making and remaking themselves in a variety of ways that are part of, but not simply reducible to, current theories about 'the nationalist project', the hegemonic nature of colonial history writing, or the evolution of truly decolonized history.

## Notes

1. I am grateful to Russell McDougall, Klaus Neumann and Alan Ward for comments upon earlier versions of this paper; also to colleagues in Kloster Andechs, Germany, and Kiribati, the Pacific Islands, for discussions and criticism.

2. Jocelyn Linnekin, 'Ignoble Savages and Other European Visions: The La Perouse Affair in Samoan History', *The Journal of Pacific History*, vol. 26, no. 1 (1991), pp. 3–26.

3. George Irwin, 'Samoan-Odyssey-III', *Blackwoods Magazine* 293 (1771), May 1963, p. 470.

4. See Margaret Mead, *Growing up in Samoa*, New York, 1961 [*c.* 1928]; Derek Freeman, *Margaret Mead and Samoa*, Canberra, 1983; and Hiram Caton, *The Samoa Reader: Anthropologists Take Stock*, New York, 1990.

5. From Sylvia Masterman, *Origins of International Rivalry in Samoa 1845–1884*, London, 1934; and Felix M. Keesing, *Modern Samoa*, London, 1934; through J.W. Davidson, *Samoa mo Samoa: The Emergence of the Independent State of Western Samoa*, Melbourne, 1967; R.P. Gilson, *Samoa 1830–1900: The Politics of a Multicultural Community*, Melbourne, 1970; P.M. Kennedy, *The Samoan Tangle: A Study in Anglo–German–American Relations 1878–1900*, St Lucia, 1974; D.K. Fieldhouse, *Economics and Empire*, London, 1973; to P. J. Hempenstall, *Pacific Islanders under German Rule: A Study in the Meaning of Colonial Resistance*, Canberra, 1978; and Michael Field, *Mau: Samoa's struggle against New Zealand Oppression*, Wellington, 1984.

6. A fairly typical heroic history of this moment is Philip J. Parr's *The Murder of Tamasese*, The Aspect Press, 1979.

7. Marshall Sahlins, 'Goodbye to Tristes Tropes: Ethnography in the Context of Modern World History', *Journal of Modern History* 65 (March 1993), p. 13.

8. Recent historiographical surveys would include David Routledge, 'Pacific History as Seen from the Pacific Islands', *Pacific Studies*, vol. 8, no. 2 (1985), pp. 81–100; F.X. Hezel, 'New Directions in Pacific History: A Practitioner's Critical View', *Pacific Studies*, vol. 11, no. 3 (1988), pp. 101–110; Max Quanchi, 'Pacific History – The View over the Breakers', *Australian Historical Association Bulletin* 61 (December 1989), pp. 9–17; Peter Hempenstall, 'The Line of Descent: Creating Pacific Histories in Australasia', in *Historical Disciplines and Culture in Australasia*, ed. John Moses, *Australian Journal of Politics and History* 41, Special issue (1995), pp. 157–70.

9. The words are Sahlins's again, 'Goodbye to Tristes Tropes', p. 6.

10. M. Meleisea and P. Schoeffel-Meleisea (eds), *Lagaga. A Short History of Western Samoa*, Suva, 1987, preface, pp. vii–ix; Peggy Fairbairn-Dunlop, 'Samoan Writing: Searching for the Written Fagogo', in Paul Sharrad, *Readings in Pacific Literature*, University of Wollongong, 1993, p. 139.

11. This section draws on Davidson, *Samoa mo Samoa*, pp. 69–71, 81,

202, and on discussions in 1993 and 1994 with Dr Te'o Ian Fairbairn, the distinguished economist, who is the present holder of the Te'o title.

12. Davidson, *Samoa mo Samoa*, p. 202.

13. Br Henry, *History of Samoa*, Apia, 1979 (also Br Henry, *Samoa: An Early History* [revised by Tofa Pule, Nikalao I. Tuiteleleapaga], American Samoa Department of Education, 1980); and Leulu Felise Va'a, 'The Parables of a Samoan Divine. An analysis of Samoan texts of the 1860s', MA thesis, Australian National University, 1987.

14. Jocelyn Linnekin 'Representing Samoan History: Indigenous, Colonial and Post-Colonial Genres', unpublished ms., p. 41.

15. M. Meleisea, *Change and Adaptations in Western Samoa*, 1988 Macmillan Brown Lectures, Canterbury, 1992, p. 22.

16. Fairbairn-Dunlop, 'Samoan Writing', pp. 137–9.

17. Linnekin, 'Representing Samoan History', pp. 12, 39. Linnekin's paper is a perceptive exploration of the way Samoa's past has been historicized, and was the original inspiration for this chapter.

18. Geoffrey M. White, *Identity through History: Living Stories in a Solomon Islands Society*, Cambridge, 1991, p. 2.

19. 'Mimic men' is an expression of V.S. Naipaul, from his book of the same title (London, 1967). Naipaul has himself been accused of being a 'mimic man' because of his longing for the civilization and order of the centre, represented by England. See Bill Ashcroft, Gareth Griffiths and Helen Tiffin, *The Empire Writes Back*, London, 1989, pp. 88–91. For a useful summary of 'lit. crit.' views on post-colonial literature, see Anne Maxwell, 'The Debate on Current Theories of Colonial Discourse', *Kunapipi*, vol. xiii, no. 3 (1991), pp. 70–84.

20. Homi K. Bhabha, 'Signs Taken for Wonder: Questions of Ambivalence and Authority under a Tree outside Delhi, May 1817', in Francis Barker et al. (eds.), *Europe and Its Others*, Colchester, 1985, p. 104.

21. The story of the *mau e pule* is in Hempenstall, *Pacific Islanders under German Rule*, pp. 55–72. According to Meleisea, a copy of the history is with I'iga Suafole, Apia.

22. C.G.A. McKay, *Samoana: A Personal Story of the Samoan Islands*, Wellington, 1968, p. 22.

23. Meleisea, *Change and Adaptations*, has the best definition of the repertoire of values and relationships that *aganu'u a Samoa* comprises (p. 52).

24. I'iga Pisa's story is in McKay, *Samoana*, pp. 21–36. Lauaki did not reach Samoa in 1915, dying of dysentery in Tarawa in the Gilbert Islands on the way back.

25. Knowledgeable Europeans agreed: the European Chief Justice in Apia in 1898, W.L. Chambers, declared Lauaki's speech in 1898, anointing Mata'afa Josefo as the rightful heir to the High Titles, as the finest speech he had heard in Samoan. J.W. Davidson, 'Lauaki Namulauulu Mamoe. A traditionalist in Samoan politics', in J.W. Davidson and D. Scarr (eds.), *Pacific Islands Portraits*, Canberra, 1976, p. 288.

26. Davidson, 'Lauaki', p. 296.

27. White, *Identity through History*, p. 5, is illuminating on the way the present is created through 'idioms of remembrance'.

28. In an interesting symmetry, I'iga Pisa was also a Petaia by marriage.

29. They are also being interpreted through imperfect English translations, from my First World position, which has its own kind of historicity and power relations built into it.

30. Meleisea, *Change and Adaptations*, p. 52. Meleisea has also claimed (interview with author, 20 February 1992) that the Samoans today lack any Samoa-wide sense of a national history.

31. This applies very much to that sacred icon of Samoan history (at least for western historians), the *mau* movement of the 1920s, which deserves a complete dissection from the Samoan side, exposing its varied directions and contradictions.

32. E.P. Thompson, quoted in Bain Attwood, *The Making of the Aborigines*, Sydney, 1989, p. 147.

33. See Ranajit Guha (ed.), *Subaltern Studies: Writings on South Asian History and Society*, Delhi, 1982.

34. A point made by David Hanlon in relation to Pohnpeian history writing in 'The Path Back to Pohnsakar: Luelen Bernart, his Book and the Practice of History on Pohnpei', *Isla*, vol. 1, no. 1 (1992), pp. 13–36.

35. M. Meleisea, 'Pacific Historiography: An Indigenous View', *Journal of Pacific Studies* 4 (1978), p. 40; Fairbairn-Dunlop, 'Samoan Writing', p. 137; Linnekin, 'Representing Samoan History', p. 38.

# 6

# 'The Kava Ceremony is a Prophecy': An Interpretation of the Transition to Christianity in Samoa

## THOMAS BARGATZKY

I want to place before you an anthropological riddle and two attempts at its solution.[1] The riddle is the speedy adoption of Christianity by the Samoan population in the nineteenth century. This process, I argue, has been misinterpreted both by missionaries and by some western anthropologists. I will sketch briefly the history of the transition to Christianity. A summary of the received anthropological opinion will follow, and finally my own explanation will be given. I argue that missionaries and anthropologists share some basic western preconceptions concerning religion, despite their disagreement in many fields. This has prevented a number of them from appreciating the importance of a paramount ritual (the Kava Ceremony) for both the political *and* the religious domain.

## Missionaries, Anthropologists and Samoan Religiosity

It is a fact established beyond all doubt that relations between anthropologists and missionaries have generally been strained and uneasy. Prejudices and animosities against one another still dominate their relations today. It seems to be especially hard for anthropologists to overcome their long-standing ambivalence towards missionaries and Christianity, despite the scientific achievements of men like Sahagún, Lafiteau, Codrington and Schebesta, to mention only a few names.[2] For many western anthropologists, it has long been difficult to approach Pacific Christianity, because Christianity seems familiar and is so embedded in European colonial experience. They continue to view Christianity primarily as a missionary imposition, especially in Melanesia,[3] and the same can be said regarding the attitude of many western observers towards Christianity in Polynesia. Yet western anthropologists and missionaries are of the same stock; they share the same general culture and some of its basic tenets and assumptions, their more overt disagreement on many issues notwithstanding. This has resulted, at times, in a misunderstanding and misinterpretation of foreign ways of life. Among other things, anthropologists and missionaries share some basic ideas about religion that have been deeply rooted in western civilization since the era of the Renaissance and Reformation. This common heritage has resulted in a misinterpretation of pre-Christian religion in Samoa.

The process of Christianization in Samoa can be called without doubt a 'success story'. The main events in the transition are well known and will be only briefly summarized here.[4] Conversion to Christianity took place rather smoothly and incredibly speedily, despite a moment of crisis in 1839. In 1830 the missionaries John Williams and Charles Barff of the London Missionary Society (LMS) landed in Samoa, leaving behind, after a stay of about ten days, eight Polynesian catechists – six from the Society Islands, and two from Aitutaki (Cook Islands).[5] The first Wesleyan Methodist missionary, Peter Turner, arrived in Samoa in 1835, to be followed in the same year by LMS missionaries Platt and Wilson, and in 1836 by a group of six resident European LMS missionaries. Yet the Samoans had been exposed to Christianity well before 1830. In 1826, for example, the Wesleyan Methodist Mission gained a permanent foothold in Tonga and probably for centuries there had been relations between the dominant parties of Tonga and Samoa.[6] It can be inferred that this was one channel for the spread of information about Christianity in Samoa. The first resident white messengers of Christianity, however, were a class of people who have been labelled 'beachcombers', that is, European craftsmen, sailors or convicts who had settled in Samoa since early in the nineteenth century.[7] They seldom settled in groups but entered into a patron–client relationship with an influential chief as the patron. Due to the intensity of the rivalry between chiefs in Samoa, chiefs were eager to possess a tame white man, especially if he was skilled.[8] Religious knowledge attributed to these foreigners rated paramount among these skills, as a communication by commander Charles Wilkes of the US Exploring Expedition, who visited Samoa in 1839, shows. Some years before the arrival of the missionaries a shipwreck occurred and the cargo was seized by the Samoans, but the crew were well treated.

> The captain advised his crew to turn missionaries, and set them the example himself. He met with much success, and succeeded in building churches ... It is not probable that even the captain was deeply versed in religious knowledge, and very certain that the crew could not have been...[9]

Initially every white man was probably looked upon as a messenger of a powerful new religious system which the indigenous people wanted to make their own. Later, when the missionaries arrived, they 'were from the very first taken under the protection of the most powerful chiefs, and have never received either insult or injury from any of the natives'.[10]

During his visit to Samoa in 1836, the LMS missionary Charles Barff noted in his diary on 26 June that 'It was truly gratifying to see the Samoans keep the Sabbath so strictly.'[11] At that time, the Polynesian catechists had been in Samoa for six years and the resident white LMS missionaries for about one month. By 1839, if we can trust the statistics of the mission, almost one-quarter of the Samoan population had turned to Christianity.[12] In 1844 the LMS Theological College at Malua was established, and in the following year Roman Catholic missionary activity commenced on the island of Savai'i.

In a book published in 1861, LMS missionary George Turner writes that,

> On the reception of Christianity, temples were destroyed, the sacred groves left to be overrun by the bush, the shells and stones and divining cups were thrown away, and the fish and fowls which they had previously regarded as incarnations of their gods were eaten without suspicion or alarm. In a remarkably short time, under God's blessing, hardly a vestige of the entire system was to be seen.[13]

The period of transition was not entirely without strains, however. Adherents of the old religion and converts, followers of the LMS and Wesleyan Methodist missions, partisans of the sailor sects and disciples of the Samoan prophet and healer Sio Vili,[14] vied with one another. The Sio Vili Cult is of special interest in this connection, since it was an early, and at times very popular, attempt to see Christianity through Samoan eyes and through Samoan culture and custom.[15] Sectarian rivalry at times caused severe social stress marked by extreme emotionalism.[16] Yet on the whole a tremendous zeal was aroused for the new religion and Samoans also adopted the new standards of behaviour imposed by the missionaries.[17] About 1850, therefore, the process of Christianization seems to have been completed – 20 years after the establishment of the Christian mission. Today, even the most casual observer 'is impressed with the religiosity and devoutness of the Samoans, who have transformed Christianity into a unique indigenous complex of beliefs and practices'.[18]

This success, however, did not really satisfy the missionaries. On 4 December 1854, for example, George Stallworthy wrote in a letter that

> The impulse of the first love has spent itself. The novelty of Christianity no longer attracts the people. Many who embraced it under shallow and false impressions and expectations have discovered their mistake. They find that they have been drawing water from the wrong fountain.[19]

It became a recurrent complaint among the missionaries that 'Christianity, *instead of bursting the bonds of the old life*, has been eaten up by it', as one missionary confessed to Felix M. Keesing.[20] The words of the same missionary quoted by Keesing are worth giving in full:

> from the Christian viewpoint the missions have been rather a failure in Samoa. Instead of accepting Christianity and allowing it to remould their lives to its form the Samoans have taken the religious practices taught to them and fitted them inside Samoan custom, making them a part of the native culture. Christianity has changed Samoan theology a little, that is all. Otherwise the people are mentally arrested; there is no religious questioning or conflict – everything is easy-going.[21]

Now it is interesting to note that such views have been echoed by anthropologists. Margaret Mead's portrayal of the Samoans as an easy-going people, without deep emotions and with easy solutions for every problem[22] has been instrumental in the creation of the received anthropological opinion concerning Samoan religiosity. In *Social Organization of Manu'a,* for example, she writes: 'chiefly concerned ... with their social pattern, the Samoans have time for little else. Pondering upon the exigencies of ordered society, they take small interest in the world of the supernatural'.[23] Quite the contrary is true, as we know today, since there now exist excellent and authoritative works on pre-Christian and contemporary Samoan religion.[24] Yet for a long time there has been agreement among anthropologists and other social scientists that the conversion to Christianity was superficial and nominal only,[25] due to 'the light stress laid upon religion and ritual in Samoa, which distinguishes the culture from other Polynesian areas ... The religious life is not marked, evidently, by ethical, moral or aesthetic axiomatics of any great strength.'[26] To another investigator, the motives of conversion, together with the 'convenient elasticity in religious thinking', suggest that 'Samoans did not in general experience any fundamental change of heart or reach a deep understanding of any new truth.'[27] Yet while the missionaries, for obvious reasons, disapproved of this state of affairs, anthropologists accepted it more or less tacitly. Missionaries and anthropologists are agreed, however, with respect to the extraordinary ease with which Samoan religious life was ultimately penetrated by formal Christianity, and they concur in the opinion that the adoption of Christianity did not fundamentally alter the *fa'aSamoa,* the Samoan way of life.

I will now summarize the received anthropological opinion concerning the causes of the success of Christianity in Samoa. Following this, I will give reasons for my partial disagreement with this view and offer my own explanation of the transition to Christianity.

### The Received Opinion

The missionary John Williams, an astute observer with much comparative ethnographical knowledge at his disposal, was one of the first Europeans to notice that the religious system of the Samoans differed essentially from that which obtained in eastern Polynesia.[28] Modern anthropologists agree with him that in pre-contact Samoa, religious values and organization were under-stressed[29] and that religion 'was not everything'.[30] Compared to eastern Polynesia, the received anthropological opinion would hold that the structure of Samoan religious life was unorganized.[31] The LMS missionaries, accustomed to the religious practices of Tahiti, recorded some striking absences: no idols, no spectacular temples, no polytheistic pantheon, no differentiated, institutionalized priesthood, no splendid public religious rituals. Overt religious rituals were not connected with social life. It is hard to find religious connections with the social organization; rituals were performed privately in the family, the titled family head (*matai*) acting as family priest and ensuring the family's welfare by seeking the favour of the family god (*aitu*). There was no religious centre in Samoa comparable to the *marae* of eastern Polynesia, the sacred temple compound housing the idols, which served religious as well as social functions. The Samoans, therefore, unlike east Polynesians, did not have to pass the traumatic test of destroying *en masse* the paraphernalia of their old religion. The Samoan *malae*, the community's public square, was just a meeting place and village green serving merely social functions and was without religious importance. Hence there were no vested public interests which stood in the way of the expansion of a new faith.

Above all, there was no priestly caste whose power and prestige could have been threatened or demoted by Christianity. On the contrary, status rivalry among the kings and high chiefs, together with the secular and pragmatic attitude toward religion, were favourable conditions for the propagation of the new religion. To the Samoans their material culture was god-given, and when they came to learn of the white man's religion they concluded that the great God Jehovah was in the same way responsible for all those coveted foreign riches. This pragmatic attitude explains the ambition of the chiefs to possess a resident white man as a teacher of religion, which manifests itself in the early hunt for European beachcombers, and later for missionaries. While no European missionaries were available and when, after 1835, they were still very rare, sailors and escaped convicts, too, were considered capable of teaching the secrets of the religion of the white man. Individual European castaways in Samoa took advantage of this state of affairs, some with good and honest intentions, others with less honourable ones. They became the founders of the so-called 'sailor sects', which arose well before 1830 and petered out only after the missionary presence in Samoa was strengthened.

The position of the *matai* as family head and family priest, however, was affected neither by the changes in Samoan customs, nor by the doctrinal and institutional changes in the wake of the missionary enterprise. *Matais* continued to conduct the daily family prayers, simply substituting Jehovah for Tagaloa, the supreme god of pre-Christian days, and for other traditional *aitu* like their family gods. Hence the traditional power structure remained intact. Real institutional changes such as the establishment of the office of pastor did not come into conflict with the *matai* system because of the customary separation between rank and power. This means that social eminence is not necessarily translated into political power. The pastor, in the absence of a traditional priestly class, was just put on top of the hierarchy of ranked titles. Thus he was accorded the highest honours, but political government remained in the hands of the *matai* as before. When more and more Samoans became pastors and the white missionaries (except for Roman Catholic priests and nuns) gradually withdrew from the country, the Samoans took over the most important missionary organizations and held them firmly. The 'imprisonment of Christ in *fa'aSamoa*', as one observer would have it,[32] was complete. The genius of the Samoans lay in social and political fields rather than in religious or philosophical matters. Hence religion in Samoa was never as highly organized as elsewhere in Polynesia. *Matais* simply became deacons in the new village churches. Missionaries and, later, indigenous pastors took over the socially sanctioned role of spirit-medium (*taula aitu*).

Thus far the received opinion. I agree with much of it, especially with Watters' useful summary of the factors involved in the composite reaction of Samoan society to western culture.[33] According to this author, the economic motive – the yearning for the material benefits of the transition – played a major part.[34] Next, missionaries taught *converts* to read and write; and when a printing press was landed in 1838, printed matter, including the Gospel, was a considerable incentive to turn to Christianity.[35] Conversion of a *matai* was almost invariably followed by that of his kinsfolk, and the conversion of a community (*nu'u*) was often followed by that of allied communities. In local power politics it was an advantage to turn to Christianity if the missionaries supported the dominant party (*malo*). Status rivalry was instrumental as an entry channel for the new religion, since increased social status followed admission to church membership; and new taboos such as the observance of the Sabbath and the new moral precepts were readily accepted, as they replaced old ones of equal severity. I also agree with the received opinion that the *matai*'s position as family priest has not changed to a large extent since pre-Christian days, and that the political influence of the pastor has been neutralized through the traditional separation between power and rank.

Yet I consider the received opinion to be completely mistaken concerning the fundamentals of Samoan religious life. I shall argue that: (1) the separation of religion and the public domain reflects modern western concepts and is invalid when applied to a society such as Samoa; (2) the Samoan *malae*, like its eastern Polynesian counterpart, was and still is a community centre of major religious importance; (3) traditional Samoan religion was not merely a private family affair; religious rituals were also inseparably connected with political organization. Hence, (4) the conversion to Christianity was so successful not because the Samoans were religious pragmatists and their religion was practised only in the family, but, on the contrary, because it was constitutive for the organization of the body politic, the polis (*nu'u*). The most important public ceremony, the Kava Ceremony, is the key to our understanding of the real significance of religion in pre-contact Samoa, and of what it still means today.

## The Samoan Kava Ceremony

Kava (*piper methysticum*) is cultivated in Polynesia for ordinary use, but it is also an essential element in social usage and ceremonial.[36] The Samoan form of the name 'kava' is *'ava*, and in Samoa nothing of any importance can be commenced without a preliminary bowl of kava. There are many forms of kava use, but the most important was the ceremonial drinking of kava in an assembly house at the *malae* by the *matai*s. There are different myths concerning the origin of the first kava plant.[37] For example, the plant is said to have originated as the result of a sacrifice made to Tui Manu'a, the holder of Samoa's highest kingly title, who was accorded divine status in pre-contact times. In a famous variant, the first Kava Ceremony was enacted by Tagaloa and Pava, a war god on the south side of Upolu.[38] The social *and* religious character of kava drinking in Samoa and Tonga has been stressed by

E.S.C. Handy,[39] and a sense of sacredness adheres to the ceremony to the present day; nobody may break into the Kava Circle, and noise or disturbance of any kind is forbidden inside or outside the assembly house when the ceremony is being performed.[40] As one contemporary Samoan observer, a pastor himself, has stated: the recipient of a kava cup utters a few words in the form of a prayer, 'giving thanks and asking for guidance and blessing. As he speaks he pours a little kava onto the floor as an oblation, *originally intended for the ancestor gods, but now often addressed to Almighty God.*'[41]

The deeply religious significance of the Kava Ceremony in pre-Christian Samoa can be gleaned from the traditions. The Gods were believed to assemble in the Ninth Heaven, the dwelling-place of Tagaloa the creator (Tagaloa-fa'a-tutupu-nu'u) and Tagaloa the immovable (Tagaloa-lê-fuli), when the various decrees were made concerning the creation of the world. Kava was served on this occasion.[42]

The Kava Ceremony and the Christian service of communion, the Eucharist, are homologous in structure, and this, I argue, paved the way for the ultimate identification of the Christian way of life and the *fa'aSamoa*. If this is correct, the *matai* performing the Kava Ceremony were not merely family priests. On the contrary, they were the real, original priesthood of traditional Samoa. All they had to do in the Christian era was to consecrate the Kava Ceremony to Jehovah. This they did, and thus it became possible for them to continue to behave as Samoan chiefs and to be Christians at the same time.

The identification of the most important and meaningful traditional Samoan ritual with the Eucharist manifests itself strikingly in a booklet published in 1973 by the Roman Catholic Church in Samoa, entitled *The Kava Ceremony is a Prophecy*.[43] In it, the authors state that the kava root can represent Jesus Christ who was presented as a heavenly Kava Root at Bethlehem,[44] and the distribution of the kava cup is seen as a reminder of the apostles distributing Holy Communion.[45] In the foreword, the Bishop of Samoa and Tokelau, Cardinal Pio Taofinu'u (the first cardinal of Samoan origin), addresses his countrymen with the following words: 'Samoa! You have to, deeply, reconsider your Culture. Your Culture is your inheritance, the foundation of your life, from God.'[46]

As a clergyman, the cardinal avails himself of a strategy of incorporation familiar to Christian theology. As early as the second century AD, Justinus Martyr (100–167), for example, in a letter to the Roman Emperor, Antoninus Pius, portrays Heraclitus and Socrates as predecessors of Jesus Christ. Through the divine *logos spermaticos*, they have partial access to the knowledge of God's divine and eternal truths.[47] In the same way, Cardinal Pio describes the Kava Ceremony as a 'prophecy', which revealed to the Samoans, in their own cultural idiom, God's eternal truths well before the advent of the missionaries.

Yet Cardinal Pio is not the only Samoan clergyman who explains the Kava Ceremony as a powerful symbol of a contextual theology in the Pacific. Similar views have also been expressed recently in the *Pacific Journal of Theology* by a minister of the Methodist Church in Samoa.[48] To this author, the Kava Ceremony is both a cultural performance and a traditional act of worship; and the sacredness of the experience of worship, he suggests, was strengthened by the introduction of Christianity! The pounded *ava* root is interpreted as a symbol of Christ who was crushed on the cross. 'From the cross His blood (the liquid *ava*) was poured out to redeem, reconcile and unify the world as God's people.'[49] Hence, from a theological point of view, the kava root 'should be understood as a locally created material which can be used to manifest the sacramental reality of God's creation'.[50]

Anthropologists should take such views seriously and not dismiss them as theologians' speculations. Quite independently, the similarity of the Eucharist with certain major Polynesian rituals has been pointed out by western scientists in regard to Fiji[51] and Tikopia.[52] From a comparative point of view the Eucharist and the Kava Ceremony are essentially ritual commemorations. They bring to mind *archái*, sequences of events involving mythic substances that recur in identical form, as *real presence*, in the actions based upon them.[53] In Mircea Eliade's[54] terms, the Eucharist would belong to a class of polyvalent, universal hierophanies which can be translated into many diverse local cultural expressions. In traditional Samoa, I suggest, this hierophany found its expression in the Kava Ceremony performed on the *malae*. It is a political ritual and at the same time a religious one, and this was the case well before the introduction of Christianity. We should always bear in mind that in Samoa, the *malae* is *pa'ia*, *sa* (sacred), attributes also given to the Christian God.[55] The religious character of the Kava Ceremony, however, has remained hidden to missionaries and many anthropologists alike. I suggest that this is because they share some basic western preconceptions, despite their disagreement in many other fields. Yet the transition to Christianity in Samoa demands a rethinking of some of our basic concepts, such as *religion* and *politics*, in order to be properly understood.

A major element of pre-Christian Samoan religion was 'a sense of integral relationship between religious practices and the general welfare of the community', as Derek Freeman puts it so aptly.[56] The Kava Ceremony, I argue, is the trait in which this aspect of Samoan religiosity is most impressively expressed. That this has not generally been recognized by western observers is due to the fact that in the West, in accordance with St Augustine and Lactantius, the word 'religion' is commonly derived from *religare* – to fasten, to bind. In its figurative sense *religare* refers to that bond which unites the human individual to God.[57] This etymology stresses the highly individualistic relationship between God and the single human being, and espouses a concept of morality that dissociates the striving for *individual* salvation from the commitment to the common good. It agrees well with the central position of the individual in modern western thought, which has blossomed in the wake of the development of civil society and the modern market economy. What is more, since the Reformation, and since René Descartes inaugurated the great anthropocentric shift in philosophy through his distinction between *res cogitans* and *res extensa*, western religion – while retaining external expressions – has placed ever-increasing emphasis on the more inward-turning, on religion as a matter of the mind, of cognitions and beliefs, and of sentimental attitudes. This, I suggest, is the concept of religion shared by missionaries and anthropologists (whether the latter are believers or not does not matter).

There is another concept of religion, however, which does not relate religion to a sum of dogmas, beliefs and attitudes. It is M. Tullius Cicero's concept,[58] for he derived *religio* not from *religare*, but from *relegere*. The literal meaning of this word is 'to read again'; in its figurative sense, however, it means *to observe scrupulously ritual duties and regulations*. Hence, among the several meanings of the word *religio*, the *Oxford Latin Dictionary* lists the following: 'a religious practice, custom, ritual'; 'punctilious regard for one's obligations, consciousness'; 'scrupulous regard (for)'. And one of the meanings of the adjective *religiosus* is 'scrupulous with regard to accuracy or correctness'.[59] The proper statesman is one who furthers the common good by punctiliously discharging his ritual public duties, either by being most conscientious about correctly performing them himself, or by showing the utmost care in providing for the correct performance of public rituals by specialists, for example priests.

All the keynote speakers at the Sixteenth Congress of the International Association for the History of Religion held in Rome in September 1990 agreed that this is a concept of religion that can be applied fruitfully in cross-cultural comparison.[60] Religion, in this sense, has been labelled *Observanzreligion* (religion of observance). This is the kind of religion we encounter in old and modern Samoa. Its climax is the Kava Ceremony held during the *fono*, the assembly of *matai*, on the *malae*.[61] It is enshrined in the speeches, the etiquette, the full splendour of Samoan ritual culture. It is a public religion, a political religion which can be carried on in the name of Jesus Christ. The crux of the matter lies in the concept of 'politics', of course, and the significance that is attributed to this word when applied to pre-capitalist societies outside Europe. The family of words embracing the words 'political', 'politics' and 'politician' originates from the Greek word 'polis', a town, a castle, municipality or their inhabitants. One particularly interesting sideline in this connection leads to 'politeia', in the sense of constitution, or internal order in a polis.[62] Hence political activity, in this sense, is directed towards maintaining unity, public order and security. However, there is hardly any type of activity in a society like Samoa that is more political than cult and ceremonial activities. And there is hardly any type of activity, we can add, that is more religious. Hence we can hardly be more mistaken than to claim that the transition to Christianity took place so easily because the Samoans were without 'a widely articulated sacred ethic'.[63] The contrary is true: Chiefs *had to* embrace Christianity, because by so doing, by adapting a new cult, they believed that they would further the common good. In turning to Christianity, the Samoans have been continuing to practise their established religion of observance. Samoans, and many other Pacific islanders, were not just passive clients of foreign missionary activity. Right from the beginning they were active participants in their own conversion. They created new forms of religion that are both Oceanic and part of world Christianity.[64] Hence Christianity in Samoa, and in the Pacific in general, finally deserves to be taken seriously by those western intellectuals who still claim that it is a religion false to Oceanic cultures.[65]

Paradoxical as it may sound, the transition to Christianity in Samoa took place not because the old religion could be replaced so easily, but because turning to the new cult conformed with the logic of the old system. In this sense, the Kava Ceremony has really been a Prophecy.

## Notes

1. I thank John Charlot and John Mayer, University of Hawai'i at Manoa, Honolulu, who discussed earlier versions of this chapter and shared valuable information with me. The final version was prepared during my stay as an Official Visitor at the East–West Center in Honolulu, in October and November 1994. I would like to thank Geoffrey White, Director of the Center's Program for Cultural Studies, and his staff for their patience and assistance and for providing the facilities which enabled me to write this chapter. Thanks are also due to the Roman Catholic Diocese of Samoa and Tokelau, especially to His Eminence, Cardinal Pio Taofinu'u, for his assistance and encouragement of my researches. Father Michael Allen and Father Simon Bourke shared valuable information with me during my short visit in 1995. Sister Ancillita and the Sisters of the convent at Savalalo are remembered with gratefulness for their help and generous hospitality offered during our stay in 1980–81. Ethnological fieldwork in Western Samoa was supported by the Deutsche Forschungsgemeinschaft, Bonn.

2. Excellent summaries of the missionaries vs. anthropologists issue are given by Daniel T. Hughes, 'Mutual Biases of Anthropologists and Missionaries', in J.A. Boutilier, D.T. Hughes and S.W. Tiffany (eds.), *Mission, Church, and Sect*, University Press of America, Lanham, pp. 65–82; and Claude E. Stipe, Anthropologists versus Missionaries', *Current Anthropology* 21 (1980), pp. 165–79. See also *Zeitschrift für Mission*, vol. 12, no. 4 (1986).

3. John Barker, Introduction, in John Barker (ed.), *Christianity in Oceania: Ethnographic Perspectives*, University Press of America, Lanham, 1990, p. 8.

4. For historical accounts of the transition to Christianity in Samoa, see J.W. Davidson: *Samoa mo Samoa: The Emergence of the Independent State of Western Samoa*, Oxford University Press, Melbourne, 1967, pp. 31–45; John Garrett, *To Live Among the Stars: Christian Origins in Oceania*,

World Council of Churches/University of the South Pacific, Geneva and Suva, 1982; R.P. Gilson: *Samoa 1830–1900: The Politics of a Multi-Cultural Community*, Oxford University Press, Melbourne, 1970; Niel Gunson, *Messengers of Grace: Evangelical Missionaries in the South Seas 1797–1860*, Oxford University Press, Melbourne, 1978; Lowell D. Holmes, 'Cults, Cargo and Christianity: Samoan Responses to Western Religion', *Missiology*, vol. 8, no. 4 (1980), pp. 471–87; Sharon W. Tiffany, 'The Politics of Denominational Organization in Samoa', in Boutilier, Hughes and Tiffany (eds.), *Mission, Church, and Sect*, pp. 423–56; R.F. Watters, 'The Transition to Christianity in Samoa', *Historical Studies*, vol. 8 (1959), pp. 392–99.

5. Richard M. Moyle (ed.), *The Samoan Journals of John Williams 1830 and 1832*, Australian National University Press, Canberra, 1984, p. 75.

6. See Niel Gunson, 'The Coming of Foreigners', in Noel Rutherford (ed.), *Friendly Islands: A History of Tonga*, Oxford University Press, Melbourne, 1977, pp. 90–113. The Samoan genealogies collected by Augustin Krämer contain many references to marriages between members of the Samoan and Tongan nobility. See *Die Samoa-Inseln*, vol. 1, Schweizerbartsche Verlagsbuchhandlung, Stuttgart, 1902.

7. Concerning beachcombers, see H.E. Maude, 'Beachcombers and Castaways', *JPS*, vol. 73, pp. 254–93; Thomas Bargatzky, *Die Rolle des Fremden beim Kulturwandel*, Klaus Renner, Hohenschäftlarn, 1978; see also T. Bargatzky, 'Beachcombers and Castaways as Innovators', *The Journal of Pacific History*, vol. 15 (1980), pp. 93–102.

8. See Ian C. Campbell, *European Transculturists in Polynesia 1789–ca. 1840*, Ph.D. thesis, University of Adelaide, 1976, pp. 275–6.

9. Charles Wilkes, *Narrative of the United States Exploring Expedition During the Years 1838, 1839, 1840, 1841, 1842*, Lea & Blanchard, Philadelphia, 1845, vol. II, p. 128.

10. Ibid., pp. 128–9.

11. Charles Barff, *Journal*, 26 June 1836, London Missionary Society, South Seas Journals, Box 8, No. 112. The observance of the Sabbath has been noted, too, by a sailor like Charles Erskine, a member of Commander Wilkes' expedition, who was in Samoa in 1839. See his *Twenty Years before the Mast with More Thrilling Scenes and Incidents while Circumnavigating the Globe under the Command of the Late Admiral Charles Wilkes 1838–1842*, published by the author, Boston, 1890, p. 85.

12. Wilkes, *Narrative*, vol. II, p. 130. See Tiffany, 'The Politics of Denominational Organization', for a critical discussion of missionary censuses.

13. George Turner, *Nineteen Years in Polynesia: Missionary Life, Travels, and Researches in the Islands of the Pacific*, John Snow, London, 1861, p. 243.

14. Concerning Sio Vili, see J. Derek Freeman, 'The Joe Gimlet or Siovili Cult: An Episode in the Religious History of Early Samoa', in J.D.

Freeman and W.R. Geddes (eds.), *Anthropology in the South Seas*, Thomas Avery, New Plymouth, 1959. See also D.J. Inglis, 'The Siovili Cult', in John Hinchcliff, Jack Lewis and Kapil Tiwari (eds.), *Religious Studies in the Pacific*, Colloquium Publishers, Auckland University, Auckland, 1978, pp. 37–44.

15. Inglis, 'The Siovili Cult'.

16. Alan Gavan Daws, 'The Great Samoan Awakening of 1839', *JPS*, vol. 70 (1961), pp. 326–37.

17. See Wilkes, *Narrative*, vol. II, pp. 76–9, 82, 91, 107, 133–4, 138–40; Turner, *Nineteen Years*; John B. Stair, *Old Samoa, or Flotsam and Jetsam from the Pacific Ocean*, Religious Tract Society, London, 1897.

18. Tiffany, 'The Politics of Denominational Organization', p. 424.

19. Letter, London Missionary Society, South Seas Letters, Box 25, Folder 8, Jacket C.

20. Felix M. Keesing, *Modern Samoa: Its Government and Changing Life*, Allen & Unwin, London, 1934, p. 410, italics mine. This view is quoted by W.E.H. Stanner, *The South Seas in Transition: A Study of Post-War Rehabilitation and Reconstruction in Three British Pacific Dependencies*, Australasian Publishing Company, Sydney, 1953, p. 292.

21. Keesing, *Modern Samoa*.

22. Margaret Mead, *Coming of Age in Samoa*, William Morrow, New York, 1928.

23. Margaret Mead, *Social Organization of Manu'a*, Bernice P. Bishop Museum Bulletin 76, Honolulu, 1930, p. 85.

24. Horst Cain, *Aitu: Eine Untersuchung zur autochthonen Religion der Samoaner*, Franz Steiner, Wiesbaden 1979; see also Derek Freeman, *Margaret Mead and Samoa: The Making and Unmaking of an Anthropological Myth*, Harvard University Press, Cambridge Mass., 1983, ch. 12.

25. Keesing, *Modern Samoa*, p. 408; Dorothee Schneider-Christians, 'Die alte Religion und das Christentum Samoas', D.Phil. dissertation, Bonn University, 1992, p. 13.

26. Stanner, *The South Seas in Transition*, p. 309.

27. Watters, 'The Transition to Christianity', pp. 397, 396.

28. John Williams, *A Narrative of Missionary Enterprises in the South Sea Islands, with Remarks upon the Natural History of the Islands, Origin, Languages, Traditions, and Usages of the Inhabitants*, John Snow, London, 1838, p. 464.

29. Stanner, *The South Seas in Transition*, p. 304 n.5.

30. Tiffany, 'The Politics of Denominational Organization', p. 429.

31. This view is expressed in accounts by missionaries such as George Turner, *Nineteen Years*, p. 239; and in *Samoa A Hundred Years Ago and Long Before*, Macmillan, London, 1884; George Brown, *Melanesians and Polynesians. Their Life-Histories Described and Compared*, Macmillan, London, 1910, pp. 227–8; and Stair, *Old Samoa*. The summary of the received anthropological opinion presented in this chapter is based on the

works of the following authors: Stanner, *The South Seas in Transition*, pp. 310–11, 317; Keesing, *Modern Samoa*, pp. 399–402; Gilson, *Samoa 1830–1900*, pp. 73–74; Davidson, *Samoa mo Samoa*, pp. 33, 37; Freeman, 'The Joe Gimlet or Siovili Cult'; Watters, 'The Transition to Christianity'; Tiffany, 'The Politics of Denominational Organization', pp. 428–9; Lowell D. Holmes, *Samoan Village*, Holt, Rinehart & Winston, New York, 1974, pp. 58–64; Gerda Kröber, *Das MATAI-System in Samoa: Rekonstruktion seiner traditionellen Ausprägung und Analyse seiner Resistenz gegenüber dem Akkulturationsdruck*, D.Phil. dissertation, Freie Universität Berlin, 1975, pp. 81–3; Douglas L. Oliver, *The Pacific Islands*, revised edn, The University Press of Hawai'i, Honolulu, 1975, p. 213; Jukka Siikala, *Cult and Conflict in Tropical Polynesia: A Study of Traditional Religion, Christianity and Nativistic Movements*, FF Communications No. 233, Academia Scientiarum Fennica, Helsinki, 1982, pp. 174–6, 195, 200–201.

32. Stanner, *The South Seas in Transition*, p. 317. Cf. ibid., p. 292.

33. Watters, 'Transition to Christianity'.

34. Cf. J.D. Freeman, 'The Joe Gimlet or Siovili Cult'.

35. Many accounts of Samoan history would give 1839 as the year in which a printing press was landed in Samoa. Yet according to Archibald Wright Murray, one of the six resident LMS missionaries who arrived in Samoa in 1836, the missionary John B. Stair arrived in Samoa on board the missionary ship *Camden* in September 1838. 'Mr. Stair was a printer, and came furnished with a printing-press and everything needful for the exercise of his calling.' See A.B. Murray, *Forty Years' Mission Work in Polynesia and New Guinea, from 1835 to 1875*, Robert Carter & Brothers, New York, 1876, p. 99. Printed matter, including psalms, hymns and religious tracts, printed at the LMS press in Huahine (Society Islands) and later in Rarotonga, may have been available in Samoa even before this date. See William Churchill, 'The Earliest Samoan Prints', *Proceedings of the Academy of Natural Sciences of Philadelphia*, vol. 67 (part 2), 1915, pp. 199–202.

36. For descriptions of kava cultivation and use, see Mead, *Social Organization of Manu'a*, pp. 102–12; Te Rangi Hiroa, *Samoan Material Culture*, Bernice P. Bishop Museum Bulletin 75, Honolulu, 1930, pp. 147–64.

37. O. Stuebel, *Samoanische Texte, unter Beihülfe von Eingeborenen gesammelt und übersetzt*, Veröffentlichungen aus dem königlichen Museum für Völkerkunde Berlin, 4(2–4), Dietrich Reimer, Berlin, 1896, pp. 68–70, 168–9.

38. Turner, *Samoa A Hundred Years Ago*, pp. 42–3. A different spelling of the name is 'Paoa'. Paoa is claimed as one of the ancestors of the Maori of New Zealand. See W.E. Gudgeon, 'Paoa', *JPS*, vol. 1 (1892), p. 76.

39. E.S. Craighill Handy, *Polynesian Religion*, Bernice P. Bishop Museum Bulletin 34, Honolulu 1927, p. 322.

40. Tevita Amituana'i, 'Kava in Samoa', in Gweneth and Bruce Deverell

98     EUROPEAN IMPACT AND PACIFIC INFLUENCE

(eds.), *Pacific Rituals – Living or Dying?*, University of The South Pacific, Suva, 1986, p. 39.

41. Ibid., p. 37; italics mine.

42. John Fraser, 'The Samoan Story of Creation', *JPS*, vol. 1 (1892), p. 172; T. Powell and G. Pratt, 'Some Folk-Songs and Myths from Samoa', *Journal of the Royal Society of New South Wales*, vol. 24 (1890), p. 211. See also 'O le Solo o le Va', in 'Folk-Songs and Myths from Samoa', p. 25, edited by John Fraser, *JPS*, vol. 6 (1897), pp. 19–36.

43. *O le 'Ava o se Pelofetaga: The Kava Ceremony is a Prophecy*, with a foreword by Cardinal Pio Taofinu'u, dated 8 September 1973; second edition, enlarged, 1995.

44. Ibid., p. 2.

45. Ibid., p. 7.

46. Ibid., p. 1.

47. Apologia I, 46; II, 8, 13. *Patrologia Graeca*, ed. Migne, VI, column 397, 457, 465.

48. Urima Fa'asi'i, 'Gospel and Culture in the *Ava* Ceremony', *Pacific Journal of Theology*, series II, no. 10 (1993), pp. 61–3.

49. Ibid., p. 63.

50. Ibid.

51. John Charlot, 'Oceanic Customs/Coutumes Océaniques', *L'Osservatore Romano* 11:3; 27:5 (1968).

52. Raymond Firth, *The Work of the Gods in Tikopia* (second edition with new Introduction and Epilogue), Athlone Press, London, 1967, pp. 156–9. Incidentally, the parallel between kava and *sua* (the food for honoured guests that goes with the presentation of kava) and the bread and wine of Communion was pointed out by Robert Franco in an unpublished seminar paper given at Chico, California State University, in 1975. This paper was not available to me, but a reference to it is given by L.D. Holmes, 'Cults, Cargo, and Christianity', p. 482. Holmes, too, concludes that traditional Samoan religion had much in common with Christianity (ibid., p. 484).

53. For ethnological parallels, see Adolf E. Jensen, *Mythos und Kult bei Naturvölkern*, Franz Steiner, Wiesbaden, 1960. For Indo-European variants, see Bruce Lincoln, *Myth, Cosmos, and History: Indo-European Themes of Creation and Destruction*, Harvard University Press, Cambridge Mass., 1986. For an encompassing epistemological treatment of the ontology of myth and ritual, see Kurt Hübner, *Critique of Scientific Discovery*, University of Chicago Press, Chicago, 1983; and especially Hübner's *Die Wahrheit des Mythos*, C.H. Beck, Munich, 1985.

54. Mircea Eliade, *Die Religionen und das Heilige: Elemente der Religionsgeschichte*, Insel, Frankfurt am Main, 1986, p. 25 (originally published under the title *Traité d'histoire des religions*, Payot, Paris, 1949).

55. Information given by John Mayer, University of Hawai'i at Manoa.

56. Freeman, *Margaret Mead and Samoa*, p. 180.

57. See Wilhelm Traugott Krug, *Allgemeines Handwörterbuch der philosophischen Wissenschaften, nebst ihrer Literatur und Geschichte*, F.A. Brockhaus, Leipzig, 1833, pp. 497–501.

58. *De natura deorum* II, 72.

59. P.G.W. Glare (ed.), *Oxford Latin Dictionary*, Clarendon Press, Oxford, 1982, p. 1606.

60. See Ugo Bianchi (ed.), *The Notion of 'Religion' in Comparative Research* (Selected Proceedings of the XVI IAHR Congress), 'L'Erma' di Bretschneider, Rome, 1994. Cf. Peter Antes, '"Religion" einmal anders', *Temenos* 14 (1978), pp. 184–97; Ulrich Berner, 'Religio und Superstitio. Betrachtungen zur römischen Religionsgeschichte', in Theo Sundermeier (ed.), *Den Fremden wahrnehmen: Bausteine für eine Xenologie*, Gerd Mohn, Gütersloh, 1992, pp. 45–64.

61. The deep religious significance of the Kava Ceremony also obtains for pre-Christian Tonga: 'The presentation and drinking of *kava* was an essential part of the visit and supplication to gods.' See E.E.V. Collocott, 'Kava Ceremonial in Tonga', *JPS*, vol. 36 (1927), p. 43. Cf. ibid., pp. 39, 45.

62. See Hans Maier, 'Politik I. Geschichte und Systematik', in: *Staatslexikon*, vol. 4, 7th edition, Herder, Freiburg im Breisgau, 1988, col. 431–5; Dolf Sternberger, *Drei Wurzeln der Politik*, vol. I, Insel, Frankfurt am Main, 1978, p. 25; Thomas Bargatzky, 'Politik, die "Arbeit der Götter"', in Thomas Schweizer, Margarete Schweizer and Waltraud Kokot (eds.), *Handbuch der Ethnologie: Festschrift für Ulla Johansen*, Dietrich Reimer, Berlin, 1993, pp. 263–83.

63. Stanner, *The South Seas in Transition*, p. 317.

64. See Barker (ed.), *Christianity in Oceania*, p. 15 (cf. n.2 above).

65. See, for example, Jeff Dunn in a letter to the University of Hawai'i newspaper *Ka Leo O Hawai'i*, 28 October 1994, p. 5.

# 7

# Zealotry among the Converted: American Board Missionaries in Micronesia, 1852–1919

## ARTHUR J. KNOLL

### 'The Other'

No more difficult enterprise of social transformation could be visualized: an ascetic and puritanical group of missionaries from Boston, sent out by the American Board of Commissioners for Foreign Missions (ABCFM),[1] descended on Micronesia in 1852 to convert the extroverted, *lebensfreudige* islanders of the Carolines and the Gilberts. Their task was to transform a this-worldly behaviour pattern into a life style of ascetism, pacificism and preparation for the next world. In the words of two researchers of Pacific history: 'For the missionaries of the ABCFM who went to Micronesia, matters of morality were stark black and white, there could be no compromise with evil.'[2] After a series of initial lean years, given the means at its disposal, the mission was quite successful in converting people and in changing their life styles on islands like Ponape, Nauru, Kusaie, and in the Marshalls.[3]

The first mission task was to confront and to dominate 'the other'. This is a useful concept which describes abundance, primeval existence, wildness, naturalness, and exotic behavior. Michael Taussig wrote of the 'imputation of mystery and demonic by the more powerful class to the lower – by men to women, by the civilized to the primitive, by the Christian to the pagan...'[4] 'The other' is also 'the spirit of the unknown and the disorderly,

loose in the forest encircling the city and the sown land...'.[5]
Taussig's model of primitivism versus civilization is derived from
his investigation of the exploitation of local people along the
Putumayo River of south-western Colombia for rubber and other
plantation products during the nineteenth and twentieth centuries.
It is a concept useful enough to be used in the encounters of
Europeans and Americans with those in traditional societies.

American Board missionaries in Micronesia described 'the other'
in these terms: as 'the darkest night of spiritual desolation', as 'a
degradation the sight of which makes one shiver to the bone'. It
was manifest in 'heathen dance ... conducted with wild madness
and most licentious practices' and done 'to propitiate the evil
spirit...'.[6] Missionary Phillip Delaporte, reflecting in 1910,
described the 'revolting immoral scenes' he had witnessed fifteen
years previously.[7] Missionary Edward T. Doane viewed Ponapeans
as 'a loathsome mass of depravity', at least before their redemption by Christianity.[8] The perceived promiscuity of the Marshall
islanders caught the attention of visitors such as the Capuchin
missionary, August Erdland, who depicted practices which, to him,
seemed licentious: that the first-born son had sexual access to the
wives of his younger brothers; that in the absence of the elder
brother it became the turn of the younger brothers to have intercourse with his wife; that women essentially gained in stature
through the frequency of intercourse.[9] Erdland also reported about
the 'murderous free intercourse' which killed 'thousands of men
and women' as a result of infectious venereal disease.[10] Missionary
insistence upon monogamy and sexual abstinence, conceived for
religious reasons, represented on this occasion sane health practice.

How did one do this, transform 'the other'? It would be a daunting
task. August Erdland called the Marshall islanders 'indolent and
lazy, ... that their mendacity is far surpassed by their sensuality',
that they have no word for nakedness, and that 'there is no spiritual
and moral education'.[11] Erdland's perception was essentially that of
the missionaries. Missionary Sarah L. Garland thought that taming
the primitive other would require much effort given 'the accumulated evil tendencies of generations of heathen ancestors...'.[12] Such
assessments presaged a degree of social engineering that would root
out the traditional in favour of the western and the modern.[13] The
mission was definitely not in the tradition of Jean-Jacques Rousseau
and Paul Gauguin in praising the natural life. The natural life of

'the other' did have one advantage for missionaries: they saw it as the opportunity to shape virgin material as one wanted.

Apparently American missionaries measured islanders in Micronesia by religious standards developed for religious communities in New England, where the emphasis was upon work, self-denial, and preparation for the hereafter. Missionaries also prized order, direction and propriety, virtues that the Ponapean life style seemed consistently to violate.[14] These congregationalists were exclusive in the sense that they removed from their midst those who fell short of their standards. As a result of this sort of spiritual boycott, only the redeemed would be left and those who could not or would not conform would be asked to leave because they represented a tempting alternative to the faithful. Congregationalists were also specialists in small group dynamics; they relied upon initiative and incentive from below rather than upon direction from the top. Authority patterns which emanated from below represented an inversion of the traditional hierarchical authority structure of Ponape or the Marshalls.

When mission models of approved conduct were applied in the Pacific, islanders fell short of the standards prescribed for them by the American Board. Missionaries observed that islanders had fallen prey to whaling and beachcomber communities who introduced them to alcoholic beverages. The result was a great 'craving for drink', often encouraged by local political elites who profited from sales in tobacco and alcohol. The potential for violence was also great, given the Marshall Islanders' possession of weapons and alcoholic drink.[15] If the mission were to succeed, it would have to bend not only beachcombers and whalers to its will, but also those who dabbled in the trade.[16] The power of chiefs would also have to bend to the will of the faithful in Christian committees and groups. Constraining chiefs would be a difficult task since, in the beginning at least, the missionary 'belonged' to the chief within whose territory he worked. On the other hand, the missionary offered his aid to the chief in restraining the more refractory elements on Ponape.[17]

## The New Technology

Unfortunately the mission documents are mostly silent about islander perceptions of the new arrivals with their new order of priorities. From the works of Hermann Hiery, Paul Mark Ehrlich and David Hanlon we do, however, have an idea of what the islanders found remarkable about the missionaries. For one thing local people reacted enthusiastically to the new implements that the missionaries brought. On the island of Ponape these could be used by adaptable Ponapeans to gain advantage and leverage in their own culture. It was very important in a competitive society like Ponape to get ahead. Ponapeans perceived the mission as offering important advantages in this regard.[18] Similarly, in New Guinea, as Stewart Firth noted: 'The Melanesian villager valued the missionary, at least initially, not for what he preached but for what he possessed, gave away or traded.'[19] Thus 'Christianity's immediate appeal (not its ultimate one) sprang from its political and material aspects.'[20]

Hermann Hiery has pointed out that the respect engendered by technology has not been properly credited by historians.[21] The power of these *Wunderdinge* was demonstrated in August 1854 when a smallpox epidemic ravaged Ponape. Missionary Dr Luther H. Gulick inoculated against the disease in spite of the opposition of priests who sought to impede him. Gulick reported success: 'This is a considerable triumph; for the Nanakin and his sons were a short time since among the most active in threatening to shoot me. They now pay me every respect.'[22] Islanders now perceived the Christian faith as having both power and utility.

Hermann Hiery has also indicated that Micronesians did not necessarily feel intellectually, socially or culturally inferior to the European possessors of technology. Rather they respected foreigners for their acquisitions and they tended to be wary of what these users of technology might do with it.[23] Thus on the island of Mogemog in the central Carolines, Hans Damm, one of the researchers for the Thilenius' South Seas Expedition of 1908–10, related how the islanders scrupulously obeyed the orders of the *Bezirksamtmann* on Yap because they thought he could control them from his island seat, possibly through his access to the new technology.[24]

Other islanders, such as those on German Samoa, were not content simply to bemoan their low status in the eyes of the German residents. They analysed the cause of their humiliation and concluded that Germans didn't respect them because they were perceived as being rooted in ignorance. Determined to transform this perception, Samoan elites advocated a speech pattern without stuttering and hesitation (to impress the Germans); they also sought input into the legal decisions of the *Bezirksamtmann*.[25]

## Creating the New Social Order

Missionaries began their evangelical work with behaviour-transformation through schools, informal contact, and teaching by example. First of all, indolence had to be removed. There could be no lolling about. The work ethic had to be implanted. Paul Hambruch, the German ethnologist, had described the islanders as enthusiasts for eating, drinking and sleeping, but difficult to motivate for work.[26] The means to get islanders to work in the sense that the mission wanted them to work could be best achieved through the acquisition of western goods. Once the islanders saw such objects in mission houses they might be inspired to work for them.

The second step was to enrol local elites for one's conversion programme. In hierarchical societies, such as on the Marshalls or on Ponape, chiefs and elders seemed the right choices. Thus on Ponape the chief's son moved into the mission in 1853 and missionary Benjamin R. Snow confidently reported: 'He is sort of a guardian angel to us; for no native will dare to meddle with anything of mine, while he is near.'[27] Similarly in the Marshalls and at a much later date (1919), missionary C. R. Heine reported that chiefs not only attended church services but also contributed financially to the mission. All the chiefs and underchiefs except one had converted to Christianity.[28] But the German government also sought to make use of the elites for its own purposes. The *Bezirksamtmann* of Truk wanted to enrol in a future government school only the children of influential subjects, such as those of prominent chiefs. The aim of official schooling was clearly stated: 'The government school will surely help to strengthen the confidence of the leading natives in the methods and aims of the German administration.'[29]

Initially chiefs stood to lose a great deal if they followed the mission path. Not only could they not deal in tobacco or alcohol, with their attendant profits (since temperance became a 'ready symbol for distinguishing Christians from heathen'[30]), but their power would also be circumscribed by church committees. Further, chiefs who wanted to convert and still practised polygamy could retain only one wife. The others had to be set aside as 'concubines'.[31] Nevertheless, many chiefs, perhaps seeking an additional legitimacy, converted. By the 1880s, on Ponape at least, missionary Edward T. Doane reported: 'Christian converts and missionaries were becoming the major political power',[32] while in eastern Micronesia the American Board eventually bested all competitors except the German colonial authorities.[33]

A third way to tame 'the other' was through institutional transformation. For the mission the practice of collective land tenure had to be supplanted by individual ownership and responsibility. Only in this way way could work be effectively assigned and completed. In the words of the mission: 'Wives, children, lands, property, belong to everybody and to nobody. In this state of things, there is and can be but little desire to improve or acquire.'[34] The mission suggested, and the people on Ponape adopted, a sevenmember legislature which introduced the concept of individual ownership of property. The mission exulted: 'This law is the most radical of any they need, as it strikes at the root of the great evil here, – a kind of socialism, quite destructive to all our efforts to *fix* them as to place or property.'[35] John Locke (1632–1704), British philosopher and political theorist, would have been delighted with his mission disciples. They, like Locke, felt that man abandoned his 'natural liberty' in the state of nature to enter 'Civil Society' in order to secure his property.[36]

Another step toward institution-building was the creation of a sort of congregational consistory, which supervised morality on Ponape. Its principal work was to guard against excessive drinking. The mission gladly reported that, not only was intemperance under assault, but that this group worked against adultery, stealing and fighting.[37] In achieving these successes the mission supplanted a previously dominant influence in the life of the islanders: the trader. Phillip Delaporte, born in Germany and subsequently naturalized in America, reported from Nauru in 1906: 'Formerly the trader's verandah was the meeting place of the majority of the population, but the coming of the missionary has changed all this – instead of drinking bad gin and smoking worse tobacco in the trader's house, the Christian natives go about their business...'[38] That is, they went about their business as productive and pious citizens according to the definition of the mission.

In accomplishing behavioural and institutional transformation,

American Board missionaries did not want to relegate their charges to a secondary or subordinate role in society. Rather they were grooming their converts to become teachers and preachers. Thus the American Board sought to put itself out of business as soon as possible. For the fulfilment of this aim, missionaries needed to treat converts and potential converts as far as possible as equals, or, failing that, as potential equals once they had subscribed to and practised the moral norms of the mission. As a result, in the literature of the American Board one would hardly find a statement the equivalent of the following from the Rhenish Mission in German South West Africa: 'Since our native population has eventually to accustom itself to being in a serving capacity, the school must first of all take this factor into consideration...'[39]

Some mission leaders had a wider view of their enterprise than simply one of conversion to a puritan style of Christianity. They saw their task as that of commercial modernization, of placing their converts in the ranks of a civilization which had already produced the railroads and the telegraph. Thus Samuel B. Capen, at an address in Boston in December 1899, extolled his brothers and sisters for 'opening up many new markets for America's manufacturers', particularly in the Pacific, and for pushing into retreat 'the old religions of the East.'[40] The idea of connecting mission enterprise with national commercial progress also excited German colonial enthusiasts. They were convinced that the Americans had hit on a method which would both save souls and augment the national coffers. Thus Carl Meinhof of the Seminar of Oriental Languages in Berlin advocated that the American example of encouraging the consumption of manufactured products by local people be followed.[41]

## Conversion Enthusiasm

Mission converts sometimes exceeded the expectations of their mentors. In their enthusiasm for the new-found faith, and the moral or civil power which might derive from it, they embarked upon tasks which put the mission in difficulty with the government. Foremost among these was a quest for power on the part of the new church committees. At Mejuro in the Marshalls a church committee 'thought to hasten the salvation of their fellow men' by passing a law that no person should embark in a canoe on Sunday. Church officials had to explain to the committee that it was not for its members to make laws; that was the chiefs' prerogative. According to Clinton Rife, the committee should obey the chief and try to strengthen his hand.[42]

Rife reported that one church committee asked Landeshauptmann Eugen Brandeis at Jaluit that it be vested with the authority over all people on the island including the resident traders. Rife exclaimed that fulfilment of this request would give the committee more power than the chiefs. 'Of course', he said 'it was entirely out of the sphere of a church committee. I had been aware for the past two years that these committees were becoming too important, and were taking upon themselves authority which did not belong to them...'. Rife then proceeded to curtail the functions of this committee and to reiterate that temporal power did, indeed, belong to the chiefs.[43]

Another initiative of the converts was to prevent the arrival of goods which the mission despised, such as tobacco and beer. A mission convert at Jaluit, Seanien, forbade church members to carry these articles to shore when they unloaded freight from ships because they brought harm to converts. Clinton Rife was perplexed: on the one hand he would have liked to support this initiative so in line with mission policy; on the other he did not want to jeopardize good relations with the government. He asked for advice from home.[44] The answer that he received is not recorded.

Although convert enthusiasm seemed to validate the mission's presence in Micronesia, the record was not one of unblemished success. Retreat from conversion and Christian vows occurred if islands received no regular missionary or teacher visits. In the Marshalls, for instance, visitations to locally run churches by American missionaries occurred but once annually. For some missionaries, like Clinton Rife, the most serious issue was the 'marriage question' because local people often broke marriage vows or they had multiple wives.[45] Chiefs particularly found it difficult to put aside other wives when the mission insisted upon the retention of one. Other missionaries wondered about the depth of conversion among their charges. Thus Elizabeth Baldwin on Kusaie: 'There is so little of the deep conviction of sin, and consequently but a slight appreciation of the cost of our redemption.'[46] Phillip Delaporte on Nauru reasoned that the gulf separating the 'heathen condition' from the lowest rung on the Christian ladder was so enormous that the process of transformation would necessarily be a long one.[47]

## Conversion and Ambition

What explains why so many islanders converted to Christianity and adopted attitudes of moral reconstruction when conversion and reform, particularly under the puritanical American Board, represented a seemingly radical break with their own traditions? First, conversion opened the road of upward mobility in both mission and colonial service to ambitious young people, many of whom lived in essentially static societies where opportunities for socio-economic advancement tended to be limited. The mission offered the prospect of employment in the prestige positions of teachers and preachers. In the colonial hierarchy an islander might work as an interpreter, a scribe, or in some technical capacity. Although it is not fashionable today to view traditional societies as unprogressive or stagnant, as Karl Marx did, for instance, when he wrote about the progressive impact of British imperialism in India,[48] it is probable that islanders thought that they could find better opportunities in the colonial or mission hierarchy than they could at home. Thus in the Carolines the highest office that the world held for a Pingelap boy was that of minister in the mission church.[49] Similarly, colonial administration jobs as interpreters or clerks conferred a measure of power and prestige upon their holders.

Second, conversion to Christianity presented the opportunity to increase control of one's own destiny. On the islands the elements made life uncertain at best. Typhoons overwhelmed islands. On 27–28 March 1907 a typhoon caused great destruction on Ifaluk in the central Carolines. Local tradition recorded that in about 1760 a typhoon killed all of the inhabitants of the central Carolines except two women.[50] Since the whites obviously had command of an effective technology, perhaps they could master the elements, or, failing outright mastery, they could divert them in another direction. Life was uncertain, and the islanders, as masters of hedging their bets, would seek means to make life more secure and predictable. Conversion to Christianity provided such an option.

Third, conversion also fitted nicely into the existing value structure on Ponape. It provided the means to get ahead of one's neighbour. In an extremely competitive society such as that of Ponape, status was relative to performance and 'men especially had to demonstrate their superiority to one another'.[51] As a result, there was intense competition 'for personal prestige, higher titles, and the rights which accrued'.[52] To become a Christian on Ponape was obviously a benefit because one was thought to be 'strong' and able to deal with westerners.[53]

One is entitled to ask about the seriousness of the converted, even if missionaries did not delve too deeply into the motives of their new charges. Did conversion represent an attitudinal change or merely acquiescence to the exterior, more formal requirements of Christianity? It is difficult to know the answer, although Christianity's message of the equality of all believers before God held out real advantages for the underprivileged in Ponapean society. As David Hanlon points out, women and lesser chiefs particularly stood to benefit materially 'from the commercial and educational aspects of the Protestant mission's civilizing strategy'.[54] Thus these converts obtained a double advantage: material benefit in this life and the chance for salvation in the hereafter.

The classic example of the great competitor, the one who really succeeded in both traditional and in western society, was Henry Nanpei (1862–1927), a 'new man' on Ponape. Born into a noble clan on his father's side, Nanpei quickly learned about hard work and Christianity from his American Board tutors. In turn, the missionaries viewed Nanpei as their 'prize student, model convert, and irreplacable supporter'.[55] Nanpei demonstrated his business sense early. He planted and harvested copra rather than engaging in pagan festivals and feasts.[56] The profits he then turned to land purchase. Nanpei's acceptance of Christianity and its work ethic demonstrated to other Ponapeans that one could synthesize aspects of the traditional clan and ruling system with its tribute, rank and privileges, with the requirements of the new Christian faith.[57] As an intensely acquisitive man who eventually owned about 25 per cent of the land on Ponape, Nanpei demonstrated how Christianity was no impediment to the exercise of one's competitive energies.[58]

A less charitable view of Nanpei is that he was an 'extremely ambitious man with a marked propensity for manipulation...'.[59] More importantly, from the mission point of view, Nanpei remained true to the faith during the Spanish period on Ponape from 1885 to 1899, which was also the period of expulsion of the American Board. Other islanders viewed Nanpei as 'enlightened (*marain*) in the ways of the white man, and this gave him special influence among traditional leaders...'.[60] He was a man who had dealt with foreigners and purchased their Remington and Winchester rifles for only forty dollars per weapon.[61] Clearly Nanpei was adaptive, resourceful and, on occasion, opportunistic in his dealings with a succession of Spaniards, Germans and Japanese. He understood the modernization reshaping traditional Ponapean society and how to profit from it.[62]

## Mission and Government

Mission and government often pursued an ambiguous and strained relationship with one another. First, they competed for the same personnel, particularly after the Germans arrived in the Carolines and the Marianas in 1899. German administrators made it their priority to enrol the children of elites in their schools. Some officials, like Eduard Haber, the Acting Governor after Albert Hahl left New Guinea early in 1914, wanted to transform independent chiefs into functionaries of the government.[63] Governor Albert Hahl noted the competition between mission and government at various levels and made his famous and oft-cited observation: 'I know the mission from my work in the East Carolines. I have always found their impact to be a markedly political one.'[64]

The government, in the eyes of the mission, also relied too heavily upon traders, the evil overlords of commerce. Clinton Rife complained about the Governor in Jaluit: 'He seems to be influenced more by the evidence of a single white man ... than by the evidence of several natives, even though they may be good Christians. We find it a hard matter to preach that "every soul be subject to the higher powers".'[65] Implied in Rife's statement is his perception that once an islander converted to Christianity, he rose to the standing of the western population and therefore deserved equivalent treatment. Rife further objected to high taxation, excessive regulation, and trade restrictions as they existed in the Carolines.[66]

Mission reliance upon church committees exercised the government, which saw them as competitive of its own authority. In the Ebon Affair, well described by Stewart Firth, a church committee on the island of Ebon fined a foreign trader 200 Chilean dollars for a misdeameanour. When the trader refused to pay, the committee boycotted his business. The commander of a German warship, the S.M.S. *Nautilus*, in turn fined the mission for endangering

the authority of the chiefs.[67] As a result of this and related incidents, Firth concluded that 'American missionaries were surely
not supporters of German colonial rule'.[68] Wolfgang Treue carries
this argument further in his article on the Jaluit Gesellschaft. He
portrays the American Board as not only a hindrance to trade, in
that it encouraged chiefs to boycott German firms, but also as a
threat to peace in the Marshalls.[69]

From the articles of these two authors, one might conclude that
mission and government were always at loggerheads, and that the
mission sought to undercut the work of the secular authorities.
Actually there were a number of areas in which the desires of
mission and government tended to converge. The last State
Secretary of the German Colonial Office before the outbreak of
the First World War, Wilhelm Solf, remarked eloquently how
missions not only furnished psychological insights concerning local
inhabitants, but how they created understanding among locals for
the intent of administrative measures.[70] *Bezirksamtmann* Merz
credited the American Board with teaching the inhabitants of both
the Ralik-Ratak chains in the Marshalls reading and writing.[71]
Hermann Kersting attested to the success of mission work on
Ponape: 'The people love their Christianity. With considerable
talent, the old and the young sing daily in and out of the church,
their beautiful spiritual songs ... one doesn't hear anymore pro-
fane singing.'[72] Phillip Delaporte had earlier reported from Nauru:
'The songs of the heathen priest are heard no more...'.[73]

There were so few Germans in Micronesia that it was to the
government's advantage to view missionaries as potential aides in
creating the proper climate of understanding among subjects, as
Solf had in mind, rather than as adversaries. Naturally, this recourse was not by desire, but rather by need, given the thin staffing
of administrators throughout the islands.

American Board missionaries were often well pleased with
German officials, and on many occasions enjoyed their support.
Missionary Ida C. Foss reported home in November 1900 that Dr
Hahl 'is a kind, genial man interested in our welfare, and seems
favorable to our work'.[74] Foss also felt that German rule was a
marked improvement over that of the Spanish in the Carolines.[75]
In a similar vein, missionary Jessie R. Hoppin extolled Dr
Hermann Kersting as 'a man of high rank and a just and kind
ruler, much loved by the people' for his work in the Carolines and

the Marshalls.[76] Even Clinton R. Rife, perhaps the most assertive of the American Board missionaries and sometime *bête noire* of the German authorities, had good things to say about the government. Rife reported in 1902 that in the last eight years he had had no serious difficulties with Landeshauptmann Brandeis in Jaluit. Furthermore, Rife had taken it upon himself to curb the authority of church committees in the Carolines. Missionary Phillip Delaporte reported about his work on Nauru that: 'The German officials, with one or two exceptions, have always been friendly to our work. Perhaps being natives of Germany has something to do with this.'[77]

The American Board also addressed the issue of teaching German in primary schools – a constant demand by German administrators. The mission hired Phillip Delaporte and his wife, both of whom were born in Germany. They taught German in the Carolines. The teaching of English was also dropped there. As Clinton Rife said: 'the English language is not taught, the Fourth of July is not commemorated, and we are endeavoring in every way possible to comply with the wishes of the officials without compromising our work.'[78]

The attitudes of Clinton Rife, Ida Foss, Jessie Hoppin and Phillip Delaporte are to be compared with those of the German Capuchins who established the Apostolic Vicarate of the Marianas and the Carolines. Gerd Hardach has related in his *König Kopra* how German officials resented the extreme 'Machstreben' of the Capuchins on these islands, and their desire, upon every occasion, to demonstrate their independence of the government. *Bezirksamtmann* George Fritz even went so far as to accuse the Capuchins of partial responsibility in causing the Sokehs Rebellion on Ponape in October 1910.[79] American Board–government relations scarcely ever reached this low ebb. There was no need for a George Fritz to pen an *Ad majorem Dei gloriam!* against the American Board.

What was responsible for this consensus between American mission and German government which, however, might at any time be disrupted by arbitrary officialdom or islander initiatives? In the last analysis Wilhelm Solf said it correctly: 'In this very difficult area of native policy, the mission is the faithful colleague and ally of the colonial administration.'[80] It was a matter of reciprocity. The mission relied upon the executive arm of the government for the preservation of law and order, however slowly this might come. The government relied upon the mission for the tasks of education, socialization westernization and, if possible, Germanization. Essentially this reciprocity weathered the many frictions which occurred when two different institutions, mission and government, sought to remould subject populations, each in its own image.

This often abrasive 'togetherness' of mission and government basically supports Horst Gründer's thesis that the mission functioned as part of the colonial apparatus. As spiritual mentor, the mission had the ultimate task, so nicely stated by the Catholic historian Joseph Schmidlin, of the intellectual and spiritual assimilation of the islanders to Christian and western values.[81] In this line of thinking, mission and colonial authority are simply reverse sides of the same coin.[82]

To cast the American missionaries as willing partners of the German imperium would be to overstate the argument. Certainly mission and government had their differences over things like taxes, church committees, teaching German, traditional customs, liquor, and traders. The mission saw its task as spiritual development, whereas the government seemed to be interested only in pecuniary matters, according to F.M. Price on Ruk.[83] Philosophically, however, both could agree on the primacy of productive labour, on the need to control feasting on Ponape, and on the idea that the proper role of the subject is to obey the civil authorities. Particularly Colonial Secretary Bernhard Dernburg's reformist imperialism stressed the importance of subjects' work: 'the manual labor of the natives creates the most important factor...' in colonial development.[84] Congregationalist missionaries, specialists in ascetism and hard work, often acted as if they sought implementation of Dernburg's policy.

## Notes

1. One frequently hears the term 'Boston Mission' applied to the congregationalist missionaries sent forth by the American Board of Commissioners for Foreign Missions from their Boston headquarters. See, for instance, the article by Stewart Firth, 'Die Bostoner Mission in den deutschen Marschall-Inseln', in Klaus J. Bade (ed.), *Imperialismus und Kolonialmission. Kaiserliches Deutschland und koloniales Imperium*, Franz Steiner Verlag, Wiesbaden, 1982. To my knowledge, neither the Board itself nor its missionaries ever used this title.

2. Mac Marshall and Leslie B. Marshall, 'Holy and Unholy Spirits', *Journal of Pacific History*, vol. XI (1976), Part 3, p. 151.

3. The total expenses for the Micronesian mission in 1903 were reckoned to be $18,125. For the year ending 1903 there were 907 communicants on Ponape, 3,812 on Kusaie and the Marshalls, 1,205 on Ruk and the Mortlocks, and 715 on the Gilberts. Statistics for the Year Ending 1903, Documents, Minutes, Reports, Micronesia Mission, vol. 14, Papers of the American Board of Commissioners for Foreign Missions, Research Publications, Woodbridge, Ct., Unit 6, Microfilm 851 (hereafter *RP*).

4. Michael Taussig, *Shamanism, A Study in Colonialism, and Terror and the Wild Man Healing*, University of Chicago Press, Chicago, 1987, p. 215.

5. Ibid., p. 219.

6. *The Missionary Herald*, vol. XCI, no. XII (December 1895), p. 504 (hereafter *MH*). F.M. Price, 'Notes on Ruk and the Mortlock Islands', *MH*, vol. XCI, no. VIII (August 1895), p. 314, Microfilm Reel 1243, vols. 89–94, January 1893–December 1898.

7. Phillip Delaporte, *Ninth Annual Report of the Nauru Mission*, Marshall Islands, Nauru, 1910, p. 8, Reel 855.

8. Quoted in David Hanlon, *Upon a Stone Altar: A History of the Island of Pohnpei to 1890*, University of Hawai'i Press, Honolulu, 1988, Pacific Islands Monographs Series, no. 5, p. 90.

9. August Erdland, *The Marshall Islanders: Life and Customs, Thought and Religion of a South Seas People*, Anthropos Bibliothek, Münster, 1914, trans. 1942 by Yale University Cross-Cultural Survey, Human Relations Area File, 1961, p. 197.

10. Ibid., p. 83. Alfred Crosby pointed out how the Maoris were also particularly susceptible to venereal disease because of their unrestricted sexual practices. Alfred W. Crosby, *Ecological Imperialism. The Biological Expansion of Europe, 900–1900*, Cambridge University Press, New York, 1993, p. 231.

11. Erdland, *The Marshall Islanders*, pp. 22, 97, 106, 107.

12. Sarah L. Garland to Dr Barton, 27 July 1906, Letters A–H, vol. 15, Micronesia Mission, 1900–1909, Microfilm Reel 852, RP.

13. Hermann J. Hiery, *Das Deutsche Reich in der Südsee (1900–1921). Eine Annäherung an die Erfahrungen verschiedener Kulturen*, Vandenhoeck & Ruprecht, Göttingen, 1995, p. 274.

14. Hanlon, *Upon a Stone Altar*, pp. 92, 103.

15. Wolfgang Treue, 'Die Jaluit-Gesellschaft auf den Marshall-Inseln, 1887–1914', in *Schriften zur Wirtschafts-und Sozialgeschichte, Band 26*, Duncker & Humblot, Berlin, 1976, p. 33.

16. Marshall and Marshall, 'Holy and Unholy Spirits', pp. 136, 145, 157.

17. Hanlon, *Upon a Stone Altar*, p. 95.

18. Paul Mark Ehrlich, 'The Clothes of Men: Ponape Island and

German Colonial Rule, 1899–1914', Ph.D. dissertation, History–Anthropology, SUNY Stony Brook, 1978, pp. 39, 41. The mission could also interpret the many ordinances which the German government showered upon the islanders.

19. Stewart Firth, *New Guinea under the Germans*, Melbourne University Press, Melbourne, 1982, p. 156.

20. Hanlon, *Upon a Stone Altar*, p. 203.

21. Hiery, *Das Deutsche Reich*, p. 268.

22. Journal of Dr Luther H. Gulick, Ponape, August 1854, Micronesia Mission, vol. 1, Documents, Reports, Letters, 1852–1859, Reel 854, RP.

23. Hiery, *Das Deutsche Reich*, p. 269.

24. Hans Damm, 'Zentralkarolinen', II. Halbband in G. Thilenius (ed.), *Ergebnisse der Südsee Expedition, 1908–1910*, II. Ethnographie: B. Mikronesien, Band 10, De Gruyter & Co., Hamburg, Friederichsen, 1938, p. 299.

25. Bericht über das Fono (Ratsversammlung), 5 February 1914, copy, BAP: RKolA 2760, pp. 4, 6.

26. Ibid., p. 299. This perception of the 'vice of idleness' is not a unique German view of the islanders. Rather it is frequent in European attitudes toward Africa and the Middle East where, in the latter area, it became an important component of orientalism. Linda Nochlin, *The Politics of Vision: Essays on Nineteenth-Century Art and Society*, Harper & Row, New York, 1989, pp. 38–9.

27. *MH*, February 1854, vol. L, no. 2, p. 52, Microfilm Reel 1237. Unfortunately Missionary Snow specified neither the chief's name nor that of his son.

28. 'Report of the Influence of the Protestant Religion in the Marshall Islands', 14 March 1919, Reel 855, Micronesia Mission, 1910–1919, Documents, Reports, Letter, Part I, vol. 18, RP.

29. Eduard Haber to State Secretary of the Colonial Office, 2 June 1914, BAP: RKolA 2756, p. 103B.

30. Marshall and Marshall, 'Holy and Unholy Spirits', p. 161.

31. Edward T. Doane, Report from Ponape, *MH*, vol. LXIX, no. VII (July 1873).

32. Ibid., p. 160.

33. Ibid., p. 166.

34. *MH*, vol. LXX, no. VIII (August 1874), p. 253. Reel 1240.

35. Ibid.

36. John Locke, *Two Treatises of Government*, ed. Peter Laslett, Cambridge University Press, New York, 1988, pp. 330–31.

37. Robert Logan from Renan Station, Ponape, *MH*, vol. LXXII, no. X (October 1876), pp. 310–11.

38. Phillip Delaporte to Rev. Enoch Bell, 22 March 1907. Report of the Nauru Mission, 1906, p. 11, Reel 851, RP.

39. Jahresbericht of the Rhenish Mission Society, 1906–07, p. 65, included in RKolA: BAP 6538. Of course, this pronouncement was made

in the context of a settler society of which there were essentially none in Micronesia.

40. Samuel B. Capen, 'The Supreme Opportunity', *MH* Extra Edition, 12 December 1899, Reel 851, RP.

41. Carl Meinhof to the State Secretary of the Colonial Office, 22 March 1908, Evangelische Missionstätigkeiten in den Kolonien, 1907–1913, BAP: RKolA 6909.

42. Clinton Rife to Judson Smith, 2 February 1898, vol. 13, American Board of Commissioners for Foreign Missions, Micronesia Mission. From the originals in the Houghton Library Harvard.

43. Clinton Rife to Judson Smith, 16(?), 18(?) June 1902, vol. 17, Micronesia Mission, pp. 3–4, Reel 854, RP.

44. Clinton Rife to Judson Smith, 12 January 1895, vol. 13, Micronesia Mission, 1890–99, Houghton Library, Harvard.

45. Clinton Rife to James L. Barton, 27 March 1909 and 15 May 1909, Micronesia Mission, vol. 17, 1900–1909, Letters R–W, Reel 854, RP.

46. Elizabeth Baldwin to Mr Bell, 4 April 1913, Micronesia Mission, 1910–1919, Part I, Documents, Reports, Letters, Reel 855, RP.

47. Ninth Annual Report of the Nauru Mission, 1909, Marshall Islands, Nauru, 1910, pp. 9–10, Reel 855, RP.

48. Lewis H. Gann and Peter Duignan, *Burden of Empire*, Frederick A. Praeger, New York, 1967, p. 17.

49. Report of Mr and Mrs Gray, *MH*, April 1905, vol. CI, no. 4, p. 185.

50. Hans Damm, 'Zentralkarolinen', II. Halbband in G. Thilenius (ed.), *Ergebnisse der Südsee Expedition, 1908–1910*, pp. 6–7, 227.

51. Ehrlich, 'Clothes of Men', p. 41.

52. Ibid., p. 39.

53. Ibid., p. 127.

54. Hanlon, *Upon a Stone Altar*, p. 202.

55. Paul Ehrlich, 'Henry Nanpei: Preeminently a Ponapean', in Deryck Scarr (ed.), *More Pacific Islands Portraits*, Australian National University Press, Canberra, 1978, p. 131.

56. Ehrlich, 'Clothes of Men', p. 64.

57. Ehrlich, 'Henry Nanpei', p. 142.

58. Ibid., p. 131.

59. David Hanlon, 'Another Side of Henry Nanpei', *The Journal of Pacific History* 231 (1988), p. 40.

60. Ehrlich, 'Clothes of Men', p. 68.

61. Ibid., p. 83.

62. Ehrlich, 'Henry Nanpei', pp. 152–4.

63. Eduard Haber to the State Secretary of the Colonial Office, 2 June 1914, BAP: RKolA 2756, p. 103B.

64. Governor Hahl to the State Secretary of the Colonial Office, 10 July 1911, Report no. 382, BAP: RKolA 2761, p. 139.

65. *MH*, August 1902, vol. XCVIII, no. VIII, p. 331.

66. Clinton Rife to Judson Smith, 16 or 18 June 1902, vol. 17, Micronesia Mission, Letters R-W, Microfilm Reel 854, RP.

67. Firth, 'Die Bostoner Mission', p. 259.

68. Ibid., p. 265.

69. Treue, 'Die Jaluit-Gesellschaft', pp. 167–8.

70. Wilhelm Solf, *Mein politisches Vermächtnis*, Berlin, 1919, p. 93, in Treue, 'Die Jaluit-Gesellschaft', p. 167.

71. Merz on the Marshalls, 29 December 1917, BAP 3077, pp. 4–5.

72. Hermann Kersting to the State Secretary of the Colonial Office, September 28, 1911, BAP 6520, p. 81. Kersting did say, however, that the depth of conversion seemed to him to be superficial (p. 81).

73. Phillip Delaporte to Enoch Bell, 22 March 1907, Reel 857, RP.

74. Ida C. Foss to Judson Smith, 7 November 1900, Reel 852, RP.

75. Ida C. Foss to Judson Smith, 31 January 1901, Reel 852, RP.

76. Jessie R. Hoppin to Kate G. Lamson, 29 May 1913, Reel 855, RP. There is a considerable dispute about the evaluation of Kersting's colonial performance, particularly in Togo. A historian of German imperialism, Peter Sebald, portrays Kersting as sort of a latter-day Hernando Cortes who led sixteen armed expeditions against the Togolese from 1897 to 1902 (Peter Sebald, *Togo, 1884–1914. Eine Geschichte der deutschen 'Musterkolonie' auf der Grundlage amtlicher Quellen*, Akademie Verlag, Berlin, 1988, p. 218). Kersting also figured prominently in the discussion of the 'colonial scandals' in the Reichstag which led Chancellor von Bülow to close the 140th Session on 13 December 1906 (140th Session, December 13, 1906 in BAP: RKolA 7258, Reichstagssachen, p. 291). On the other hand, J. Macmillan Brown, a perceptive and important anthropologist engaged in Pacific island studies, credited Kersting with extreme tact in dealing with the islanders. Brown saw Kersting as one who avoided force for the gentler means of persuasion and concluded: 'Rarely have I come across an administrator so capable of dealing with native races' (J. Macmillan Brown, *Peoples and Problems of the Pacific*, T. Fisher Unwin, London, 1927, p. 124). Lewis Gann and Peter Duignan have described the advantages possessed by Germany's physician-administrators, one of whom was Kersting: they were steeped in a discipline which emphasized acute observation of phenomena; they were taught to help themselves and others in critical situations; they fared well, as members of the middle class, in publicizing their exploits before the reading public (Lewis H. Gann and Peter Duignan, *The Rulers of German Africa*, Stanford University Press, Stanford, 1977, pp. 57–8).

77. Phillip Delaporte to Enoch Bell, 22 March 1907: Report of Work in 1906, pp. 4–5, Reel 851, RP.

78. Clinton F. Rife to Judson Smith, 15 or 18 June 1902, vol. 17, Letters R-W, Reel 854, RP.

79. Gerd Hardach, *König Kopra, Die Marianen unter deutscher Herrschaft, 1899–1914*, Franz Steiner Verlag, Stuttgart, 1990, pp. 189–91.

80.  Solf, *Kolonialpolitik*, p. 93, quoted in Treue, *Die Jaluit-Gesellschaft*, p. 167.

81.  Cited in Horst Gründer, *Christliche Mission und deutscher Imperialismus*, Ferdinand Schöningh, Paderborn, 1982, pp. 330–31.

82.  Horst Gründer, 'Kolonialpolitik und christliche Mission im Zeitalter des Imperialismus: Entwicklungslinien und Forschungsperspektiven', *Jahrbuch der historischen Forschung in der Bundesrepublik Deutschland*, Berichtsjahr 1983, K.G. Saur, Munich, 1984, p. 36.

83.  F.M. Price, *M.H.*, vol. LXXXIX, June 1893, no. VI, p. 216, Reel 1243.

84.  'Die manuelle Leistung des Eingeborenen das wichtigste Aktivum bildet...' Bernhard Dernburg, *Zielpunkte des deutschen Kolonialwesens: Zwei Vorträge*, Ernst Mittler & Sohn, Berlin, 1907, p. 7.

# PART II

---

# Impact Unleashed:
# European Contact and the Environment

## JOHN M. MACKENZIE

## The Environmental and Medical History of the Pacific

Two of the greatest growth areas of recent world historiography
have been environmental and medical history. It is possible to use
the word 'world' because these sub-disciplines have contributed
perhaps more than any others to historical globalization. Microbes,
pathogens and the agents of ecological transformation are no
respecters of political, ethnic or even natural boundaries. Moreover, whereas political, diplomatic and military history often deal
with the interaction of individuals – their ideas, policies, techniques and objectives; their projected outcomes and successes and
failures – environmental and medical history deal with vast and
impersonal forces that seem largely out of human control. Although
human migrations and economic practices of all sorts profoundly
shape the speed, scale and destructiveness of such forces, they are
almost always unintended, the potent results of a destructive combination of human restlessness, cupidity and ignorance.

This helps to explain why the western historiographical tradition has been so behind-hand in studying these vital effects of the
interaction of humans with each other and with the environment.
In the late nineteenth and early twentieth centuries, this tradition
was still obsessed with progressivist notions of expanding knowledge and growing control, with a formal and informal imperialism
that represented the onward march of strikingly new forms of

technological competence, with the expansion of the industrial complex and the consequent oscillations of nationalist and internationalist contexts. In its own way, the Marxist response was equally impervious to ecological change, focusing as it did upon the invariably deterministic social and political changes consequent upon transformations in modes of economic production.

The historian's obsession with the document, particularly the official document, also inhibited much environmental and medical awareness. Documents are not of course entirely free of material relating to such specialisms, particularly when death rates or environmental degradation impinge upon power, political control or economic and military success, but they had to be read in new ways both to yield up their evidence and facilitate fresh analytical morphologies. Historians had to escape their obsession with policy, with top-down approaches, to be able to develop some understanding of forces which seemed so often to be out of control. Moreover, they had to form *rapprochements* with a whole range of other disciplines, both in the sciences and the social sciences, to discover the full range of sources and interpretive opportunities.

Imperial history has been the most successful milieu in which these developments have taken place. Imperialism was the great globalizer of the modern world. It turned the globe into a laboratory in which experiments – as we now know not always controlled experiments – took place. Data was accumulated, collated and analysed in vast quantities and a whole range of publications and disciplines were generated or profoundly influenced by this copious taxonomic archive. However, as McNeill points out in Chapter 8, imperialism is subject to many different definitions. In recent times, the significance of direct political rule and the even more narrow criterion of settlement have been much reduced as prerequisites of the imperial relationship. Economic, social and cultural relations conducted within contexts of inequalities of power (invariably accelerating as the relationship grows) have come to be seen as the central norms of imperialism. This definition has perhaps greatly facilitated environmental and medical studies, although there is no reason why they should not equally be encompassed within narrower concepts of imperialism.

The globalizing potential of these studies was well illustrated by W.H. McNeill's *Plagues and Peoples* and Alfred Crosby's *Ecological Imperialism*. But there have also been environmental and medical histories that have concentrated on specific regions and territories. Although American scholars seemed to command this field for a period, particularly rich work has been developed in Indian, African and Australasian historiography. In recent years the Pacific has also provided much detailed scholarship. The articles in this section offer valuable analytical syntheses of much of this work.

The European social and economic impact on the Pacific, with its attendant and often highly destructive environmental and medical pressures, occurred primarily between the late eighteenth and early twentieth centuries. Although this was later than similar effects in the Americas, it was largely coterminous with parallel changes taking place as imperial commerce and rule spread in India and Africa. Moreover, the Pacific, with its combination of strikingly large and small islands, also exhibited complex patterns of accessibility and inaccessibility which affected both the chronology and speed of the environmental and medical impact.

These two were of course closely interrelated. Traders brought exotic and fatal diseases to remote populations, while the commodification of nature for international trade produced dramatic depletions and extinctions. Invasive animals and plants could create new social and economic contexts in which diseases could thrive (plantations are the classic example). Death-dealing epidemics could so reduce populations as to lead to dramatic changes in the balance between humans and their environments. As Crosby demonstrates, these effects could continue in remoter districts of New Guinea until the mid-twentieth century. Meanwhile other imports, like the sweet potato, could help to produce population growth.

It is of course dangerous to set western medicine, with its concentration on acute rather than chronic illness, its dominant physical approach rooting out the invasive element, and its remote and somewhat overbearing practitioners, within the same sorts of progressivist paradigms as those used within imperial rule itself. In examining the full effects of environmental and medical change we need to discover a great deal more about indigenous knowledge, local modes of understanding based upon the richly practical knowledge of survival systems. We also need to comprehend indigenous medicine, with its tendency to emphasize the chronic, the spiritual and the environmental context. A greater interaction between anthropology and history will greatly help here, as it has done in many African and Indian studies.

Progressivist notions of conservation should also be abandoned. Conservation ideas are usually deeply embedded in economic and cultural contexts. As Bolton suggests in his overview of comparative developments on either side of the Tasman Sea (Chapter 9), conservation pressures have often emerged out of specific indigenous objectives and competition over land, holy places and prestige. More relativist approaches to conservation help to confirm that throughout all these studies of environmental and medical history we should be wary of both apocalyptic and developmental approaches. Environmental change can generally only be understood within much longer time-scales. There can be little doubt that commercial and imperial pressures, with the often shattering introduction of international market forces, produced rapid changes previously unheard of in human history, but such transformations have to be set into longer cycles in which ecological forces have ebbed and flowed like the human migrations with which they have been closely bound up. As our perspectives upon the imperial period open out, the interrelationships of these longer cycles with shorter-term change are becoming more apparent. As they do so, it may be that the irruption of Europeans and their markets in this vast region will be viewed less as an apocalypse than as an accelerator, hugely destructive certainly, but only in inducing a much more dramatic swing of an environmental pendulum that has been in motion since humans first interacted with nature.

# 8

# Pacific Ecology and British Imperialism, 1770–1970

## J.R. MCNEILL

Pacific island ecosystems, like all island ecosystems, are prone to rapid change. Their first human occupants altered them considerably upon arrival, and continued to do so ever after. But the arrival of European mariners, especially after the eighteenth century, produced ecological change of an intensity and extent unprecedented in Pacific history. The European impact, here considered mainly in its British versions, made itself felt through the mechanisms of demographic collapse, exotic species invasion, and intensified pressure on selected vegetation and soils. After an initial stage that lasted a century, the European impact shifted slowly from a hunting and gathering pattern of resource exploitation to one that featured reorganized production. After the 1880s, island ecosystems changed comprehensively so as to produce more plantation crops, resulting in a vegetation mosaic that largely endures to this day. In what follows I will chart some of these ecological changes, and assess the role of imperialism in bringing them about.

## Pacific Ecology

The pre-human Pacific was an Asian lake. Almost all its life forms derived from Southeast Asia. The great majority of islands were born barren of life, volcanic pimples on the sea's surface. The species these islands eventually acquired came by air or sea, usually drifting over great distances. Some immigrated with the help of birds. In any case, the difficulty of getting to most islands screened out large numbers of species. Only good floaters and drifters arrived alive and ready to propagate. Only the very best made it as far as the eastern Pacific: Easter Island, even after Polynesians brought their contributions, had only 30 plant species, whereas Bougainville in the Solomons had several thousand. As bio-geographers put it, the Pacific had (and still has in modified form) an attenuated Indo-Malayan biota.[1] As a rule of thumb, the further from Indonesia the more impoverished the biota. This holds well for land species, less well for marine species, and scarcely at all for oceanic birds.

Immigrant species to Pacific islands evolved in isolation from the continental hothouses of terrestrial evolution. Vacant niches invited the creation of new species (through what biologists call adaptive radiation), a process that yielded numerous species found nowhere else in the world: endemics. Remoter islands had very high rates of endemism, as much as 99 per cent. This isolated evolution meant that Pacific species had no experience comparable to that of most of the victorious species in struggles for continental niche space: the Pacific biota was well-adapted to its (various) climatic and soil conditions, but highly vulnerable to disruption in the event of biological invasion from outside the Pacific. This ecosystem-wide vulnerability to rapid change ecologists call lability. In the Pacific, lability derived from evolutionary isolation – and from the late arrival of humankind.

People first came to the western Pacific about 50,000 years ago. They moved beyond New Guinea only 12,000 years ago. They found the first atolls of Micronesia and Polynesia only about 3,500 years ago, and finally reached the remote corners of the Polynesian triangle, Easter Island (c. 400 AD) and New Zealand (c. 1000 AD) only a few human generations ago – and within the lifetime of some trees now standing. In most parts of the Pacific, plants and animals have evolved in the absence of human impact, and have had very little time to adjust to it. They have paid a heavy price for this. Pacific animals were often dangerously naive: in the Galápagos Islands, Darwin found birds that would let him approach within arm's length. Pacific plants had minimal resist-ance to fire, because natural fire was rare on most islands. In contrast, continental species were much warier of human beings, having had millions or hundreds of thousands of years to get used to us. And they were much more resistant to fire, having had long experience of either natural or human fire. In short, the Pacific biota was unusually labile, vulnerable both to invasive species and to human impact.

## The Pre-European Pacific

The first human settlers of the Pacific islands arrived with a limited tool kit and a very limited repertoire of domesticated species. Armed with stone tools and fire, and accompanied by only three or four useful animals and a few more cultigens, they nevertheless set about changing the new-found landscapes to suit their purposes. They succeeded to a great extent, especially in lowlands, and in so doing inadvertently brought other environmental changes, such as extinctions, deforestation and erosion. They were, after all, not ecological angels but human beings, living not in paradise but in highly labile ecosystems. Thus when European mariners began to frequent the Pacific, the inhabited islands they saw were anthropic landscapes, created and maintained by islanders' labour and fire.[2]

## The Age of Cook, 1769–1880

James Cook first sailed into Pacific waters 250 years after Magellan. Yet Cook found a world little touched by European influence. Magellan and all his successors before Cook had seen about 100 Pacific islands and had set foot on about 30. But no European had dallied anywhere for long except Guam, which after 1668 was a regular stop on the Spanish Manila galleon route from Acapulco. Outside Guam, Europeans scarcely affected the ecological isolation of the Pacific. There had been no 'Magellan Exchange' of plants, animals and diseases across the Pacific, no analogue to the Columbian exchange in the Atlantic.[3] Thus the 1770s, not the 1520s, were the Pacific's equivalent to the 1490s in the Atlantic World.

The impact of Cook and his successors was, by the leisurely standards of previous Pacific environmental history, sudden and thorough. It took three main forms: human depopulation, alien species introduction, and depletion of the most valuable and readily accessible native species.

The evidence concerning depopulation is far from optimal, but permits a general picture. It conforms to the dismal pattern of the Americas after 1492. Under the impact of alien diseases, indigenous populations declined sharply after contact, sometimes by 90–95 per cent. Land expropriation, violence and labour recruitment played lesser roles. In most cases, population declines lasted 120–150 years, as in the Americas. Given the isolation of islanders' immune systems from the prevailing infections of Eurasia, anything other than this sweeping tragedy would be epidemiologically surprising.[4]

The rapid decline in human numbers destabilized the anthropic landscapes of the Pacific. Cultivated area shrank dramatically, opening land for opportunistic colonizers, animal, vegetable or human. An American captain in 1840 found agriculture on Tonga 'entirely neglected'.[5] In Fiji the bush reclaimed land from numerous villages around 1860.[6] Secondary forest growth spread widely in the wake of depopulation, often stabilizing landscapes once more. But where islander farming had relied on terraces or irrigation, as in Fiji, Hawai'i and elsewhere, labour shortage brought these to ruin, accelerating soil erosion. More widely, newly introduced species took advantage of the massive fallowing that came with population decline.

Alien grazing animals, weeds and new crops prospered mightily in the disturbed conditions of the nineteenth-century Pacific. Their full effect was first to contribute to the destabilization of island ecosystems, then to further the homogenization of the islands – just as original human settlement had done.

Grazing animals, intentionally introduced by European sailors, found good forage on abandoned lands. Tall forest would have suited them less well. Goats, pigs and cattle colonized widely in the absence of predators and (initially) of diseases. Their hooves and teeth were new enemies to the plants of the Pacific, many of which could not withstand the pressure of grazing and gave way to alien weeds better adapted to life under the hoof.

Unintended invaders also flourished. The brown rat and Norway rat, wily opportunists and prolific breeders, accompanied Europeans to the Pacific and disembarked at every stop. Herman Melville knew them well from his whaling ship days: 'They stood in their holes peering at you like old grandfathers in a doorway. Often they darted in upon us at meal times and nibbled our food

... every chink and cranny swarmed with them; they did not live among you, but you among them.'[7] Rats decimated the native bird life of the Pacific islands. They influenced the species composition of forests by their preference for certain seeds and nuts. They displaced the Polynesian rat. In many cases they were the single most consequential animal intruder, and together with smallpox, measles, and other pathogens, formed the shock troops of ecological imperialism in the Pacific. Rats' attention to crops provoked efforts to control them through the introduction of cats, weasels and stoats in New Zealand, and mongooses in Fiji. But the hired assassins generally ignored their mandate and fell upon the native birds themselves.

Europeans brought plants as well as animals to the Pacific. In the early nineteenth century, one Hawaiian valley acquired watermelon, maize, cabbage, beans, oranges, limes, lemons, guava, cucumber, squash, red peppers and rice. These arrivals greatly improved food production possibilities. The valley, Anahulu on Oahu, also acquired coffee and tobacco, less beneficial perhaps, but no less popular among Hawaiians. Many of these new plants ran wild, colonizing widely in the gashes left behind by the retreat of cultivation.[8] And of course European ships brought their own weeds, tropical ones such as clidemia, and temperate ones such as gorse and broom.

All told, the arrival of Europeans and their 'portmanteau biota' spelled disaster for lowland and lagoon organisms and their soils in the Pacific. Many native species suffered extinction; many more found their range reduced under the onslaught of invaders. All this disturbance, extinction and replacement involved unconscious ecological teamwork, as one invader cleared the path for the next. By killing islanders, microbes paved the way for livestock to graze in widowed lands, which in turn helped grasses and weeds to gain footholds. The process resembles the ecological imperialism of temperate lands outlined by Alfred Crosby, except that outside New Zealand it did not require or involve significant European settlement.[9] Occasional European visits and the extreme lability of island environments sufficed.

Economic action supplemented biological invasion in transforming Pacific ecologies. With the arrival of Europeans, Pacific ecosystems were linked not merely to other ecosystems, but to other economies as well. British, Australian and Yankee traders linked the lagoons, reefs, forests, fields, gardens and high seas of the Pacific to zones of intense demand, most notably China. In consequence, islanders and aliens (chiefly British and American) scoured the Pacific for seals, whales, sandalwood, timber, mother-of-pearl, *bêche-de-mer*, and several other species, now treated as commodities.

In 1784 Britain reduced its import duty on tea by 90 per cent, bringing tea from the palace to the cottage and bringing the world to Canton (Guangdong). British and other traders sorely needed items to trade for tea, and among the solutions to this persistent problem were Pacific products. First came sealskins. Fur seals maintained colonies on the cooler shores of the Pacific, generally far from any human presence. Before the 1770s, Pacific islanders hunted seals only haphazardly, and rarely anywhere but New Zealand. After 1790, Australians and Americans descended on New Zealand, butchering seals in their millions and selling the skins in Canton. It was good business while it lasted, which in New Zealand was only until about 1810. Bleaker outcrops of land in the Pacific subantarctic – the Chatham islands, Macquarie, Auckland, Campbell – all these islands attracted sealers keen to tap the Chinese market. By 1830 Pacific sealers had worked so well that they put themselves out of business.

Whalers showed no more restraint. If they learned anything from the brief history of Pacific sealing it was urgency not conservation. Pacific whaling opened up in the 1780s. East India Company monopoly rights kept Britons and Australians out of the business until 1801, giving the Americans and French a headstart. By the 1840s, sperm whales alone attracted 500–700 ships and 15–20,000 men to the Pacific in any given year. Americans accounted for 80–90 per cent of these. By 1860 whalers had depleted their quarry so as to make continued hunting of right, sperm and humpback whales uneconomical. Not until new technology put larger whales at risk (around 1900) would whaling revive. Whaling also had some impact on island vegetation, because reducing whale-blubber to whale-oil required fuelwood.[10]

Smaller creatures fared little better. Sea-slugs (*bêche-de-mer* or *Holothurioidea*) have long appealed to the Chinese as delicacies and aphrodisiacs. Through the efforts of British and Yankee traders after 1820, countless sea-slugs found their way into Chinese soups. Fiji provided the lion's share, especially 1828–50, until its lagoons were depleted. Drying sea-slugs for shipment required fires day and night. A million cubic feet (about 100,000 m³) of Fijian timber, including valuable palm groves, went up in smoke this way.[11]

Smaller trades had smaller ecological impacts. Early colonial Australia had difficulty feeding itself, so Sydney's demand for pigs and pork provoked a boom in Tahitian hogs (1793–1825), with profound consequences for Tahitian vegetation. Tortoiseshell, pearls, pearl shell, mother-of-pearl, coral moss and birds' nests all found markets in China in the nineteenth century. Between 1802 and 1820 about 150,000 tons of mother-of-pearl left the Society Islands and Cook Islands for China. The oyster beds have not recovered 175 years later.[12]

Long-lasting ecological changes derived from long-distance trade affected Pacific forests as well as lagoons. Sandalwood (*santalum*), a genus of aromatic tree that reaches 20 metres in height, was common throughout the tropical Pacific before the nineteenth century (it was also widespread in south and south-east Asia). Chinese demand, long fed from south Asia, focused on the Pacific as well after 1800. Fiji (1804–16), the Marquesas (1815–20), Hawai'i (1811–31), and the New Hebrides (1841–65) all contributed most of their sandalwood to Chinese boxes, chests, furniture and incense. Sandalwood-gatherers burned large tracts of forest to make their targets easier to find (only the heartwood was valuable, so charred trunks were of no concern). Sandalwood has never recovered. The link between Pacific ecosystems and Chinese markets, forged by British and Yankee merchants, has had a durable impact on the species composition of Pacific forests.[13]

New Zealand forests also felt the impact of nineteenth-century trade. Northern New Zealand once had tall stands of kauri, a hardwood much admired by shipbuilders. These stands vanished between 1790 and 1860, primarily to help satisfy the timber needs of the Royal Navy. The British market for wool, and after 1882 for refrigerated meat and dairy products, led to the clearance of millions of hectares of New Zealand forest. In the 1890s alone, British settlers torched forests equivalent to 14 per cent of New Zealand's land area, making it one of the most active frontier zones in the world. Kauri is rare nowadays, and New Zealand in all has one-third as much forest as in 1840.[14]

Throughout the nineteenth century, commerce that meant comparatively little to China, Britain, America or Australia had powerful repercussions on Pacific islands. This was obviously and understandably true politically and economically, but no less true ecologically. Thus far I have offered two reasons for this: the inherent lability of Pacific ecosystems, and the focusing of concentrated demand of millions of consumers upon small sources of supply. There is a third reason, more cultural than ecological or economic.

In nineteenth-century Oceania, existing political and cultural systems had matured over several centuries. They had developed so as to fit historical circumstances, not to face the sudden changes that European traders, whalers and occasionally settlers brought. Where firm political hierarchy prevailed, as in Fiji or Hawaii, the extractive trades appealed to chiefs and kings. They organized the necessary labour to extract sandalwood or sea-slugs, monopolized exchange with British or American traders, and generally became addicted to the goods received in return. So extractive trade continued, with little regard for ecological costs. In some cases, the chiefs' and kings' political position required continued trade for European goods, lest guns fall into the hands of potential enemies. At any rate, political structures sometimes conduced to the rapid ecological transformation of Pacific islands.

Beyond this, the constraints island societies had often devised against resource-depletion usually disintegrated with the culture change of the nineteenth century. Christianity lacks taboos on resource depletion, although it has strong ones on abortion and infanticide. It is a continental ideology, not an atoll one. Mission education and its public successors generally neglected local ecological knowledge, so each generation knew less and less of the cycles of nature than the last. The price mechanism and doctrine of individual advancement contributed to the corrosion of constraints on overexploitation. So the forests, lagoons and reefs of the Pacific suffered nearly the same fate as the seal rookeries and whaling grounds. Chaotic culture change converted these often well-regulated common resources into poorly regulated or entirely unregulated commons, leading to the unhappy effects noted by observers from Aristotle to Garrett Hardin.[15]

Taking the very long view of evolutionary biology, the entire Age of Cook is merely a punctuation mark in the punctuated equilibrium of Pacific evolution. From the less Olympian heights of history, however, one can see an era of accelerated change from about 1790 to about 1850, followed by a slackening from 1850 to

1880. The important exotic species (micro-organisms and mammals) had arrived early in the century. The rate of human depopulation slowed and in most islands stopped before the end of the century. The slackening was mild, indistinct, and impossible to demonstrate given the overlapping complexities of population biology among dozens of introduced and native species. Much clearer is the slackening derived from the decline of the Chinese market.

Whale oil aside, the major products hunted and gathered for export in the Pacific after 1780 went to China. By 1850, however, Chinese tea and silk could be had without hunting down the last seals or sandalwood. After the Treaty of Nanking (1842), Bengali opium provided the key that unlocked the China trade. Soon thereafter, the great Taiping Rebellion (1850–64) convulsed China, reducing its appetite for Pacific speciality goods. After decades of hunting and gathering, the China trade had skimmed off the cream of readily accessible and marketable resources. Until commercial production replaced commercial hunting and gathering, the ecological impact of Europeans in the Pacific would temporarily abate.

## The Age of Plantations, 1880–1970

Toward the end of the nineteenth century, the plantation complex[16] – cash crops, unfree and often imported labour, export orientation – came to many islands of the Pacific. As plantation agriculture developed, so too did regular networks of transport and communication, organized within the context of colonial empires and economies. The old extractive trades often continued, or were replaced by new ones made economic by new technology, new transport, or new markets. The plantation economy did not so much replace the ecological effects of the extractive economy as overshadow them. In consequence of the cumulative impact of both economies, environmental change accelerated once again. The formal end of colonialism in the mid- and late twentieth century did not make much difference, at least in environmental matters. The organization of the islands' landscapes still reflects the new arrangements forged a century ago. Here I will consider biological invasions, plantations, the modernized extractive trades of logging, mining and whaling, and population growth.

The variety of alien organisms able to make it to the Pacific increased with steamships. As in the Age of Cook, advances in human transport led to considerable ecological change, almost all of it unintended and unforeseen. Most of the important exotic species introductions to the Pacific took place before 1880. Naturally it took time for the invaders to spread, so their colonizations and consequences rippled throughout Oceania into the twentieth century. Cats in the Cook Islands, introduced in the nineteenth century, devoured native birds throughout the twentieth. Rabbit and deer, late nineteenth-century additions to the New Zealand biota, nibbled and browsed so voraciously on the native bush and imported pasture grasses as to provoke vigorous control measures after 1930. New invaders arrived all the time, adding their disruptive effects: Hawaii, which acquired new species at the rate of one every 100,000 years in prehuman times, now hosts an average of 20 invasive invertebrates alone every year. Most arrive by plane.[17]

Most tropical Pacific islands received the giant African snail (*Achatina fulica*) sometime after 1930. It originated in East Africa, but was deliberately brought to Mauritius and Réunion so that French planters could enjoy outsized escargots. From there it made its way to India, the Philippines, and the South Pacific following the circuitry of the plantation complex. It is a major crop pest, afflicting cocoa, rubber, banana, sweet potato, cassava, yams, breadfruit and papaya among others. It has also brought many indigenous snails to the brink of extinction. In this it was helped by an American snail introduced to control the African, but which instead turned on the native species. This is typical: in the twentieth century about one hundred species have become extinct through biological pest control gone awry.[18]

Numerous other crop pests have become established in the Pacific since 1880, assisted by improved transport, by the Panama Canal (1914), and by plantation monocrop agriculture. The golden age of Pacific shipping, from 1914 to 1965, with its regular services to dozens of islands, saw rapid dispersion of diseases, beetles, rabbits and other pests. Vast fields of sugar-cane or groves of coconut palms presented ideal environments for the rhinoceros beetle, coconut beetle, and several others.

Plantation agriculture meant much more than the easy dispersion of crop pests. Broad expanses were cleared to plant crops. Sugar-boiling required endless amounts of fuelwood and the harvest needed endless labour. Thus Fiji lost much of its remain-

ing forest and acquired its Hindu population with the establishment of sugar. Sugar dominated Saipan, Tinian and Rota under
Japanese rule (1919–45), and led to similar devastation of
vegetation and rapid immigration. Hawaii, the Society Islands and
countless copra islands experienced parallel changes in vegetation,
as sugar, pineapple, cotton or coconuts replaced wild bush. Land
clearance proceeded out of all proportion to island population,
because now the islands were producing for millions of consumers
around the Pacific Rim and indeed the world.

Livestock plantations, commonly known as ranches or runs, also
developed greatly after 1880, most notably in Hawaii and New
Zealand. After European settlement began in 1840, but much faster
after the introduction of refrigerated shipping in 1882, New
Zealanders converted their native bush to pasture. Grassland
doubled in extent between 1840 and 1980, most of it sown with
imported seed. New Zealand has done comparatively well out of
this ecological transformation. Despite its deep economic dependence on Britain, New Zealand in 1940 was in per-capita terms the
richest society in the world, with the longest life expectancy and
the lowest infant mortality. This bounty came at the cost of exposing New Zealand soils to the risk of accelerated erosion, which
ravaged parts of the country after 1860. Since 1950, pastoral
productivity and general prosperity have depended on the liberal
use of chemical fertilizers, most of which derives from phosphate
deposits on other Pacific islands. New Zealand has not made the
most of its ecological transition – millions of cubic metres of good
timber went up in smoke – but other Pacific societies have fared
worse, partly because they had less control over the process.

The creation of plantations and livestock runs is the first aspect
of environmental change in the Pacific that was strongly linked to
imperialism. Previous extractive trades generally took place in the
context of indigenous societies. In some cases plantations did so as
well, but generally they flourished only where European authorities
took at least partial control of law, land and labour.

The plantation complex added new momentum to ecological
change, but some extractive industries continued, some re-
awakened, and some new ones were born after 1880. Mining did
not necessarily require colonialism, but certainly expanded greatly
because of it. Colonial authorities routinely proved sympathetic to
those seeking mining concessions. Nowhere did mining affect the

ecology more than Nauru and Banaba (formerly Ocean Island).
Here, over millennia, seabirds left rich guano deposits, almost pure
phosphate, which until 1905 were covered by topsoil, forest and
small-scale horticulture. Mining began in 1905 and will end very
soon. About 100 million tons have been extracted, two-thirds of
which went to Australian pastures, more than a quarter to New
Zealand's sheep runs and dairy farms, and the balance to Britain,
Malaysia and Japan. Four-fifths of Nauru consists of pits dug to
6–7 metres' depth amid limestone pillars that show where the
earth's surface once was. This ecological barbarity did not necessarily require imperialism, but imperialism certainly helped. The
destruction of Nauru and Banaba has made good the declining
fertility of much of the British Empire and Commonwealth.[19]

Whaling in the twentieth-century Pacific was an extractive
industry that required no assistance from imperialism. The mori-
bund business revived around the turn of the century thanks to
technological innovations made chiefly by Norwegians. They introduced the explosive harpoon gun, faster steam-powered ships, and
pumps to inflate big rorquals (big, fast whales that sink when dead).
By 1914 they invented the factory ship, which processed whales at
sea, freeing them from regulations imposed by colonial authorities
in the Pacific (and elsewhere). In 1850 whalers had hunted their
prey like Pleistocene mammoth hunters, throwing a spear into the
giant creatures. By 1914 whaling had entered the industrial age.
By the late 1930s, blue whales, the largest and most valuable
rorqual, had grown scarce. Fin whales became depleted by 1960,
sei whales by 1975. Sonar and satellite have brought all but Minke
whales, the smallest and least valuable of rorquals, to the edge of
extinction. Colonialism has had nothing to do with it: market forces
and technology have sufficed.[20]

The plantation complex and the extractive economies grew as
they did with the assistance of a burgeoning population in the
twentieth century. After 1900, population growth asserted its
influence again, as it had in many islands in pre-contact times.
Natural increase and immigration filled most islands to historic
maxima by 1950. At that date Oceania's population was growing
by 3 per cent per annum, as fast as it had been declining a century
before. In most cases this growth led to heightened pressure on
vegetation, reefs and lagoons. In addition to secular growth in the
twentieth century, temporary surges of population associated with

war or tourism brought instability and attendant ecological problems ranging from waste disposal to the wartime depletion of all
edible creatures. Population flux is inherently destabilizing wherever humankind is the ecological dominant.

## Imperialism and the Driving Forces of Ecological Change

In general, imperialism played a modest role in the ecological transformations of the modern Pacific. Three of the four great driving
forces operated independently of formal imperialism: transport
advance, concentration of dispersed demand, and population. (The
inherent lability of Pacific ecosystems is a condition, not a force.)
The fourth driving force was geopolitics, very much a matter of
imperialism.

Military occupations had brought forced depopulations of some
islands in the seventeenth-century (Spanish) Marianas. Franco-
British rivalry inspired much of the voyaging, mapping and inven-
torying of the Pacific islands in the late eighteenth century. By the
late nineteenth century, ambitious great powers needed Pacific
colonies, especially coaling stations for their steam navies. Geo-
political impact on Pacific ecology, however, remained slight until
the Second World War. That war led to a burst of changes, from
the effects of combat to flurries of biological invasions. It involved
Americans and Japanese but generally not European imperial
powers, and falls outside the scope of this chapter.

The post-war nuclear programmes of the great powers may
account for the most important environmental effects of geo-
political rivalry. It is difficult to know because the French and
British carefully guard all information concerning their tests. The
Americans were less secretive, and studies of atolls where they
tested nuclear weapons reveal – not surprisingly – massive
ecological changes.[21] Presumably the same could be found in the
Gilberts, where Britain used to conduct hydrogen-bomb tests, and
the outer atolls of French Polynesia, where France did its testing
after 1962. Between them, the French, British and Americans
exploded some 250 nuclear devices in the Pacific before a 1992
moratorium. The effects, great or small, will be durable.
Substances created in these blasts will still be lethal in 24,000
years, six times as long as humanity has graced Micronesia and
Polynesia.

If one uses the term imperialism in its broad sense, then virtually every environmental change since Cook can be ascribed to it. But if one uses it in a stricter sense, as I have, to refer to political dominion, then imperialism had no appreciable bearing on Pacific environmental history in the Age of Cook, and a modest one since then. In the entire period since 1769, economic ties to the great economies, and epidemiological ties to the great centres of population mattered more than imperial ties to the great powers. What mattered most of all, however, was the long isolation of Pacific ecosystems and human populations. This isolation conferred extraordinary power on biological and cultural agents of all ranks. Ecosystems, socio-political systems, and individuals' immune systems all proved vulnerable. It could hardly have been otherwise. Any economic, epidemiological, and biological contact, whether in the context of formal imperialism or not, would have profoundly disrupted the Pacific. Imperialism contributed to a burst of environmental changes brought on by the end of isolation.

## Notes

1. Exceptions to this include New Zealand, which had its own life forms when it spun off from Gondwanaland some 80 million years ago, and thereafter remained (until recently) a sanctuary for Cretaceous species; and several of the westernmost Pacific islands which acquired migratory species by land in times of lower sea level such as the ice ages.

2. See P.V. Kirch, 'Man's Role in Modifying Tropical and Subtropical Polynesian Ecosystems', *Archaeology in Oceania* 18 (1983), pp. 26–31; M.S. McGlone, 'The Polynesian Settlement of New Zealand in Relation to Environmental and Biotic Changes', *New Zealand Journal of Ecology* 12 (1989) [supplement], pp. 115–30; Ben Finney, 'The Other One-Third of the Globe', *Journal of World History* 5 (1994), pp. 273–97; J.R. McNeill, 'Of Rats and Men: A Synoptic Environmental History of the Island Pacific', *Journal of World History* 5 (1994), pp. 299–349.

3. Alfred W. Crosby, *The Columbian Exchange*, Greenwood, Westport, Conn. 1972.

4. The best guide to this subject concerns chiefly the French Pacific: J.-L. Rallu, *Les populations océaniennes aux XIXe et XXe siècles*, INED, Paris, 1990. See also Ian Pool, *Te iwi Maori*, University of Auckland Press, Auckland, 1991; A.O. Bushnell, *The Gifts of Civilization: Germs and Genocide in Hawai'i*, University of Hawai'i Press, Honolulu, 1993; Alfred W. Crosby, 'Hawaiian Depopulation as a Model for the American Experience', in T. Ranger and Paul Slack (eds.), *Epidemics and Ideas*, Cambridge University Press, Cambridge, 1992, pp. 175–201; and David Stannard,

*Before the Horror*, University of Hawaii Social Science Research Institute, Honolulu, 1989.

5. Charles Wilkes, *Narrative of the United States Exploring Expedition during the Years 1838, 1839, 1840, 1841, 1842*, 5 vols, Gregg Press, Upper Saddle River, N.J., 1970 [1845], vol. III, p. 32.

6. Harold Brookfield and John Overton, 'How Old is the Deforestation of Oceania?', in John Dargavel, Kay Dixon and Noel Semple (eds.), *Changing Tropical Forests*, Centre for Resource and Environmental Studies, Canberra, 1988, p. 91.

7. Quoted in Carolyn King, *Immigrant Killers: Introduced Predators and the Conservation of Birds in New Zealand*, Oxford University Press, Auckland, 1984, p. 68. Two healthy rats in three years can generate 20 million descendants. If all went well – it never does – in ten years they could produce 50 quadrillion ($5 \times 10^{17}$) progeny. Soon they could encase the globe in a squirming ball of rat flesh expanding with a radial velocity greater than the speed of light.

8. P.V. Kirch and Marshall Sahlins, *Anahulu: The Anthropology of History in the Kingdom of Hawaii*, 2 vols, University of Chicago Press, Chicago, 1992, vol. II, p. 169.

9. *Ecological Imperialism: The Biological Expansion of Europe, 900–1900*, Cambridge University Press, New York, 1986.

10. Hawaii at one point produced half-a-million barrels of whale oil per year, which implies burning mountains of fuelwood. Tasmania and Russell (NZ) were the other main whaling ports, and presumably supplied plenty of wood too. Whalers routinely stopped at tropical islands when hunting the sperm whale, and would have burned their wood as well.

11. R.G. Ward, 'The Pacific Bêche-de-mer Trade with Special Reference to Fiji', in R.G. Ward (ed.), *Man in the Pacific: Essays on Geographical Change in the Pacific Islands*, Clarendon Press, Oxford, 1972, pp. 117–18.

12. John M.R. Young (ed.), *Australia's Pacific Frontier: Economic and Cultural Expansion into the Pacific, 1795–1885*, University of Melbourne Press, Melbourne, 1967; Ward, 'The Pacific Bêche-de-mer Trade'; B. Salvat, 'The Living Marine Resources of the South Pacific – Past, Present, and Future', in N.A. Shilo and A.V. Lozhkin (eds.), *Ecology and Environmental Protection in the Pacific Region*, Nauk, Moscow, 1981, pp. 119–45.

13. Dorothy Shineberg, *They Came for Sandalwood*, University of Melbourne Press, Melbourne, 1967; Mark Merlin and Dan Van Ravensway, 'The History of Human Impact on the Genus *Santalum* in Hawai'i', in *Proceedings of the Symposium on Sandalwood in the Pacific*, US Forest Service Pacific Southwest Research Station, Berkeley, 1990, pp. 46–60.

14. A.H. Reed, *The Story of Kauri*, Reed, Wellington, 1951; M.M. Roche, 'The New Zealand Timber Economy, 1840–1935', *Journal of Historical Geography* 16 (1990), pp. 295–313.

15. Gary A. Klee, 'Oceania', in Gary Klee (ed.), *World Systems of Traditional Resource Management*, Edward Arnold, London, 1980, pp. 268–

71; F.R. Fosberg, 'Past, Present, and Future Conservation Problems in the Pacific', in A.B. Costin and R.H. Groves (eds.), *Nature Conservation in the Pacific*, Australian National University Press, Canberra, 1973, pp. 209–15; Garrett Hardin, 'The Tragedy of the Commons', *Science* 162 (1968), pp. 1243–8; Aristotle, *Politics* 2.3.

16.  The term is Philip Curtin's: *The Rise and Fall of the Plantation Complex*, Cambridge University Press, New York, 1990.

17.  According to Alan Holt of The Nature Conservancy, Honolulu. *The Economist*, 10 April 1993, p. 92.

18.  E. Dharamaraju, 'Transport and Spread of Crop Pests in Tropical Polynesia', in M. Laird (ed.), *Commerce and the Spread of Pests and Disease Vectors*, Praeger, New York, 1984, pp. 264–6; Francis G. Howarth, 'Environmental Impacts of Species Purposefully Introduced for Biological Control of Pests', *Pacific Science* 46 (1992), pp. 388–9.

19.  Philippe L. Hein, 'Between Aldabra and Nauru', in W. Beller, P. d'Ayala and P. Hein (eds.), *Ss.ustainable Development and Environmental Management of Small Islands*, UNESCO and Parthenon Publishing, Paris, 1990; Barrie MacDonald and Maslyn Williams, *The Phosphateers*, Melbourne University Press, Melbourne, 1985; Christopher Weeramantry, *Nauru: Environmental Damage under International Trusteeship*, Oxford University Press, Oxford, 1992. Nauruans got virtually nothing from this before independence in 1968; since then they have grown very rich. Banaba was mined out before the money began to flow.

20.  J.N. Tonnessen and A.O. Johnsen, *The History of Modern Whaling*, University of California Press, Berkeley, 1982; Jeremy Cherfas, *The Hunting of the Whale*, Penguin, Harmondsworth, 1989. The timber trade is another extractive economy that has had little connection to formal colonialism. I exclude it here because it is primarily a post-1970 affair.

21.  F.R. Fosberg, 'Vegetation of Bikini Atoll', *Atoll Research Bulletin* 315 (1988), pp. 1–28; W.B. Jackson, 'Survival of Rats at Eniwetok Atoll', *Pacific Science* 23 (1969), pp. 265–75.

# 9

# Acclimatizers: European Environmental Impact in Australia and New Zealand/Aotearoa

## GEOFFREY BOLTON

Until recently, New Zealand has been largely ignored by Australian historians, and the opportunity of drawing comparisons across the Tasman Sea is seldom taken. When in 1980 I published a short environmental history of Australia[1] it did not occur to me to look at the New Zealand experience as an instructive source of comparison and contrast. Yet the two countries were connected quite closely during the nineteenth century. Before the Treaty of Waitangi in 1840, the governor of New South Wales exercised a vague oversight over New Zealand, and missionaries and traders from New South Wales settled there. Australian volunteers crossed the Tasman in the 1860s to take part in the Maori wars, and miners prospected for gold on both sides of the sea. Australians have never quite understood why New Zealand was so reluctant to join the federated Commonwealth in 1901. That contact did not cease during the twentieth century is demonstrated by the excessive number of New Zealand-bred horses that have won the Melbourne Cup, Australia's leading sporting event.

Environmental history might seem a less fruitful field than political history for comparative studies. Australia is a continent of some 7.5 million square kilometres with a large arid centre fringed by a monsoonal north and a more or less Mediterranean south-east and south-west. New Zealand consists of two elongated islands and some smaller outliers totalling less than 270,000 square kilometres but including mountains towering far above Australia's highest. Much of Australia endures marked seasonal variations, to which the characteristic eucalyptus has shown notable powers of adaptability. New Zealand has no well-defined dry season, and before human settlement much of its land surface was covered by hardwood and beech forest, with some poorer fern and scrub lands on South Island. The Australian environment shows the effect of continuous human contact longer than almost any other part of the world. The ancestors of the Aborigines arrived at least 50,000 years ago; perhaps 115,000 years if we accept Singh's theory that the change from deciduous species to eucalypts in the Lake George district near Canberra reflects the coming of fire through human agency.[2] A hunter-gatherer people whose needs did not impel them to take the step to systematic agriculture, the Aborigines in many regions of Australia used fire to burn off the country as a means of driving out game and encouraging the regeneration of new grass. They are thus credited with creating the park-like country which attracted European pastoralists in the nineteenth century. In New Zealand, on the other hand, human settlement of any kind did not occur until the 9th century AD. The settlers arriving from Polynesia increased faster than the Aborigines. In the late eighteenth century, the Maori population reached an estimated peak of between 125,000 and 150,000, whereas after fifty centuries of habitation there were still probably only about a million humans in Australia. But although in New Zealand the Maoris cleared the native timber for villages and farming, they had not time to leave such a deep imprint on the country as the first Australians.

In both countries the human presence brought with it new animal species to compete with indigenous fauna. In Australia humans in quest of a rich source of protein hastened the extinction of the diprotodon, a cousin of the wombat about the size of a hippopotamus. Asian seafarers brought the first dingo to northern Australia around 5,000 years ago. More efficient in the pursuit of small game, the dingo competed successfully with an earlier carnivore, the thylacine tiger, which survived only in a Tasmania already separated from the mainland. In less than a thousand years the Maori also managed to make inroads into the indigenous fauna of New Zealand. They hunted the last moas to extinction and, by introducing dogs and rats, eradicated the tuatura except on a few small islands. But neither the Australian Aborigines nor the Maoris of Aotearoa transformed their environments as comprehensively as the largely British settlers who began to arrive at the end of the eighteenth century.

The newcomers lived by ideologies significantly different to those of their predecessors. The culture and religion of the Australian Aborigines identified humans with their landscapes, and their disciplines as a hunter-gatherer people largely protected their country from over-exploitation. A similar reverence may be seen in the Maori custom that no tree was felled until traditional rites had been performed over it in order to propitiate the forest god Tane for the death of one of his children. The British of the late eighteenth and nineteenth centuries carried with them an ideology that regarded property as the essential hallmark of a citizen, and the efficient economic development of property as an overriding and socially beneficial goal. Although the Romantic movement was placing a new stress on the beauty and value of wilderness, this attitude had not had time to influence political and economic behaviour. An orderly cultivation was seen as satisfying the aesthetic ideal no less than the imperatives of productivity; and when the young naval officer, John Lort Stokes, encountered in 1841 the open country that lay beyond the mangroves fringing the Gulf of Carpentaria, it was not thought ridiculous that he should name it 'the plains of promise' or to predict that before long the landscape would be dotted with the spires of Christian villages.[3]

Stokes' calm certainty that the British settlers could impose their own cultural and economic patterns on the landscape reflected the official doctrine that before white settlement the Australian continent was *terra nullius*, no man's land, to which the indigenous inhabitants possessed no title. But as Henry Reynolds has shown, the British authorities in the 1830s and 1840s were far from sure of the justice of the *terra nullius* doctrine.[4] When New Zealand passed under British sovereignty in 1840, the Treaty of Waitangi, with all its imperfections, recognized the Maori presence and ensured that, in future, pakeha and Maori would each influence the other's traditions of land stewardship.[5] By contrast, the Australian settlers very largely ignored the accumulated experience of the Aborigines in coming to terms with the environment, though in practice Australia's pastoralists and even Australia's road-builders owed unacknowledged debts to Aboriginal precedent. In both countries, however, the impact of European settlement came with devastating rapidity. The white settlement of New Zealand took place within a dozen years of 1840. Over the much larger land surface of Australia the process took longer, but after a slow start in 1788 occupation spread with a rapidity matched only by the conquistadors' of Latin America. Some Aborigines lost their lives in conflict,[6] more through introduced disease, beginning with a smallpox epidemic in 1789. By 1888, only the desert remained undisputed in Aboriginal keeping.

Such rapid expansion meant inevitably that the newcomers gave themselves no time for coming to terms with the Australian environment, despite its obvious differences from anything they had experienced in Britain. Similarly, their assessment of New Zealand was coloured by its superficially closer likeness to the climate and topography of familiar regions in the northern hemisphere. As it happened, the first major environmental impact arising from settler economic activity was to be found in the seas around Australia and New Zealand. The American War of Independence had displaced the British whaling industry from its old hunting grounds off Greenland and Canada. It was no coincidence that some of the shipping transporting early consignments of convicts to New South Wales was provided by whaling companies, nor that as early as the Third Fleet in 1791 one enterprising captain, having dumped his convict cargo at Sydney, turned to the harpooning of whales migrating along the coast. Between 1800 and 1840 the maritime industries of whaling and sealing were a major staple of the Australian economy, with crews ranging along the entire south coast of the continent, east across the Tasman and south as far as Macquarie Island. Though a rough and dangerous trade, which contributed much to the destruction of coastal Aboriginal peoples, whaling and sealing provided opportunity for ex-convicts, attracted American and French interlopers, and contributed to Hobart's boom in the 1820s. But accessible seals were nearly exterminated in Australian waters by the 1830s and in New Zealand a decade or two later. By the 1850s the whaling harvest also was dwindling fast. The final discouragement came after 1859, when the commercial development of petroleum competed successfully with that of whale oil, but by that time the carnage was thorough.

On land, the major staple industry in both Australia and New Zealand was sheepfarming, although the nature of the ecological impact was necessarily different in each. In Australia, with its emphasis on wool-growing, merino sheep became the dominant breed, partly because of their capacity to survive in dry conditions. But merino sheep are dainty feeders, and in many regions they soon eradicated the most nutritious native grasses and hastened their replacement by coarser competitors and introduced weeds. Besides, they concentrated on the frontages of rivers and watercourses where no hoofed animal had ever trodden before, so that in many districts of northern Australia soil erosion resulted within twenty years of occupation. Nor was it helpful that much pastoral land was held by leasehold by graziers with neither the will nor the resources to think in terms of long-term family occupation. In New Zealand, on the other hand, the decades of pastoral leasehold gave way by 1900 to a pattern of smaller holdings under freehold occupation. Fencing and stock control came more readily, necessarily because after the development of the frozen meat trade in the 1880s New Zealand exporters were concerned as much with lamb and mutton as with wool. As we shall see, New Zealand also had its problems with soil erosion but it was possible to blame other agents of change besides sheep.

The ecological impact of European settlement in Australia was charted in 1966 by leading zoologist Jock Marshall. The thrust of his book is shown in its title: *The Great Extermination: A Guide to Australian Cupidity, Wickedness and Waste*.[7] Marshall's main theme was the destruction of native fauna by the settlers and their beasts. In the first generation of pioneering, settlers were understandably reluctant to sacrifice their own livestock for food, and instead hunted for native game. Between 1806 and 1813 the commissariat of Van Diemans Land offered payment – in hard times up to a shilling a pound – for kangaroo meat. Matthew Flinders considered that the wombat 'resembled lean mutton in taste and to us acceptable food'.[8] Bandicoot was thought to resemble sucking pig, and even the spiny ant-eater, the echidna, was not safe from the cooking pot: 'it is exceedingly fat, the flesh has a somewhat aromatic taste and was thought delicious'. Even when the times of scarcity were over, native fauna were hunted. To the ex-convicts and other working-class settlers, it was an important mark of Australian freedom that there were no game laws to forbid poaching. When in the 1860s Australian colonial governments belatedly realized the need for legislative action to prevent the extinction of native animals and birds, they encountered strong opposition from working-class representatives with bitter memories of Britain's game laws. The higher classes in Australia regarded hunting as the characteristic pastime of the British gentry, whom they strove to emulate, but many would have agreed with Captain Foster Fyans, old army man and magistrate at Geelong, who wrote: 'For an idler or a sportsman this country affords nothing and for a military officer it is the most damnable quarter in the world.'[9]

To those who thought thus, the obvious remedy was the introduction of exotics, but it was not until the prosperous years following the goldrushes of the 1850s that the acclimatizers succeeded. Fallow deer were released in the forests east of Melbourne from 1863 and throve so well that later generations declared them vermin. Aspiring foxhunters found it more difficult to acclimatize their quarry, and at late as the 1860s young bloods in hunting pink had to be content with galloping after dingos and kangaroos. But the Melbourne Hunt Club, established in 1864, was more successful, and by 1885 foxes were at home in over 12,000 square kilometres of south-eastern Australia, and were proving a pest to sheep farmers. Their capacity for damage was far outdone by that of the rabbit. Responsibility is usually attributed to the Victorian squatter Thomas Austin, who had to make three attempts before shipping out a strain of rabbits hardy enough to acclimatize in Australia, but there are earlier reports of rabbits in the bush in Tasmania and South Australia and the point still needs clearing up.[10] Undeniably after the 1860s the rabbit population exploded irresistibly. Rabbits competed with the pastoralists' sheep and cattle for feed and water. It has been estimated that their presence eventually went close to halving the value of Australia's wool production. But no native predator could cope with the rabbits' powers of multiplication, and the introduction of cats and ferrets only added to the ecological imbalance. In any case, to the small farmer who added rabbit to his family's diet, to the trapper who made a living from rabbit pelts and meats, and to the working-class Sydney household eking out its budget by recourse to the 'rabbit-oh', the disaster had its ample compensations. Hence scientific attempts at a solution were not strongly supported by politicians alert to working-class sympathies. In the early years of this century, the Western Australian government erected three rabbit-proof fences spanning hundreds of kilometres in a futile attempt to keep out the invaders. Coming so soon after Western Australia's reluctant entry into the federated Commonwealth, the rabbit-proof fence probably stood as a symbolic barrier against other intruders rather than a practical measure of control.

Eric Rolls, a practising grazier, in a provocative book entitled *They All Ran Wild*,[11] points the finger at the well-intentioned Acclimatization Societies of the mid-Victorian period for introducing many undesirable immigrants into Australia's fauna. In the 1860s, Victoria and New South Wales both supported influential Acclimatization Societies whose members considered the Australian bush 'dull and lifeless' and released skylarks and sparrows to enliven the bush, attack farmers' crops and foul the streets of Australian cities. In New Zealand, over-enthusiastic acclimatizers carry a long list of responsibilities, starting with Captain James Cook, who, on his second voyage in 1773, released pigs and goats in an effort to boost New Zealand's protein supplies. After 1840, New Zealanders showed themselves slow to learn from Australian experiences. Rabbits, sparrows and foxes established themselves in the teeth of Australian precedent. Not sharing the qualms of Australian ex-convicts about the game laws, the gentlemen of New Zealand from 1851 made repeated attempts to acclimatize deer, particularly on South Island, and by the end of the century it was becoming clear that their efforts had been all too successful. Yet as late as 1907, when the Austrian Kaiser, Franz Josef, presented New Zealand with a brace of chamois, nobody seems to have foreseen that their descendants might also contribute to the problems of mountain erosion. Precisely because the New Zealand landscapes seemed more temperate than most of Australia, the impression apparently prevailed that its ecology would prove more tolerant of European imports.

If Australia and New Zealand had been more enlightened in their forestry policies, some of the damage, especially erosion, could have been averted. But as Sir Keith Hancock observed as early as 1930, the early settlers hated trees.[12] Between 1800 and the 1880s the magnificent stands of cedar along the east coast of Australia were cut down, with enormous waste. Timber cutting was largely a poor man's occupation, offering independence and quick profit, and it was difficult to police. In 1847 an official calculated that the Big Scrub on the Richmond River in northern New South Wales could not be cleared for five or six centuries.

Within thirty years dairy farmers were rounding up their milkers on the same country. In the North Island of New Zealand, kauri similarly became a major export from the 1850s, and from the 1860s Western Australia's jarrah and karri forests were open to exploitation. More than the timber trade, however, it was the pastoralists and farmers who hastened the clearing of indigenous trees and scrub. Burning off was found difficult to control and sometimes resulted in calamitous bushfires. An alternative method of clearing, known as ringbarking, was practised in the Hunter valley region of New South Wales as early as 1826. This consisted of cutting a section around a tree trunk so that the tree eventually died for want of nourishment and could be felled easily. The practice did not become widespread until after 1860 when the labour shortages caused by the discovery of gold impelled landowners into paddocking and fencing, but it then caught on rapidly in both Australia and New Zealand. This led to a major debate in New South Wales in the early 1880s because some observers, including qualified foresters, conjectured that the wholesale clearance of trees would discourage rainfall, whereas many pastoralists asserted that on the contrary 'springs had been found gushing up where they had never been found before, because the water had been absorbed by the trees'.[13] I have been so far unable to discover whether comparable debates were taking place in New Zealand at the same time, but recent research suggests that the pessimists were correct. Western Australian wheatlands cleared since the early years of this century have suffered a decline in rainfall, whereas the originally drier country inland had undergone a gradual increase. Comparative material from New Zealand would be instructive.

The mining industry was also greedy for timber. Firewood was used in huge quantities as fuel for steam engines: the goldmines of Kalgoorlie consumed half-a-million tonnes in 1902. In New Zealand, where goldmining lost its significance before the beginning of the twentieth century, the scale of the damage may not have been quite as great, but note should be taken of the ecological impact of widespread sluicing. Nor should we underestimate the continuing demand for firewood for domestic purposes. I have not found an estimate earlier than 1925, but in that year New South Wales and Victoria between them consumed a million tonnes of firewood for domestic purposes. In both Australia and New

Zealand in the first half of the twentieth century, many rural electric power stations were fuelled by firewood.

Australia and New Zealand's slowness to practise enlightened forest husbandry was to a large extent inherited from the British, who, with comparatively little remaining of their original forests, lagged far behind France and Germany in silviculture. The main centre of scientific forestry in the later-nineteenth-century British Empire was India, where a leading part was played by a forester named Ribbentrop. It is relevant to note that the first significant initiatives towards improved forestry was the work of German immigrants. South Australia, soon after its foundation in 1836, acquired a significant intake of Lutherans from Prussia and the Rhineland, and the architecture and landscape of a major wine-growing district, the Barossa valley, still bear a distinctive German imprint.

South Australia's timber resources were markedly smaller than those of the other Australian colonies and New Zealand. The problem attracted the notice of the eminent botanist Ferdinand von Mueller. He had a friend from the same part of Schleswig-Holstein, one Heinrich Krichauff, who, having carried a banner in the 1848 rising in Berlin, departed for South Australia later that year and was a member of parliament there by 1870. In that year Krichauff moved for the creation of forest reserves in South Australia. He found an ally in the curator of the Adelaide botanical gardens, Robert Schomburgk, who had long lamented what he called 'the wasteful destruction of our forests' and urged that municipal councils should be subsidized to plant vacant lands with a mixture of Australian and European timber.[14] Krichauff and Schomburgk circulated a questionnaire among prominent citizens and landowners, and, despite a mixed response, persuaded the South Australian authorities in 1875 to set up a board of management for forestry. This was followed by a government department in 1882, and the appointment of a conservator of forests three years later. Victoria, New South Wales and Tasmania all followed this example quickly, but Queensland, Western Australia and New Zealand took little effective action until around 1900. Perhaps they believed their forest reserves to be greater; perhaps they needed more Germans in politics. Eventually, between 1907 and 1920, forestry commissions were set up in each Australian state, and a New Zealand royal commission appointed in 1913 brought about reforms there, although their implementation was delayed by the 1914–18 war. The export of Kauri was brought to a halt, and policies of reafforestation began, though much of this effort, both in New Zealand and Australia, was concentrated on the acclimatization of pine as softwood offering comparatively quick commercial returns. Once again a minority of conservationists wondered whether pine, which discouraged undergrowth and hence provided a home to few native birds or animals, was an appropriate addition to antipodean landscapes.

Well before the end of the nineteenth century, some governments had become aware of the need to set aside areas of wilderness for future generations. The United States showed the way in the 1860s and 1870s with the reservation of striking natural features such as Yosemite and Yellowstone, but Australian governments were suprisingly early on the scene. From the 1860s, the practice arose of reserving the foreshores of lakes, rivers and the ocean for public use, even although the beach would not become a major source of relaxation until after 1900. As early as 1866, the New South Wales government declared a reserve at Jenolan Caves, and in 1879 Sir Henry Parkes, the grandiose but often imaginative premier of New South Wales, declared 73,000 acres of bush south of Sydney as the Royal National Park 'for the use of the public forever'.[15] This in practice meant a mixture of uses, from bushwalking to family picnics, without any clear understanding of the impact of such use on the bush. If the government could have afforded it they would have introduced deer. But it was a constructive initiative and Parkes followed it in 1888 by the establishment of Centennial Park in Sydney itself, which is arguably still Australia's best example of a multi-purpose recreational park serving an area of high population density. Characteristically, he also proposed – unsuccessfully – that a mausoleum should be erected in which Australia's most eminent citizens should be interred. There are no prizes for guessing whom the 73-year-old Parkes saw as chief figure at the opening ceremony.

In the formation of Royal National Park and Centennial Park we note the influence of one person in authority. Parkes' example was followed in Victoria in 1887, and in the other colonies in the 1890s, when Tasmania began to take a lead with legislation for scenic preservation designed with a conscious eye on the growing tourist trade from the Australian mainland. It will be noted that of course the Australian Aborigines lacked opportunity to voice any opinions about the concept of wilderness preservation. It was otherwise in New Zealand, where the initiative for a national parks policy came not from a pakeha statesman but from a prominent Maori. Following the eruption of Tarawera in 1886 and the destruction of the remarkable Pink and White Terraces, New Zealanders were alerted to the vulnerability of their cherished landscapes. The psychological moment was seized by a chief, Te Heuheu Tukioro IV, who offered to donate a substantial portion of his people's lands for the formation of a national park in perpetuity, provided that the government took responsibility for the proper maintenance of the ancestral tombs included in the area. So it was that New Zealand acquired Tongarino, its first National Park, in 1887. (James Belich informs me that some quite complex concepts about restitution of honour lay behind the offer: Te Heuheu had been on the losing side in the Maori wars a decade earlier.) Since the New Zealand government established only one more national park in the next half-century – Mount Egmont, set aside in 1900 – this initiative invites notice. Although the governments of the Australian states proclaimed a number of national parks between 1898 and 1915, these were intended for public recreation rather than the preservation of wilderness in its pristine state. It was only in the 1920s and 1930s that the Australian states and New Zealand legislated for the protection of native plants, and it was only in those same years, with New Zealand tending to take the lead, that adequate measures for soil conservation began to be enforced.

This slowness to come to terms with the native environment is readily explicable. It was not until the last decades of the nineteenth century that Australia held an adult population of whom a majority were Australian-born, and it took a little longer in New Zealand. Especially in Australia, where so little systematic use was made of Aboriginal experience, it would require time and observation before the problems and opportunities could be adequately appreciated. To put the Australian and New Zealand response to their environments in due perspective, it is necessary keep hold in mind some under-appreciated statistics. Neither the United States nor China has a land mass more than 20 per cent greater than Australia, yet the United States supports more than 200 million inhabitants and China more than 900 million. In all the millennia of human existence there are probably fewer than 100 million human individuals who have survived early childhood to experience the Australian environment at first hand. There are possibly not more than 10 or 12 million who have ever experienced New Zealand. It should be no surprise that those who live in Australia and New Zealand should still be finding out about the potential and the limitations of their environments. In some respects it is impressive that they have adjusted so quickly – always remembering, as an exception, the Australian Aborigines with their uniquely long record of occupation and their consequently greater sense of affinity with their country. But there is still plenty of room for humility and the sustained application of human intelligence.

## Notes

1. Geoffrey Bolton, *Spoils and Spoilers.: Australians Make Their Environment*, Allen & Unwin, Sydney.
2. Josephine Flood, *Archaeology of the Dreamtime* (revised edn), Melbourne, 1995, pp. 114–16.
3. John Lort Stokes, *Discoveries in Australia*, vol. II, London, 1846, p. 319.
4. Henry Reynolds, *Dispossession: Black Australians and White Invaders*, Allen & Unwin, Sydney, 1989.
5. Cf. Claudia Orange, *The Treaty of Waitangi*, Port Nicholson Press, Allen & Unwin, Wellington, 1988.
6. Cf. Bruce Elder, *Blood on the Wattle: Massacres and Maltreatment of Australian Aborigines since 1788*, Child & Associates, Frenchs Forest, 1988. Also, Ann McGrath (ed.), *Contested Ground*, Angus & Robertson, Sydney, 1995.
7. Alexander James Marshall (ed.), *The Great Extermination: A Guide to Anglo-Australian Cupidity, Wickedness and Waste*, Heinemann, London and Melbourne, 1966.
8. Ibid., chapter 2.
9. T.F. Brine, *Letters from Victorian Pioneers*, Melbourne, 1898 (reprinted 1969), pp. 191–2.
10. Eric C. Rolls, *They All Ran Wild: The Story of Pests on the Land in Australia*, Angus & Robertson, Sydney, 1969, chapters 1–9.
11. Ibid., pp. 236–42.
12. Cf. William Keith Hancock, *Australia*, Ernest Benn, London, 1930.
13. New South Wales, *Parliamentary Debates*, 1880–81, p. 1211.
14. South Australia, *Parliamentary Papers*, 1870–71, no. 147; 1873, vol. 2, no. 26.
15. G.C. Bolton, *Spoils and Spoilers: Australians Make their Environment, 1788–1980*, Allen & Unwin, Sydney, 1981, p. 104.

# 10

# Papua New Guinea,
# its Demographic History and
# Infectious Diseases

ALFRED W. CROSBY

It is a truism among epidemiologists that when a large, dense, cosmopolitan population abruptly comes into contact with an isolated and smaller population the latter will suffer a decline in numbers, even a crash.[1] This happened over and over again during the age of expansion of Europeans into the Americas and Oceania.[2] There is, however, an impression abroad that there is one great exception to the rule, and that is the experience over the last century of the people of Papua New Guinea or, to extract from that category its most distinctive fraction, most particularly the people of the highlands.[3] Their case poses an instructive puzzle for epidemiological and demographic historians.

Papua New Guinea is far too large and various to examine as a homogeneous unit. The obvious division is between the mainland and the islands. A more significant division for the former is one of altitude, the division at 1,200–1,500 metres altitude between the coastal plus riverine lowlands and the highlands – that is, the division between lands that are hot and lands that are cool. The highlands of the offshore islands are relatively insignificant in altitude, area and population compared to those of the mainland, and so we will place the smaller islands entirely in the first category, along with the lowlands of the mainland.[4]

The isolation of Papua New Guinea, both lowlands and highlands, has been the dominant element in its history.[5] Papua New

Guinea's remoteness, however, was not so extreme as to isolate it from Chinese and Malay traders, nor the arrival of tropical diseases: filariasis, yaws, various other kinds of skin disease, several sorts of internal parasite, and, above all, malaria, overwhelmingly endemic in lowland areas of the mainland and present but usually less ferocious along the coasts of the islands.

Papua New Guineans were isolated from without, and the inhabitants of the lowlands were isolated from those of the highlands. The terrain was formidable and New Guinea's shortage of wild sources of food between the coasts and the highlands – travellers had to carry nearly everything they ate – made long treks logistically difficult.[6] Trading was carried on in short pulses – from one locality to the next and from there to the next – and lowlanders and highlanders hardly ever saw each other until the past two or three generations. The first Europeans to penetrate the highlands in the 1930s found some steel axes that had been traded up from the coast, but these were so old that they were worn down nearly to the eye that held the haft.[7]

Another kind of isolation arose from the distrust and hostility felt by each indigenous people on the mainland towards every other, often including those immediately adjacent. Many individuals travelled no more than a few kilometres from their birthplace in their entire lives.[8] The outstanding proof of their proclivity for keeping away from each other is their languages: they speak over 700 different languages – not dialects.[9]

The degree of isolation of some individual tribes challenges credulity. The Etoro, to cite one example, had no contact whatever with whites, theoretically the administrators of their part of the world, until the 1930s, and then at most a glancing and momentary contact. The next contact did not come until the 1960s.[10] The Gebusi first met outsiders in 1940, not again until 1963, and for the next twenty years saw but one official patrol a year.[11]

The Papuans' isolation from the outside world began to diminish sharply in the nineteenth century. Naturalists like the Russian Nikolai Nikolaevich Mikloucho-Maclay, and the Italian Luigi Maria D'Albertis, were too curious about New Guinea's flora, fauna and people to be daunted even by the ferocity of the people and the promise of malarial infection.[12] Christian missionaries, determined to save heathen souls, came to the mainland to stay in the 1870s. Diplomats, captains, colonels and administrators came treading on the heels of naturalists and evangelists.

An immediate effect of increasing contact between Papua New Guinea and continental peoples was the passage of the lowland populations through a gauntlet of virgin- or nearly virgin-soil epidemics. In 1872 Mikloucho-Maclay, then on the north coast of the mainland, noticed that the face of a Melanesian aquaintance, 'bore traces of smallpox. He explained to me that the illness came from the north-west and that many died from it.'[13] There was certainly one epidemic among the peoples of the south coast, and probably more, in the nineteenth century. In the early 1880s, a European on that coast met Papuans who spoke tearfully of 'the frightful disease' that had, sixteen years before, 'carried away their children and friends'. We know for sure that measles arrived on board the London Missionary Society steamer, *Ellengowan*, at Port Moresby in 1875. It spread far and wide; how far and with what result we do not know, but it is worth noting that Fiji's first epidemic of measles, also in 1875, killed one-fifth and possibly one-quarter of the population.[14]

The Europeans who followed the naturalists and missionaries to Papua New Guinea were intent on founding plantations throughout the Pacific's torrid latitudes to produce crops for the world market. They staffed their plantations with indentured labourers drawn from Oceania, mostly from Melanesia (also from Malaysia, India and China, but these continental peoples are outside our purview, except as disease carriers).

Pacific Island labourers often found themselves poorly fed and jammed into fetid quarters, at sea and ashore, with people with alien infections. Pacific island men often found themselves where the only women available to them were prostitutes. Pacific island women (a minority in the labour trade, but a significant element) found themselves sexually exploited by European masters and male labourers.

Before recruiting ended in the early twentieth century, about 100,000 Melanesians, mostly from the New Hebrides and Solomons, left home to work for the whites. The coastal regions of the mainland of New Guinea, relatively unknown and of bad reputation before the First World War, supplied and received no more than a few thousand labourers until after 1920, but enough to ensure the transfer of infections. Thereafter, scores of thousands

of indentured labourers drawn from the communities of the mainland worked in the plantations, bringing face to face peoples who
had had no epidemiological contact before.[15]

The demographic effects of the trade on indigenous societies
was often devastating, especially in the early years. Some of the
labourers, nearly all of them young adults, were seduced by the
attractions of the wider world and remained abroad, withholding
themselves and their potential offspring from their homelands. Of
greater influence were the depopulating effects of diseases of the
outside world, first upon the workers while under contract, and
then upon their families and clansfolk if and when they returned
home. We have few precise statistics on the latter tragedy, but we
can gain some notion of its possibilities from the mortality rates of
labourers during their indenture.

The death rates of the Pacific islanders who went to Queensland and Fiji (that is to say, the great majority of the recruits)
were high, especially in the early years: for instance, 82 per
thousand annually in the decade beginning in 1879.[16] To cite an
even more extreme example, 21.5 per cent of the labourers who
left the Bismarck Archipelago and the German Solomons for the
German plantations in Samoa between 1887 and 1912 – 5,285 in
total – died while under contract.[17] The ships' captains, recruiters
and plantation managers often treated the labourers poorly, but
there were other factors, too. Travel from a malaria-free or only
periodically malarial region to a malaria-drenched environment
guaranteed high mortality.

What was the effect of all this on the indigenes who stayed at
home in the lowlands of Papua New Guinea? Generalizations are
impossible, beyond saying that the morbidity and mortality rates
must have been high. In 1922, a collection of articles, admittedly
impressionistic, but all by outsiders of long experience in Papua
New Guinea and environs, was published, called *Essays on the
Depopulation of Melanesia.*[18]

Let us begin with the diseases most abrupt in individual onset
and purely epidemic in schedule – that is, those that came and
departed most swiftly and unambiguously – and then make our
way on to the more stately infections. The swiftly communicable
breath-borne diseases called crowd or childhood diseases on the
continents – smallpox, measles, chicken-pox, mumps, whooping
cough – had great impact, but only periodically and briefly. The

island populations did not provide enough fuel to sustain these micro-organic wildfires.

Smallpox may have appeared in Papua New Guinea in the mid-nineteenth century, as we saw in Mikloucho-Maclay's account above. In June 1893 it arrived (again?) in German New Guinea in the person of a Malay stoker on the steamer *Lübeck*. The malady spread along the coast to other German settlements and native villages, attacking the indigenes 'with great severity'. It lasted from June until April or so the following year and 'claimed many victims'.[19] Smallpox did not reach British New Guinea in 1893–4, and never figured significantly again in the western half of New Guinea, though there were epidemics in the Netherlands' half of the mainland.[20]

Influenza exploded again and again, particularly in the world-wide pandemic years, such as the early 1890s and 1920s, becoming with pneumonia a major cause of mortality.[21] In 1931, a foreign ship brought influenza to Lae on Papua's coast, and 'without exception the whole population came down with it'. At the close of the epidemic one-third of the children of Lae had neither father nor mother.[22] In 1932, an influenza epidemic killed up to 10 per cent of those it afflicted in the hills of Papua.[23] Pneumonia, which trailed after influenza and often dealt the *coup de grâce*, also spread in epidemics of its own, in contrast to its usual behaviour on the continents.[24]

Most important of the swift epidemic infections in its repeated assaults on the peoples of Papua New Guinea and elsewhere in the South Pacific was water- and food-borne dysentery, encouraged by filthy conditions on board ship, in the plantations and, later, in the gold fields.[25] It struck again and again, retreating only in the dry season (where there were dry seasons) and where and when officials enforced sanitation and dug deep wells – and, probably, where and when islanders built up resistance the hard way.[26]

As usual, statistics are better for indentured labourers than for local natives: in fact, they are the only statistics we have. Between 1909–10 and 1912–13 dysentery accounted for 40 to 75 per cent of all labourers' deaths in Papua.[27] The 1909–10 annual report of German New Guinea proclaimed the disease, by then endemic 'everywhere' and virulently epidemic every rainy season, as 'the real scourge of the country, claiming many victims among the natives'.[28]

Of the maladies we usually think of as spreading at a slower rate than the above, the most important demographically were malaria, tuberculosis and venereal disease. Malaria, where it was endemic, killed chiefly the new-born and newly arrived adults; where it or one of its strains was newly present, it killed at every age level.[29] Tuberculosis came ashore, probably for the first time, and killed many outright, but was probably more important as an underlying cause of death. A study published in 1924 tells of a 30 per cent positive rate for those given the tuberculin test at Rabaul, New Britain.[30]

Gonorrhoea killed fewer among the lowlanders than any of the other imported diseases cited above, but in all likelihood it was a more important cause of population decline, because it prevented recovery of the losses caused by other diseases and by emigration. It seldom killed adults, but often sterilized them, and snuffed out future mothers and fathers as foetuses, babies and toddlers. Syphilis was very rare among the peoples of Papua New Guinea because of the prevalence of a closely related disease, yaws. Infection with yaws produces immunity to its venereal cousin.[31] Gonorrhoea, however, was widespread.[32]

There is no doubt that lowland population declined, in some places radically,[33] but we know too little to do more than sketch a general picture. At present our best guide is R.F.R. Scragg, who made an analysis of the documentation on the decrease of the people in New Ireland, which may be the demographic bellwether of lowland Papua New Guinea, and has studied the demographic history of lowlanders of the mainland in so far as the statistics are available in mission records. He has verified the emigration of indentured labourers as a significant cause of depopulation of New Ireland, acknowledged the losses to dysentery and the various respiratory diseases, but has concluded that it was malaria, a killer long present but in new distribution geographically, and gonorrhoea, a sterilizer newly debarked, that dictated demography.[34]

Scragg judges that by 1920 epidemics of whatever identity had ceased to be the decisive factor in the demographic history and composition of the people of New Ireland, but that gonorrhoea was still preventing a restoration of population.[35] That judgement provides a basis for speculation about the lowlands of Papua New Guinea as a whole. If we assume that the rest of the Papua New Guinean lowlanders, who had not been subjected to continual contact with the outside world as early or as fully as the New Irelanders, were lagging twenty or so years behind the latter in demographic results of that contact, as Scragg's study of the populations of Yule Island and Mekeo on the south coast of the mainland seem to suggest, and if we venture a guess that venereal disease, for the same reason, was not so widespread among them, then we can theorize that the lowlanders were poised for demographic recovery by 1940.[36]

The Second World War delayed that recovery. At the end of the war Papua New Guineans were probably fewer and less healthy than for centuries[37] – but recovery did follow.[38] Its schedule is confused. As the lowlanders began to recover, the highlanders, perhaps as much as 40 per cent of the total Papua New Guinean population,[39] may still have been in a period of demographic decline.

In the 1930s, Australian explorers and gold-seekers penetrated New Guinea's high country. They found not the empty land that conventional wisdom predicted, but the mainland's heaviest densities of population.[40] The demographic and epidemiological history of Papua New Guinea is not a unit. It happened in two sequences of events, one for the lowlands, which we have sketched, and another for the highlands. The two were barely connected until the 1930s.

The highlanders were the largest population in the world not yet exposed to the majority of humanity's most important infections. None had been exposed to the foreigners' smallpox, measles or influenza, and few to even the lowlanders' malaria. The high country had the anopheles mosquitoes to spread the disease, but no or very few sources of malarial plasmodia, that is to say, no or few humans with active cases of the fever.[41] If epidemics of such breath-borne infections as smallpox had swept the highlands before the middle of the nineteenth century, then they sputtered out after using up all the susceptibles.

Increased contact with the coasts opened the high country to the endemic diseases common in the lowlands. Dysentery, never absent for long, was rife in the gold-fields between the wars, and worse during the Second World War.[42] Yaws, a nuisance infection, spread up from the lowlands, as did the deadly malaria.[43] Post-war intermingling of lowlanders and highlanders, especially when the latter migrated to work on coastal plantations and then returned home, accelerated the spread of infections, including tuberculosis and venereal diseases, to mountain and plateau peoples.[44]

There have been a number of severe, fast-moving, usually localized epidemics of respiratory diseases in and around the highlands. Influenza sickened and killed considerable numbers in the 1940s.[45] Measles and influenza roved the Papuan plateau in tandem in 1948–49. In 1950 there was a twin epidemic of measles and mumps in Fasu country, which soon spread among the Etoro and Onabasulu. Influenza struck the Foi sometime in the 1950s.[46] The 1969 Hong Kong influenza hopped and skipped across the mainland's interior, hardly troubling some communities and killing up to 10 per cent of others.[47] Anthropologist Raymond C. Kelly was with the Etoro of the Mount Sisa area when this epidemic hit them, accounting for 71 per cent of all deaths in a fifteen-month period. That epidemic killed 5.7 per cent of all Etoro, most of these in one week.[48]

Impressionistic reports have it that the peoples of the Chimbu and Bismarck regions suffered population losses between 1930 and 1945. Nancy Bowers, a careful researcher, has discerned clear evidence of population loss among the inhabitants of the Upper Kaugel and Upper Mendi valleys west of Mount Hagen – that is, disproportionately low numbers among the cohorts born 1930–1945.[49] Raymond C. Kelly estimates that the Etoro declined by half between the mid-1930s and mid-1970s. According to his interpretation of a 1968 population pyramid of the Etoro, the twin epidemics of measles and influenza in 1948–49 alone reduced the population by 15 per cent.[50]

Carol Jenkins, Mary Dimitrakakis, Ian Cook, Ray Sanders and Neville Stallman have supplied us with the clearest picture of what happens to an isolated community upon contact with the greater world, in this case the Hagahai who live in the valley of the Yuat River at the western corner of the Schrader Range, Madang Province, at altitudes ranging from 350 to 2,400 m. The study was conducted from 1984 to 1989 while the Hagahai were experiencing their first sustained contact with outsiders. It is based on firsthand testimony and reinforced with seroepidemiological testing.

There were a few instances of contact with outsiders before 1984, but firm contact did not begin until that year, when missionaries, at Hagahai invitation, established themselves in the indigenes' country. The latter's motive in inviting missionary medical personnel to come and live with them may have been the series of epidemics that they had undergone in the previous few decades, epidemics in which the victims, according to elder informants, coughed blood, produced blood with their stools, and suffered red skin rashes. Serological evidence indicates that at least one of these epidemics, a particularly bad one, was of one of the South Pacific's most effective killers, measles.

More epidemics came with more contact. In the period 1985–86 the Hagahai had to endure, in addition to malaria, filariasis and other endemic infections, epidemics of influenza, parainfluenza, mumps, hepatitis, respiratory syncytial virus and adenoviral infections, and possibly more. In 1986–87 their gross mortality rate was 53 per thousand per year. Over half of all infants were dying.[51]

The recent history of the Hagahai, the Etoro, and other inland communities of Papua New Guinea indicates that their experience has been similar to that of other Pacific peoples, Eskimoes and Amerindians upon contact with people from Eurasia and Africa. The chief difference between the highlanders' experience and that of the others is that the former do not seem to have suffered as extreme a population decline and certainly did not do so for so long as the others.[52] Why not?

The answer pertains to location and timing. Highlanders were never in danger of being displaced by Europeans. Europeans have never been attracted in large numbers to New Guinea. Hubert Murray, the Australian who was lieutenant-governor of Papua from 1908 to 1940, started out with the typical European's attitudes towards the heat and mosquitoes: 'There is no doubt that this is an abominable country, and there are times when I feel inclined to curse the luck that brought me here.'[53]

In 1910 there were only 700 Europeans in all of British New Guinea. In 1914 there were only 1,130 Europeans, 1,377 Chinese, and two hundred or so other foreigners in all of German New Guinea.[54] By 1930, when whites penetrated the highlands, the part of Papua New Guinea most comfortable and healthy for them, the great age of Europe's emigration was coming to a close. (More about timing in a moment.)

Topography slowed foreign invasion and the spread of infection: the swamps and the mountains made every colonialist advance difficult. The profusion of tribes and languages made efficient conquest impossible. Papua New Guinea had no centres – not one and not one hundred – no emperors and no capitals whose subjugation rendered large fractions of the population open to contact and exploitation, often prerequisites for epidemics. That is to say, linguistic and general cultural differences and age-old distrust played the role that rods of graphite play in atomic piles. They prevented explosions.[55]

The highlanders' contact with the outside world was delayed until the worst dangers had passed. For example, the worst of the nineteenth century's cholera epidemics swept round the world and dissipated before the Germans, British or Australians established permanent settlements in Papua New Guinea, and long before they trekked up through the mountains and into the interior valleys. Full contact between outsiders and Papua New Guineans held off until the whites were beginning to realize that they had a moral responsibility and an economic motive to protect their colonial subjects from decimation. And by this time the whites were, of all the people on earth, the most advanced in medical science and its application to public health problems. Hence regulation of travel to and from the highlands to limit the spread of disease; hence widespread utilization of quarantine, the building of clinics and hospitals, the digging of deep wells; hence the instruction of indigenes in sanitary practices and modern medicine.[56] The deadly epidemic of dysentery during the Second World War would have been far deadlier but for the thousands of sulphaguanadine tablets flown in and distributed by Allied forces.[57]

It may be that nothing was more important than vaccination in the recent history of Papua New Guinea. Vaccination, not a universal but a common practice in Europe and its overseas extensions in the nineteenth and twentieth centuries, reduced the chance of the transportation of smallpox to, and the spread of the disease in, Papua New Guinea. First the Germans and then the British and Australians vaccinated thousands of indigenes against the disease.[58] That disease appeared and spread in Dutch New Guinea in the twentieth century but never on the coasts of the eastern half after 1894, and *never* in its highlands. That fact alone makes the history of the mainland's highlands profoundly different from that of most of Europe's overseas colonies; very different, for instance, from the history of the Mexican and Peruvian highlands. Inoculation against tuberculosis followed upon vaccination against smallpox after the Second World War.[59]

The greatest killer of highlanders of the other breath-borne diseases has probably been influenza. What would have been the mortality if the 1918 influenza – a uniquely deadly strain, which killed millions in the most medically advanced societies, over 10 per cent of all Tahitians and at least 20 per cent of the people of Western Samoa[60] – had reached the high country? Australians saved themselves from the pandemic in 1918 by imposing a maritime quarantine on their ports. Papua New Guineans, whose connections with the world ran through those ports, benefited equally. The virus of 1918 did not reach Papua until 1921, by which time it had lost much of its virulence. Even so, it killed over half of all indentured labourers who died that year, and more of them than any influenza had ever killed before or has since.[61]

Contact between the eastern and western hemispheres since the late fifteenth century brought large numbers of invaders, brutal exploitation, and wave after wave of new diseases to the Amerindians, and population crash. There were positive benefits from the contact, too – for instance, the introduction of wheat and rice, and of domesticated animals like horses and cattle, but the demographic benefits of these for the indigenes were much slower in effect than the negative factors.[62]

The ingredients of European expansion into the lands of the Papua New Guineans were much the same: invasion, exploitation, new diseases, new foods (new domesticated animals, too, but with relatively little influence). But the demographic results for the indigenes differed because the proportions of the ingredients and the sequence of their arrival differed markedly.

First came a benign import, the sweet potato from America, probably via the Philippines and Indonesia centuries before the first European attempts at colonization in Papua New Guinea. The plant was more productive in the high country than taro or the other traditional crops, and proved to be especially well suited to what is New Guinea's healthiest region for humans, the stratum between malaria and frost, 1,700–2,200 metres. If James B. Watson's interpretation is correct, acquisition of this new crop set off a population explosion in the highlands.[63]

Then, long after, the Europeans arrived to stay, exploited lowland peoples, tempted them off to adventures elsewhere, moved them from the disease environments of their births to others often teeming with unfamiliar infections, and subjected them wherever they were to new and often fatal illnesses. But the outsiders, Europeans and indentured servants from elsewhere, did not come in large numbers and did not penetrate the highlands for many years. Lowland New Guineans suffered a population decline of considerable magnitude from no later than the middle decades of the nineteenth century to the middle of the twentieth. Starting in the 1930s, highlanders suffered diseases spawned abroad, and endemic lowland infections seeped into the high country. We know only fragments of the demographic history of the highlanders, but these suggest that in total they underwent a demographic decline. The picture is complicated spatially and temporally in that the epidemics were of the 'hop-and-skip' kind, rather, for instance, than the imporous and unremitting kind that devastated the dense and integrated populations of the highlands of sixteenth-century Mexico.

Whatever may have been the angle of the decline of the high-landers, we can be sure that the duration of that decline was much briefer than in the Americas, Australia, New Zealand or Hawai'i. Of all the isolated peoples snatched into the great world in the past half-millennium, Papua New Guinean highlanders have in all likelihood weathered the trauma the best.


## Notes

1. I want to thank John McNeill of Georgetown University, USA, and Carol Jenkins and Michael P. Alpers of the Papua New Guinea Institute of Medical Research for trying to minimize the number of errors of fact and interpretation in this paper.

2. Henry F. Dobyns, 'Disease Transfer at Contact', *Annual Review of Anthropology*, vol. 22 (1993), pp. 273–91; Jean-Louis Rallu, *Les Populations Océaniennes aux XIXe et XXe Siècles*, Institut National d'Études Démographiques, Presses Universitaires de France, Paris 1990.

3. N.D. Oram, 'Population', in *Encyclopedia of Papua and New Guinea*, vol. 2 (1972), p. 951; Glenn Dennet and John Connell, 'Acculturation and Health in the Highlands of Papua New Guinea', *Current Anthropology*, vol. 29 (1988), pp. 273–99.

4. Bryant Allen, 'The Geography of Papua New Guinea', in Robert D. Attenborough and Michael P. Alpers (eds.), *Human Biology in Papua New Guinea: The Small Cosmos*, Oxford University Press, Oxford, 1992, pp. 38, 43, 44; Jacqueline A. Cattani, 'The Epidemiology of Malaria in Papua

New Guinea', in Attenborough and Alpers (eds.), *Human Biology in Papua New Guinea*, p. 304.

5. Ian Lilley, 'Papua New Guinea's Human Past: The Evidence of Archaeology', in Attenborough and Alpers (eds.), *Human Biology in Papua New Guinea*, p. 159.

6. Jared M. Diamond, 'The Last First Contact', *Natural History*, 1988, p. 28.

7. Bob Connolly and Robin Anderson, *First Contact: New Guinea's Highlanders Encounter the Outside World*, Viking Penguin, New York, 1987, pp. 50–52, 120–6, *passim*; Michael J. Leahy, *Explorations into Highland New Guinea*, University of Alabama Press, Tuscaloosa, 1991, pp. 98–9, 128, 194.

8. Bryant Allen, 'Human Geography of Papua New Guinea', *Journal of Human Evolution*, vol. 12 (1983), p. 19; Bryant Allen, 'Infection, Innovation, and Residence: Illness and Misfortune in the Torricelli Foothills from 1800', in Stephen Frankel and Gilbert Lewis (eds.), *A Continuing Trial of Treatment: Medical Pluralism in Papua New Guinea*, Academic Publishers, Dordrecht, 1989, p. 37.

9. Sean Dorney, *Papua New Guinea: People, Politics, and History since 1975*, Random House, Milsons Point, 1990, p. 31.

10. Raymond C. Kelly, *Etoro Social Structure: A Study in Structural Contradiction*, University of Michigan Press, Ann Arbor, 1974, pp. 25, 27.

11. Bruce M. Knauft, *Good Company and Violence: Sorcery and Social Action in a Lowland New Guinea Society*, University of California Press, Berkeley, 1985, p. 12.

12. Donald C. Gordon, *The Australian Frontier in New Guinea, 1870–1885*, Columbia University Press, New York, 1951, p. 65; Gavin Souter, *New Guinea: The Last Unknown*, Angus & Robertson, Sydney, 1963, pp. 30–43; J.L. Whittaker, 'New Guinea: The Ethnohistory of First Culture Contacts', in *The History of Melanesia*, Research School of Pacific Studies, Australian National University, and the University of Papua and New Guinea, 1969, p. 630; Nikolai Nikolaevich Mikloucho-Maclay, *New Guinea Diaries, 1871–1883*, Kristen Press, Madang, 1975.

13. Mikloucho-Maclay, *New Guinea Diaries*, p. 91.

14. Andrew D. Cliff and Peter Haggett, *The Spread of Measles in Fiji and the Pacific*, The Australian National University, Canberra, 1985, pp. 22–30, 35; Nigel Oram, 'Environment, Migration and Site Selection in the Port Moresby Coastal Area', in John H. Winslow (ed.), *The Melanesian Environment*, Australian National University Press, Canberra, 1977, p. 92; I. Maddocks, 'Communicable Disease in Papua and New Guinea', *Papua and New Guinea Medical Journal*, vol. 13 (1970), pp. 120–21.

15. Allen, 'The Geography of Papua New Guinea', p. 53.

16. Ralph Shlomowitz, 'Epidemiology and the Pacific Labor Trade', *Journal of Interdisciplinary History*, vol. 19 (1989), p. 597.

17. Stewart Firth, *New Guinea under the Germans*, Melbourne University Press, Melbourne, 1982, p. 179.

18. W.H.R. Rivers (ed.), *Essays on the Depopulation of Melanesia*, Cambridge University Press, Cambridge, 1922.

19. *German New Guinea, The Annual Reports*, ed. and trans. Peter Sack and Dymphna Clark, Australian National University Press, Canberra, 1979, p. 81; British Sessional Papers, House of Commons, 1896, *Colonial Reports – Annual. no. 168 British New Guinea. Annual Report for 1894–5*, pp. 36–7.

20. British Sessional Papers, House of Commons, 1896, *Colonial Reports – Annual. no. 168*; Frank Fenner, 'Viral Infections', in Peter Ryan (ed.), *Encyclopedia of Papua and New Guinea*, Melbourne University Press in Association with the University of Papua and New Guinea, Melbourne, 1972, vol. 2, p. 1174.

21. Ralph Shlomowitz, 'Mortality and Indentured Labour in Papua (1885–1941) and New Guinea (1920–1941)', *Journal of Pacific History*, vol. 23 (1988), p. 72; Shlomowitz, 'Epidemiology and the Pacific Labor Trade', p. 602.

22. Ian Willis, *Lae: Village and City*, Melbourne University Press, 1974, p. 112.

23. R.F.R. Scragg, 'Historical Epidemiology in Papua New Guinea', *Papua New Guinea Medical Journal*, vol. 20 (1977), p. 744.

24. Maddocks, 'Communicable Disease in Papua and New Guinea', p. 122; R. Fleming Jones, 'Tropical Diseases in British New Guinea', *Transactions of the Royal Society for Tropical Medical Hygiene*, vol. 5 (1910–11), p. 102; Allen, 'Infection, Innovation, and Residence', pp. 45–6.

25. Allen, 'Infection, Innovation, and Residence', pp. 43–4.

26. Jones, 'Tropical Diseases in British New Guinea', pp. 98–9; Rivers (ed.), *Essays*, p. 63; Shlomowitz, 'Mortality and Indentured Labour', pp. 72, 76.

27. Shlomowitz, 'Epidemiology and the Pacific Labor Trade', p. 601; B. Jinks, P. Biskup and H. Nelson (eds.), *Readings in New Guinea History 1973*, Angus & Robertson, Sydney, p. 199.

28. *German New Guinea, The Annual Reports*, pp. 43, 52, 66, 162, 213, 281, 297, 310.

29. R.F.R. Scragg, *Depopulation in New Ireland: A Study of Demography and Fertility*, Minister for Territories, Papua and New Guinea, Port Moresby, 1957, p. 125.

30. Parliament of the Commonwealth of Australia, *Report to the League of Nations on the Administration of the Territory of New Guinea from 1st July, 1921, to 30th June, 1922*, p. 37; Maddocks, 'Communicable Disease in Papua and New Guinea', p. 122.

31. Donald Denoon, *Public Health in Papua New Guinea: Medical Possibility and Social Constraint, 1884–1984*, Cambridge University Press, Cambridge, 1989, p. 12.

32. Ian. D. Riley, 'Population Change and Distribution in Papua New Guinea: An Epidemiological Approach', *Journal of Human Evolution*, vol. 12 (1983), p. 129.

33. Heather Radi, 'New Guinea under Mandate, 1921–4', in W.J. Hudson (ed.), *Australia and Papua New Guinea*, Sydney University Press, Sydney, 1971, pp. 92–3.

34. Scragg, *Depopulation in New Ireland*, p. 125.

35. Ibid., p. 117.

36. Scragg, 'Historical Epidemiology in Papua New Guinea', pp. 104, 108.

37. Souter, *New Guinea*, p. 238; Denoon, *Public Health in Papua New Guinea*, p. 63.

38. Allen, 'The Geography of Papua New Guinea', p. 55; Riley, 'Population Change and Distribution in Papua New Guinea', p. 126.

39. Riley, 'Population Change and Distribution in Papua New Guinea', p. 125.

40. Ben R. Finney, *Big-Men and Business: Entrepreneurship and Economic Growth in the New Guinea Highlands*, University Press of Hawai'i, Honolulu, 1973, pp. 20–21.

41. J. Radford, H. van Leeuwen and S. H. Christian, 'Social Aspects in the Changing Epidemiology of Malaria in the Highlands of New Guinea', *Annals of Tropical Medicine and Parasitology*, vol. 70 (1976), p. 22.

42. Edward L. Schieffelin and Robert Crittenden, *Like People You See in a Dream: First Contact in Six Papuan Societies*, Standford University Press, Stanford, 1991, p. 270; J.T. Gunther, 'From Stone Age to Parliamentary Government in a Decade', in Colin Simpson, *Plumes and Arrows: Inside New Guinea*, Angus & Robertson, Sydney, 1971, p. 405; Allen, 'Infection, Innovation, and Residence', p. 44.

43. Robert H. Black, 'The Epidemiology of Malaria in the Southwest Pacific: Changes Associated with Increasing European Contact', *Oceania*, vol. 27 (1956), p. 138; Schieffelin and Robert Crittenden, *Like People You See in a Dream*, pp. 135, 187, 262, 264, 270, 275; Shlomowitz, 'Mortality and Indentured Labour', p. 76; Maddocks, 'Communicable Disease in Papua and New Guinea', p. 122; Robin Radford, *Highlanders and Foreigners in the Upper Ramu*, Melbourne University Press, Melbourne, 1987, pp. 14, 144, 147, 168; R.F.R. Scragg, 'Medical Demography', in Peter Ryan (ed.), *The Encyclopedia of Papua and New Guinea*, Melbourne University Press in association with the University of Papua and New Guinea, 1972, vol. 2, p. 744; Leahy, *Explorations into Highland New Guinea*, pp. 77–8; Denoon, *Public Health in Papua New Guinea*, p. 31.

44. Cattani, 'The Epidemiology of Malaria in Papua New Guinea', p. 304; A.P. Vines, 'Disease Prevalence (Morbidity)', in *The Encyclopedia of Papua and New Guinea*, ed. Peter Ryan, Melbourne University Press in Association with the University of Papua and New Guinea, vol. I, p. 261; Ian D. Riley and Deborah Lehmann, 'The Demography of Papua New

Guinea: Migration, Fertility, and Mortality Patterns', in Attenborough and Alpers (eds.), *Human Biology in Papua New Guinea*, p. 76.

45. Dennett and Connell, 'Acculturation and Health in the Highlands of Papua New Guinea', p. 279.

46. Charles M. Langlas and James F. Weiner, 'Big-Men, Population Growth, and Longhouse Fission among the Foi, 1965–79', in James F. Weiner (ed.), *Mountain Papuans*, University of Michigan Press, Ann Arbor, 1988, p. 98.

47. R.M. Garruto and D.C. Gajdusek, 'Unusual Progression and Shifting Clinical Severity, Morbidity, and Mortality', *American Journal of Physical Anthropology*, vol. 42 (1975), pp. 302–3.

48. Kelly, *Etoro Social Structure*, p. 30.

49. Nancy Bowers, 'Demographic Problems in Montane New Guinea' in Steven Polgar (ed.), *Culture and Population*, Schenkman Publishing, Cambridge, 1971, pp. 13–22.

50. Kelly, *Etoro Social Structure*, pp. 28–31, 172.

51. Carol Jenkins, Mary Dimitrakakis, Ian Cook, Ray Sanders, and Neville Stallman, 'Culture Change and Epidemiological Patterns Among the Hagahai, Papua New Guinea', *Human Ecology*, vol. 17 (1989).

52. Finney, *Big-Men and Business*, p. 38.

53. Hubert Murray, *Selected Letters of Hubert Murray*, ed. Francis West, Oxford University Press, Melbourne, 1970, p. 48.

54. Jones, 'Tropical Diseases in British New Guinea', p. 94; Firth, *New Guinea under the Germans*, p. 166.

55. Norma McArthur, 'The Demographic Situation', in *New Guinea on the Threshold*, University of Pittsburgh Press, Pittsburgh, 1968, p. 112.

56. J.T. Gunther, 'Medical Services, History', in *Encyclopedia of Papua and New Guinea*, p. 754; Rowley; Connolly and Anderson, *First Contact*, pp. 85–6, 170, 216–17.

57. Gunther, 'From Stone Age to Parliamentary Government', p. 405; Finney, *Big-Men and Business*, p. 28.

58. British Sessional Papers, House of Commons, 1896, *Colonial Reports – Annual. no. 168*, p. 37; *German New Guinea, The Annual Reports*, pp. 81, 122, 268, 296; Fenner, 'Viral Infections', p. 1174; Gunther, 'Medical Services, History', p. 754.

59. Radford, *Highlanders and Foreigners*, p. 103.

60. Alfred W. Crosby, *America's Forgotten Pandemic: The Influenza of 1918*, Cambridge University Press, Cambridge, 1988, p. 234.

61. Shlomowitz, 'Mortality and Indentured Labour', p. 72; Shlomowitz, 'Epidemiology and the Pacific Labor Trade', p. 602.

62. Alfred W. Crosby, *Ecological Imperialism: The Biological Expansion of Europe, 90–1900*, Cambridge University Press, Cambridge, 1986, pp. 171–216.

63. James B. Watson, 'The Significance of a Recent Ecological Change in the Central Highlands of New Guinea', *JPS*, vol. 74 (1965); Paula

Brown, *Highland Peoples of New Guinea*, Cambridge University Press, Cambridge, 1978, pp. 100, 102, 104; V. Watson, 'Papua New Guinea Highlands Prehistory: A Social Anthropologist's View', in D.K. Feil (ed.), *The Evolution of Highland Papua New Guinea Societies*, Cambridge University Press, Cambridge, 1987, pp. 27, 29; Bowers, 'Demographic Problems in Montane New Guinea', pp. 22–5.

# PART III

# Traditional and European Concepts of 'Justice' and their Influence on One Another

## HERMANN J. HIERY

'What is truth?' Pontius Pilate asked Jesus of Nazareth and thereby set the historical example of the judge who is cynical about his ethical task of differentiating between good and bad, right and wrong, preferring instead to assess whether or not a set of rules and regulations had been adhered to. But how important is establishing *real* justice, meaning some form of fairness, or at least the attempt to achieve this sort of justice, for a government, and in particular a colonial one? It might be argued that any colonial government is *per se* unjust. So were the British and German decisions to introduce their respective legal systems simply the result of a more general desire to impose their own structures wherever their will was command, regardless of traditional concepts and views?

As we can see from the contributions to this section, historians have, as always, to differentiate. Sione Lātūkefu in Chapter 11 demonstrates that the introduction of the British concept of justice in Tonga can be considered a successful implementation of the rule of law even by a non-European population. Before the British arrived with their version of Christianity and legal procedures, Tonga possessed only an extreme form of class justice. The will of the *Tu'i Tonga* was law even if it demanded cruelties like the wanton killing of children. His arbitrary decisions could not be questioned by the people who lived, says Lātūkefu, in constant fear of punishment for violating the chiefly taboos. The 'bulk of the population ... had no rights socially, politically, economically or religiously.... The commoners were believed to exist for the sole purpose of serving their chiefs ... to have no souls, and upon death were destined to become vermin.' Rulers were not accountable in any way and any idea of social justice or liberty was non-existent before European contact.

Contact with Europeans necessarily implied contact with European ideas. But, as Lātūkefu claims, it was an indigenous decision to adopt their view of the world and put it into Tongan practice. Tongan society being as strict as we have shown, such a change could only come from above. Two factors were decisive: the Christian teaching of equality in the sight of God and a political strategy by the Tongan king who sought to limit the powers of his rival chiefs by giving rights to commoners. From its beginnings in 1838 the new principles of liberty, equality and justice were systematically expanded until a Tongan constitution, promulgated in 1875, officially instituted a *Declaration of Rights* with all the freedoms known from European examples. Today there is a growing demand among Tongans to rid themselves of the remaining traditional bonds and structures.

Does this mean that the British rule of law and the concept of equality (which is certainly *a* if not *the* foundation of modern European law) did indeed bring about more justice? If we accept Lātūkefu's argument, the answer has to be in the affirmative. It could be put even more strongly: there was no justice before the arrival of the British. But was it intended? Or was it only a side-effect that grew out of all proportion when the Tongan king opened a new box of European strategies that could be used as weapons against his chiefly rivals?

Whatever may have been the case in Tonga, Peter Sack states categorically that justice 'has never been and will never be the goal of any form of government'. Sack presents in Chapter 12 a number of colonial court cases which involved the Melanesian population of German New Guinea. What they reveal, incidentally, is that Tok Pisin had been accepted in the court proceedings of German New Guinea as early as 1890. They also demonstrate the readiness of the Melanesian side to manipulate the other,[1] including an attempt to offer compensation to the government, but in fake shell money. For most German colonies the records of legal proceedings involving indigenous disputes have been all but lost, but hundreds of these files have survived in German New Guinea. They illustrate vividly the day-to-day problems that occurred in the colonial setting, and it is therefore surprising that in the past historians have chosen to disregard them. While Sack is therefore right in claiming that they 'represent the meat of German colonial rule in Melanesia', his more general conclusions, including the assertion that no one was really concerned with justice, will evoke opposition.

Sack, a specialist in colonial law, presents his arguments well. But for a historian different interpretations emerge. The final judicial example dating from March 1910 quoted by Sack offers a case in point. Here an indigenous man claimed compensation from the mission for shooting one of his pigs. The fact that eventually he was given his rights proves to Sack that the rule of law had finally arrived in German New Guinea after a long period which he sees as having been 'essentially abnormal'. But while the Melanesian man To Urakaga probably was in the right, *de jure* he would have achieved nothing. He would even have been punished. A legal technicality meant that he would get no compensation and was liable to pay the court costs as well because the European defendant was a missionary bound by his vow of poverty and thus without money to pay. The decision by the *Bezirksamtmann* to rebuke the mission and to find a way out of this European legal maze was a political one. It was influenced by his desire for the Melanesian side to experience the German legal system as just and fair, a system that established equity. Only this intervention by the government could achieve anything like 'justice'. This approach was taken because it was justice that mattered, not a mere theoretical rule of law or the implementation of a set of judicial rules and paragraphs that would have been completely beyond the understanding of the indigenous population. The plaintiff eventually got what he had asked for, not in spite of belonging to the native side, but *because* he was a member of the indigenous population. As I show elsewhere in this volume, a legal system, and even more a colonial government without sufficient military force to implement its rules, relies heavily on acceptability. If there is no general acceptance, it breaks apart.

In his chapter about German rule and colonial law in Micronesia (Chapter 14) Gerd Hardach maintains that 'traditional indigenous law co-existed with imported German law.' I agree with him that the colonial administration respected traditional custom and law 'as long as these did not conflict with German concepts of law and order, or with important objectives of colonial policy'. German interference was limited as long as peace was maintained. The colonial government was short of staff and money. Therefore even in those cases where European concepts openly clashed with local traditions, a cautious approach was necessary.

There can be no doubt that neither British nor Germans were prepared to accept traditional behaviour that was in their eyes barbarous, inhumane and un-Christian. Practices such as cannibalism, head-hunting or the strangulation of widows were condemned, not because they were proscribed as crimes in English or German law – indeed they did not even exist under English or German law, a fact that contributed to the difficulty of prosecuting them legally – but because they were found to offend against human rights that were considered universal. There was also a deeply rooted feeling that Europeans not only had a right to eradicate such habits, but were almost obliged to do this in order to distribute justice to those who most obviously suffered from the consequences of these customs.[2]

But the Melanesians of German New Guinea were persuaded rather than forced to abandon such inhumane habits. The colonial government actively renounced its right, if not its duty, automatically to persecute all criminal offences in its territory. A criminal police did not exist in German New Guinea, and only in cases which were explicitly brought to their attention did the authorities start proceedings. Even then the judges did not strictly follow German legal procedures but established a colonial practice that regarded traditional behaviour as a mitigating circumstance. The punishment depended on how much European contact the accused had had in the past.[3] Without being aware of it, the colonial authorities also introduced a new concept: clemency.

The question of which traditions were regarded as acceptable by European standards was much disputed at the time. Abortion was probably the greatest bone of contention with regard to German New Guinea. The anthropologist Richard Neuhauss conducted a private vendetta against the colonial authorities because he was of the opinion that the administration was interfering too rigorously with what was 'simply a very ancient habit'.[4]

For Sack, the European side had no intention of integrating traditional Melanesian ways into their system of justice. If we look at legal books or colonial laws it is indeed hard to find such elements. But the reality of colonial life is simply not sufficiently covered by metropolitan regulations. Very often what was done on the spot was in contempt of, if not in contradiction to, these regulations. In this light, it was not the legal situation in the colony that was 'essentially abnormal'; metropolitan guidelines proved to be inapplicable in the colony because they were drafted with norms in mind that were more often than not at variance with the situation in Melanesia. To put this right, German colonial officials – many of them legally highly qualified – tried to exert the legal leeway still left to the judge in the German judicial system. More research certainly needs to be done in this area. But there are many indications to support the interpretation that the colonial administration of justice had indeed accepted traditional Melanesian patterns. The most important factor was the adoption of the principle of compensation even in criminal proceedings. In metropolitan law compensation claims had to be dealt with separately in civil cases. This sharp distinction was given up as impracticable in Melanesia.[5] The integration of the Melanesian concept of redress into a German legal principle in colonial New Guinea contributed decisively to the Melanesian acceptance of the German administration of justice. In most cases Melanesians indeed felt that they were being treated 'justly'.

Hahl's decision to create Melanesian officials must not be necessarily seen as 'essentially abnormal'. Nor were their judicial powers 'limited' in a Melanesian sense. The bulk of Melanesian disputes and quarrels were settled by them and without German interference. It was an important decision by the colonial authorities because it was tantamount to German approbation of the traditional Melanesian system of settling conflicts by internal arbitration. These officially recognized Melanesian arbiters, it was thought, might gradually develop into a body of judges who would sit in common to hear and judge indigenous cases.[6] The idea was based on Melanesian world-views that placed more importance on society and the group as a whole than on the individual. To be sure, the inauguration of a Melanesian Bench was a long-term aim of the colonial administration, not a temporary exception.

The timid beginnings of this process were halted when the Australian administration took over, as Allan Healy shows in Chapter 13. An aggressive assimilationist approach replaced the

German gradual process. The rule of law the Australians brought with them had no room for indigenous concepts let alone indigenous participation in legal procedures. For Healy this 'represented the very antithesis of the British approach'. He explains it as a specific Australian form of racism that was central to the development of Australian nationalism. In addition, there was also a widespread Australian phobia about alien powers that focused on the neighbouring island in the north. Strategic motives were paramount in the acquisition of New Guinea. But as long as the island could be used as a buffer, Australians did not care much about what actually happened there. While the first British governor of what came to be called Papua had originally followed a course quite similar to Governor Hahl's in the north, from 1914 on Australian attitudes dominated the entire eastern part of New Guinea: 'Papuans had no recognized say in the framing or implementing of the law, at any level.' This policy continued until the 1960s. It was even supported by the few Australian academics interested in New Guinea, including the (then) Dean of Pacific Studies at the Australian National University.[7]

Australian policies only changed when pressure exerted by the United Nations and the United States in particular became too strong. But as Healy argues, the rush to independence failed to deliver a home-grown system of justice. Instead, much of what is today Papua New Guinean law is in fact a direct copy of Australian legislation. There are many legal absurdities which have since long become defunct in Australia but are still observed in Papua New Guinea. The official age for marriage being set at twenty-one is just one example. A treaty with the newly independent state secured Australian political authority over the islands right on New Guinea's doorstep. Thus something of the buffer status which Papua New Guinea had held in Australian eyes was retained.

Most of Micronesia originally lay outside the Australian sphere of interest. Nauru is the most important exception to this rule and it is only recently that bilateral problems dating back to colonial times have been solved.[8] The German impact on legal structures is demonstrated by Gerd Hardach in Chapter 14; the recent British influence by David Murray in Chapter 15. While in most islands under German influence, traditional patterns of land tenure, and family and inheritance law, prevailed until the end of Germany's colonial era, land rights in Ponape/Pohnpei, with its much-debated

Sokeh revolt, were changed to a system of male primogeniture. I am not sure whether the German intervention in what was, to European eyes, a basically feudal society can be adequately explained by reference to the colonial 'reforms' that were introduced in the metropolis, as Hardach claims, in common with many other historians before him. Be that as it may, the social and economic changes that had been planned for the Marshall Islands as well were postponed because of the violence that had erupted in Ponape. A squabble between the monopoly holder Jaluitgesellschaft and the Australian company Burns Philp had convinced the German government to put an end to this last German form of colonial rule by a concession company in 1907.[9]

It is fitting that David Murray ends this section with a closer look at British legal influence on the former British colonies in Micronesia when they became independent and worked out their own constitutions. In Tuvalu (formerly the Ellice Islands) the colonial elites favoured retaining the characteristic features of the Westminster model.[10] The reason for their unanimity in this matter was, according to Murray, 'their concern to safeguard the existing structure and their own positions within it.' Constitutional developments in Kiribati (formerly the Gilbert Islands),[11] however, took a completely different form. Here there was more general indigenous participation in the drafting of the constitution. The discussion showed that a belief in individual rights had struck roots with the Kiribati people. Kiribati solutions could be found on issues as understood and interpreted in the light of Kiribati experience and tradition. While British elements and British influence should not be underrated,[12] Murray argues convincingly that, in contrast to the Tuvalu constitution, the Kiribati constitution is a symbiosis between British and Kiribati conceptions.

## Notes

1. See my *Das Deutsche Reich in der Südsee. Eine Annäherung an die Erfahrungen verschiedener Kulturen*, Göttingen, 1995, Chapter 3.

2. In principle, this view has not changed over the years, though there have been attempts in the more recent past to use 'traditional' (European traditions excluded, of course) as a synonym for 'righteous' and thereby excuse the inexcusable. Cannibalism (or head-hunting, the strangulation of widows, etc.) were not justified outright. Rather, those who used this argument tried to condone these practices by claiming that 'they were not

so bad', or tried to deny their very existence. While this 'enlightened view' is far from questioning the European concept of universal human rights as such (it is on the contrary only a radical offshoot of this belief), the contemporary Asian accusation that the concept of 'human rights' is nothing but an exclusively occidental view of the world is much more fundamental. In this view, the European attempt to make the acceptance of human rights universal is as much a colonial undertaking as European policies had already been in the past.

3. Hiery, *Das Deutsche Reich in der Südsee*, pp. 122–30.

4. R. Neuhauss, *Deutsch-Neuguinea*, vol. 1, Berlin, 1911, pp. 152, 183.

5. A mass of court files provides evidence of this.

6. *Bezirksamtmann* Dr Klug, Mioko, 30 November 1911, about a provisional attempt to start with such an institution; AAC: AA 1963/83 Bun 66.

7. J.W. Davidson, commonly regarded as the 'first Pacific island historian', is indeed a problematic figure. Although he left behind an influential group of scholars who have long dominated Pacific historiography, his political record and influence on Pacific island policies has yet to be properly investigated. There is a poignant note to the close association between Australian academics and politicians in regard to Papua New Guinea. Allan Healy's original Ph.D. thesis was locked away by the library of the Australian National University in a 'poison cupboard' for decades, and denied to other researchers – a practice only too reminiscent of otherwise undemocratic states where something like academic freedom existed on paper only.

8. *Rehabilitation and Development: Co-operation Agreement between the Government of Australia and the Government of the Republic of Nauru*, Australian Government Publishing Service, Canberra, 1994 (concluded at Bridgetown, Barbados; entry into force: 5 May 1994). *Exchange of letters constituting an agreement between the government of Australia and the government of New Zealand relating to Nauru*, Department of Foreign Affairs and Trade, Canberra, 1994. For the conflict, see Christopher Weeramantry, *Nauru. Environmental Damage under International Trusteeship*, Oxford, 1992.

9. The German view is in Wolfgang Treue, *Die Jaluit-Gesellschaft auf den Marshall-Inseln 1887–1914. Ein Beitrag zur Kolonial- und Verwaltungsgeschichte in der Epoche des deutschen Kaiserreichs*, Berlin, 1976, pp. 120–22; the relevant files are in BAP: RKolA nos. 2772–7. The view of the Australian company is in K. Buckley and K. Klugman, *The History of Burns Philp: The Australian Company in the South Pacific*, n.p., 1981, pp. 148–51.

10. Among the three principles that are given prominence in the preamble is also 'the Rule of Law' (the others are Christianity and Tuvaluan customs and tradition); *Pacific Constitutions*, vol. 1, Suva, n.d., p. 389.

11. Here the preamble stresses 'the principles of equality and justice'. *Pacific Constitutions*, vol. 2, Suva, 1983, p. 332.

12. See, for example, section 127: 'The provisions of this Constitution shall be published in a Kiribati language text as well as this English text, but in the event of any inconsistency between the two texts this English text shall prevail.' Ibid., p. 379.

# 11

# The Impact of the British on the Tongan Traditional Concept of Justice and Law

## SIONE LĀTŪKEFU

Tonga is a member of the wider Polynesian cultural and linguistic family situated within the well-known Polynesian triangle in the eastern Pacific – 1,100 miles north-east of New Zealand, 420 miles south-east of Fiji and 500 miles south of Samoa. The total land area is only 260 square miles, made up of 150 small islands, 36 of which are inhabited, the main island, Tongatapu, being only ninety-nine square miles.[1] At present Tonga's total population is about 98,000, and probably more than 60,000 Tongans live overseas, mainly in New Zealand, Australia and the United States of America.[2]

In order to understand and appreciate the significance of the British impact on the Tongan traditional concept of justice and law, a clear discussion of the latter is necessary. Before European contact, which was sparse during the seventeenth and eighteenth centuries and more intensive in the nineteenth century, Tongan society, being non-literate, lacked codified laws and relied entirely on the oral transmission of knowledge of customs and traditions from one generation to the next. Like other Polynesian societies in the Pacific, Tonga had a chiefly system; it was a stratified society in which chiefs ruled and developed customs and traditions over centuries to perpetuate, protect and legitimize their status, powers and privileges through a process now referred to by some scholars as 'traditioning'.[3]

Tonga was undoubtedly the most highly stratified society in the Pacific. At the apex of the social pyramid were the *ha'a tu'i*, royal dynasties. By the eighteenth century there were three of them: Tu'i Tonga; Tu'i Ha'atakalaua; and the Tu'i Kanokupolu. A separate honorific language was used to address them. In the next stratum were the *hou'eiki*, the chiefs, and a separate honorific language was used for them as well. The third level were the *kau mu'a*, the gentry, who were offspring of 'illegitimate' unions between chiefs and *matāpule* (their attendants). The fourth, the *kau matāpule*, were chiefs' attendants; the majority of the people were the *kau tu'a*, commoners, and at the bottom of the social hierarchy were the *kau pōpula*, slaves.[4] Each class had its own internal divisions, and mobility was possible within each one through arranged marriages or distinguished achievements in a variety of fields.[5] It was virtually impossible, however, to cross the lines that divided the main strata of the social pyramid, particularly the one between chiefs and commoners.[6]

Political control was in the hands of the titled chiefs. When one inherited a title one inherited an office which brought with it powers over a particular *tofi'a*, tract of land and the *kāinga* (localized socio-political unit which inhabited it). Both the land and the inhabitants of a particular *tofi'a* belonged to the title holder,[7] whose powers over them were absolute and arbitrary.

The source of these powers derived mainly from two basic and closely related notions of *mana*[8] (supernatural power, sacredness) and *tapu*[9] (customary prohibition or taboo). *Mana* was believed to be an attribute of the gods. The first Tu'i Tonga (ruler of Tonga), 'Aho'eitu, in about the tenth century AD, was claimed to be descended from a god of the sky, Tangaloa 'Eitumatupu'a, and an earthly woman,[10] Va'e Popua, thereby bestowing considerable *mana* on 'Aho'eitu and the Tu'i Tonga dynasty. Early missionaries to Tonga described the manner in which Tongans revered the Tu'i Tonga thus:

> Tuitonga appears, and all prostrate themselves and kiss his feet.... The Tongans refuse him nothing, exceeding his desires. If he wishes to satisfy his anger or some cruel fancy, he sends a messenger to his victim who, far from fleeing, goes to meet death. You will see fathers tie the rope round the necks of their children, whose death is demanded to prolong the life of this divinity.[11]

*Above:* Melanesian craftsmen trading with German ethnologists at the River Sepik. From *E. Freiherr von Spiegel*, Meere, Inseln, Menschen. Vom Seekadetten zum U-Boot-Kommandanten, Berlin 1934.

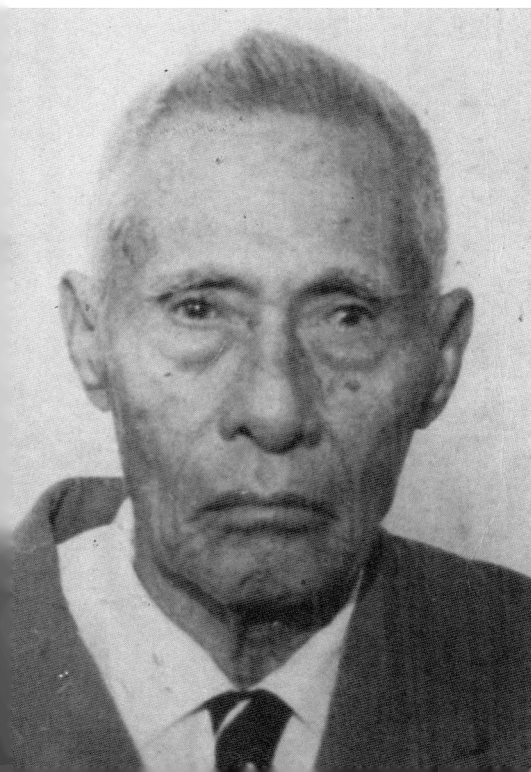

*Left:* I'iga Pisa in his later years. Private collection.

*Above:* The *Fitafita*, the Samo[an] Police, welcomes German Admiral Gühler, ex-*Scharnhorst*. Apia, 1909. Archives of the German Naval Institute, Mürwik.

*Left:* The Samoan traditionalist Lauati with his wife and daughters, on the wa[y] to exile in 1909. Archives of t[he] German Naval Institute, Mürwik.

*Left:* Father Aniseto del Carmon, Arch-Priest of the Spanish Marianas, with Christianized Caroline boys. Photographed in 1876 by the crew of the German ship "Hertha". Archives of the German Naval Institute, Mürwik.

*Below:* Lutheran baptismal procession, Sattelberg, German New Guinea. Lutheran Archives, Neuendettelsau.

The first draught animal in New Guinea, ox *Stern*, in Sattelberg. The indigenous drover is Mitiang. Lutheran Archives, Neuendettelsau.

Performing an operation in the Lutheran mission hospital, Finschhafen. Lutheran Archives, Neuendettelsau.

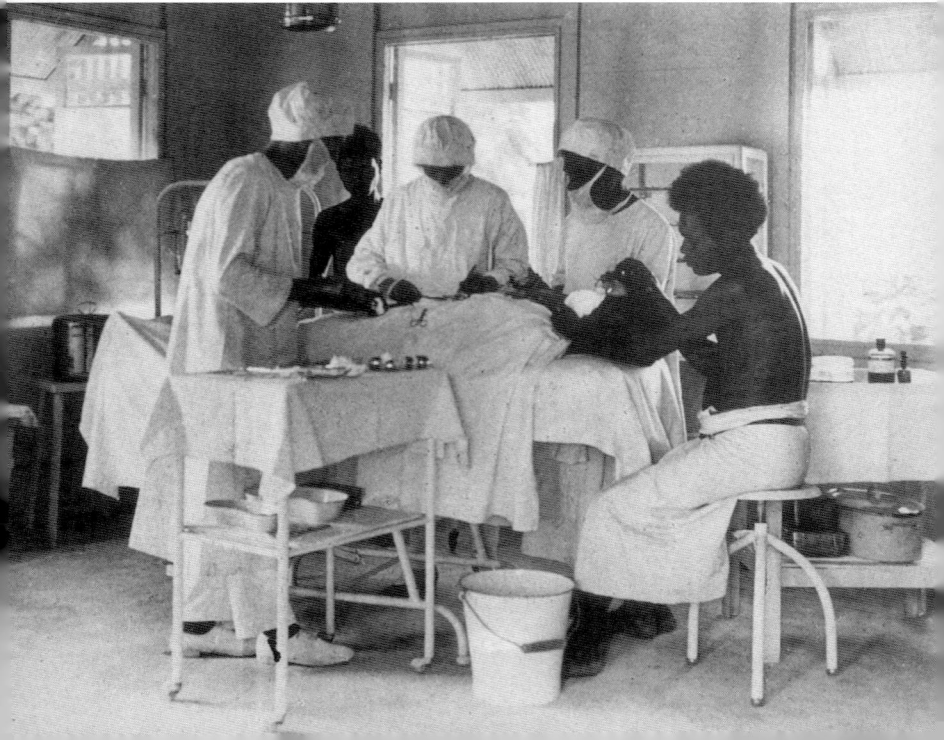

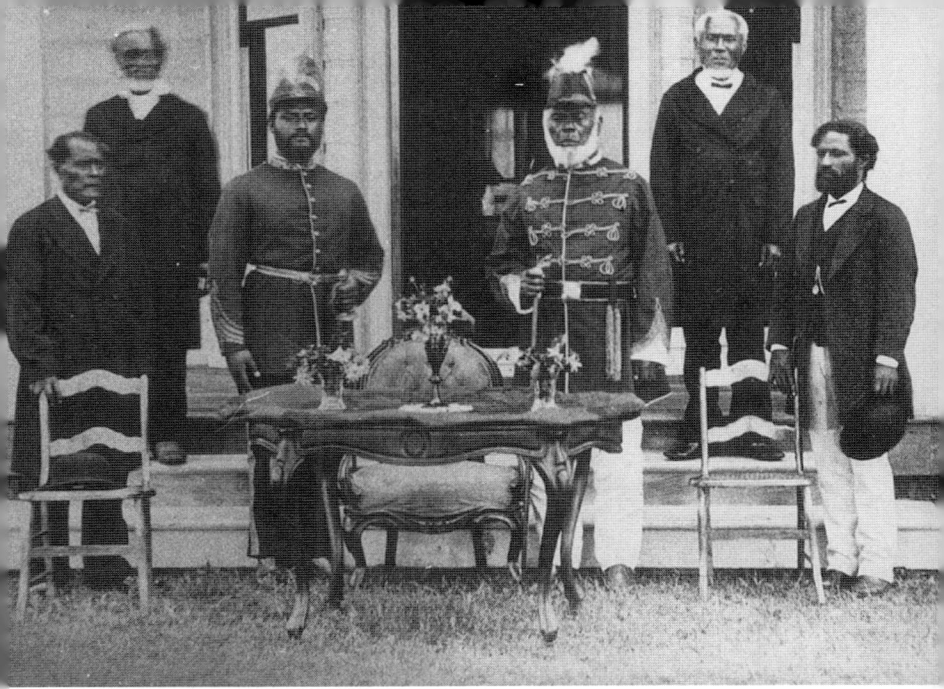

King George Tupou I of Tonga with Prince Wellington and his cabinet.
Photographed in 1876 by the crew of the German ship "Hertha".
Archives of the German Naval Institute, Mürwik.

German Luluai from Matupi with his family. Linden-Museum Stuttgart.

German Melanesian Police in the Baining Mountains. Museum für Völkerkunde, Berlin.

Australian "Field Punishment No.1 for Natives". Marie von Hein Collection, Mitchell Library, State Library of New South Wales.

Phosphate Mining on Angaur in German times. Theodor Hagedorn Papers, Bonn.

Adele Klink, daughter of Hans Klink, the German *Stationsleiter* of Morobe, and the Melanesian woman Ambo, with Lutheran missionaries and her half-caste husband. Lutheran Archives, Neuendettelsau.

Samoan women and German sailors. Museum für Völkerkunde, Berlin.

Palauan *armongol* in the *bai*. Museum of Mankind, London.

Cook reported that if the Tu'i Tonga entered a house belonging to a subject it became *tapu* and could never be inhabited by its owners, so there were houses specially built for his reception when travelling.[12]

As most of the chiefly titles originated directly or indirectly from the Tu'i Tonga line they, in varying degrees, derived *mana* and thereby chiefly powers through birth. At the same time, one had to demonstrate one's inherited *mana* in outstanding performance. Prowess on the battlefield and proven gifts of leadership in both war and peace enhanced one's *mana*. Succession to chiefly titles was decided according to the claimant's proven degree of *mana* through clearly demonstrated gifts for leadership. Loss of *mana*, on the other hand, was believed to be due to conduct contrary to the will of the gods.[13]

The *tapu* system was designed to protect and uphold the *mana* of chiefs, acknowledging their sacredness and power and setting them apart from those of lesser rank who lacked their privileges and powers. *Mana* and *tapu* were intimately related to the traditional religious system, which reinforced the societal values that the various strata must accept and strictly observe.[14] Thus the bulk of the population, especially commoners, were obliged to observe all the social, economic and religious taboos, whereas the chiefs were allowed to violate them, and the lack of ill effects were interpreted as further indication of the degree and effectiveness of their *mana*. Murder, for instance, was a crime only if the victim was of the same or higher rank, and theft similarly was an offence only if the property was sacred or belonged to someone of the same or higher rank.[15] A chief's person and his possessions were *tapu*. As all land and sea resources belonged to the chiefs, they could place *tapu* on the best of everything that the commoners produced or caught from the sea, under chiefs' supervision, and for the exclusive use of the chiefs.[16] As a consequence, the sweetest variety of coconut (*ta'okave*), the best varieties of yam (*kahokaho*) and turtle were forbidden to commoners. Any variety of yam, plantain, banana or fish reaching a certain size was termed *'eiki* (chiefly) and was *tapu* and consequently for exclusive consumption by the chiefs. Any violation of these taboos resulted in severe physical punishment administered by the chief himself or his powerful henchmen, or in divine retribution that resulted in sickness or death. Fear of these consequences of violating taboos kept the commoners in their place and the chiefs in control. Commoners were believed to exist for the sole purpose of serving their chiefs. Although they made up the bulk of the population, they had no social, political, economic or religious rights. They played no part in decision-making, had no share in exercising authority, owned no property or wealth, and had no say in the means of production. Even in the cosmology, they were believed to have no souls, and upon death were destined to become vermin, hence the term *kainangaefonua* (derived from *kaifonua*, meaning eaters of the earth or soil) was applied to them. By contrast, chiefs had souls and, by virtue of their birth, were believed after death to become secondary gods in paradise (*Pulotu*).[17]

The principle of reciprocity applied in the operations of the traditional Tongan chiefly system, when it was at its best and not abused by tyrannical individuals. Wise rulers understood the extent of their dependence on the commoners for almost everything – production of food for daily subsistence, wealth for ceremonies and exchanges, and personal and communal security. Those who were more caring and fostered goodwill in acts of kindness were able to gain the complete loyalty and devotion of their *kāinga* in reciprocation.[18] However, this was not common and most chiefs for most of the time relied heavily on fear and repression as their means of controlling and gaining what they wanted from the people.[19]

From the above discussion it is abundantly clear that Tongan traditional concepts of justice and law were intimately bound up with their traditional world-view or cosmology.[20] There was no acceptance of liberty or social equality under any circumstances; there was no idea of social justice for commoners who were the majority of the population; and for most of the time there was no accountability among those who ruled and who regarded commoners as completely under their subjugation. In short, Tongan traditional concepts of justice and law were essentially based on the premiss that 'might is right', supported by the dual notions of *mana* and *tapu* which maintained the power and privileges of chiefs by a combination of supernatural sanctions and physical repression.

In the present day, these traditional concepts of justice and law have been significantly modified, largely through British influence. However, it must be noted that British influence on Tongan culture was mainly indirect, since Britain never formally annexed Tonga, as she had other Pacific islands. Initially British influence was exerted through the British Wesleyan Methodist missionaries who successfully re-established their mission in 1826, after an earlier failed attempt.[21] A treaty of friendship and protection was foisted on King George Tupou II and his government in 1900, and was amended by Britain in 1905, with the dual purpose of stopping corruption in the government and protecting British interests in the region and internationally.[22]

British colonial policy favoured minimum intervention in the case of small countries such as Tonga with little prospect of economic returns, and it encouraged indigenous governments, supported and guided by missionaries and responsible settlers, as long as no other world power exerted undue influence over these governments.[23] Internal political events in Tonga in the nineteenth century enabled Britain to pursue this policy. It was made possible owing to the rise to power of King George Tupou I, who brought about the eventual unification of Tonga and was renowned throughout the Pacific at that time as a uniquely sophisticated and effective warrior statesman.[24]

After five years of struggle and painful uncertainty, the Wesleyan Methodist missionaries began to pin their hopes for success on an ambitious young chief, named Tāufaʻāhau, with remarkable gifts for leadership, who was one of the claimants to the temporal rulership of Tonga, the Tu'i Kanokupolu dynasty. In 1820 he had assumed the rulership of Ha'apai, the middle group of islands, succeeding his father upon the latter's death, and in 1833 he took over the rulership of the northern group of Vava'u, after the death of its ruler, Finau 'Ulukalala. He had been baptized in 1831, and had become known prior to that as King George.[25] He could see that the support of the missionaries would facilitate his quest for rulership in Tonga. Indeed his close relationship with the missionaries had helped to broaden his political sophistication, and he desired to rule his people in a similar way to that of Britain, the homeland of the missionaries.

King George foresaw the tidal wave of European impact and, like the expert navigator that he actually was, opted to ride the wave rather than go against it. He clearly perceived that the Tongan traditional cosmology was inadequate to explain the power, technology and wealth of the European intruders, and when the missionaries came, he quickly accepted their teachings and their world-view. After his conversion, he became the champion of their work, and they supported and encouraged his desire to unite Tonga into a kingdom. It was mainly through this marriage of convenience that most of the changes to the Tongan traditional concepts of justice and law were effected.

King George had learned from the missionaries that the King of Britain had laws with which to govern the people, and he requested their help in drawing up a code of laws, and so the first written code of laws was born – the Vava'u Code which had been tried out in Ha'apai in 1838 and then officially promulgated in Vava'u in 1839.[26] It was a simple code of eight provisions, supposedly of Tafa'ahau's own composition with some help from the missionaries, as was evident in the long preamble, written in Biblical language.

Significantly, it provided the first small but vital step in legislation towards accepting the concepts of equality in the eyes of the law, liberty among the people, and social justice and accountability among the rulers. The adoption of these new principles resulted directly from a subtle combination of the missionaries' teachings that all people were equal in the sight of God, which was clearly contrary to traditional beliefs, and King George's determination to limit the powers of his rival chiefs, consolidating thereby his own political authority.

King George had decided, soon after his conversion, to work towards limiting the powers of the chiefs and to emancipate or liberate the commoners from their bondage. In the Code he was quoted as saying in Provision 3: 'My mind is this. That each chief ... show love to the people you have under you ... also that you divide to each one of them land for their own use, that each one may have means of living'; and Provision 4 says: 'I make known to you it is no longer lawful, for you to hunuki or mark their bananas for your use, or to take by force any article from them, but let their things be at their own disposal.' This was the first attempt to limit or control the absolute powers of the chiefs.

The Code also placed strong emphasis on peace, prohibiting actions that would disturb the peace, such as 'Murder, Theft, Adultery, Fornication and the retailing of ardent spirits', and encouraged those actions which would promote peace, such as attending worship and keeping Sunday sacred. It also emphasized the importance of industrious habits, proper cultivation of the land, and designing ways to prevent pigs from destroying crops (Provision 5). Finally, judges were appointed to try serious offences (the minor ones being taken care of by local chiefs).

These principles of liberty, equality, social justice and accountability were further developed in the 1850 Code and 1862 Code, culminating in the Constitution of 1875. In the 1850 Code,[27] section I, clause 3 states: 'Whatever is written in these laws, no Chief is at liberty to act in opposition, but to obey them together with his people.' Section III, clause 3 and sub-section 1 reads: 'There shall be no respect of persons with the Judges in their trial of offenders. Though the offender be a Chief, or next in rank, he shall be tried according to these Laws; it being unjust to differ between the trial of a Chief and that of a common man.' And, in an obvious attempt to ensure impartial justice and prevent corruption, sub-section 2 of the above clause reads: 'On no account for the Judges to receive food or payment from those about to be tried: should any one so receive, and it be discovered, he shall be deposed from his office, having acted unjustly.' In the 1862 Code,[28] the Emancipation Edict – clause XXXIV – the Law concerning Tribute stated:

2. All chiefs and people are to all intents and purposes set at liberty from serfdom, and all vassalage from the institution of this law; and it shall not be lawful for any chief or person, to seize, or take by force, or beg authoritatively in Tonga fashion, anything from anyone.

3. Everyone has the entire control over everything that is his.

6. And the chief shall allot portions of land to the people as they may need, which shall be their farm, and as long as the people pay their tribute, and their rent to the chief, it shall not be lawful for any chief to dispossess them, or any other person.

7. And the King affectionately recommends that the size of the farms be increased according to the number of the family.

All these developments reached their zenith in the promulgation of the Tongan Constitution in 1875.[29] It has a *Declaration of Rights* as the first of its three main sections which states:

Seeing it appears to be the Will of God for man to be free, as He has made of one blood all nations of men, therefore shall the people of Tonga be for ever free, and all people who reside or may reside in this kingdom. And the lives and bodies and time of all people shall be free to possess and acquire property, all doing as they like with the fruits of their hands, and using their own property as they may see fit.

Freedom of worship, of speech, of the press and of assembly, and the right to petition the King or Parliament, among other matters, followed.

In Part II, *Form of Government*, and in relation to the Legislative Assembly, Clause 63 declared that: 'The Legislative Assembly shall be composed of the Ministers ... and the Nobles and representatives of the people.' The representatives of the people were equal in number to those of the nobles. For the first time, the commoners were allowed the opportunity to join the chiefs in decision-making. Considering the time and the nature of the traditional society, where commoners had been treated as mere chattels to be used or disposed of by chiefs at will, this was a remarkably radical and brave innovation. It helped, legislatively at least, to break down the formidable barriers between chiefs and commoners in traditional Tonga.[30]

Indisputably, these remarkable changes were due to the influence of the British Wesleyan Methodist missionaries and other British officials, as well as British common law. Legal authorities in New Zealand were consulted when law codes were drawn up, and the author of the 1875 Constitution, the Reverend Shirley Baker, was given a copy of the Laws of New South Wales when he was preparing the Constitution.[31] The Tongan Constitution in clause 32 declares: 'And should any foreigner be judged and there shall be no Tonga law to meet the case, he shall be judged according to the British law which shall be held to be the law of Tonga in such cases, until a law has been passed by the King and Legislative Assembly to meet the same.'

King George Tupou I died in 1893 and was succeeded by his 19-year-old great-grandson, Tāufaʻāhau, who became King George Tupou II. The young king was lamentably ill-prepared for the weighty responsibilities of his position, and the early stages of his reign were marked by corruption, social unrest and political instability.[32] The British government became alarmed by the possibility of a hostile power exploiting the situation to gain a foothold in Tonga, and imposed the Treaty of Friendship and Protection in 1900, taking over foreign affairs and defence and, in the 1905 amended Treaty,[33] demanding major reforms to the government, and that the King should rule according to the Tongan Constitution. These interventions did not produce significant alterations to the changing Tongan concept of justice and law. What they did was to force King Tupou II and his reformed government to improve the implementation of change embodied in Tongan laws and the Constitution.

The continuing tug-of-war between, on the one hand, introduced principles of equality, social justice, honesty and accountability, and, on the other, traditional culture, has not yet been completely resolved, even to the present day. It was not easy to terminate the deeply entrenched social customs and traditions. The powers of the chiefs have continued 'unofficially', although flagrant abuses are usually brought under control. It has not been unusual for serious offences committed by members of paramount chiefly families to be ignored by the authorities as if they had never occurred, hushed up by the community and never reported, particularly if the victims of such offences or crimes happened to be lowly commoners. I can still recall from my youth in the early 1930s, a certain elderly paramount chief, Nuku'alofa, a near neighbour of my maternal aunt in the capital, who used to sit in the back seat of his horse-drawn carriage, holding a long whip which he would mercilessly swipe at any passer-by on the road who forgot to bow or salute as he was driven along the public road. People talked about it, but no one ever complained or questioned his traditional right to do as he did. A decade or two earlier, protocol still required that when our high-ranking chief was at home in his newly built European-style house, any passer-by was expected to bow his or her head, and if on horseback to dismount and lead the horse along with head bowed. The same applied to those driving carts. Failure to behave correctly often resulted in the offender being seized by members of the chief's household, who would administer punishment such as whipping or forcing the offender to hit the trunk of a large tree with clenched fists.[34] These customary ways of showing respect to chiefs are declining except in the case of high-ranking nobles and members of the Royal family, and the traditional sanctions are no longer enforced.

The brave decision by King George Tupou I to limit the powers of the chiefs by his introduction of the rule of law and to foster the notion of equality in the eyes of the law, irrespective of birth and social rank, have gradually become integrated into modern

Tongan culture. The *mana* of the chiefs and the strict *tapu* system surrounding them has significantly declined, and the sanctions, both punitive and supernatural, that once enforced the *tapu* system are no longer present, though in many cases strong social pressures continue to exist. As higher education, growing political awareness and increasing contact with the outside world have brought considerable social changes to Tonga, particularly during the past 30 years, ordinary people are gaining greater economic independence and freedom of expression (Tonga now has a growing independent press), and there is increasing demand for society to abide by the introduced concepts of liberty, equality, social justice and accountability.

## Notes

1. E.W. Gifford, *Tongan Society*, Honolulu, 1929, p. 5; S. Lātūkefu, *Church and State in Tonga*, Canberra, 1974, p. 1; A.H. Wood, *History and Geography of Tonga*, Nuku'alofa, 1932, pp. 70, 70–85.

2. This rather conservative estimate includes not only Tongans migrated overseas, but also their children and, in some cases, grandchildren.

3. Ted Campbell, a prominent American Church historian, recently defined the term 'traditioning' as 'the process by which communities selectively and critically connect themselves to their past ... not all of the past, but the past which we value and select and which we choose to "hand on" ... to new generations'. T.A. Campbell, 'Wesley's Use of the Church Fathers', 5 July 1994, World Ecumenical Conference on 'Sanctification in the Benedictine and Methodist Traditions', Mondo Migliore Institute, Rome.

4. Gifford, *Tongan Society*, p. 111; Lātūkefu, *Church and State*, p. 9.

5. Within the chiefly class there were high chiefs and lesser chiefs. Upward social mobility was determined by marrying a person of a chiefly family higher than one's own. Arranged marriages were commonly organized with this principle in mind. A young chief with a record of achievements that proved his high degree of *mana* improved his prospects of marrying upwards.

6. No commoner was ever permitted to marry into a chiefly family. Any male commoner caught in an affair with a chiefly woman was put to death. The accused partner would be ostracized or even suffer the same fate for bringing disgrace to the family. Although such harsh measures no longer apply, even in present-day Tonga there have been instances where marriages between commoners and those of high chiefly rank were annulled, through social pressures.

7. In other parts of the Pacific, land belonged to a corporate land-

owning group, such as the *'ainga* in Samoa, the *mataqali* in Fiji or the *iwi* among the Maori of Ao-tea-roa (New Zealand). A group of land-owning titleholders, such as in Tonga, was absent.

8. Gifford, *Tongan Society*, pp. 326–7; Lātūkefu, *Church and State*, pp. 4, 85. See also R. Firth, *History and Traditions of Tikopia*, Wellington, 1961, p. 64; R. Firth, 'The Analysis of Mana: An Empirical Approach', *Journal of the Polynesian Society*, vol. 49, 1940. Firth states that 'a description in terms of mana often appears to be a symbolic way of expressing the special qualities attributed to a person of status and authority in a society, and of providing sanctions for their actions'. R. Firth, 'Mana', in *Encyclopaedia Britannica*, vol. 14, 1969, p. 746.

9. Lātūkefu, *Church and State*, pp. 2, 9. For further discussion, see R. Firth, *Elements of Social Organisation*, London, 1951, pp. 115–17; Gifford, *Tongan Society*, pp. 16–19, 187–90, 342–5.

10. Gifford, *Tongan Society*, p. 52; Wood, *History and Geography of Tonga*, p. 5.

11. Lātūkefu, *Church and State in Tonga*, p. 2; R.W. Williamson, *The Social and Political Systems of Polynesia*, Cambridge, 1924, pp. 1, 151.

12. James Cook, *The Voyages of Captain James Cook Round the World*, London, 1809, V, p. 428, Lātūkefu, *Church and State*, p. 2.

13. Gifford, *Tongan Society*, p. 326; see also R. Firth, *Rank and Religion in Tikopia*, London, 1970, p. 37.

14. For a further discussion of this topic, see R. Firth, *Essays on Social Organisation and Values*, London, 1964, pp. 225–93.

15. In a case of a commoner murdering another commoner or stealing from another commoner, neither act was regarded as a serious offence, except in so far as it disturbed the peace, and the chief of the *kāinga* concerned would settle it. See S. Lātūkefu, *The Tongan Constitution*, Nuku'alofa, 1975, pp. 11–13.

16. Lātūkefu, *Church and State*, pp. 8–9; J. Martin, *An Account of the Natives of the Tonga Islands*, vol. II, Edinburgh, 1827, pp. 122–4.

17. Gifford, *The Tongan Society*, pp. 289–90; Lātūkefu, *Church and State*, p. 5; Wood, *History and Geography*, pp. 3–4.

18. Lātūkefu, *Church and State*, p. 9; *The Tongan Constitution*, pp. 9, 11.

19. For generations the commoners had been conditioned by their chiefs to believe, and to teach future generations, that it was their fate, imputed by the gods, to accept in total submission whatever treatment was meted out to them by their chiefs, whom they were born to serve.

20. Lātūkefu, *The Tongan Constitution*, pp. 18–20; *Church and State*, pp. 96–7.

21. Lātūkefu, *Church and State*, pp. 26–8; Wood, *History and Geography*, pp. 44–5.

22. Lātūkefu, *The Tongan Constitution*, pp. 70–73.

23. I.C. Campbell, 'British Treaties with Polynesians in the Nineteenth Century'; S. Lātūkefu, 'The Treaty of Friendship and Tongan Sovereignty',

in W. Renwick (ed.), *Sovereignty and Indigenous Rights*, Wellington, 1991, pp. 69 and 83.

24. There were outstanding warriors in the Pacific at the turn of the eighteenth and nineteenth centuries, who, using European technology and military skills, managed to unite their countries – for instance Kamehameha I of Hawaii, Pomare I of Tahiti, and Cakobau of Fiji – and others, such as Tamafainga of Samoa, who were unsuccessful. However, none of them became outstanding statesmen except King George Tupou I. His receptiveness of the new values and cosmology advocated by his missionary mentors enabled him to become the most outstanding warrior-statesman of his day. Historians have designated him the 'Grand Old Man' of the Pacific. S. Lātūkefu, 'King George Tupou I of Tonga', in J.W. Davidson and D. Scarr (eds.), *Pacific Islands Portraits*, Canberra, 1970, pp. 55–76; Lātūkefu, *Church and State*, p. 219; Wood, *History and Geography*, p. 61.

25. Lātūkefu, *Church and State*, pp. 219–20.

26. Ibid., pp. 121–7. Appendix A contains the full text of the 1839 Code of Laws, pp. 221–5.

27. Ibid., pp. 128–32. For the full text of the 1850 Code of Laws, see Appendix B, pp. 226–37.

28. Ibid., pp. 171–9. For a full copy of the 1862 Code of Laws, see Appendix C, pp. 238–51; see also N. Rutherford, *Shirley Baker and the King of Tonga*, Melbourne, 1971, pp. 18–21.

29. For the full text of the 1875 Constitution and its 1975 version, see Lātūkefu, *The Tongan Constitution*, pp. 90–140.

30. Tongans take this remarkable event for granted since it has been part of their political life for over a century now, but at the time when the Constitution was promulgated it was indeed revolutionary.

31. Lātūkefu, *The Tongan Constitution*, pp. 40–41; Rutherford, *Shirley Baker and the King of Tonga*, pp. 55–9.

32. I. Campbell, *Island Kingdom*, Christchurch, 1992, pp. 110–16; Lātūkefu, *The Tongan Constitution*, pp. 69–71; N. Rutherford (ed.), *Friendly Islands: A History of Tonga*, Melbourne, 1977, pp. 183–5.

33. Campbell, *Island Kingdom*, p. 115; Lātūkefu, *The Tongan Constitution*, pp. 72–3; Rutherford, *Friendly Islands*, pp. 186–7.

34. Siosiua Lātūkefu, the present writer's father, personal communication.

# 12

# Colonial Government, 'Justice' and 'the Rule of Law': The Case of German New Guinea

## PETER SACK

### I

When I was asked to consider how European and Melanesian concepts of 'justice' had influenced each other during the period of German colonial rule in the Pacific, my first reaction was puzzlement, since the historical record suggested that the issue of 'justice' had played no significant part in either the exercise of German colonial rule or the Melanesian responses to it. To be sure, I could have ignored these 'historical' warning lights and embarked on a comparative analysis of modern European and traditional Melanesian concepts of 'justice'. But while this could have been jurisprudentially exciting,[1] it was unlikely to be historically rewarding. It then dawned on me that my response had itself been prompted by a German concept of 'justice'. The question I was meant to consider took on a different complexion if it was viewed from a British perspective, because 'justice' then turned from an ethical concept into an administrative activity: the administration of justice – a linguistic absurdity in German because '*Gerechtigkeit*' cannot be administered.[2]

This fundamental difference between the British and German concepts of 'justice' also caused the familiar claim that the British acquired colonies because they desired to bring 'the natives' the advantages of 'British justice' – the height of hypocrisy from a German perspective – to appear far more realistic, because they did not promise *Gerechtigkeit* but merely the benefits of an orderly administration of justice in accordance with the, naturally vastly superior, British model. Still, the contrast between the British and German approach to colonial rule remains striking, since German colonial officials stressed time and again, with an almost masochistic honesty, that Germany had acquired colonies not for the benefit of their indigenous inhabitants but because it served German economic interests. Yet this assessment did not prevent German observers from noting with satisfaction – especially after the end of German colonial rule – that 'the natives' had experienced this rule as 'hard but just'.

Neither this self-congratulatory cliché, nor its British counterpart, impressed 'the natives' after they had achieved political independence, at least in the case of Papua New Guinea. Its first 'Minister for Justice' (!) – a Tolai from the centre of German colonial activity – declared all colonial law to have been a fraud because it had failed to deliver 'justice' to the local people. It is unlikely, however, that his ancestors experienced German colonial law in those terms when they were subjected to it, just as it is unlikely that they experienced German colonial rule as hard but just, or that their Papuan counterparts cherished the altruistic gift of 'British justice'. The simple but disturbing fact is that 'justice' in a substantial sense (whatever that may mean) has never been and will never be the goal of any form of government – colonial or metropolitan, German or British – and that Melanesians were 'traditionally' far too pragmatic to believe otherwise.

On the other hand, this suggested a constructive way of approaching my topic: I had to move my attention away from 'justice' and focus instead on 'the rule of law' and its German equivalent, the *Rechtsstaat*. At first glance this shift may not seem to amount to much, because we are all conditioned to identify 'the rule of law' with 'justice', and, to a lesser extent, the *Rechtsstaat* with a commitment to *Gerechtigkeit*, but if we look behind this ideological smokescreen, it is plain that 'the rule of law' does not mean a 'just' rule but a rule *in accordance* with the law. It means a rule-governed, bureaucratic form of government that uses law primarily as an instrument of government rather than as an instrument for the control of the executive by an independent judiciary.

It was probably something like this pragmatic perception of 'justice' that 'the natives' had in mind when they described

German colonial rule in terms that their non-Melanesian (and not necessarily German) audience eagerly interpreted as 'hard but just'. Their assessment had nothing to do with 'justice' but with 'predictability'. The Germans, so the ideologically much less satisfying message went, were tough masters, but they played by the book and one knew where one stood.

Seen in this light, the task I had to face was taking the following shape. I had to investigate whether the history of German colonial rule over Melanesians could be described as a movement from the discretionary exercise of political power towards the 'rule of law'; to what extent German colonial rule was shaped by traditional Melanesian law; and how German colonial law had altered the way of life of Melanesians.

The first step was comparatively easy: a description of the legal framework which prescribed what the Colonial Government could do in relation to its Melanesian subjects. But how was I to accomplish the second step of giving an account of the Colonial Government in action, let alone the third step of ascertaining how its Melanesian subjects, who had left hardly any written records of their own, had responded to these activities? Or was it my 'real' task to demonstrate that this was impossible and that it was high time to adopt more modest and realistic approaches to history instead of producing increasingly surrealistic phantom narratives?[3]

## II

The Imperial Charter granted to the Neu-Guinea-Compagnie in 1885 gave it two main governmental responsibilities: the economic development of the colony and the cultural advancement of its indigenous population, with whom peaceful relations were to be established and maintained and for whose protection the Government of the Reich would enact (unspecified) regulations. The Charter, by stating that the *Kaiser* had (unilaterally) assumed sovereignty, implicitly denied that 'the natives' held 'public' rights, but it took the recognition of their 'private' rights for granted, by specifying that the Company's land acquisition monopoly included, apart from ownerless land, the contractual acquisition of land and land rights from them. The Charter was silent as to the recognition or otherwise of native law, but there is no doubt that it could be legally abolished whenever the Colonial Government chose to abolish it.

The most important exclusion from the Company's governmental powers was the administration of justice (*Rechtspflege*), which was to be 'organized' (*ordnen*) by the Government of the Reich. This was done by the 1886 Protectorates Act, which applied to all German colonies, and by general or colony-specific implementation legislation. Taken together, these rules and regulations established a dual system of colonial 'justice': one for non-natives, which essentially applied German metropolitan civil, criminal and procedural law, and one for natives, in relation to whom the *Kaiser* retained full governmental discretion.[4]

In the case of German New Guinea, the *Kaiser* used his discretion to delegate his powers to the Neu-Guinea-Compagnie, which, in turn, enacted a Native Penal Ordinance in 1888. It was essentially a procedural code, which established special courts for natives (*Stationsgerichte*) with an exclusively criminal jurisdiction. Natives could be punished by these courts only for acts that constituted serious offences (*Verbrechen* and *Vergehen*) under German metropolitan law (or had been prohibited by local police ordinances). This meant that natives could *not* be judicially punished for 'customary' offences that were not also punishable under German law, but they could be so punished for acts that fell into the latter category although they were *not* a 'customary' offence. However, the courts were given discretion not to prosecute, and the Administrator's Implementation Regulations stressed that this primarily called for a consideration of the 'intellectual and moral development' of the native in question. This consideration was also relevant under the heading 'mitigating circumstances', which could justify a reduction of the otherwise prescribed punishments. The most direct reference to 'custom' was contained in a 'compensation' provision. It authorized the courts to order an offender, in addition to his punishment, to compensate the victim, where he had to do so in accordance with 'the views and habits' (*Anschauungen und Gewohnheiten*) of the natives.

The Native Penal Ordinance remained in force until the end of German colonial rule. Its only significant amendment occurred in 1908 when the 'negative' discretion *not* to prosecute acts constituting serious offences under metropolitan German law was replaced by a 'positive' discretion to prosecute whenever the competent official decided, on a case-by-case basis, that a prosecution before the Station Court was appropriate. This amendment appears to be a step away from 'the rule of law'. It was doubly problematic because it ran directly counter to the *'nulla poena sine lege'* principle enshrined in the German Criminal Code.[5] Yet the pre-history of this amendment, which I do not wish to go into here, shows that it intended to *extend* 'the rule of law', by enabling the Colonial Government to deal with all forms of 'offensive' native behaviour judicially, and therefore in accordance with the formal procedures prescribed in the Native Penal Ordinance, rather than 'administratively' and hence 'informally', since the 1905 Imperial Ordinance defining the administrative, coercive powers of the colonial authorities did not, in the case of German New Guinea, apply to 'the natives'.

Apart from the Native Penal Ordinance, and the local police ordinances supplementing it, natives in German New Guinea thus remained in principle subject to the administrative discretion of a Colonial Government that preferred to deal with matters concerning native administration in the form of internal administrative instructions (*Dienstanweisungen*), rather than in the form of legislation that gave natives judicially enforceable legal rights and duties.

An 1887 Ordinance by the Neu-Guinea-Compagnie's administrator concerning property disputes among natives was never put into practice. The administration of civil justice in relation to natives generally remained an administrative task. There was only one attempt to codify their substantive 'civil' law: an ill-fated 1904 ordinance dealing with certain aspects of the family law of the Tolai in the north-eastern Gazelle Peninsula. This lack of action amounted to a *de facto* recognition of customary law, in so far as it had not been replaced by colonial law and in so far as the official dealing with a particular matter chose to apply it.

A 1908 Imperial Ordinance confirmed this state of affairs. It empowered the Chancellor of the Reich to legislate in relation to the substantive law of the natives as well as in relation to the exercise of jurisdiction over them, even in cases involving non-natives. A non-native could therefore not take a native to court but had to appeal to the administrative authorities for relief, whereas a native could take a non-native to court, with the consequence that the native plaintiff was then also subject to the colonial law applying to non-natives.

The entire area of administrative coercion, let alone the use of military force in relation to natives, remained legally a grey area until the end of German colonial rule. It should be stressed, however, that the criminal law applying to non-natives did not distinguish between non-natives and natives as victims, so that colonial officials were as much subject to criminal prosecution for their behaviour towards natives as towards non-natives. Legally, nothing changed on that score from the beginning of German colonial rule. To go out to shoot a few natives as a punishment for a crime committed in their area was as illegal in 1889 as it was in 1914. But this did not mean that the use of military force against natives was always illegal. It was legal in 1889, as well as in 1914, if it was necessary to remove a continuing danger to public order and safety. But during these 25 years, not only did the actual conditions in the colony change, but also the awareness of the legal position, and the manner in which executive action was rationalized.[6] It was a gradual process of 'normalization', including a normalization in the distribution of military power between the Government and those whom it tried to govern. In 1889, German New Guinea was far from being an ordinary polity. It consisted of a few small and weak colonial enclaves, surrounded by potential enemies, who still had to be 'subjugated', and were not yet part of 'the public' whose safety the Colonial Government protected. Its subjects consisted, in fact, exclusively of the inhabitants of the colonial enclaves, primarily the non-natives, but also the natives employed by them.

It was natural to 'punish' natives living outside these colonial enclaves only for 'crimes' committed against inhabitants of these colonial enclaves, primarily against non-natives, and to use military means to effect the 'punishment', because outside the colonial enclaves a primordial state of war was assumed to persist. There was no need for the Colonial Government formally to declare a state of war before taking military action in particular instances, because the extraordinary was the norm under these extraordinary circumstances. It was unusual to be able peacefully to arrest natives accused of having committed 'crimes' outside the colonial enclaves and unlikely that they would be handed over by their group to the Colonial Government for punishment.

This changed as the colonial enclaves grew, by 'pacifying' and 'organizing' neighbouring areas, which had the effect of making their inhabitants part of 'the public' whose safety the Colonial

Govenment had to protect, and of incorporating these areas into a domain within which public order had to be maintained, and where conditions were thus becoming increasingly 'normal'. This process of normalization accelerated under its own steam, as the Government's 'means of power' grew, allowing it to become proactive: embarking on systematic pacification efforts; organizing natives administratively; compelling them to carry out public works, to refrain from using self-help and from following other 'abnormal' customs, such as cannibalism and infanticide, and from leading a lazy, unhygienic or otherwise 'irrational' life.

It is tempting to see some aspects of the approach taken by the Colonial Government during the early phase of colonial rule as an adoption of traditional Melanesian ways of doing things. The historical record indeed shows that German officials and contemporary observers repeatedly referred to what they saw as traditional Melanesian acceptance of 'group responsibility' for acts performed by one of its members, in order to justify punitive expeditions, the taking of hostages or the indiscriminate destruction of property. They also referred to what they saw as a traditional Melanesian acceptance of 'strict liability' to justify the punishment of individuals in cases where their individual 'guilt', their awareness of having done wrong, could not be established.[7]

Still, it would be wrong to interpret this as an attempt to find a synthesis between traditional Melanesian and modern European notions of 'justice'. There is no question that German officials regarded punitive expeditions at least theoretically as a necessary evil, which could be made more palatable by claiming that its targets did not complain because they would have done the same. Indeed, the belief that Melanesians felt justified in avenging on all non-natives the misdeeds of particular non-natives could justify punitive expeditions or other governmental action even in cases where violent acts against a non-native had been provoked by its victim.

The same applies to other, less dramatic 'concessions', involving a temporary departure from normal modern European standards, including the appointment of 'government chiefs' with limited judicial and police powers, or the imposition of corvée labour. All this was essentially abnormal. People everywhere were meant only to pay taxes, just as crimes were meant to be punished only by the courts. In short, in German New Guinea 'the rule of law' was treated from the start as the norm to which all its inhabitants had to adjust as soon as practical.

So much is clear, but this amounts historically to very little. The historical challenge is to depict how this process of 'normalization' actually took place, and I want to illustrate the magnitude and the character of this challenge by two clusters of cases dealt with by the authorities towards the beginning and the end of German colonial rule in the north-eastern Gazelle Peninsula.

## III

1. On 15 February 1890, Octave Mouton informed '*la Cour Imperial a Karawara*' that Emon, one of his Tolai traders, had been violated by three natives, two fellow-Tolai, Towatup and Tokirenil, and Jimmy, a Solomon Islander, who traded for 'Queen Emma' Forsayth.[8] Two days later the Imperial Chancellor, Georg Schmiele, investigated the matter, taking evidence from the victim, the three accused and one witness, Towando, another Tolai trader, who worked for the Deutsche Handels- und Plantagen-Gesellschaft. The hearing was conducted in '*Pidgen Englisch*' and, where this proved impossible, with the help of Mouton as a Tolai/French interpreter. It was recorded in German by Surveyor Linnemann, who acted as clerk of the Station Court, re-translated and then signed by the natives with their crosses. The following story emerged.

Tokirenil had seduced the wife of Emon. Emon had demanded the 'customary' compensation of 10 fathoms of shell-money. When Tokirenil had refused to pay, Emon had seized a roll of 100 fathoms of shell-money as a 'customary' pledge from Tokirenil's house during the latter's absence. When Tokirenil discovered what had happened, he secured the help of Towatup and Jimmy, who was to receive one fathom of shell-money for his trouble, and went to Emon's house to 'negotiate', as he claimed. Tokirenil and Towatup climbed in through a not fully closed window, Jimmy through another, which he forced open with a tomahawk he had brought with him. A struggle ensued, during which Emon's shell bracelets were broken and a small oil lamp was smashed. After a while Jimmy appeared on the verandah, with the retrieved roll of shell-money, and Tokirenil and Towatup carried out Emon – watched by Towando, who had accompanied the three accused and denied that they had threatened to kill Emon (as the latter asserted).

Schmiele found the three accused guilty of criminal trespass and the two Tolai also guilty of criminal damage. He fined Jimmy, whom he held mainly responsible for the violence (and who had at first denied that he had been paid or that he had carried a tomahawk), 30 Marks and the two Tolai 6 Marks each, ordering them in addition to compensate Emon for his broken shell bracelets. Schmiele did not bother to consider any of the complex legal issues that the case could have raised because he regarded the whole affair as 'an ordinary quarrel among natives', which hardly justified his judicial intervention.[9]

2. On 31 July 1890, Richard Parkinson, then manager of the Neu-Guinea-Compagnie's new station in Herbertshöhe, reported to Schmiele that Harry, an 'independent' trader from the New Hebrides, had been killed by natives. Schmiele regarded this as important enough to inform the Imperial Commissioner in Finschhafen and the Commander of SMS *Alexandrine*, which happened to be in Matupi harbour.

Three days later it turned out that Harry was alive and well, but that another trader from the New Hebrides, another Jimmy, had been killed. Schmiele's investigation established that Jimmy had fallen victim to a plot hatched by chief Toparapor, from Ragunai, inland from his coastal station, because he had 'sexually used' Toparapor's daughter without paying the 'customary' compensation.[10] Schmiele was told that there was no chance that Toparapor – or the actual killer – would voluntarily appear before him, that twenty men would be sufficient for a 'successful expedition' (presumably in order to arrest him), but that the Ragunai people might be willing to pay compensation.

Since it was too late in the day to march inland, and since Jimmy had seriously offended against 'custom' (and presumably because Jimmy, as the Imperial Commissioner was later to spell out in his report to Berlin, was himself only a native), Schmiele decided to send a message demanding the return of Jimmy's Winchester rifle and a fine (*Busse*) of 300 fathoms of shell-money. He also took no action against Jimmy's Tolai neighbours who, according to Harry, had started to loot Jimmy's station – perhaps because they had done so 'in line with local custom' (*nach Landessitte*).

The Ragunai people refused his demands, but Schmiele had arranged to go on an 'expedition' on SMS *Alexandrine* to the remote Nissan Islands, so that it was mid-September before he could pursue the matter. It had in the meantime taken on a different complexion because the Ragunai people had started a noisy campaign of defiance, boasting that the warship had not dared to fight them and that their women had polished plenty of stones for their slings, should Schmiele be foolish enough to come near them.

Schmiele ordered a punitive expedition. It failed to reach Toparapor's village, or to capture shell-money or prisoners, but met with stiff resistance. Nevertheless, Schmiele expressed himself satisfied to the Imperial Commissioner because 'the enemy' had suffered substantial losses, whereas there had been no casualties among Schmiele's men. Two days later Harry came to Schmiele with a mixed bag of news. Chief Tolakit from Vuneram and chief Towutnapir from Rambitnamgunan had asked him to take a roll of shell-money from each of them to Schmiele to buy immunity for their areas in case of further military activities. On the other hand, Harry had heard that Toparapor was still ready to fight, and that he had brought his shell-money treasures to Tolakit as a precaution. In addition, chief Tokinkin, who had been Schmiele's chief guide during the expedition, was accused of taking the opportunity of stealing large amounts of shell-money from natives who had nothing to do with the matter.

While Tokinkin defended himself convincingly,[11] Schmiele also learned that his main opponents during the expedition had not been Ragunai people at all, and that the two shell-money rolls he had been sent were not the genuine article but rather a wooden frame covered with only a thin layer of shells. He therefore decided on a second punitive expedition. But it had to be delayed by several weeks because Schmiele's feet took so long to recover from the effects of the first. It set out on 21 October, reinforced by twelve of 'Queen Emma's' Buka boys, armed with Snider rifles.

With Tolakit as a guide, it reached Toparapor's part of the Ragunai district, but since it had been 'evacuated' several weeks earlier, only the gardens could be destroyed. There was some fighting, but the enemy refused to make a stand and vanished in the broken terrain. When the expedition returned to Tolakit's village, Schmiele used him as a second, easier target. Although Tolakit denied that he was 'harbouring' Toparapor's shell-money, he could not wriggle out of the matter of the fake shell-money rolls that he and Towutnapir had sent to Schmiele. He was handcuffed and taken to Herbertshöhe because the full amount of 50 fathoms of shell-money that he had now agreed to pay was brought only in dribs and drabs from the bush.

Tolakit was sent to the capital, Finschhafen, to see with his own eyes the 'means of power' the colonial authorities had at their disposal, but he was ransomed by his people through various intermediaries and released on 19 December 1890. The ransom was sent straight to 'Queen Emma' in recognition of her assistance. This payment does not appear as part of the costs of the second Ragunai expedition, which Schmiele specified as having amounted to 16.90 Marks for trade tobacco, and six metres of yellow and red cloth at a total cost of 2.40 Marks, after having removed from his clerk's draft list the much larger expense of the 400 or so Mauser cartridges that were apparently used. However, the use of the ransom was later formally approved by the Imperial Commissioner, who was also happy with Schmiele's distribution of the 24 fathoms of shell-money that the expedition itself had yielded. Ten fathoms went to Harry, who had earlier been authorized to keep what was left of Jimmy's belongings, 10 fathoms were shared among the police soldiers and 'Queen Emma's' labourers, and 4 fathoms were paid to Tolakit for his valuable services as a guide.

The file 'concerning the punishment of the chief Toparapor ... for the murder of the trader Jimmy'[12] does not tell us whether any further action was taken against Toparapor. It is unlikely, however, not so much because Schmiele believed that Jimmy's actual killer had been among the casualties of the punitive expeditions, but because such expeditions, as the Imperial Commissioner, Fritz Rose, took pains to stress in his report to Berlin, were by no means routine measures. They were undertaken only where this was necessary to protect the life or the property of 'the Whites', or the prestige of the Government. Their aim was not the punishment but the education of natives, which, in order to be effective, had to correspond to 'their views and the level of their culture'.[13]

3. The file 'concerning the judicial investigation of the accusation of cannibalism against chief Turrulem'[14] begins with a record of an interview, dated 3 April 1891, with three Tolai from Nodup: Towagurie, alias Alik; Tomarut, alias Bob; and Towando (probably the same man who had appeared before Schmiele as a witness in our first case). Their spokesman, Alik, demanded the punishment

of Turrulem, who, four years earlier, had killed and eaten four of their relatives – Tomaeng, Tomidir, Tomakurru and Topurra – on Pidgeon Island (between the Gazelle Peninsula and the Duke of Yorks). They had believed that the four men had drowned in a storm, until the wife of Tolituro had told them that Turrulem had himself confessed that he was responsible for their deaths. They had thereupon searched the (uninhabited) island and found a human skull and a thigh bone (which they produced).

Schmiele succeeded in arresting Turrulem, who lived inland of Ralum, without incident two days later. When confronted with his accusers he denied everything. They then named the Methodist teacher, Rupeni, in Raluana, as someone who could confirm their accusation. Schmiele summoned Rupeni through his superior, Missionary Oldham, and remanded Turrulem in custody. On 7 April Turrulem was questioned again, Oldham acting as (Tolai/English) interpreter. He once more denied everything but now, with the help of Oldham, in much greater detail, for example by denying categorically that he had spoken to Yaliwute, the wife of Tolituro. Rupeni, on the other hand, confirmed the accusation, giving his colleague Anassa, in Nodup, as his source. He also rejected the alternative explanations, which had surfaced in the meantime, of the origin of the human bones found on Pidgeon Island, including one according to which Tokinkin and other Raluana people had killed and eaten a woman on the island some ten years ago.

Tokinkin was heard as a witness, but in connection with the accusations against Turrulem rather than the ones directed against himself. He pronounced Turrulem innocent and the whole story as arising from gossip among women. He was backed by Tolituro who expressed himself satisfied that the four men had perished in a storm. His wife, Yaliwute, simply denied any knowledge, even after she had been confronted with the evidence of Alik. Predictably Turrulem's brother and two cousins protested his innocence as well, suggesting that Alik was only demanding Turrulem's punishment because he had refused to pay the compensation Alik had demanded.

Anassa, on the other hand, when heard a week later, strongly supported the accusations. Yaliwute, whom he identified as Turrulem's 'own' sister, had told him that Turrulem had confessed to her during a visit to Nodup. Tolituro had also known about the matter and had even admitted that he had lied when he had given evidence, presumably because he had feared that Turrulem would take revenge if he had told the truth.

Confronted with this evidence, Turrulem finally made a limited confession: he had killed two (not four) Nodup people on Pidgeon Island but he had definitely not eaten them. Schmiele had no intention of pushing the matter further. He established through Anassa that not Tolituro but Tombola was the leading chief of Nodup and summoned him, in addition to Tolituro and Yaliwute, for the following day.

Tombola took a diplomatic approach in his evidence. He stressed that he was no enemy of Turrulem, that it was not he who was pressing charges against him and that he left it to Schmiele to decide whether and how much compensation was to be paid. Not to be outdone, Schmiele asked Turrulem how much he was prepared to pay, on the basis of his confession that he had killed but not eaten two men, and Turrulem offered 100 fathoms of shell-money.

This left the matter of the false evidence of Tolituro and Yaliwute. It was quickly resolved; they meekly confessed that they had lied because they had been afraid, not of Turrulem, it appears, but of 'all the men' inside and outside the courtroom. Schmiele now pronounced his orders. Turrulem had to pay 100 fathoms to Tombola, as compensation, and 150 fathoms to him, as a fine for the confessed murder of two men. Tolituro had to pay a fine of 10 fathoms for himself and his wife for a breach of their duty as witnesses. Turrulem was ordered to remain in custody until the 250 fathoms were paid, which was hardly necessary because they were produced on the spot.

Schmiele's first step in justifying these orders was the exclusion of the 1888 Native Penal Ordinance, on the grounds that it had not yet been in force when the crimes were committed. This gave him full administrative discretion but did not stop him from explaining its exercise. As a second step, he therefore argued that the case nevertheless required governmental action because the natives could not appreciate the technical reasons which prevented its judicial treatment; because it was necessary to strengthen the confidence of the native victims of crimes in the colonial authorities by acting on their behalf; and because inactivity would have created the danger of renewed blood feuds. The third step was to demonstrate that the course of action he had taken had been appropriate. The ground was already prepared. The main task of the Government was to preserve the peace and to persuade the natives to abandon such inhuman habits as cannibalism. Under these circumstances, a combination of compensation of the victims' relatives and essentially educational fines had been called for. Such an educational fine had also been necessary in the case of the two witnesses, because they had to learn to support the colonial officials in their search for the truth. In his report to the Imperial Commissioner, Schmiele gave additional reasons for the light punishment he had imposed on Turrulem. Not only had justice in accordance with the circumstances and pedagogical considerations required a light punishment, but a harsh punishment would have created strong opposition among the natives, which the Administration did not have 'the means of power' to control. He had also thought it wise to treat Turrulem gently – who was obviously a force to be reckoned with – for the same reason he had treated the chief Talili gently (no details are given): he was hopeful that, as a result, Turrulem and his people would hand over one of the murderers of Queen Emma's Filipino overseer Moses (whose killing had created a great deal of unrest a year earlier).

4. Let us skip twenty years or so and look at a second complaint of Alik, then himself a prominent 'government chief'. On 13 December 1912, he appeared fuming in Governor Hahl's office because the *Bezirksamtmann*, Dr Klug, had just publicly called him a liar, because Klug had decided to believe the lies of his 'accuser' To Urakaga. He was 'beside himself', Alik told Hahl (who, in contrast to Schmiele, spoke Tolai), and demanded an investigation.

According to the file,[15] Alik had little reason to be upset. To Urakaga had complained to Klug about a letter Alik had written to 'the Pater in Nodup'. In it, Alik had claimed that To Urakaga had placed a young woman, Ja Kukuna, at 'the disposal' of his people. Since he had heard about the letter, To Urakaga had been ashamed to go to church on Sunday – with good reason, because the priest had told the entire congregation that this evil deed would earn To Urakaga three years 'in Kaewieng' (in northern New Ireland where Tolai had to serve longer prison sentences).

This had deeply wounded him in his honour because the accusation was totally without foundation. It was mere talk, invented by two young men, To Ropiam and Tatunie, who had told the story to Ja Kukuna's brother, To Bunbun, who, in turn, reported it to his *tamana* (classificatory father), Alik.

To Urakaga had come well prepared, bringing with him a number of witnesses. To Ropiam and Tatunie admitted that they had passed on a rumour, which they had heard from To Manuke, To Mang and To Vutie, to To Bunbun. To Bunbun admitted having reported it to Alik, after To Ropiam and Tatunie had repeatedly assured him that it was true. Alik admitted having written to Pater Hoffmann, because the latter did not want the people to continue to do 'such evil things'. He had written that To Urakaga did not stop his people from giving the girl *malira* (love magic), and that some said that To Urakaga himself had given her *malira*. Alik had believed the story to be true and had tried to check it with To Urakaga. He now realized that it would have been better if he had refrained from writing the letter until he had done so. Ja Kukuna denied that she had been given *malira* or that anyone in Nodup had 'chased after her' (*nachstellen*). Finally, Taliva confirmed that Pater Hoffmann had indeed pronounced in church that the *malira* business could earn To Urakaga three years 'in Kaewieng'.

Klug wrote to Pater Hoffmann, asking him for the letter he had received from Alik, for details of what he had said in church, and for his evidence of the truth of the accusations against To Urkaga. He, Klug, had gained the impression that they were only malicious gossip, but he could not imagine that Pater Hoffmann had accepted what Alik had written without having additional reasons for doing so. Since Klug intended to deal with the matter during the next regular sitting of the Station Court, on 20 December, he requested a speedy response.

Alik's complaint to Hahl, which caused the latter to ask Klug for 'clarification' (*Aufklärung*), probably did not improve the mood in which the *Bezirksamtmann* received the Pater's 'clarification' two days later. But its substance did not help either. He had become involved in the matter, Pater Hoffmann claimed, because Ja Kaba had complained to him that To Urakaga had threatened 'to judge' her (*richten*) because she had informed Hoffmann of the *malira* story. [16] He had told Ja Kaba that this was not true because

he had known it already from Alik's letter. Besides, it was none of
To Urakaga's business if she came to him to tell him what the
Nodup people were up to, because no *kanaka* chief had jurisdiction over him. After his sermon he had therefore publicly prohibited Ja Kaba from attending To Urakaga's court, because
everybody was free to come to him and no chief was entitled to
judge anyone who did. He had added that it was not Ja Kaba who
had informed him about the *malira* business but 'this letter' (which
he presumably waved in the air at that point). If To Urakaga
wanted to take him to court because he did not allow him to judge
Ja Kaba, he should by all means go 'to [the District Office in]
Rabaul'. He, Pater Hoffmann, would then simply take 'this letter',
since it included information that could earn To Urakaga three
years in Kaewieng.

What he had had in mind had been To Urakaga's 'polygamy',
which the letter had also mentioned, rather than the *malira* story.
Since he had never linked that story with To Urakaga, it was
quite superfluous and beside the point to substantiate it. He had
no idea how Taliva had arrived at his version of what had been
said in church, because it did not fit at all in the train of thought
that he, Pater Hoffmann, had been expressing.

The copy (!) of Alik's letter – in Tolai – which was attached to
this explanation indeed places the main emphasis, as far as I am
able to tell, on To Urakaga's relationship with his 'illegal' second
wife, Ja Kokop, whom To Urakaga kept, as Pater Hoffmann elaborated in an appendix, as a 'concubine' in Bai (Alik's bailiwik),
while his 'legitimate' wife, Ja Padala (whom he had married in
church), was living in Nodup. Ja Padala herself had confirmed her
husband's adulterous relationship with Ja Kokop, about which
Alik's letter had complained. Moreover, To Etira from Bai had
stressed that To Urakaga and Ja Kokop, who had two children
together, wanted to live together as husband and wife.

The *Bezirksamtmann* was not impressed. Instead of hearing To
Urakaga's complaint against Alik in the Station Court, Dr Klug
blasted Pater Hoffmann 'administratively' behind closed doors,
fortunately recording the main points in the file.[17] He told Pater
Hoffmann that he had improperly interfered in native matters by
prohibiting Ja Kaba from appearing before To Urakaga's court,
and warned him not to misuse his position again in a similar
manner. He also told Pater Hoffmann (over whom he had no

judicial jurisdiction) that he regarded him as guilty of slander because he had admitted to having said in church that To Urakaga would be sent to prison if he were to report this prohibition to the authorities. He informed him, finally, that he had decided not to punish Alik for writing this letter, as he had initially intended, because Pater Hoffman's public statements had been a far more serious attack on To Urakaga's honour than this private letter.

Here the matter appears to have rested until the new year. On 2 January 1913, To Urakaga and Alik were summoned and 'advised' (*belehrt*). The file does not show what this 'advice' consisted of, but we can safely assume that they were told as much as was regarded appropriate about the stand which Klug had taken when he had blasted Pater Hoffmann two weeks earlier.

Whatever Alik was told, he made no further complaints to Governor Hahl, and Hahl was satisfied with Klug's treatment of the matter when he was subsequently sent the file for his information. Klug formally closed it a day later, without taking any action against To Urakaga for his 'bigamous' relationship with Ja Kokop.[18] Perhaps he knew more about its history than Pater Hoffmann had bargained for.

5. Back in October 1907, Heinrich Fellmann, the head of the Methodist Mission, had complained to the District Office, then still in Herbertshöhe, that the manner in which To Urakaga was changing his wives was causing a public scandal. The complaint was referred to the Government Station in Simpson Harbour, which summoned To Urakaga and several witnesses, including the three women named by Fellmann.

It appears that To Urakaga's evidence was regarded as sufficient to close the matter — at least my notes do not show what further action, if any, was taken. The record of interview[19] reveals the following: To Urakaga had been told by 'the Judge in Herbertshöhe' two years earlier that he, as a Christian, was allowed to have only one wife. He had decided in favour of Ja Kokop, with whom he had, since then, lived.[20] According to To Urakaga, everything had been fine until Pater van Berkel had demanded that he should send away Ja Kokop and marry (the presumably Catholic) Ja Padala instead. To Urakaga had refused, but the Pater had kept on urging him and had become so angry that he had finally bought Ja Padala for 30 fathoms of shell-money. However, he had never lived with her and had no intention of doing so. He was happy to stick to the decision of two years before, when the Court had declared Ja Kokop to be his wife. He requested the Government to approach the Catholic Mission so that it would stop Pater van Berkel from forcing him to marry Ja Padala. He further asked for permission to take back the shell-money he had paid for her, thereby revoking the purchase.

This obviously had not happened. Instead To Urakaga had been persuaded to marry Ja Padala in church and to send Ja Kokop (presumably a Methodist) back to her people. Nevertheless his relationship with Ja Kokop had continued, as shown by their youngest child who, at the time of Pater Hoffmann's attack on To Urakaga's 'polygamy' in December 1912 ,was only eighteen months old. It was thus conceived around the time when To Urakagahad had taken Pater Hees, the successor of Pater van Berkel in Nodup, and the predecessor of Pater Hoffmann, to court in a quite different matter, involving pigs rather than women.

6.  On 13 March 1910, To Urakaga had come to the District Office demanding 100 Marks compensation from Pater Hees, who had shot a pig belonging to him, a large boar with well-developed tusks, which he used for breeding.[21] Pater Hees refused to pay, demanded that To Urakaga be officially warned to control his pigs, and foreshadowed counter-claims, demanding compensation for the damage they had caused. To Urakaga had been repeatedly warned, but instead of controlling his pigs he had threatened 'to judge' Pater Hees' Tolai houseboy if he reported their presence in the Mission garden. Besides he, Pater Hees, had not killed the pig. He had merely exercised a firmly established right by ordering the shooting of an uncontrolled pig, which was causing damage. Finally, the claim that the pig had been worth 100 Marks was ridiculous.

Dr Klug, who was already serving as *Bezirksamtmann*, responded by pointing out that Pater Hees was only legally entitled to refuse the payment of compensation if the requirements of Section 228 of the German Civil Code were met – which stipulated, applied to this case, that the damage caused by the killing of the pig be not out of proportion to the damage it was causing – a question which would have to be decided by the District Court, should this prove necessary.

Pater Hees replied that he was familiar with Section 228, and that the damage caused by the pig had far exceeded its worth. Besides, To Urakaga could have substantially reduced his loss if he had slaughtered the pig, which had only been wounded. He could have easily done this if he had discovered its disappearance when it did not turn up in the evening expecting to be fed, but he never bothered to feed his pigs, preferring them to get fat at other people's expense. Pater Hees applied for a rejection of To Urakaga's complaint, and requested to admit Pater Schinke as his legal representative, should it come to a formal hearing.

Since To Urakaga stuck to his demand, Klug appointed Police Sergeant Bernicke as *his* legal representative, and asked the latter to begin formal legal proceedings. Bernicke presented a written statement of claim to the District Court, which set a hearing for 29 April. To Urakaga, who had reduced his claim to 50 Marks, achieved a full victory: Pater Hees was ordered to pay that amount plus costs. The District Court Judge, Dr Stübel, found that it was not necessary to consider the question of the proportionality of the damage caused and avoided, because an application of Section 228 was already excluded by the fact that the shooting of the pig had not been *necessary* to prevent further damage, since this could have been achieved simply by chasing it away. Nor did it matter that Pater Hees had not shot the pig himself but had ordered Brother Dehm to do so, since he was liable for the damage caused by the latter's actions under Section 831 of the Civil Code.

On the other hand, it looked as if To Urakaga's triumph was going to be short-lived, because Pater Hees declared himself unable to pay, by reference to his vow of poverty. But Bernicke was not prepared to give up. He tried unsuccessfully to have the judgement executed and, when the Mission did not respond to his request to pay on Pater Hees' behalf, threatened to sue it, after forcing the Pater to declare himself officially bankrupt.

At this point Klug decided that it was time to involve the Governor, or rather the Acting Governor, Dr Osswald, since Governor Hahl was on home leave. Osswald asked the Mission to reconsider its refusal to pay on the Pater's behalf because it would seriously undermine the still embryonic confidence of the natives in the Government if they saw that a 'white', who had access to wealth far beyond their own reach, did not have to make a compensation payment that had been judicially ordered. How could the natives ever learn to trust 'our legal system' if they felt that it was unable to assure that their judicially acknowledged rights were honoured, as it was bound to look to them in this case?

While the Mission considered, an even darker cloud appeared on the horizon. The new District Court Judge, Weber, decided that under the relevant German metropolitan law, in view of Pater Hees' inability to pay, To Urakaga was liable to pay the court costs of his successful action. When Osswald learned about this decision he instructed his staff to contact Weber immediately by phone, requesting him to postpone its implementation.

Fortunately Pater Schinke, as representative of the 'Sacred Heart Mission, Limited Liability Company', agreed to pay the 50 Marks compensation to To Urakaga, but not the costs, which, he suggested, should be cancelled. Pater Schinke stressed that the Mission would usually have been happy to pay on behalf of one of its members under circumstances of this kind, although it was not legally obliged to do so, but that this was an unusual case because the decision of the District Court, which was not appealable because the amount at issue had been less than 300 Marks, had been a misguided departure from established practice, which had acknowledged that the shooting of straying native pigs and dogs was the only effective way in which settlers could protect their property. If the natives learned that the Europeans were no longer able to defend themselves, they would be only too delighted 'to outwit' them and their law (*ein Schnippchen schlagen*). Still, if Osswald felt that it was necessary for political reasons that To Urakaga be paid because it was no longer possible to set aside this unfortunate judgement, the Mission was willing to oblige as a demonstration of its goodwill towards the Government.

Osswald was startled by Schinke's assessment of 'the native character' but relieved that this particular matter could now be settled. He thanked the Mission, cancelled the court costs and ordered that the cash expenses of Police Sergeant Bernicke, as To Urakaga's legal representative – mainly the lunch he had consumed at the hotel '*Deutscher Hof*' on the day of the hearing – be refunded by the Treasury.

Now back to what, at least for our purposes, is the crux of the matter: the 'revolutionary' decision of the District Court under Dr Stübel. It had, legally speaking, little choice but to find in favour of To Urakaga because the strict requirements of Section

228 of the Civil Code were plainly not fulfilled.[22] Legally speaking, it also had little choice but to refuse, as it did, to deal with the counter claims of Pater Hees, because the District Court had, formally, no jurisdiction over native defendants, although that had not stopped it from dealing with actions of this kind in the past. But it appears that Stübel also felt that the time was politically ripe for a decision of this kind, although the judgement gives no indication that he thereby broke, as Pater Schinke claimed, with an established practice.[23]

Stübel did acknowledge, however, that his decision would create considerable practical difficulties for 'the settlers' in the future. Yet he insisted that the fact that it would not be easy for them to obtain compensation from the native owners of pigs that had damaged their property did not justify their interfering in an even more serious way with the property rights of others by shooting the animals. Even if they belonged to natives, and even if they were causing more damage than they themselves were worth, the shooting of domestic animals was no longer 'on' in German New Guinea. The rule of law, it appears, had arrived and the rough 'private justice', which might have been unavoidable during the early pioneering phase, had become intolerable.


## IV


What can we do with these two clusters of cases, considering that accounts of hundreds of equal relevance have survived as part of the historical record; that thousands more were handled by the colonial authorities, the records of which have been lost or which were never recorded in similar detail; and that they might tell, or would have told us very different stories.

It is plain that these cases represent the meat of German colonial rule in Melanesia, so that an adequate history of this rule cannot be written without taking them into account. But how can we utilize this vast and at the same time vastly incomplete mountain of information of always questionable reliability, if we are not satisfied with mining it as a quarry for a few colourful anecdotes to enliven a narrative which has been distilled from other sources?

It hardly needs saying that a quantitative approach is unsuitable, not only because much of the historically most interesting information is impossible to quantify but also because the surviving historical record is too incomplete and uneven to provide statistically reliable data. Moreover, German New Guinea was probably a historical stage[24] which was throughout too small and unsettled to produce statistically meaningful trends. For example, the jurisdiction of the first Station Court in its eastern Melanesian section initially comprised the entire Bismarck Archipelago and the northern Solomons – including Choiseul and Ysabel – whereas five Station Courts operated in 1914 in the same geographic area – minus Choiseul and Ysabel – and at least one further Station Court (Simpson Harbour) had come and gone in the meantime. Besides, hardly any of the decisions of three of these Station Courts (Manus, Namatanai and Kieta) have survived and the survival rate of the oldest (Kerawarra/Herbertshöhe/Rabaul) probably is, all told, less than 10 per cent.

By the same token there is far too much information still available to be handled 'narratively' – and ignoring the unmanageable surplus does not help because its presence is bound to make an account of the history of German colonial rule which ignores it demonstrably counterfactual, if anyone bothers to check it against the available sources. Yet the problem is not so much the difficulty of giving a factually accurate account of what happened in the past, or the impossibility of interpreting historical events 'objectively', as a deeply rooted expectation that historiography, at least if it is written by professional experts, is somehow capable of capturing a manageable middle ground of generality in the field of history that actually does not exist, neither in the past nor in the present or the future. Put differently: the problem is a misguided ambition on the part of historians not simply to tell what happened in the past, but to do so in a manner which purports to be a form of history that gives the past retrospectively an ideologically satisfying meaning.

While the desire at least to make sense of the past, since we are obviously unable to understand what is going on around us in the here-and-now, is understandable, it is unlikely that an attempt to satisfy this desire can be turned into a respectable academic enterprise. It would thus seem that intellectually honest historiographers have the choice between pursuing this irrational, pre-modern ambition – and to admit that they are engaged in creating myths rather than in advancing our knowledge of the past – and settling for a more modest and realistic, but perhaps no longer marketable, approach that acknowledges that 'history' can no more be written than 'justice' can be administered, and that academic historiographers do not study history but the surviving historical record, which determines what they can and cannot do.

Since it would be professional suicide to adopt openly the first position, we can dismiss it.[25] Does this mean that academic historiographers have no choice but to adopt the second position and become slaves of the historical record instead of sucking narrative nectar from a selection of its most attractive flowers? Of course not, since they can instead continue to pretend that the past is an insoluble mystery. Hence it is only to be expected that history is simultaneously unique and typical, meaningful and unpredictable, subjective and factual, so that historiographers can make it answer any question they choose to put to it, including the one I was invited to consider. I am afraid, however, this is a job which calls for a professional historian who has been initiated into the ancient rituals of this particular tribe, and regards its blinkers as perfectly natural and indeed necessary.

Ironically, these rituals probably did make sense, until 'the rule of law' emerged and started to produce a historical record of a different kind from that produced during the Dark Ages, where historians still prefer to lead their professional lives because a narrative longbow is the only weapon they are willing and able to use, irrespective of the nature of their target. Yet this matters little as long as their target remains the same age-old, imaginary struggle between good and evil and they are merely trying to dress their leading actors in different period costumes and to vary the details of the set accordingly.

Who really wants to know how European and Melanesian concepts of 'justice' influenced each other during the exercise of German colonial rule in the Pacific? And who, among those who do, is prepared to digest the detailed information and analysis necessary to provide a genuine answer? At least the answer to this last question is simple: no one. I might as well leave it at that.

## Notes

1. See, for example, Peter Sack, 'Law, Morals and Religion: A Melanesian Perspective', *Rechtstheorie*, vol. 12 (1991).

2. The 'functional' German counterpart of the administration of justice, namely the *Rechtspflege* (= law-care, which is concerned with *Rechtsprechung*, the determination of what is 'right' in particular cases) is conceptually a very different enterprise, and the linguistic counterpart, *Justizverwaltung*, is yet another kettle of fish. (For a discussion of the different conceptual structuring of 'law' in German and English, see Peter Sack, 'Law and Custom: Reflections on the Relations between English Law and the English Language', *Rechtstheorie*, vol. 18 [1987].)

3. For a case study of the 'phantomization' of one particular episode in the history of German colonial rule in the Pacific, see Peter Sack, ' "The Sokehs Rebellion" and the "Phantomization" of History', forthcoming.

4. It is worth noting that the term 'native' was defined as covering 'members of foreign coloured tribes' as well as the 'local' natives.

5. According to this 'no punishment without a law' principle, people could be punished only for an act that had been declared punishable by law before they performed it.

6. There is ample anecdotal evidence that colonial officials, up to the highest level, throughout the period of German colonial rule, did not understand the legal relationships between criminal and disciplinary punishments, and between punishments and the use of administrative coercion or military force. (This legal ignorance still prevails among historians, and contributes significantly to a 'phantomization' of their accounts of German colonial rule. For a discussion of one such example, see Sack, ' "The Sokehs Rebellion" '.)

7. Whether this was a 'true' perception of traditional Melanesian law is another matter.

8. I want to avoid the old 'problem' of which proper names to use and how to spell them, and shall therefore produce the form which appears in the sources, although I have improved 'consistency', where this was desirable, to prevent confusion.

9. For example, Schiele did not consider whether the removal of a 'customary' pledge also qualified as '*Pfandkehr*' under the German Criminal Code, which would have elevated the case, legally, into a far more serious category. The case is fully documented in AAC: AA63/83, B39.

10. The German term used to translate the natives' evidence is '*beschlafen*', a 'euphemistic' term which indicates neither that Jimmy had raped the woman (or girl) nor that he lived with her without buying her. (It should also be noted that any 'customary' compensation would have been 'in principle' due to the woman's matrilineal relatives rather than to her father.)

11. Tokinkin admitted, however, that his people had captured two 'muskets', which he would now hand over to Schmiele.

12. AAC: AA63/83, B39.

13. See BAP: RKolA 2979, Fol. 137.

14. AAC: AA63/83, B39.

15. AAC: AA63/83, B68.

16. The term 'judge' (*richten*) is used in the sense of punishing a person rather than in the sense of judicially deciding whether an accusation against a person is justified.

17. AAC: AA 63/83, B68.

18. Nor, as far as I know, was Pater Hoffmann prosecuted for slander.

19. AAC: AA 63/83, B62.

20. This statement suggests that To Urakaga had been reported for bigamy in 1905, but that he had been saved by Section 1 of the Governor's Implementation Regulations to the 1904 Native Marriage Ordinance, because it provided that even in cases where polygamy constituted a criminal offence under that Ordinance, the guilty parties were to be released in the first instance, after an earnest admonishment.

21. The file is in AAC: AA 63/83, B78.

22. A legally more adventurous court might have used the 1900 version of the Protectorates Act to argue that a departure from Section 228 was called for because of the different circumstances obtaining in German New Guinea at the time, but this is not a line Stübel wanted to take.

23. I am not at all sure that the District Court had, in fact, consistently rejected compensation claims of this kind in the past, as Pater Schinke claimed. I also have other doubts about the factual accuracy of the information contained in the files, which I have reported here. (For example, Alik's complaint to Hahl strongly suggests that he still believed that his *malira* accusations against To Urakaga were true.)

24. I am using this term in the 'theatrical' rather than 'evolutionary' sense.

25. The same applies to the postmodern alternative of deconstructing history instead of writing it, as it can only lead into, at best, a fascinating blind alley.

# 13

# Colonial Law as Metropolitan Defence: The Curious Case of Australia in New Guinea

## A.M. HEALY

The recent discrediting of Marxism and its derivatives should have cleared the way for a more rational assessment of the modern colonial regimes. The era of anti-colonial nationalism since the Second World War has produced a plethora of broad censorious analyses stemming from the basic preconception that 'colonialism' as a whole was inherently nasty, exploitative and oppressive. It should now be possible, however, to re-examine the primary evidence in a less jaundiced way, recognizing that modern colonial administration, which undertook to create new nations from tribal aggregations, was the most difficult and complex of all forms of government. The various European powers differed in their approaches and must be judged separately; but, together, they re-shaped the world.[1]

The essential hermeneutic question is: which criteria may properly be applied in any reassessment? What was it that made some colonial regimes more effective than others in drawing disparate, pre-modern societies together into new states? It is suggested here that we should examine the means used to integrate novel concepts and Western institutions with traditional cultural bases. Unless that was handled with appropriate sensitivity and flexibility, the emerging national system would lack meaning and credibility, and would therefore be dysfunctional. In short, we have to look, *as a primary measure*, at the ways in which the colonial regimes attended to cross-cultural realities, working through the inevitable anomalies, rather than trying to assume or decree an exogenous model.

Lord Hailey wrote many years ago that the best index to the nature of a colonial regime lay in the field of law, because it was there that cultural rigidities tended to be most obvious.[2] In law, meaning custom, precedents and statutes as a whole, basic cultural divergences, extending to the ideas of the self, of social order, and the very nature of power, really stood out. As Epstein put it in relation to Melanesian societies, the western notion of individual and abstract justice conflicted with the indigenous objective, which was to 'restore or redress the equilibrium within society'.[3] Those divergences had to be handled with understanding by a colonial regime if the dominant and dependent cultures were to be brought together in a functional way, and if the ultimate legal institutions and usages were to have meaning, and so attract allegiance and respect.

Hailey and many other scholars have made out a strong case for modern British colonial administration, essentially pragmatic, flexible, and inclusive, to be regarded as having been most effective. In Sir Ernest Barker's cogent phrase, the general British aim was to create 'civilizations *sui generis*' within self-governing states;[4] and that implied a recognition of indigenous law. It also implied a recognition of the essential processes of acculturation and legal syncretism, meaning that imported elements were adapted, not adopted, according to the patterns of the receiving cultures. Traditional societies never simply yielded to the new; rather, they responded to it and, with encouragement, developed functional syntheses, in both substance and procedure. Effective colonial administration provided for that via appropriate bridging institutions.

The imperial record testifies to very considerable success. India represented a major learning experience for British administrators, who, under Hastings, began the long process of systematizing and codifying Hindu and Muslim law, while simultaneously introducing English law. As Fieldhouse has written, this blending of apparently incompatible juridical traditions turned out to be 'possibly the greatest British achievement in India'.[5] Similarly T.O. Elias, the first Attorney-General of independent Nigeria, paid tribute to the British approach in gradually bringing together a wide variety of African and English legal usages.[6]

In dependencies where the indigenous peoples lacked kings and chiefs and traditional state structures, the British created Native Authorities by, first, encouraging gatherings of elders to make rules and to adjudicate over both custom and matters delegated to them; and, second, gradually formalizing such gatherings into indigenous councils and courts, under flexible central monitoring, so that they could become statutory institutions of local government, with form and functions developing *pari passu* with general social change and administrative sophistication.[7] Obviously, this did not eliminate generational and role conflict; but it progressively brought together indigenes with traditional status and those with wider experience in local decision-making, parallel adjudicating, and the redefining of custom.

In that light, Australia's record in legal administration in Papua New Guinea appears difficult to explain, because it represented the very antithesis of the British approach. Australia, of course, is a federation of former British colonies which inherited, and continue to respect, English law; and it was the major Australian colonies that, in 1884, pressured Britain to annex Papua.[8] Britain agreed, but only on condition that the Australians paid the recurrent costs. In return, the Australians had a major say in policy until 1906, when the new federation formally assumed full control. Australia also took over former German New Guinea as a League Mandate after the campaign of 1914–15. Thus, Australia effectively defined law and government in east New Guinea until the Territory's independence in 1975. But the entire bent of Australian policy – well illustrated in the legal system – amounted to an attempt at decreed grassroots assimilation, grounded in entirely ethnocentric postulates, and ignoring or overriding indigenous tradition. How is that to be explained, and what were the implications in law and legal administration?

Some British officials in the region in the 1880s had foreseen an unfortunate outcome, recognizing that formative influences in the Australian colonies would dictate policy in New Guinea. For example, Sir Arthur Gordon, High Commissioner for the Western Pacific, counselled London that the Australians, having for decades kidnapped Melanesians for virtual slavery on Queensland plantations, were 'unfit to be placed in charge of native races'.[9] He saw a tradition of unrelieved oppression of blacks as an indicator, and a warning. Treatment of the Australian Aborigines supported such a view. They had been driven off the land, and many had been murdered. By the 1880s, the miserable survivors were being herded onto reserves, there to be forcibly 'protected' and 'civilized' – to the extent that their perceived 'low natures' allowed. Aboriginal culture was dismissed as primitive, worthless and expendable. New Guineans and their cultures tended to be regarded similarly. As Humphrey McQueen has noted, racism was central to the development of Australian nationalism.[10]

The other major determinant in Australia was fear of alien powers or influences, and this gradually focused on the region to the north.[11] Thus, New Guinea was seen as a defence buffer which had to be dominated by, and made dependent on, Australia. That implied total and indefinite Australian control, which would be threatened by any form or degree of indigenous self-expression, at any level. That being so, Australian institutions, methods, concepts and precedents became, almost from the beginning, the essential referents.

Only in the first four years, under the Protectorate (1884–88), did white officials work *with* traditional 'big men' and elders, acting as observers, advisers and mediators rather than overlords; and the reason for this was uncertainty about their legal powers.[12] Once the Colony came into being, however, doubts about their right to dictate from the centre, and to enforce official decisions, evaporated. Nevertheless, the pioneer British governor, Sir William MacGregor (1888–98), initially sought consultative relationships with the Papuans, and he set about appointing Government Chiefs with whom officials could liaise. White officials were empowered as magistrates; but MacGregor recognized that western mores encapsulated in law were quite alien, so he established a Native Regulations Board to frame laws appropriate to village society. He believed that, after indigenes had gained some experience and a little education, they could serve on the Board, where they would help gradually to codify and update custom. That would subsequently assist the authorizing of elders to hear village cases, under official supervision.[13] In fact, however, none of this eventuated.

The difficulty was that MacGregor was expected by the Australian colonies rapidly to pacify the coast, to facilitate the work of planters, traders and missionaries. He had a minuscule, poorly educated staff, and slender funds (perennial problems in later administration), and the Australians showed little interest in progressive relations with the Papuans. Thus, he was gradually reduced to appointing hundreds of Papuans as Village Constables, who were instructed to bring offenders against the Native Regulations before patrolling white officials for punishment.[14] Inevitably, the VCs faced impossible role conflict; but that was ignored, and the system became entirely coercive, being dictated by ideas, values and intentions that were alien to Papuan societies. Opportunities for consultation, and for indigenous inputs, quickly slipped away.

MacGregor himself knew that his administrative-cum-judicial arrangements were rudimentary, and he thought of them as stopgap;[15] but, remarkably, they remained the standard methods into the 1960s. Papuans had no recognized say in the framing or implementing of the law, at any level. They remained subject to official edicts, perceived as civilizing instruments. The formal transition to full Australian control in 1906 saw the final abandoning of any consultative ideals. A Royal Commission of inquiry into the future administration showed interest only in basic law and order, economies in funding, and the potential for economic development by whites. 'Native policy' was ignored, except to the extent that Papuans might be 'civilized' by pressure to work for whites. As Judge Hubert Murray testified to the Commission, 'the Papuans have been placed on a pedestal for far too long, with absolutely no result'.[16] Unsurprisingly, Murray was named in 1908 as Lieutenant-Governor (Administrator), a post he retained until he died in office in 1940 at the age of 78 (in itself a testament to Australian indifference).

Murray was urbane and highly educated, with an Oxford First in Classics. He also had a deep interest in 'the natives', and read widely in anthropology and comparative administration. He wrote with charm and conviction. Australian politicians were happy to let him get on with governing, as long as costs were low and the natives quiet. So he cemented in place what became known as 'the Murray Tradition', which was accepted in Australia as the last word in humane colonial administration. In fact, it defined a regime of unrelieved paternalism, predicated on the antique notion of a natural hierarchy of peoples and cultures. Indefinite white tutelage was thus the only way to go, the only moral course. It was the role of Papuans gradually to learn white ways, to the limited extent that they were capable. Murray believed that Papuans were 'deficient in natural gifts', and that their own cultures would eventually fade away.[17]

Consequently, any positive role they might have was problematic; and formalizing custom would have been pointless. As Murray wrote in 1938, after he had been running the government for 30 years: 'Some day it may be possible to hand over petty acts of administration and trivial native cases for Papuans themselves to deal with; but when that day will come is hard to tell.'[18] Anything that Papuans *might* do would be allowed them by whites; they had no immanent customary rights of administration or adjudication. Murray knew of Britain's Native Authorities, but he had the perfect answer: similar institutions were impracticable in Papua because the situation was unique, the natives much more primitive, more in need of white direction and moral suasion. (This 'uniqueness' argument became a stock Australian defence.)

In the same way, Murray shrugged off occasional criticism from foreign social scientists. Although he came to realize, along with his government anthropologist, F.E. Williams, that his system was wholly punitive, he had created a Catch-22 from which there was no escape.[19] Real consultation and devolution had become impossible. That being so, the number of Native Regulations governing almost every aspect of indigenous life continued to multiply, along with penalties imposed by white officials, backsliding by Village Constables, and evasion by Papuans generally. The Regulations represented the juridical arm of assimilation. They laid down how indigenes should behave, dress, wash, build houses, garden, observe curfews, abjure 'objectionable' practices, and generally please patrolling white officials. In Papuan eyes, 'the law' was something arcane and extraneous. As custom remained outside the ambit of the official legal system, it could not be officially monitored, modified, or invoked by accord to influence acculturation. Lord Hailey, who observed Papua New Guinea from a seat on the League of Nations' Permanent Mandates Commission, concluded that the Murray Tradition amounted to 'a benevolent type of police rule'.[20]

Meanwhile, over the border in what had been German New Guinea until 1914–15, an Australian administration led by a succession of retired army officers established a very similar pattern of uncompromising white control. In the process they extinguished some promising initiatives of the German governor Albert Hahl (1902–14), whose progressive thinking on devolution never resurfaced. In areas of heavy contact, such as the Gazelle Peninsula, Hahl had encouraged indigenes under recognized headmen (*luluais*) to run their own affairs, including the administering of courts with jurisdiction over custom, some civil matters (within defined limits), and minor criminal offences (with specified penalties). Some effort was also made to form 'political unions', grouping villages together under paramount *luluais*, with the object of expanded indigenous jurisdiction.[21] This was similar to what was encouraged within Britain's Native Authorities (for example, in East Africa, which had similar small-scale socio-political units based on segmentary lineages).

Under Australian control, however, the New Guineans, regardless of their level of acculturation, had to submit to Murray-type overrule. A recommendation of 1924 by the British administrator John Ainsworth, that the judicial functions of *luluais* be formally recognized, was rejected.[22] Instead, an avalanche of Native Regulations descended on the indigenes, particularly after the Rabaul Strike of 1929, which threw terror into the white community. New Guineans had to be subordinated. They were explicitly forbidden to 'lodge or wander in company' with whites.[23] Underlying resentment of, and cynicism about, Australian rule became a permanent factor among New Guineans, especially those, such as the Tolai of the Gazelle Peninsula, who had been accorded some measure of local self-government by Hahl.

The death of Murray in 1940, and the Japanese invasion in 1942, gave some temporary promise of a dramatic change in Australian policies. Many indigenes came into contact with aliens from advanced societies (Japanese and Americans) expressing anti-colonial views. As Stanner puts it, this 'brought about significant changes of outlook and behaviour in many areas ...; the simple acceptance of European authority and prestige seemed to be no longer assured'.[24] Some indigenous leaders, such as Paliau on Manus, took practical steps toward local self-government (which later led to his being classed as a dissident and jailed by the returning Australians).[25] Yet the wartime administration, ANGAU, which had brought in outsiders, including anthropologists, had proved liberal (or realistic), and advocated giving at least the more 'advanced' indigenes their own councils and courts (which were specifically promised to the Tolai and the Motu).[26] In January 1945 a spokesman for Canberra's (Labor) Minister for External Territories announced that the post-war government would encourage 'increasing participation by the natives in the administration of justice'.[27]

The immediate difficulty as the war ended was that no-one knew how to go about it, especially in the face of demands that priority be given to making the Territory economically viable (i.e. helping Australian enterprises). The new administrator, J.K. Murray (no relation to Hubert), was a total amateur; and in 1946 he was faced by a body of experienced senior officials steeped in the 'Murray Tradition', determined to reassert white control and the *status quo ante*. (A retiring age of 65 meant that many of these men were influential into the 1960s.) The Chief Justice, J.B. Phillips, made it clear that any suggestion of native courts was anathema to him.[28] 'Justice' had to come from above.

A small seed of British-style reforms had been sown; but it was destined to lie in acid soil. However, one young official, David Fenbury, in 1946 was actually sent to the British Colonial Office in Tanganyika, and he came back full of enthusiasm for Tanganyika's Native Authorities (already in the process of being copied in the neighbouring British Solomons, where Native Courts had been given statutory form in 1942).[29] In 1949 an ordinance providing for Native Local Government Councils in Papua New Guinea was eventually promulgated, in the face of general hostility from senior officials.[30] But they had nothing to worry about. Drafting in Canberra meant that it was a monstrous piece of legislation, along metropolitan lines, offering unlimited opportunities for central control, and totally at variance with comparable provisions in British dependencies. In practice, it facilitated the establishing of a handful of putative councils, under the thumb of white supervisors, in areas threatening dissidence, such as Manus, the Gazelle Peninsula and Port Moresby. These councils were, first, control mechanisms; and second, long-term educative institutions under the mantle of assimilation. They gave negligible scope for indigenous self-expression.[31]

What particularly worried Fenbury, who had been assigned to introduce this emasculated form of local administration, was the lack of any parallel provision for native courts, which would have represented some real local empowerment. He saw them, most importantly, as having the potential to bring custom, and the consultative regulating of culture change, within the aegis of a more relevant legal system. The few councils theoretically had the power to make rules, which appeared to open the way to the codifying of custom; but in practice it quickly became clear that central supervision, especially from Crown Law officials, was stifling that potential. Councils ended up adopting 'model rules' framed by white supervisors. That made the authorizing of native courts all the more imperative.[32]

With only one honourable exception (C.J. Lynch), Crown Law officials, and Chief Justice Phillips, resisted the proposal, which represented a test of the assimilationist, regulatory thinking behind direct rule. Native courts then remained under discussion *for nine years*. During that period the Labor government in Canberra was replaced (December 1949) by a conservative regime headed by Robert Menzies, who was appalled by the break-up of the British empire and by decolonization in Southeast Asia. To Menzies, the new nationalists were dangerous people. Australia had to see that they did not appear in Papua New Guinea, which was sealed off from the world and made subject to more detailed control from Canberra. Simultaneously, the policy of assimilation, directed primarily at the Aborigines and phrased in terms of a moral responsibility, came to be more clearly articulated. This carried over to discussion on Papua New Guinea and further militated against any devolution of authority.

In 1951, the Ministry of External Territories passed to a reluctant ex-diplomat, Paul Hasluck, who became the *de facto* governor of Papua New Guinea for the next (crucial) twelve years. Hasluck was totally without colonial experience, though a published advocate of assimilation for the Aborigines.[33] Despite that, he was convinced that he had the answers. In fact, his whole approach was indistinguishable from that of Hubert Murray two generations earlier: Australia had a prime responsibility to adhere to a phased, long-range plan that would teach the natives ('primitive savages', as he called them) the elements of civilization, Australian-style. Precisely because they *were* savages they could have no say in that; once they *had* learned the elements – perhaps in fifty or a hundred years – they could become junior partners. An insistence on 'uniform development' meant that the general pace of advance had to be that of the slowest: very convenient for those who wanted

Papua New Guinea to be dependent indefinitely. Rapid movements toward self-government elsewhere in the colonial world were branded either irrelevant or reprehensible.[34]

Hasluck's reinvigoration of the 'Murray Tradition', emphasizing the primacy of white controls, concepts and values, conflicted with any suggestion of ceding local powers to indigenes. When he learned of the native courts proposal he was outraged; and he delivered the *coup de grâce* in a lengthy and caustic memo in January 1955, which showed, *inter alia*, his abysmal ignorance of the sociology of law in its most basic form. He was incapable of understanding why anyone would make such a proposal, ignoring the long history of native courts and accommodations to customary law in scores of diverse British dependencies: 'is it only proposing something that looks judicial but is in fact designed to meet the convenience and to serve the purposes of administration of native affairs?'[35] His mind worked only in western models. He was transferring to the Papua New Guinea situation the same kind of functional compartmentalization he expected in an Australian context, with a separation of powers, and the judicial arm monitoring the executive. In a cross-cultural environment such minds are dangerous. It was not surprising that he went on to say that primitive societies had absolutely nothing to offer when it came to law and justice. Justice was outside the ken of primitives, being 'a gift that we have brought to them'. He then added a sentence that epitomized both his attitude to the legal system and Australia's entire administrative philosophy: 'I believe there is a great deal to be said for presenting the idea that the Queen ... is the fount of justice and the courts are the Queen's courts.'[36]

Obviously, the judicial prerogatives of Australian lawyers, and of patrolling white officials, were not going to be challenged in Hasluck's New Guinea. In vain did Lynch, a professional lawyer, pinpoint the crucial flaws in the Minister's stance: 'First of all, he appears to consider the Common Law of England as the fount of all justice and, secondly, he ignores the fact that the term 'justice' has a meaning only in relation to a specific social and cultural environment.'[37] Just as seriously, Fenbury pointed to the practical results of long-standing policy, warning Hasluck that the irrelevance of the existing judicial system had led to the development of a parallel, unauthorized and unsupervised system of illicit tribunals operating throughout the Territory, dealing with matters from murder to land disputes and virtually everything encompassed by custom. These could not be brought within official cognizance while the indigenes were deemed to have no customary judicial role. At the same time, indigenes had no chance of serving within the official judicial system, because they lacked the education, which had been restricted to little more than upper-primary level. Hasluck made no bones about policy there: in Africa things had got out of hand, he opined, because some of 'the natives' had been given too much education 'prematurely'. He had no intention of encouraging the emergence of what he called 'native demagogues'.[38] Thus, Hubert Murray's old Catch-22 persisted – but now in an era of galloping decolonization.

Unfortunately, public comment in Australia reflected ignorance and complacency comparable to Hasluck's. Assimilationist policies towards both the Aborigines and the New Guineans had bipartisan political support, as the leader of the Labor Opposition, A.A. Calwell, made clear at the 1958 conference of the Australian Institute of Political Science. No one wanted an unpredictable independent state within sight of Queensland, particularly one that might depart from Australian ideas and ideals. Even the few interested academics endorsed Hasluck's *festina lente* paternalism: the Dean of Pacific Studies at the Australian National University commented at the same conference that Australia could thereby avoid 'the sort of crisis' (i.e. decolonization) facing Britain.[39]

However, the Territory could not be kept insulated from increasingly critical opinion in international forums, notably from United Nations Visiting Missions. In providing for detailed triennial inspections by multinational teams, the UN had made a salutary advance on the old Mandates system. Throughout the 1950s, successive UN Missions listened to indigenous opinion, which had been ignored by Australia, especially from the Tolai, among whom frustration simmered just below the surface.[40] These missions recommended the rapid extension of real local government institutions and, as a matter of priority, native courts.[41] By the end of the decade Australia was running out of arguments and time, while Papua New Guinea's legal establishment was, if anything, becoming even more die-hard in its resistance to any departure from English/Australian precedents. As one indication, in 1959 the new Chief Justice, Alan Mann (a Hasluck appointee), rejected outright the very limited proposal that indigenous assessors might assist in certain cases, as being 'quite inconsistent with our own legal practice'.[42]

With a new UN inspection pending, in 1961 Hasluck commissioned a conservative academic, Professor D.P. Derham, to make what was said to be an independent review of the Territory's legal system. Unsurprisingly, he recommended a quick move to the metropolitan model, with both blacks and whites being subject to the same courts applying the same laws. These courts would be separated completely from local authorities (and, therefore, from local inputs and influence). 'Allowance' for customary law could be made within this jurisdiction (though how that might be done was not spelled out). Indigenes were to be trained as magistrates for the regular courts – patently a long-term proposition.[43]

Such 'reforms' represented one further step along the road to decreed assimilation. They addressed none of the key problems, especially those of relevance and acceptability. They made the law even more remote, alien and mysterious: a fact made evident by the abolition (1963–66) of the old Courts for Native Matters, which, though run by white officials, at least had been basic in procedure and relatively open to village argument.

Efforts to implement Derham's recommendations conflicted with the general tenor of the highly critical report of the 1962 UN Mission, led by Britain's Sir Hugh Foot, a man of immense colonial experience. Foot stressed that the groundwork had to be laid, promptly, for self-government. To counter continued Australian resistance to devolution, he set target dates for an elected assembly, for the establishing of a university, for New Guineans to move into senior executive positions, and for the extension of genuine institutions of local government (including appropriate courts recognizing custom) to the whole indigenous population.[44]

For the rest of the 1960s, the Territory's exclusively white legal and administrative establishment struggled to give the appearance of respecting indigenous wishes and international demands, while evading the reality. But indigenous members of the House of Assembly (first elected in 1964 and expanded in 1968) increasingly succeeded in placing the focus on local issues, because of both electoral pressures and anti-centralist perceptions. Indigenes with limited education but strong personalities, such as Michael Somare and John Guise, gained experience as 'ministerial members', with access to the Executive Council.[45] It can well be argued that these first-generation nationalists had minds better attuned to village needs than many of their more highly educated successors. They helped to promote a new proposal for village courts. By the end of the decade a few indigenous magistrates, trained in the new Administrative College, had begun sitting in the existing courts; but they were hamstrung both by the continuing dominance of English jurisprudence and by their generally adjudicating, like their white colleagues, among peoples of whom they knew little. Official 'justice' continued to lack local legitimacy.

In 1970, the conservative government in Canberra began reflecting the views of a younger generation of politicians, and abruptly showed itself more amenable to the idea of a rapid progression to self-government in Papua New Guinea; and a new and more realistic Secretary for Law took office in Port Moresby. In 1971, only four years before the Territory's independence, he at last acknowledged the inappropriateness of the Derham 'reforms', and the Assembly approved legislation authorizing village courts, the introduction of which began in 1973. One of the consultants was Nigel Oram, formerly a senior official in British East Africa, who freely owned that these courts had serious defects.[46] Their jurisdiction, though ostensibly providing for custom and other village concerns, was whittled down by Crown Law insistence that they not 'infringe' on that of higher courts. Though their procedures were kept simple and professional lawyers were excluded, they had missed the generations of development, in line with acculturation, that had made the juridical arms of Britain's Native Authorities locally effective and acceptable.[47] Those stages could not be recreated. That was, and remains, the essential problem.

More than twenty years after independence Papua New Guinea retains a conservative Bar and judiciary steeped in colonial precedents. The ingrained traditions of centralized bureaucratic control have not been overcome.[48] In consequence, the official legal system continues to be widely regarded as something to be evaded; and the country has a chronic law-and-order problem, such that tourism is almost non-existent. As a resident journalist put it recently, 'the average Papua New Guinean does not have much faith in the current system of law.'[49] In fact, the legal system has been inherently dysfunctional from the early days of administration, with its motive forces being extraneous objectives, fears and paradigms – in defence of Australian interests – rather than the need to develop law and legal structures having intrinsic cultural meaning. Papua New Guinea's leaders continue to ponder how best to incorporate customary authority (now itself in flux) and to make local jurisdiction effective, in the face of a coercive, often incongruous, legal tradition.[50]

## Notes

1. The greatest comparative studies remain the two editions (London, 1938 and 1956) of Lord Hailey's *An African Survey*, which were ignored in Australia.

2. See Hailey, *An African Survey* (1956 edn), pp. 539–42, 611–16.

3. A.L. Epstein, 'Law, Indigenous', *Encyclopaedia of Papua New Guinea*, Melbourne, 1972, p. 632. Cf. F.K. Errington, *Karavar*, Ithaca, 1974, p. 73: 'Melanesians generally do not equate the code of law with order.'

4. E. Barker, *Ideas and Ideals of the British Empire*, Cambridge, revised edition 1951, p. 156; also Hailey, *An African Survey*, p. 201.

5. D.K. Fieldhouse, *The Colonial Empires*, London, 1966, p. 282; also see L.S.S. O'Malley (ed.), *Modern India and the West*, London, 1941, pp. 110–15; 622–4.

6. T.O. Elias, *Government and Politics in Africa*, London, 1961, pp. 117–64.

7. L.P. Mair, *Native Policies in Africa*, London, 1936, pp. 12–15.

8. Some relevant correspondence appeared in *Proceedings of the Royal Colonial Institute*, vol. XIV (1882–3), pp. 247–56.

9. A. Gordon to W.E. Gladstone, 20 April 1883, cited by P. Knaplund in *Historical Studies, Australia & New Zealand*, vol. VII, no. 27 (1956), p. 330.

10. H. McQueen, *The New Britannia*, Melbourne, 1970, p. 42.

11. The country's prime weekly journal for the intelligentsia, *The Bulletin* (founded 1880), was full of crude racism and warnings about 'the Yellow Peril'.

12. G.S. Fort, *Chance or Design*, London, 1942, p. 35.

13. W. MacGregor to A. Norman (Governor of Queensland), no. 71, 31 August 1889 – AAC: CP1 (Col), Set 6. MacGregor also looked ahead to the establishing of 'Native Magistrates' Courts'.

14. Native Regulation No. 1 of 1892, *Annual Report on British New Guinea, 1892–3* (Queensland Votes & Proceedings), p. vi.

15. In 1911, when he was in semi-retirement as Governor of Queensland, MacGregor urged a federal parliamentary delegation to institute a re-examination of native policy in Papua New Guinea. *Sydney Morning Herald*, 17 June 1911.

16. *Report of the Royal Commission into the Present Condition and Future*

*Administration of Papua*, Commonwealth Parliamentary Paper 6, 1907, p. 85.

17. *Annual Report on Papua, 1919–20* (Commonwealth Parliamentary Papers), p. 104; unpublished lecture on native administration, Mitchell Library, Sydney, A.3138, I, pp. 36–7, 42.

18. *Annual Report on Papua, 1937–8* (CPP), pp. 20–21.

19. F.E. Williams to H. Murray, 27 April 1925, AAC: CP1 (Col), Set 20, 16/42; Government Instruction 124, Port Moresby, 4 June 1925, Circ. 971/A123/25. When Malinowski proved critical, Murray tried to bar his re-entry to the colony; AAC: CP1 (Col), Set 20, 16/41; CP146, 21/866.

20. Lord Hailey's foreword to L.P. Mair, *Australia in New Guinea*, London, 1948, p. xvi.

21. S. Firth, *New Guinea under the Germans*, Melbourne, 1982, pp. 60–64, 105; *Report on German New Guinea, 1907–8* (typescript, trans. Thomson, AAC), p. 7. Firth underestimates the significance of Hahl's 'communes of local government': they left important legacies in key areas.

22. *Report on Administrative Arrangements and Matters Affecting the Interests of Natives in the Territory of New Guinea*, J. Ainsworth, Commonwealth Parliamentary Paper 109, 1924. Having commissioned this report, the federal government then ignored its recommendations, largely because they conflicted with the 'Murray Tradition'.

23. E.P. Wolfers, *Race Relations and Colonial Rule in Papua New Guinea*, Sydney, 1975, pp. 101–2.

24. W.E.H. Stanner, *The South Seas in Transition*, Sydney, 1953, p. 88.

25. M. Mead, *New Lives for Old*, London, 1956, pp. 166, 192–5. There were several 'dissident' movements, usually stigmatized by the Australians as cargo cults, though many of their methods and objectives were sound; but such exhibitions of 'primitiveness' reinforced the government argument for indefinite paternal control.

26. H.I. Hogbin, 'Local Government for New Guinea', *Oceania*, vol. XVII, no. 1 (1946), pp. 38–67. Hogbin recommended native courts to an official committee in Port Moresby in 1947 (DS 14/3/15). From his research in both New Guinea and the British Solomons, he knew that Native Authorities were workable in both, if government was sympathetic.

27. See B.E. Jinks, *Policy, Planning and Administration in Papua New Guinea, 1942–52*, Ph.D. thesis, Sydney University, 1975, p. 133.

28. J.B. Phillips to J.K. Murray, 11 October and 2 December 1946, DS 14/3/15 P.M.

29. See A.M. Healy, 'Local Government in the British Solomon Islands', *Journal of Administration Overseas*, vol. V, no. 3 (1966) pp. 194–205.

30. D. Fenbury, *Practice Without Policy*, Canberra, 1978, pp. 42, 55–9. He noted (p. 20) that ignorance was a determinant: none of these senior officials had even read Hailey.

31. The problem of introducing councils was exacerbated by the insistence of conservative officials, abetted by some missionaries, that indigenes not be 'forced' into local government, leading to a policy of 'voluntary

participation' (Director of Native Affairs to Asst. Administrator, 7 September 1955, NA 14/7/9 Port Moresby). This encouraged indigenous power plays, with pro and anti factions, and ultimately led to violence in the Gazelle peninsula.

32. Fenbury, *Practice Without Policy*, pp. 92–116; D. Fienberg to Director of Native Affairs, 22 October 1952, Rabaul 14/11/6/12–1. Rabaul was the most worrying area, because the refusal to sanction native courts further antagonized the Tolai, who had kept tribunals of their own going, openly or surreptitiously, since Hahl's time.

33. P.M.C. Hasluck, *Black Australians*, Melbourne, 1942. He was later honest enough to note that his only colonial knowledge came from one undergraduate history course on British colonies. P. Hasluck, *A Time for Building*, Melbourne, 1976, pp. 4–5.

34. He reiterated these views many times during the 1950s: e.g. *Australian Policy in Papua and New Guinea*, Sydney, 1956; *Australia's Task in Papua and New Guinea*, Perth, 1956. Also see his ministerial statement of 23 August 1960 (Territories, Canberra), esp. pp. 9–10.

35. Minister Hasluck to Secretary, Dept. of Territories, 27 January 1955, Territories file A 846/5/27, AAC.

36. Ibid.

37. C.J. Lynch to Senior Native Authorities Officer (a designation that was itself an atavistic misnomer), 17 August 1955, DS 14/3/15 Port Moresby.

38. P. Hasluck, 'Australian Policy in Papua and New Guinea', in J. Wilkes (ed.), *New Guinea and Australia*, Sydney, 1958, p. 92.

39. Wilkes, (ed.), *New Guinea and Australia*: Calwell's comments, pp. 118–22; those of Professor J.W. Davidson, p. 128.

40. In 1958 frustration among segments of the Tolai led to an attack on the District Commissioner and his party. The report of the resulting official inquiry, by the Chief Justice, was so obtuse and authoritarian that it dismayed even some senior administrators. A.H. Mann, *Enquiry into the Navuneram Incident of 4th August 1958*, mimeo., Port Moresby.

41. *Report of the Visiting Mission to the Trust Territory of New Guinea*, 1953, T/1078, paras. 62–5. Ditto, 1956, T/1260, para. 216. In 1956 the Belgian delegate said he thought the prompt establishing of native courts 'a matter of first importance' (General Assembly Official Records, 11th Session, A/3170, Supp. 4, p. 305).

42. C.J. Mann to Secretary, Law Dept., Port Moresby, 4 May 1959, CJ/59, J1/59.

43. D.P. Derham, *Report on the System for the Administration of Justice in the Territory of Papua and New Guinea*, 21 December 1960, Dept. of Territories, Canberra. Cf. Fenbury's comments, *Practice Without Policy*, pp. 116–36.

44. *Report of the U.N. Visiting Mission to the Trust Territory of New Guinea*, 1962, T/1597; and A.M. Healy, 'The Foot Report and East New

Guinea', *Australian Quarterly*, vol. XXXIV, no. 1 (1962), pp. 11–22.

45. J. Griffin et al., *Papua New Guinea – A Political History*, Richmond, Vic., 1979, p. 145.

46. N. Oram, 'Grass Roots Justice: Village Courts in Papua New Guinea', in W. Clifford (ed.), *Innovations in Criminal Justice in Asia and the Pacific*, Canberra, 1979, p. 66.

47. Ibid., pp. 69, 72–6.

48. In the late 1970s a young New Guinean who headed the Law Reform Commission, Bernard Narokobi, tried and failed to incorporate 'Melanesian law' in the inherited colonial system. Colin Blair, 'White Justice on Trial', *The Australian*, 6 August 1979.

49. Mary-Louise O'Callaghan, 'Canute-like Wingti and the PNG Crime Wave', *Sydney Morning Herald*, 2 August 1993.

50. It is now said officially that local institutions are to be established 'in accordance with indigenous wishes and traditions' – a century late. *Post Courier*, Port Moresby, 19 August 1993.

# 14

# Defining Separate Spheres: German Rule and Colonial Law in Micronesia

GERD HARDACH

An ancient myth tells us that a harmonious society needs no law: 'Golden was that first age, which, with no one to compel, without a law, of its own will, kept faith and did the right.'[1] Colonial law expressed colonial tension; it was certainly a law for a society that was less than perfect. But colonial law not only defined the terms of domination and colonial exploitation; it also introduced new modes of conflict resolution, notions of individual freedom, and modern property rights, and thus changed the structure of indigenous societies. The interaction between Europeans and Pacific islanders has been described as a range of 'subtle encounters', a series of social, economic, legal, religious and educational exchanges 'that proceeded with both conflict and cooperation, and which in the process were changing all parties'.[2] This chapter focuses on some legal encounters on the islands; it is neither a systematic exposition of German colonial law, nor an attempt to summarize the vast body of ethnological research on custom and law in Micronesian societies.

## Occupation

On 15 October 1885, the German flag was hoisted on Jaluit atoll in the Ralik group.[3] Captain Rötger, the commanding officer of the warship *Nautilus*, read a declaration which placed the Marshall

Islands, including Brown Island (Enewetak) and Providence Island (Ujelang), under German 'protection'.[4] An attempt to occupy the Caroline Islands failed; Spain claimed earlier rights as a colonial power. The interest that brought Germany to the Pacific was the copra trade. Copra production on the Pacific islands was always small compared to the yield of the large plantations in Indonesia and the Philippines, yet some German companies could earn substantial profits by exploiting local resources. Trade stations and plantations were established in Samoa, New Guinea and the adjacent islands, and Micronesia. Pressed by the trading companies operating in the region, Germany annexed the north-east part of New Guinea in 1884 and the Marshall Islands in 1885.

Following the Spanish–American war of 1898, when the United States occupied the Philippines and Guam, Germany acquired the remaining Spanish possessions in Micronesia in February 1899. In autumn 1899, a German mission under Rudolf von Bennigsen, the governor of German New Guinea, travelled through Micronesia on the warship *Jaguar* and the steamer *Kudat* to take over the Carolines, Belau and the Marianas. The Spanish administrative centres on Pohnpei, Yap and Saipan, tiny remnants of an empire where once the sun had never set, were chosen for the official ceremonies announcing the transfer of sovereignty. On Pohnpei, on 13 October 1899, Governor von Bennigsen read the imperial decree which placed the Carolines and Marianas under German 'protection'.[5] He added a short speech: 'Now the flag of the German Reich waves forever over these islands, to the glory of the Reich and as a bulwark against enemies. She will bring to this land under German administration the desired happiness and a long-missed peace. But the people of this island should remember from this moment on to be loyal subjects of our beloved *Kaiser* and King.'[6] Similar ceremonies took place on 3 November 1899 on Yap for the Western Carolines including Belau, and on 17 November 1899 on Saipan for the Northern Marianas.

The flag-raising rituals and the declarations of 'protection' were symbolic actions, celebrated for the benefit of the colonizers rather than the colonized, and duly recorded to confirm Germany's claim to the new territory. Some islanders who happened to be on the spot watched the ceremony, but the full meaning may have escaped them. Sooner or later, however, Micronesians even in the remoter islands were to learn that these strange rituals affected their lives; the new flag brought new ways of living, and new ways of thinking.

## Colonial Administration

Germany was a reluctant colonial power. Colonies were established in response to the pressure exerted by commercial interest groups, and the government was not prepared to invest seriously in the administration and development of the new territories. In the political sphere, the acquisition of the colonies was far more important than their administration. The Colonial Department in the German Foreign Office, and from 1907 the German Colonial Office, had a comparatively lowly rank among the imperial and Prussian ministries, and was notoriously short of staff and funds. The prevalent doctrine was that private companies should develop the colonial economies, and defray the cost of the local administration. After the annexation of the Marshall Islands, the main German trading companies in that part of the world, Robertson & Hernsheim and the Deutsche Handels- und Plantagengesellschaft, founded the Jaluit-Gesellschaft AG in 1887 to organize the economic exploitation of the new colony. In 1888 a treaty was signed establishing a condominium of the German government and the Jaluit company in the Marshall Islands. An imperial commissioner in Jaluit was to be appointed by the German government, but all administrative costs, including the salaries of the officials, were to be paid by the Jaluit company.[7] The company regarded the Marshall Islands very much as its own colony. The colonial officers in Jaluit would occasionally protest against this state of affairs, but the Colonial Department in Berlin backed the company's claims. The German administration of the Marshall Islands was extremely small. In the early years the imperial commissioner, who had held the impressive title of a *Landeshauptmann* since 1893, ruled his island territory with the help of one secretary. By the time the condominium agreement between the German government and the Jaluit-Gesellschaft came to an end in 1906, the staff of the administration on Jaluit had doubled from two to four officials.

The Carolines and the Marianas were attached to the colony of German New Guinea as an 'island territory'; the German government had taken over the administration of the colony from the

Neu-Guinea-Compagnie in April 1899.[8] Following the Spanish example, the island territory was divided into three districts, the Eastern Carolines, the Western Carolines including Belau, and the Marianas. The administrators were Albert Hahl on Pohnpei, who was also vice-governor of the whole island territory, *Bezirksamtmann* Arno Senfft on Yap, and *Bezirksamtmann* Georg Fritz on Saipan.[9] When vice-governor Albert Hahl became governor of New Guinea in 1902, the plan to govern the island territory from Pohnpei was abandoned. Communications were poor in the island territory, and a vice-governor on Pohnpei had no more control over the *Bezirksamtmann* on Yap and Saipan than the governor in Herbertshöhe. The administration in the Carolines and in the Marianas was as small as that in the Marshall Islands. Early in the twentieth century the three administrative centres had a total staff of fourteen, including government physicians, medics and a crew of three seamen for the government schooner. When the German officials took over the administration of the Carolines and Marianas in 1899, they brought with them a small force of policemen who had been hired in the Dutch Indies and in German New Guinea; it was common practice in the German colonial empire for colonial soldiers and policemen not to be recruited from the people whom they were supposed to control. But this precaution proved unnecessary in Micronesia, and the Indonesians and Melanesians were soon replaced by local police. No German warships or military personnel were stationed in Micronesia. In a serious conflict, the colonial administration could call in warships and German marines from the naval station in Jiao-zhou (Kiaochow).

The colonial reform of 1906–10, a consequence of the failure of German colonial policy in Africa, revived the interest of the German government in its Pacific colonies. Bernhard Dernburg, who was head of the Colonial Department of the Foreign Office in 1906–07 and Secretary of the new Colonial Office from 1907 to 1910, propagated a new ideology of 'scientific colonialism', which emphasized social change and economic development in the colonial empire. The colonies, with their vast potential of labour, land and mineral resources, were intended to become important producers and exporters of food and raw materials, and markets for industrial exports.[10] The German government affirmed, somewhat belatedly, its interest in the distant Pacific colonies. There was, in the years from 1906 to 1914, a new emphasis on administrative efficiency, on economic development and on increasing revenues from taxation. The administration of Micronesia was reorganized; political control shifted from the local administrators in the islands to the governor of New Guinea. When the Australian firm of Burns, Philp & Co. protested against the exclusive privileges of the Jaluit-Gesellschaft, which violated the Anglo-German agreement of 1886, the German government seized the opportunity to cancel the treaty of 1888 and terminate the condominium of the state and the Jaluit company. The Marshall Islands were integrated into the island territory in 1906, and Jaluit became a district office under the authority of the governor of New Guinea.[11] In 1911, the district office on Jaluit was reduced to a station, and the Marshall Islands were now governed from the district office on Pohnpei.[12] In western Micronesia, the district office on Saipan was changed to a station in 1907, and the Marianas came under the authority of the district office on Yap.[13]

In the early years, the district offices were the only administrative posts in the island territory. Sometimes chiefs or other local people of importance were appointed as representatives of the German rulers. On his second visit to Belau, in 1901, *Bezirksamtmann* Senfft installed James Gibbon, an immigrant from Jamaica, as his deputy. In the Truk Group the *Bezirksamtmann* from Pohnpei appointed six high chiefs as his representatives in 1903.[14] After a few years, however, the consolidation of power and the rise of phosphate mining on Nauru and Angaur made it necessary to install some form of German authority on the major islands, even if it was represented only by a lonely station officer and a few local policemen. Stations were established on Belau in 1905, Nauru in 1906, Truk in 1909, and Angaur in 1910.

After the reorganization, the island territory was governed by district offices on Pohnpei and Yap, and stations on Angaur, Belau, Jaluit, Nauru, Saipan and Truk. The administration employed a total staff of 25 German officials in 1912, including not only administrators but also government physicians, medics, seamen, and two German teachers at the new government school on Saipan.[15] This small group of expatriate Germans was supposed to govern a vast island territory which stretched over 3,700 km from Sonsorol in the Belau Group to Miti in the Marshall Islands, and 2,200 km from the southern Caroline atoll of Kapingamarangi to Farallón de Pájaros in the northern Marianas.[16] Germany's Micronesian empire is today divided into four states and one territory: the Republic of Belau, the Republic of the Marshall Islands, the Federated States of Micronesia, the Republic of Nauru, and the Commonwealth of the Northern Marianas. The German administrators in the island territory issued decrees, travelled to the various islands on the small government ship that was at their disposal, on trading vessels or on visiting German warships, explained the new state of affairs to the people, and settled local quarrels. The district offices and stations were sufficient, with the East Asia squadron stationed at Kiaochow in the background, to maintain Germany's colonial rule. 'Islanders could be cowed by superior force and transformed into acquiescent subjects of a colonial power. They knew the powers that Europeans could wield.'[17] But it was obvious that the small group of German officials could not exercise close administrative control over their island territory. To be governed effectively, the island societies had to govern themselves.

### Law and Order

When Wilhelm Solf, the last colonial secretary in Berlin, wrote an article in defence of German colonialism in 1916, he insisted that all the colonies had been 'legitimately acquired'.[18] What he had in mind was obviously not some kind of social contract between colonizers and colonized, but the system of international custom and law by which the imperialist powers defined the rules of the game. International law specified exploration, missionary activity, trade and other claims on which colonial acquisitions could legitimately be based. It laid down certain standards of administration and jurisdiction that had to be maintained, and regulated access to the economic resources of the colonies. Legitimate colonial rule did not require any form of consent by the colonized. Even liberal politicians like Bernhard Dernburg and Wilhelm Solf, who stood for colonial reform, justified colonial rule on the presumption of 'white' superiority and 'coloured' inferiority. Colonialism was inherently racist.[19] Racism was not necessarily displayed in prejudices, insulting language or aggressive behaviour against indigenous peoples. There were other, more sophisticated colonialist ideologies that were no less discriminatory: the settler ideology of industrious traders and plantation owners who put indolent 'natives' into gainful employment; the favourite administrative self-portrait of patriarchal officials and responsive children; the Christian image of benevolent missionaries and simple-minded heathens; and its secularized version, acceptable to liberals and even to socialists, of enlightened colonizers who led the colonized onto the road of civilization. And finally, there were the legislators, bringing law and order to primitive people. These ideologies offered images not only for the colonizers to identify with but also, it was hoped, for the colonized, who had the prospect of evolution and salvation. But if colonial law was imposed, it nevertheless had to be accepted by Pacific islanders, if law and order was to be maintained in the islands' territory without a large repressive force.

German colonial law defined separate legal spheres for colonizers and colonized. 'White' people were subject to laws, decrees and institutions that satisfied the standards of the civilized community of nations. Indigenous 'coloured' people were excluded from the sphere of civilized law, and were subject to a legal system of an inferior standard.[20] The discrimination applied to laws and decrees as well as to courts and legal procedure. Germans who lived in Micronesia, and other foreign residents from countries of European culture, were privileged by comparison with the indigenous Micronesians. The status of immigrants from non-European cultures defied easy classification. In the early years of German colonialism, in controversial cases the governors decided the legal status of foreign residents in their colony. By 1900, however, the situation had become so confused that the decision was vested in the German government. An imperial decree defined Japanese citizens who lived in the German colonies as 'white' people.[21] Chinese citizens, however, had the inferior legal status of 'coloured' people. In the twisted logic of colonialism, this strange discrimination was reasonable, and even necessary. Japanese traders and labourers in Micronesia had to be 'white' as they were citizens of an imperialist power. The Chinese were colonial subjects in Kiaochow, Germany's small colony on the Chinese coast, and thus had to be defined as 'coloured'. Citizenship in Germany's colonial empire corresponded to the definition of separate legal spheres; Germans who resided in the colonies were 'imperial subjects' (*Reichsangehörige*), while the indigenous people had the inferior status of 'colonial subjects' (*Schutzgebietsangehörige*).[22]

The definition of separate spheres was rigid, and there were few exceptions. In select cases the German government could promote 'colonial subjects' to 'imperial subjects'. In the Mariana Islands the prominent Chamorro merchant Pedro Ada and his wife obtained imperial German citizenship in 1905, and became members of the 'white' population.[23] But these cases of naturalization were rare. Micronesian women who married German men became 'imperal subjects' and members of the 'white' community. Thus Mrs Capelle, the Marshallese wife of the German trader Adolph Capelle, was a Prussian citizen and *Reichsangehörige*, and their children inherited this citizenship.[24] In the early years, the colonial administration's attitude towards intercultural marriages between German men and indigenous women was fairly neutral, probably because their number was so small. Early in the twentieth century, however, when there were more Germans in the colonies and opportunities for contact multiplied, the official attitude became more restrictive. The administration feared that frequent intercultural marriages would endanger racial segregation and the myth of 'white' superiority. This applied not only to the few Germans but also to the many Japanese who wanted to marry Micronesian partners. In a specific case in 1908, the *Bezirksamtmann* on Saipan refused to register a marriage between a Chamorro woman and a Japanese man. Father Callistus, a German Capuchin who was the parish priest of Garapan, protested against the decision, but the governor of New Guinea confirmed that marriages between 'white' and 'coloured' people should not be registered.[25] Intercultural marriages remained a controversial issue during the last years of Germany's colonial rule. It was questionable whether the prohibition was legitimate; and the missions requested repeatedly that the ban should be lifted. They argued that it was morally objectionable for the government to prevent couples who lived together anyway from getting married. The children of unmarried intercultural couples had the status of 'coloured' people.[26]

Europeans and other 'white' people in the German colonies were subject to German civil and criminal law. In addition there were special colonial by-laws, which were issued not by the ordinary parliamentary procedure, but in the form of executive decrees. The foundation for this form of colonial legislation by decree was the colonial law of 1886, amended in 1888, and again in 1900. This law, which has been described as the 'constitutional law' of the colonies, vested considerable power in the executive.[27] Most colonial matters, including taxes and import duties, were regulated not by parliamentary laws but by executive decrees.

To satisfy international standards at that time, courts had to be independent of the executive. But there were few places in the German colonial empire that possessed a court with professional judges. Legal procedure in the colonies, in civil and criminal cases, was therefore an abbreviated process, based on the German consular law of 1879. Like the consuls in distant ports where no professional lawyer was at hand, the German *Bezirksamtmänner* acted as judges. They were supported by two or four assessors, depending on the importance of the case, appointed from the local 'white' community of government officials, traders, settlers, captains and missionaries. The assessors did not necessarily have to be German citizens.[28]

The judicial institutions in Micronesia were almost identical with its administrative structure. In the Marshall Islands, Germany's first Micronesian colony, an imperial court was established on Jaluit in 1886, and a higher court as a court of the second instance, also on Jaluit, in 1890. The judge in the court of the first instance was one of the lower-ranking officials, while the imperial commissioner acted as judge in the court of the second instance. Four assessors and their deputies were selected from the local 'white' population to assist in the more important cases. Not only German administrators and traders but also American missionaries were appointed as assessors to the Jaluit courts.[29] When the Carolines and the Marianas came under German rule, district courts were established on Pohnpei, Yap and Saipan. Assessors were appointed, as in the two Jaluit courts, from the local 'white' population. On Saipan, *Bezirksamtmann* Fritz appointed not only Spanish missionaries but also prominent Chamorros as assessors. When the Colonial Department insisted that assessors must be 'white', Fritz appointed the Chamorro merchant Pedro Ada, who had become a German 'imperial citizen'.[30] Saipan seems to have been the only court in the island territory with Micronesian assessors during the German era. The court of appeal for the Carolines and Marianas was the higher imperial court (*Kaiserliches Obergericht*), with a professional judge, in New Guinea.

The reforms of 1906–11 centralized not only the administration but also the judicial system. The imperial court in Jaluit became a district court in 1906, and the higher court on Jaluit was abolished;

the appeal court for the Marshall Islands was now the higher imperial court in Herbertshöhe, New Guinea. In 1911 the district court on Jaluit was abolished; the Marshall Islands came under the jurisdiction of the court on Pohnpei.[31] The district court on Saipan was abolished in 1907, and the Marianas came under the jurisdiction of the court on Yap.[32] In 1908 the German parliament suggested that a supreme colonial court should be established in Germany (*Kolonialgerichtshof*) as a court of the third instance for all colonies. The government agreed, but the war broke out before it could be established.[33]

As the 'white' jurisdiction applied only to Europeans, Americans and Japanese, its impact was always small. Micronesia was not a favoured place for immigration and settlement in those years. On the whole, the foreign communities were quite peaceful. Occasionally the *Bezirksamtmann* would impose a fine in his capacity as judge, but a court session was a rare event. The lower court in Jaluit heard on average three cases a year from 1891 to 1900; no cases at all came before the higher court.[34] The situation in the Carolines and Marianas seems to have been much the same as it had been in the earlier years in the Marshall Islands. In 1910 the district courts in Pohnpei, Jaluit and Yap together heard only four cases.[35]

In the sphere of 'coloured' law, which applied to Micronesians, traditional indigenous law co-existed with imported German law. As the colonial administration was founded on co-operation with indigenous holders of authority and power, and on the acquiescence of the people, it respected traditional custom and law as long as these did not conflict with German concepts of law and order, or with important objectives of colonial policy. The German government, and the subordinate levels of the colonial administration, could at any time by their own decree replace the indigenous customs and laws by German law and legal procedure. It was also possible for judges and courts to decide on their own initiative to apply German laws in 'native' affairs.

Learning was a reciprocal process. While the administrators explained to the islanders the essentials of German colonial law, they themselves had to become acquainted with the structure of Micronesian societies and their legal systems. Colonial officials investigated the customs and laws of their island realms. Sometimes they reported their findings to the Colonial Office. As indigenous laws, originally an oral tradition, were written down, they became available for systematic research. In 1888, Dr Hammacher, a member of the imperial diet, suggested that the Colonial Department should collect the indigenous laws of the German colonies. In 1893, two professional lawyers, Felix Meyer and Albert Hermann Post, began a comparative study of indigenous laws in the colonies of different European powers. It was published ten years later.[36] In 1893 Josef Kohler, a professor of comparative law at the University of Berlin, proposed to undertake a comprehensive study of indigenous laws in the German colonies. He designed a detailed questionnaire, with 100 items, to collect information from colonial officials, missionaries and other experts. The Colonial Department sent Kohler's questionnaire to several officials in the colonies.[37] Kohler himself, who was influenced by Bachofen and Morgan, published several articles on the customs and laws of the people in Germany's colonial empire; these studies were based on information that he received from colonial officials and missionaries.

The study of indigenous customs and laws was resumed with new vigour in 1907, when the German parliament asked the government to collect and publish the traditional laws in the German colonies in Africa and the Pacific.[38] The new Colonial Office established an academic committee under Kohler, and sent an updated version of Kohler's questionnaire to adminstrators and missionaries in the German colonies. A wealth of information was collected. No results were published before 1914, however, and with the end of Germany's colonial empire the government lost interest in the project. For several years the material gathered dust in the archives, until Ernst Schultz-Ewerth and Leonhard Adam resumed the edition in 1925. A first volume, exclusively on East Africa, was published in 1929, and a second volume was published in 1930, with articles on Kamerun, South West Africa, Togo, New Guinea, Micronesia and Samoa.[39] The publication contains an impressive collection of the traditional law of Belau, Yap, Truk, Pohnpei and Nauru.[40] Another important contribution to the collection and codification of traditional law in Micronesia was the field work of the Hamburg South Sea Expedition in 1908–10. Early in this century, old customs and traditions were declining rapidly, so the anthropologists of the South Sea Expedition devoted much of their research in Micronesia to the written registration of oral traditions.[41]

Reports by German administrators, missionaries and anthropologists provide invaluable clues to the history of Micronesia. However, they were published long after the end of Germany's colonial adventure. Colonial officials and courts in the few isolated administrative stations in German Micronesia depended on their own knowledge of indigenous custom and law, unsupported by anthropologists or academic lawyers. The German administrators and lawyers of the time thought in terms of legal universalism, a unilinear evolution from 'primitive' to 'modern' law.[42] The earlier stages were measured by modern standards, and some elements of indigenous laws were found to be more acceptable than others. One part of traditional custom and law generally regarded as incompatible with German standards of justice was the jurisdiction of chiefs in criminal cases. In the Marshall Islands, the German government immediately abolished the jurisdiction of the chiefs, and in 1890 it introduced a penal code that was a condensed version of German criminal law.[43] In some Caroline Island societies the chiefs retained the right to impose fines for minor offences, but all criminal cases of any importance were decided by German judges and courts according to German law. Traditional patterns of land tenure, and family and inheritance law were more acceptable than criminal law, and in some Micronesian communities they applied until the end of the German era.

The 'native courts' (*Eingeborenengerichte*) were a part of the administration, not an independent institution. In civil law cases the *Bezirksamtmann*, or the lower-ranking station officer, passed judgement with the help of a clerk. In criminal cases the court would consist of the *Bezirksamtmann* or *Stationsleiter* and two assessors, drawn from the local 'white' population.[44] In 1908 the German parliament voted for a separation of the 'native courts' from the administration, but even the Liberal Party (*Freisinnige*), which had initiated the resolution, assumed that the installation of an independent judiciary could only be achieved in the long run. For the time being, it was argued, only the local administration had the necessary knowledge of the 'customs and laws' of the indigenous people.[45] Over the years the impact of imported laws and legal procedure increased. German jurisdiction curbed the power of chiefs, abolished punishments that were incompatible with European standards, and redefined land rights.

**Table 1** Population of Micronesia under German Rule

|                  | 1900   | 1910   |
|------------------|--------|--------|
| Caroline Islands | 37,600 | 32,500 |
| Mariana Islands  | 1,900  | 3,200  |
| Marshall Islands | 15,000 | 10,800 |
| Total            | 54,500 | 46,500 |

*Sources: Jahresbericht über die Entwicklung der deutschen Schutzgebiete* 1899/1900, pp. 209–18. *Jahresbericht* 1900/01, pp. 92–5. *Jahresbericht* 1901/02, pp. 104–5, 258. Bericht des Bezirksamts Jap an das Reichskolonialamt, 5 August 1910. Politisches Archiv des Auswärtigen Amtes Bonn, I A Südsee 16, Bd. 2.

## Transition

Throughout the German era, Micronesia was an agglomeration of small peasant societies. The Marshall Islands had an estimated population of 15,000 in the early years of German domination, scattered over the 34 atolls and coral islands of the Ralik and Ratak chains. Population figures were reported year after year, without much belief in their accuracy.[46] When the Carolines and the Marianas had been acquired, the population of German Micronesia was, according to official estimates, 54,500 people in 1900. The population declined to 46,500 in 1910. The figures were only approximations, but the trend was real enough; contemporary observers agreed that the population of Micronesia declined during the German era.

In terms of social and authority structures, Micronesia lay somewhere between Germany's two other Pacific colonies, New Guinea and Samoa.[47] The Micronesian societies of the Caroline Islands and the Marshall Islands had a rigid class structure and organized political leadership. German administrators who used the established patterns of authority for their own purposes found these societies easier to govern than the fragmented and elusive Melanesian communities of New Guinea. However, power was decentralized in Micronesia. There was no indigenous central authority either in the Carolines or the Marshall Islands. The chiefs ruled over small islands, or districts of islands. Nowhere did Micronesian societies attain the sophisticated pattern of status and power that German administrators found so congenial in Polynesian Samoa. Where traditional systems of authority were still in force, Micronesian chiefs combined political leadership, control of the land, jurisdiction and, in some instances, religious authority. The imposition of colonial law meant more than new laws and different legal procedures; it was a transition between two complex modes of authority, from the indigenous system of paramount chiefs to a modern system of functional differentiation. The German administration deconstructed traditional patterns of authority and integrated the segments into a modern, secular system of governance, property rights and jurisdiction.

The terms of the transition from a traditional to a modern mode of authority depended not only on colonial policy but also on the structure of indigenous societies. The Marshall Islands were ruled by a class of higher chiefs (*irodj*) and lower chiefs (*burak*). Previously the *irodj* had exerted some kind of authority over the *burak* and could request their support in warfare, but in the German era the ancient ties fell into disuse. The *irodj* enjoyed higher prestige, but in every other respect the *burak* were chiefs in their own right. The common people (*kadjur*) worked the land, fished, and produced all the other necessities of life. The chiefs claimed ownership of the land and exacted from their retainers a tribute that amounted to half of the produce of the land and the sea. Between the chiefs and the commoners was a class of people whose status was not clearly defined (*leodakedak*). They depended upon the chiefs, but had special skills, for example as navigators, which set them apart from the commoners. Status was passed from generation to generation by matrilineal descent. German observers tried to translate the Marshallese social structure into the familiar categories of European feudalism. Kohler, whose study of Marshallese law was based on reports supplied by the imperial commissioner in Jaluit and his deputy, described the different social strata as sovereign (*irodj*), aristocracy (*burak*), gentry (*leodakedak*) and commoners (*kadjur*).[48] Erdland, as well as Krämer and Nevermann, divided the society into two orders, nobility and commoners, each with two sub-strata; thus there was a higher nobility (*irodj*) and a lower nobility (*burak*), there were higher commoners (*leodakedak*) and lower commoners (*kadjur*).[49] The German administration confirmed the status of the chiefs and transformed the traditional pattern of power and wealth into individual property rights. The higher and lower chiefs of the Marshall Islands were recognized as legitimate owners of the land. A land register was established in Jaluit, and all claims were entered in it. All the land in the Marshall Islands that was not owned by Europeans was the property of the chiefs. The commoners were reduced to the status of tenants.[50]

Under the new conditions, the Marshallese chiefs derived rising money incomes from their control of the land. The peasant producers sold the copra crop to the Jaluit company. The chiefs, who knew the yield of the land, collected from their tenants their six months' share in cash. Tax collection provided an additional income. The Marshallese peasants had to pay a tax in kind to the colonial administration. The collection of the tax was entrusted to the chiefs, who would receive one-third of the proceeds as a commission. In the early 1890s some chiefs owned 20–30,000 Marks in cash, a considerable amount for the time. The new mode of authority was profitable for the chiefs, and suited the colonial administration, whose power was supported by the traditional pattern of dependency. The burden of the compromise between local elites, colonial administrators and the Jaluit company fell on the peasants, who lived in miserable conditions. A contemporary observer described in detail how the chiefs, whose position was protected by the colonial administration, betrayed their authority and ruined the people by greed and sexual abuse. Oppressed by their chiefs and neglected by the colonial administration, the Marshallese succumbed to imported epidemics and venereal diseases.[51] Unimpaired by the administrative reform of 1906, which brought the Marshall Islands under the control of the governor of New Guinea, the alliance between local chiefs, colonial administrators and the Jaluit-Gesellschaft continued to test the patience of the Marshallese. In retrospect, Albert Hahl stated that the Marshall Islands were a 'peaceful and well-regulated group of islands'.[52] No change was therefore introduced in the system of 'native administration' of the Marshall Islands, which had 'functioned satisfactorily for years'.[53]

The Caroline Islands shared the Micronesian type of class structure and chiefly authority, but in many other respects the larger island societies of Belau, Kosrae, Pohnpei, Truk and Yap, as well as the innumerable small atoll communities, were quite different from the Marshall Islands, and often from each other. Pohnpei had a reputation for offering effective resistance to the forceful imposition of colonial rule, and Belau, Truk and Yap were also known to be hostile to foreign influence. The chiefs represented the old ways of living. They were not easily drawn into the capitalist world of commerce and wealth, and were much less amenable to German rule than those in the Marshall Islands. It was typical that Henry Nanpei, a wealthy Pohnpeian with the business acumen of the Marshallese chiefs and excellent connections to the German administration, had nowhere to go in the complicated Pohnpeian system of status and rank. Treading on unknown ground, the German administrators in the Carolines, vice-governor Hahl on Pohnpei and *Bezirksamtmann* Senfft on Yap, proceeded carefully. They established their authority first in their district centres, and then gradually extended their influence to other islands. Together with paramount political authority, the colonial administration claimed exclusive jurisdiction in all important cases of criminal and civil law. In criminal law, indigenous customs were replaced by German law, but in civil law the traditional patterns of land rights and inheritance were respected.

Pohnpei, where Micronesians had forcefully resisted Spanish colonial rule, became the focus of co-operation and conflict in the Caroline Islands during the German era. Vice-governor Hahl had carefully sought the co-operation of the powerful district chiefs of Kiti, Madolenihmw, Net, Sokehs and Uh. In 1901, when Victor Berg, administrator on Pohnpei from 1901 to 1907, suggested an ambitious scheme of colonial development and cultural change, the Colonial Department vetoed his plans and insisted that he should follow the 'quiet and appropriate appearance of Hahl'.[54] The moderate policy on Pohnpei was successful. The administration encountered no resistance, internal fighting between the districts ceased, and the new system of law and order was apparently well received by the Pohnpeians.

The event which unsettled the compromise between colonizers and colonized, and finally led to revolt and repression on Pohnpei, was the new doctrine of 'scientific colonialism' with its emphasis on close administrative control and colonial development. Hahl himself, who had set the standard for a moderate approach on Pohnpei, thought that the time had now come for a more determined policy. During a visit to Pohnpei in 1907, he announced a programme of social change and economic development. The key objective was a reform that would transfer the ownership of the land from the chiefs to the peasants. Hahl thought that the Pohnpeian peasants were more likely than their conservative chiefs to engage in market-oriented copra production. The new policy was implemented by Georg Fritz, the former *Bezirksamtmann* of Saipan, who came to Pohnpei in 1908. The land reform made the Pohnpeian peasants individual owners of their farms. Instead of the traditional tributes in kind to the chiefs, Pohnpeians had to pay a tax to the district office, in the form of 15 days of unpaid labour per year. The chiefs were to receive half of the money equivalent of the labour tax as compensation for their loss of privileges and income. The new labour tax was widely resented; thus the land reform did not enjoy the popular support that Hahl and Fritz had expected. Impatient with the slow progress of the reform, the Colonial Office replaced Fritz with the more aggressive *Bezirksamtmann* Gustav Boeder in 1910. It was Boeder's harsh implementation of the labour tax scheme which started the Sokehs rebellion of 1910–11. The rebellion was brutally suppressed. Fifteen Sokehs leaders were summarily tried, and executed by firing squad in February 1911. The gruesome details of the execution were long remembered on Pohnpei. The Sokehs people – more than four hundred men, women and children – were exiled first to Yap, and then to Belau. The women and children stayed on Babeldaob, while the men were sent to work in the phosphate mine on Angaur. After the defeat of the Sokehs, the land reform on Pohnpei was rapidly concluded. Pohnpeian peasants became the owners of the land. Inheritance of land was changed from matrilineal descent to the particular north German pattern that the land went undivided to the oldest male heir of the owner. The chiefs lost control over the land, but retained some degree of political authority within the German administrative system.[55]

The Sokehs rebellion with its tragic consequences was the result of the Colonial Office's and governor Hahl's haste in implementing their colonial development programme, and of the impetuous behaviour of *Bezirksamtmann* Boeder in dealing with the Pohnpeians. It was not inevitable. On Belau, Kosrae, Truk and Yap the German administration was much more careful in adjusting its policies to local circumstances. On some of the smaller atolls the intervention could be more ruthless, when there was no resistance to be feared. In a vast migration scheme, more than a thousand Carolinians were transported from their small atolls to the Marianas, with disastrous consequences. On the other hand, some islands in the Carolines were never really reached by Germany's administrative efforts, and seem to have been none the worse for it. Kapingamarangi, the southernmost atoll of the Carolines, is now part of the state of Pohnpei in the Federated States of Micronesia. In the German era Kapingamarangi belonged administratively to the 'old protectorate' of New Guinea, not to the island territory; but the difference was purely academic, as neither the governor in Herbertshöhe, nor the *Bezirksamtmann* on Pohnpei was visible to the islanders. Early in the twentieth century, the island was closely integrated into the Pacific trading system. 'First visited by a government official in April 1914, Kapingamarangi was the exclusive preserve of the Mouton company under a concession of 1902, its population of about 350 trading copra for the biscuits, sugar, tinned meat and other European commodities stocked by the Mouton trader.'[56] Domestically it seems to have been a self-contained, harmonious community. This, at least, is how the anthropologist Anneliese Eilers, whose study was based on the results of the Hamburg South Sea Expedition in 1909–10, describes the island society.[57] The people, numbering only 282 at the time of the visit, called their atoll *tenuv*, meaning 'the land', indicating that they regarded it as the centre of their world. The study described the people of *tenuv* as extremely neat and tidy, as well as friendly, engaging, hospitable and helpful. At the top of the island hierarchy was 'King' Davbi, 'an elderly, respectable, reliable man'.[58] He ruled by natural authority rather than by power. As the people were law-abiding and friendly, there was no need for strong leadership. Important decisions were taken by all the adult men of the community. As the character of the people leads us to expect, relations within the community were friendly and engaging. There seems to have been no criminal law; at least, it was not mentioned. Norms governing property rights, gifts and lending were the same as elsewhere in the South Pacific.

The Marianas were different from all the other Micronesian societies, as the indigenous Chamorro culture had long since been Europeanized.[59] The political structure was the same as in the Philippines, a colonial municipal system under the supervision of the Spanish authorities. With few exceptions, the German administration maintained the municipal structure that had been established in the Spanish era. The population of the only two inhabited islands lived in three villages, Garapan and Tanapag on the west coast of Saipan, and Rota on the western tip of the island of the same name. Georg Fritz, the *Bezirksamtmann* on Saipan from 1899 to 1907, intended to transform his three villages into a model Pacific colony. The land of Chamorro and Carolinian peasants was carefully registered. The *Bezirksamtmann* encouraged the extension of coconut cultivation as a cash crop, introduced medical care, and established the only government school in German Micronesia, situated in the village of Garapan. Immigrants from Guam and the Caroline Islands were given free land on which to establish themselves as farmers; enterprising Chamorros leased government land for plantations, engaged in trade or learned crafts. Fritz criticized the destructive impact of concession companies on colonial societies, and he was lucky that the Marianas were far from the centre of German economic activity on Jaluit and from the influence of the Jaluit-Gesellschaft.

The trade of the Marianas was oriented towards Japan. The Japanese trading companies, whose schooners visited the Marianas and the Western Carolines regularly from Yokahama, sold goods at a lower cost and paid better prices than the Jaluit-Gesellschaft in the Eastern Carolines and the Marshall Islands. The station officers who administered the small community of Chamorros and Carolinians from 1907 were sensible enough to maintain the paternalistic colonialism that *Bezirksamtmann* Georg Fritz had introduced. Farms and plantations recovered gradually from the typhoons of 1905. The government school expanded, and medical care was improved. In 1947–48, when the American anthropologists Alice Joseph and Veronica F. Murray studied the indigenous culture of Saipan, which had recently been occupied by the United States, they found that after thirty years of Japanese rule the German period was still remembered with some affection by their Chamorro and Carolinian informants. 'Several of the native officials spoke wistfuly of the days when "only seven Germans" lived on the island, and said that they had not minded the German regulations. They had known what they must do and must not do and were otherwise left in peace.'[60]

## Economic Change

Micronesia was never a settler colony in German times. Colonialism was quite popular in Germany, becoming a part of middle-class culture even in small land-locked towns far from the great ports. Books and magazines on 'New Germany overseas' (*Neu-Deutschland über See*), as the colonies were sometimes called, were widely read. But reading was a substitute for travelling; not many Germans ever went to the colonies, and very few indeed to the Pacific islands. There were some adventurous traders and settlers, but most of the Germans who boarded a ship for the long voyage of six weeks and more to Jaluit, Pohnpei, Yap or Saipan had a mission to fulfil as administrators, missionaries or employees of the ubiquitous Jaluit-Gesellschaft. When they arrived at their destination they would complain about the heat, the mosquitoes and infinite boredom.[61] The Marshall Islands had 74 'white' residents in 1892.[62] In 1912 the total 'white' population of the Carolines, the Marianas and the Marshall Islands was 425; 232 of them were Germans.[63] The small number of Germans is a recurrent theme in indigenous accounts of German rule in Micronesia. If there is one positive thing to be said about Germans as colonial rulers, it seems to have been that there were not many of them.

Copra, which had brought German traders and German colonial rule to Micronesia, for many years remained the foundation of the colonial economy, both as a subsistence plant and as a cash crop. Micronesia was a region of trade copra, a system better adapted to the small island societies than the plantation system of Samoa and New Guinea. The Jaluit-Gesellschaft and other trading companies sent small schooners to the islands to buy the copra from local producers. It was then collected and shipped to the distant markets. The Jaluit company remained essentially a trading company. It established only two small plantations, on Kili and Udjelang in the Ralik Chain. Another plantation was founded on Likiep in the Ratak Chain by Adolph Capelle and two partners, with financial support from the Jaluit-Gesellschaft.[64] These three ventures remained the only plantations during the German era, and they were modest enough; in 1901 they employed a total of 170 Marshallese labourers.[65]

When the acquisition of the Carolines and Marianas from Spain was discussed in 1898–99, the German government and the Jaluit-Gesellschaft again conjured up a future of rich plantations and thriving trade. But soon after the annexation, the programme of colonial development faltered. In 1897 the Jaluit-Gesellschaft and the local trading company, O'Keefe, had agreed to divide the

Carolines, which were then still under Spanish rule, into two spheres of interest: the Western Carolines were assigned to O'Keefe, the Eastern Carolines to the Jaluit-Gesellschaft. The agreement was concluded for 25 years, and was not affected by the German annexation of the islands. The government granted a concession to the Jaluit-Gesellschaft on the understanding that the company would organize the economic development of the Eastern Carolines. But the company decided that the existing trade system was superior to a plantation system, which would have required qualified management, considerable investment and costly wage-labour. Frustrated with the Jaluit company's lack of interest, the German government withdrew the concession for the Eastern Carolines in 1907.[66] No other company from Germany was interested in competing with the Jaluit-Gesellschaft in the Micronesian copra business. The copra trade of the Western Carolines and the Marianas was organized by some local firms, and increasingly by Japanese firms. Most of the copra from the Carolines and Marianas was supplied by peasant producers. Only a few small plantations were established by German settlers, the missions and by enterprising Chamorros.[67]

Large-scale capitalist production came to the colonial economy of Micronesia with the discovery and exploitation of the rich phosphate sites on Nauru, which then belonged to the Caroline Islands, and on Angaur in the Belau group. In 1901, the Pacific Phosphate Company was established by the Jaluit Company and a British firm, the Pacific Islands Co., to exploit the phosphate sites on Nauru and Ocean Island. The sites on Angaur were mined by the Deutsche Südseephosphat-AG Bremen, established in 1909. Phosphate from Angaur and Nauru soon replaced copra as Micronesia's major export. In 1911 phosphate contributed 83 per cent and copra 16 per cent to the total exports of 7.9 million Marks from the Carolines, the Marianas and the Marshall Islands.[68]

The absence of settlers and plantations protected the stability of Micronesian peasant societies. Conflicts over land and labour for settlers or plantations, the typical causes of colonial unrest and rebellion, were avoided. In one of his first decrees, in 1887, imperial commissioner Knappe on Jaluit prohibited the acquisition of land from Micronesians by foreigners, a legal status which in this case included German imperial citizens. Any previous land claims by foreigners were to be examined by the administration.[69]

The same policy was followed in the Carolines and Marianas; in 1900 the German government issued a decree which prohibited the acquisition of land by foreigners.[70] The administration in the island territory could grant exemptions; the purpose of the decrees was not to prevent all land sales, but to keep the disposition of land under government control. Land disputes, either among Micronesians or between Micronesian owners and German settlers, were carefully investigated by the courts. With regard to the Marshall Islands, it has been suggested that the German administration's respect for the law and the land rights of the Marshallese people compared favourably with the arbitrary decisions and the requisitioning of land by the Japanese administration, and more recently by the American administration.[71]

Economic conditions were not static in the island territory, and towards the end of the German era pressure on the Micronesian peasant economies increased. By the standards of the 'scientific colonialism' of 1906–10, the situation in the Carolines, the Marianas and the Marshall Islands left much to be desired. The copra trade had languished, tax revenue from local resources was inadequate, and Japan's economic influence had expanded to a degree which was considered politically dangerous. The Colonial Office, governor Hahl and the administrators in the island territory were determined to accelerate the economic development of the Micronesian colonies. *Bezirksamtmann* Kersting on Pohnpei defended the existing structure of small-scale production. He argued that with better education and more government support, the peasant economies had a considerable development potential. A regional monopoly would stifle any initiatives.[72] Governor Hahl, however, was frustrated by the mediocre results of Germany's colonial efforts in Micronesia, and insisted that the only solution was close co-operation between the German government and large capitalist companies.[73] The situation seemed favourable, as rising copra prices in Europe revived the interest of the Jaluit-Gesellschaft in the copra business. In 1910, the Jaluit-Gesellschaft bought copra in the Carolines and Marshall Islands for 100 Marks per tonne. It would be sold in Hamburg for 460 to 480 Marks per tonne.[74] Not surprisingly, Hahl's view of economic development prevailed; the colonial experts in Berlin had always been in favour of concession companies. A vast development programme for the island territory was designed in 1910. Three regional concession

companies were to be established under the control of the Jaluit-
Gesellschaft, for the Eastern Carolines, the Western Carolines, and
the Marianas, plus a plantation company for the Marshall Islands.
When the First World War broke out, however, only the West-
Karolinen-Gesellschaft, owned by the Jaluit-Gesellschaft and the
heirs of O'Keefe, had been established, in Hamburg in 1912.[75] The
war brought the activities of the Jaluit-Gesellschaft in Micronesia
to an end. Japan closed its Micronesian mandate to German trade.[76]

## Colonial Law: A Retrospective

The German era in Micronesia was brief. Twenty-nine years after
the annexation of the Marshall Islands, fifteen years after the annexation of the Carolines and Marianas, the time had come for
new flag-raising ceremonies. In October 1914, a Japanese cruiser
squadron swept through Micronesia, seizing Kosrae, Pohnpei,
Truk, Belau, Angaur and Saipan.[77] The *Bezirksamtmann* on
Pohnpei was away on a tour of inspection to Palikir when the
change took place in Colonia. When he saw the Japanese flag flying
on his return, he was furious. He tried to lower the flag, but was
pulled away and slapped in the face.[78] In Koror, the Japanese commander was incensed by the fact that the German administrator
had interned the Japanese civilians on the island when Japan joined
the Allies.[79] But on the whole the change was peaceful enough. On
Saipan, the German flag was lowered 'in a perfectly decent manner'
on 14 October 1914, reported the German government physician,
who was the highest-ranking official at the time.[80] In the Treaty of
Versailles in 1919, most of German Micronesia was ceded to Japan.
Nauru, which in the German era was regarded as part of the
Marshall Islands, was annexed by the British Empire and was
administered jointly by Britain, Australia and New Zealand.[81]

The short German episode was for many Pacific islanders an
important turning point, when their cultures were integrated into
a modern capitalist civilization. Pacific history is often interpreted
in terms of foreign challenge and indigenous response. This is not
to deny Pacific cultures a potential for autonomous change. But in
Micronesia, in particular, the foreign impact during the last one
hundred years must have been stunning for the island populations,
as the changing tides of imperialist politics brought a succession
of German, Japanese and American administrators to their shores.

Each imperialist power imported its own colonial system: grand political and economic schemes in which Pacific islanders played only minor roles; a cultural hardware of plantations, roads, schools and hospitals; and a cultural software of language, law, beliefs and symbols.

The impact of German colonial law on the different Micronesian societies varied. In the Marshall Islands, traditional authority, custom and law were still of considerable importance when German rule ended. The Marianas were at the other extreme: during the long Spanish administration indigenous law had been replaced by European law, and the change to German law was gradual. In between lay the many different cultures of the Caroline Islands. In all societies, however, colonial law was an important agent of change. As an instrument of repression, it spelled out the terms of domination and dependency; the definition of separate spheres of superior 'white' and inferior 'native' rights served to maintain colonial rule. But at the same time colonial law aimed to draw Pacific islanders into a process of economic development and social change. The legal system, askew as it was, established norms and orderly procedures, and thus reduced arbitrariness. It provided a pattern for emancipation and modernization, abolished traditional bonds, established modern land tenure patterns and defined individual rights. More should be known about Micronesian responses to the foreign impact; but rarely, if ever, did Pacific islanders commit their experiences to paper during the German era. Foreign perspectives on Micronesia and indigenous experiences in Micronesia are reflected in different modes of historical knowledge.[82]

## Notes

1. Ovid, *Metamorphoses*, trans. F.J. Miller, Cambridge and London, 1984, Book 1, pp. 89–90.

2. Peter Hempenstall and Noel Rutherford, *Protest and Dissent in the Colonial Pacific*, Suva, 1984, p. 152.

3. Wolfgang Treue, *Die Jaluit-Gesellschaft auf den Marshall-Inseln 1887–1914*, Berlin, 1976, p. 27.

4. Modern Pacific island names are from Lee S. Motteler, *Pacific Island Names*, Honolulu, 1986.

5. Allerhöchste Ordre, betreffend die Erklärung des Schutzes über die Karolinen, Palau und Marianen, 18 July 1899, in *Die deutsche Kolonialgesetzgebung* (hereafter *DKGG*), part 4 (1898–99), p. 80.

6. Bericht des Gouverneurs von Bennigsen, in *Deutsches Kolonialblatt* (hereafter *DKB*) 11 (1900), pp. 100–112. Translation from Helmut Christmann, Peter Hempenstall and Dirk Ballendorf, *Die Karolinen-Inseln in deutscher Zeit* (The Caroline Islands in German Times), Münster, 1991, p. 180.

7. Treue, *Jaluit-Gesellschaft*, pp. 68–78.

8. Allerhöchste Verordnung, 27 March 1899, in *DKB* 10 (1899), pp. 227–8; Stewart Firth, *New Guinea under the Germans*, Melbourne, 1982.

9. Allerhöchste Ordre, 18 July 1899 and Verfügung des Reichskanzlers, 24 July 1899, in *DKGG* 4 (1898–1899), pp. 80–84.

10. Woodruff D. Smith, *The German Colonial Empire*, Chapel Hill, 1978, pp. 183–209.

11. Verordnung des Reichskanzlers, 18 January 1906, in *DKB* 17 (1906), p. 117.

12. Verfügung des Gourverneurs von Deutsch-Neuguinea, 17 February 1911, in *DKB* 22 (1911), p. 339.

13. Verfügung des Reichskanzlers, 27 February 1907, in *DKGG* 11 (1907), pp. 120–21.

14. Christmann et al., *Karolinen-Inseln*, pp. 197, 205; *DKB* 13 (1902), p. 263.

15. Jahresbericht der Schutzgebiete 1911/12, *Statistischer Teil*, pp. 28–30.

16. Governor Hahl to Kolonialamt, 11 October 1907, AAC: G 2/K 3.

17. Hempenstall and Rutherford, *Protest and Dissent*, p. 88.

18. Wilhelm Solf, 'Die deutsche Kolonialpolitik', in Otto Hintze et al. (eds.), *Deutschland und der Weltkrieg*, vol. 1, Leipzig and Berlin, 1916, p. 153.

19. Wilfried Wagner et al. (eds.), *Rassendiskriminierung, Kolonialpolitik und ethnisch-nationale Identität*, Münster and Hamburg, 1992.

20. H. von Hoffmann, *Einführung in das deutsche Kolonialrecht*, Leipzig, 1911, p. 21.

21. Kaiserliche Verordnung, 9 November 1900, in *DKGG* 5 (1899–1900), pp. 158–60.

22. Emil Peters, 'Der Begriff sowie die staats- und völkerrechtliche Stellung der Eingeborenen in den deutschen Schutzgebieten nach deutschem Kolonialrechte', dissertation, Göttingen, 1906.

23. Bezirksgericht Saipan to Kolonialabteilung, 1 January 1906, Bundesarchiv Potsdam (hereafter BAP): RKolA 5460.

24. Landeshauptmann der Marshall-Inseln to Reichskanzler, 28 March 1897, BAP: RKolA 5430.

25. Hahl to Bezirkamt Yap, 2 November 1908, BAP: RKolA 5430.

26. I. Gestmeyer, 'Rechtliche Grundlagen, Verwaltungs- und Gerichtsorganization', in Paul Leutwein (ed.), *Dreissig Jahre deutsche Kolonialherrschaft*, Hamburg, 1912.

27. Karl von Stengel, *Die Rechtsverhältnisse der deutschen Schutzgebiete*,

Tübingen, 1901.

28. Gesetz über die Konsulargerichtsbarkeit, 10 July 1879, in *DKGG* 1 (to 1892), pp. 28–36.

29. Verordnungen, 13 September 1886 and 7 February 1890, and Dienstanweisungen, 2 December 1886 and 10 March 1890, in *DKGG* 1 (to 1892), pp. 564–83.

30. Bezirksgericht Saipan to Colonial Department, 1 May 1905 and 1 March 1905, BAP: RKolA 4786; Bezirksgericht Saipan to Colonial Office, 1 January 1906 and 20 January 1907, BAP: RKolA 5460.

31. Verfügung des Reichskanzlers, 17 January 1911, in *DKB* 22 (1911), pp. 109–10.

32. Verfügung des Auswärtigen Amtes, Kolonialabteilung, 27 April 1907, in *DKGG* 11 (1907), p. 229.

33. Friedrich Doerr, *Deutsches Kolonialzivilprozessrecht*, Leipzig, 1914; Friedrich Doerr, *Deutsches Kolonialstrafprozessrecht*, Leipzig, 1913.

34. *DKB* 3 (1892) to 12 (1901).

35. *DKB* 22 (1911), pp. 886–87, and 23 (1912), p. 1183.

36. Felix Meyer and Albert Hermann Post, *Rechtsverhältnisse eingeborener Völker in Afrika und Ozeanien*, Berlin, 1903.

37. Josef Kohler, 'Fragebogen zur Erforschung der Rechtsverhältnisse der sogenannten Naturvölker, namentlich in den deutschen Kolonien', *Zeitschrift für vergleichende Rechtswissenschaft* 12 (1897).

38. *Verhandlungen des Reichstages*, 3 May 1907, vol. 228, pp. 1356–89, and vol. 242, p. 2235.

39. E. Schultz-Ewerth and Leonhard Adam (eds.), *Das Eingeborenenrecht. Sitten und Gewohnheitsrechte der Eingeborenen der ehemaligen deutschen Kolonien in Afrika und in der Südsee*, 2 vols, Stuttgart, 1929–30.

40. Hermann Trimborn, 'Mikronesien', in Schultz-Ewerth and Adam (eds.), *Einbeborenenrecht*, vol. 2, pp. 439–541.

41. Fischer, *Die Hamburger Südsee-Expedition*, Frankfurt am Main, 1981.

42. Peter Sack, *Land between Two Laws*, Canberra, 1973.

43. Strafverordnung für die Eingeborenen, 10 March 1890, in *DKGG* 1 (to 1892), pp. 627–35.

44. Von Hoffmann, *Einführung in das deutsche Kolonialrecht*, p. 76.

45. Verhandlungen des Reichstags, 17–19 March 1908, Verhandlungen, 1908, pp. 4035–55, 4104–32.

46. *DKB* 2 (1890), p. 292 and 4 (1893), p. 383.

47. W.H. Alkire, *An Introduction to the Peoples and Cultures of Micronesia*, Menlo Park, 1977; Douglas L. Oliver, *Oceania: The Native Cultures of Australia and the Pacific Islands*, 2 vols, Honolulu, 1989.

48. J. Kohler, 'Das Recht der Marshallinsulaner', *Zeitschrift für vergleichende Rechtswissenschaft* 12 ( 1897) and 14 (1900).

49. A. Erdland, *Die Marshall-Insulaner*, Münster, 1914; Augustin Krämer and Hans Nevermann, *Ralik-Ratak (Marshall-Inseln). Ergebnisse der Südsee-Expedition 1908–1910*, vol. II B. 11, Hamburg, 1938.

50. 'Jahresbericht, betreffend das Schutzgebiet der Marshall-Inseln', in *DKB* 4 (1893).

51. Erdland, *Marshall-Insulaner*, pp. 14–18.

52. Albert Hahl, *Governor in New Guinea*, ed. and trans. Peter G. Sack and Dymphna Clark, Canberra, 1980, p. 121.

53. Ibid., p. 137.

54. Christmann et al., *Karolinen-Inseln*, p. 191.

55. Paul Ehrlich, 'The Clothes of Men: Ponape Island and German Colonial Rule, 1899–1914', Ph.D. thesis, State University of New York at Stony Brook, 1978; Peter Hempenstall, *Pacific Islanders under German Rule: A Study in the Meaning of Colonial Resistance*, Canberra, 1978, pp. 73–118.

56. Firth, *New Guinea under the Germans*, p. 127.

57. Anneliese Eilers, *Inseln um Ponape. Ergebnisse der Südsee-Expedition*, vol. II. B. 8, Hamburg, 1934.

58. Eilers, *Inseln um Ponape*, p. 66.

59. Gerd Hardach, *König Kopra. Die Marianen unter deutscher Herrschaft 1899–1914*, Stuttgart, 1990.

60. Alice Joseph and Veronica F. Murray, *Chamorros and Carolinians of Saipan*, Cambridge, Mass., 1951, p. 43.

61. 'Von den Marshall-Inseln', in *DKB* 7 (1897), pp. 243–5.

62. *DKB* 4 (1893), p. 383.

63. *Jahresbericht der Schutzgebiete 1911/12*, pp. 28–33.

64. *DKB* 3 (1892), p. 333.

65. *Jahresbericht der Schutzgebiete 1900/01*, p. 267.

66. Verfügung des Reichskanzlers, 24 January 1907, AAC: G 1/109.

67. Plantagenstatistik, *Jahresbericht der Schutzgebiete 1908/09*, Deutsch-Neu-Guinea, Inselgebiet, pp. 41–2.

68. *Jahresbericht der Schutzgebiete 1911/12*, pp. 328–33.

69. Verordnung des Kaiserlichen Kommissars betreffend den Erwerb von Grundeigentum, 8 January 1887, in *DKGG* 1 (to 1892), pp. 624–5.

70. Verordnung des Reichskanzlers, 20 January 1900, in *DKGG* 5 (1899–1900), p. 19.

71. Stewart Firth, 'Racism and Forms of Colonial Domination: The Case of the Radiation Atolls in the Marshall Islands, 1912–1990', in Wilfried Wagner (ed.), *Rassendiskriminierung, Kolonialpolitk und ethnisch-nationale Identität*, Münster, 1992.

72. Kersting to Hahl, 20 January 1912, AAC: G 2/Z 14.

73. Hahl to Colonial Office, 21 June 1912, AAC: G 2/Z 14.

74. *DKB* 21 (1910), p. 39; Bezirksamt Jap to Kolonialamt, 5 August 1910, Politisches Archiv des Auswärtigen Amtes, I A Südsee 16, Bd. 2.

75. Gesellschaftsvertrag der West-Karolinen-Gesellschaft m.b.H., Hamburg, 1912, BAP: RKolA 2471.

76. Jaluit-Gesellschaft to Auswärtiges Amt, 23 September 1921; BAP: Reichswirtschaftsministerium, 2700.

77. Mark Peattie, *Nan'yo: The Rise and Fall of the Japanese in Micronesia*, Honolulu, 1988.

78. Ehrlich, *The Clothes of Men*, pp. 215–16.

79. Felix Moos, 'Dynamics of Colonialism: Japan and Germany in Micronesia', in Josef Kreiner (ed.), *Japan und die Mittelmächte im Ersten Weltkrieg und in den zwanziger Jahren*, Bonn, 1986, pp. 109–10.

80. Regierungsarzt Dr Salecker, Bericht über die Okkupation der Marianen, San Francisco, 1 February 1915, BAP: RKolA 2622.

81. Roger Thompson, 'Edge of Empire: Australian Colonization in Nauru, 1919–1939', in Donald H. Rubinstein (ed.), *Pacific History*, Mangilao, Guam, 1992.

82. Rufino Mauricio, 'A History of Pohnpei History or Poadoapoad: Description and Explanation of Recorded Oral Traditions', in Rubinstein (ed.), *Pacific History*.

# 15

# Constitutional Instruments in Kiribati and Tuvalu: A Case Study of Impact and Influence

## DAVID J. MURRAY

Constitutions in countries of the Pacific have been regarded as strikingly conventional. In this they have been taken to reflect the singular impact of foreign cultures. They have also been described as inconsistent with basic values characteristic of the Pacific. 'Why is it', Peter Sack asked, 'that the truly 'homegrown' Pacific constitution – a constitution expressing Pacific values and adopting Pacific forms of socio/political organization – remains a utopian dream. Although everyone claims to want it and no-one seems to be satisfied with what takes its place.'[1] My aim in this study is to consider the premiss in that question by looking at one specific case – the Gilbert and Ellice Islands colony and its two successor states of Kiribati and Tuvalu. Is it correct to assert that the independence constitutions of Kiribati and Tuvalu represent the working out of British cultural influence and contain no expression of the values or socio-political organization chosen by the people of Kiribati and Tuvalu?

The early history of the contact between Britain and the islands which became the Gilbert and Ellice Islands Colony is consistent with the idea of an imposed British legal and governmental order for the colony as a whole. The instruments giving legitimacy to the exercise of British power were those of the British imperial government. The Foreign Jurisdiction Act 1890 empowered the Crown to exercise any jurisdiction it would have had under the prerogative in conquered or ceded colonies, and this applied to the islands of the Gilbert and Ellice groups, as protectorates were proclaimed in successive islands in 1892. The British Settlements Act 1887 gave general constituent powers in settled colonies, of which Ocean Island (Banaba) became one in 1890 by virtue of occupation by a British company. The Pacific Islands Protection Act 1875 and successive Western Pacific Orders in Council (1877, 1879, 1880 and 1893) established a framework for governing, first, British subjects in the Gilbert and Ellice Islands and, subsequently, the islands and islanders as a whole. This framework of British law provided the authority, in British terms, for annexing the Gilbert and Ellice Islands Protectorate in 1915 and transforming it, along with Ocean Island, into the Gilbert and Ellice Islands Colony. The Colonial Boundaries Act 1895 provided the legal foundation for successive changes that brought into the colony three northern Line Islands (1916 and 1919), the other Line Islands (1972), the Phoenix Islands (1937), and first made the Tokelau (Union) Islands part of the colony in 1916 and subsequently transferred them to the jurisdiction of the Governor of New Zealand (1926).

British Orders in Council specified the nature of government for the dependencies. The Pacific Order in Council 1893 prescribed the executive, legislative and judicial powers of the Western Pacific High Commission, whose jurisdiction included the Gilbert and Ellice Islands, and powers were further elaborated in the Gilbert and Ellice Islands Order in Council of 1915, when the office of Resident Commissioner for the colony was created. These orders and the letters patent issued under the royal prerogative set out the basis for British colonial government in the colony until 1963. The law and machinery of government was dictated by British authority on the basis of British conceptions of what was proper and necessary, and expressed in terms that accorded with the legal and governmental culture of the United Kingdom.

The same was true when developments came to be made in the status of the colony and in the machinery for its government. Seen in retrospect, an Order in Council in 1963 initiated a succession of steps which took the Gilbert and Ellice Island Colony to the threshold of independence within 11 years. The 1963 Order introduced an executive council to advise the Resident Commissioner on the exercise of his authority, and at the same time granted the Resident Commissioner a legislative authority parallel to that of the High Commissioner for the Western Pacific, thus creating for the first time a legislative authority in the colony. The Resident Commissioner then used this authority to establish an Advisory Council as a precursor of a legislative council. These developments started the colony along a path of institutional development, which in outline replicated that followed in many older British dependencies. The colony had begun to acquire an identity separate from the Western Pacific High Commission, and the executive council and embryo legislative council provided the foundation for institutional development. Thereafter progressive changes separated the colony from the Western Pacific High Commission, so that the Resident Commissioner became a Governor, and a separate judicature was established in the colony. The authority of the executive council was extended so that by 1974 it had become a council of ministers with, among its members, a chief minister and other ministers with departmental responsibilities. Likewise the advisory function of elected representatives was transformed into legislative powers in a House of Assembly, and the relationship with the executive became one in which ministers in the council of ministers were selected from the representative assembly, and became answerable to it for the management of their portfolios.[2]

The succession of changes that took place between 1963 and 1974 followed a pattern familiar in British dependencies. Institutions were established as the instruments of colonial government. Powers were specified consistent with, and in the language of, imperial law. British withdrawal involved creating a successor government, and this was done by progressively adjusting the institutions of colonial rule so that step by step they became appropriate instruments of government in a newly independent state. At each stage of adjustment, the basic logic of the institutional structure pointed the way to further change. With elected members in the executive council, the obvious issue was when the governor would cease to chair the meetings and when responsibilities reserved to the governor would be transferred to the council of ministers. Once started, the process of change tended to dictate the next issue to be addressed and who would address it. The resolution of the question meant incremental change in one part of the structure, but with an effect that was consistent with changes in other parts. There was as a result what has been described as a 'piecemeal reconstitution of the Westminster model'.[3] In 1974, the Gilbert and Ellice Island Colony was reaching the stage when there would be internal self-government exercised by ministers responsible to the elected legislature. The final outcome of the process would have seemed readily predictable: that the dominating influence on the country's law, constitution and structure of government, which the successor government inherited, was British; and that any local impact on the constitutional instrument was marginal. In practice, following a referendum in the Ellice Islands, the separation of the Gilbert and Ellice Island Colony into the two colonies of the Gilbert Islands and Tuvalu created the opportunity for observing the different outcomes of two distinct processes by which the independence constitutions in the two colonies were settled.

The Tuvalu independence constitution was decided in a manner that reflected common practice in British dependencies. The form of the constitution was largely decided by the elected legislature. Wider consultation with the public did take place, but in so far as this produced any general consensus it did not affect the decisions taken in the legislature. The British government did not seek to influence the constitution – though, partly unwittingly, it did affect it in one important matter of detail.[4] What determined the shape of the constitution was the particular interests of the members of the assembly, and these favoured retaining features characteristic of the Westminster model. Among these members there were disagreements – notably between the chief minister and his principal opponent; how the working of the process affected the balance of advantage between these two protagonists is relevant to understanding some provisions. But these were details. The main outcome was a constitution characteristic of the Westminster model, scaled down to suit the circumstances of an independent state with a population, at the time, of seven thousand. On this the members of the assembly were all agreed. Those who controlled the process of reaching this decision were those who had gained power in the existing institutions of government, and in fashioning the independence constitution they were united in their concern to safeguard the existing structure and their own positions within it.

Developments in the Gilbert Islands were interestingly different. The outline sequence of events was as follows:

*1976* The council of ministers, on the proposal of the governor, agreed to a constitutional convention being convened to give advice on the independence constitution.[5]

There followed a series of seminars, public briefings, distribution of literature and public discussion, using the radio and public meetings throughout the colony.

*1 January 1977* The Gilbert Islands Amendment Order 1976 was brought into operation, providing for internal self-government.

*21 April–9 May 1977* The Constitutional Convention met and agreed recommendations on the independence constitution.[6]

*26 July–10 August 1977* The House of Assembly met in a committee of the whole house to review the recommendations of the constitutional convention, and, with minor amendments, endorsed them.[7]

*1 February 1978* A general election was held, a new chief minister was elected nationally, using the procedure recommended by the Constitutional Convention and endorsed in the dissolved House of Assembly. The newly elected House of Assembly confirmed the proposals for the independence constitution.

*21 November–7 December 1978* A constitutional conference was held in London, after which the independence constitution was drafted.[8]

*1 May 1979* The House of Assembly approved the draft constitution.

*12 July 1979* The colony became independent as the Republic of Kiribati.

An important step in this sequence of events was the meeting of a Constitutional Convention. In terms of the formal and legal processes of the colony's government, the Convention was purely advisory. It was to offer advice to the House of Assembly on the House's work of recommending to the British government the provisions for the independence constitution. As the Council of Ministers' Memorandum expressed it, 'the convention will be in essence a public means of seeking advice from as large and as representative a group of people as possible. It is intended to try to forestall the criticism, which has to date attended every constitutional change, that "the people were not properly consulted".'[9] In these formal terms, the Convention did not affect the authority belonging to the House of Assembly, and indeed was assisting the

House in its work. As an advisory body, the work of the Convention was consistent with a normal part of the process in British dependencies of settling recommendations on the constitution after taking wider soundings – as indeed happened in Tuvalu (and also in the Solomon Islands[10]). But this was not how the Convention was perceived by many Gilbertese. It was widely seen as a determinative part of the process of settling the shape of the country's independence constitution. As the Chief Minister at the time wrote – somewhat regretfully – 'the outer island delegates thought that they themselves ... were going to draft the constitution and that whatever they decided was sacrosanct and could not be changed by anybody or any House of Assembly.'[11] This was a view that was not confined to delegates. Both at the time and subsequently, the Convention was taken to have an authority that commanded respect for its recommendations.[12]

The Convention was convened by the governor, and the members were appointed by him after the Council of Ministers had approved the basis for representation. There were three categories of member: those largely connected with the government in south Tarawa, representatives of certain national bodies, some of whose representatives came from Tarawa and some from outer islands; and representatives from the outer islands. From south Tarawa there was the Council of Ministers, heads of departments and divisions in the public service (so long as they were Gilbertese), the equivalent in paragovernmental bodies, and representatives of the public service trade union. In the second category came five representatives each of the Gilbert Islands Protestant Church and the Roman Catholic Church, single representatives of three smaller churches, representatives of the seamen's union and of university students. From each of the 21 outer islands came delegates commonly numbering five: the president of the island council, the member of the House of Assembly, one representative from the co-operative society, one representative of the women's club, and a representative of the island *unimane* association. The position of *unimane* is that of male elder who represents the kin group in the community meeting house (the *maneaba*). Unimane had lost much of the authority they once had, as had maneabas in island social organization, but nevertheless, in many islands unimane still commanded respect, influence and some authority. As Roger Lawrence wrote of social organization on Tamana in the early 1970s 'people draw the distinction between the Island Council which "stands for the Government' and the *Unimane* which 'stands only for the island".'[13] In the proceedings of the Convention, the respect accorded to delegates from outer islands, and particularly to unimane, presidents of island councils and those pastors who came from outer islands, demonstrated why the Convention achieved the impact that it did. With 161 delegates, 105 of whom came from the third group – the outer islands – the Convention was a substantial and wholly Gilbertese gathering. It was chaired alternately by two senior and respected Gilbertese, one the president of an island council and formerly the first leader of government business in the House of Assembly, and the other the speaker of the Assembly.

The convention met in the Bairiki maneaba in south Tarawa, and functioned in the traditional way for a maneaba. Delegates from each island had a post (or *boti*) for their island. Those coming to support delegates sat behind the boti on the edge of the maneaba or outside. Proceedings were conducted wholly in Gilbertese. Discussion proceeded in a way that aimed to achieve a consensus. Noise and minor commotion served to indicate levels of support for, disagreement with, or disapproval of what was being said. On occasion a vote was taken, but votes were not treated as a means of deciding a matter. They were one method of assessing the balance of views and a way of showing to those on one side the degree of support a particular view commanded. More common than a vote was checking for consensus or dissent by clapping or refraining from doing so. The loudness and generality of clapping indicated the state of opinion. A matter was only concluded when dissentients, or those in a minority, indicated that they were persuaded of, and accepted, the general view and all clapped together.

The convention, then, was a gathering of persons who collectively had experience both in the law and government of the British colony and in the custom, law and practices of island affairs. But those from the outer islands in particular did not come as experts: they presented themselves as delegates from their islands who had taken counsel on the issues to be addressed. All present were to confront questions about the future constitution of the country, using processes of deliberation characteristic of a maneaba. The Convention commanded, in the outcome, sufficient authority and respect for its recommendations to determine central features of the independence constitution. The terms in which matters were discussed, the reasons for reaching conclusions, and the basis on which recommendations were made illuminate the central question posed of the differential impact of British and Pacific cultures, in this instance on the constitutional instrument for independent Kiribati.

The questions about which there was extended debate in the Convention were directed both to safeguarding against the abuse of power and to working out how authority in the state should be checked, limited and made responsible. These concerns were first explored in relation to the office of head of state. Whether there should be a head of state as well as a head of government was discussed in the light of the potential benefit of a check on the head of government and of avoiding an undue concentration of power. Against these considerations were the points that the post of head of state or governor-general would, in the normal way, be largely honorific, lack worthwhile duties and have considerable associated costs, and the holder would be likely to meddle and interfere in a manner that would be improper. The judgement went against having a separate head of state.

The most extended discussion in the three weeks concerned the office of head of government. Debate took place on a series of fundamental questions: the method of selecting the person to fill the office, in what circumstance and by what means the holder could be removed, and how the powers of the office should be limited and checked. Considerations to the fore were that the head of government should command national support and should represent the people as a whole, and not simply a faction, single island or kin group. The result was a recommendation for the national election of the president. Whether there should be cabinet government with the president as chairman or whether there should be an executive president was settled in favour of a cabinet. The critical considerations were, first, that the cabinet was a check on what might otherwise be an undue concentration of power[14] and, second, that with ministers having to be chosen from the elected legislature, the president would be less able to appoint as ministers members of the president's own kin. Limiting the opportunity for abuse of office or the exercise of power in an arbitrary manner prompted attention to a wide range of other provisions. The outcome of these find expression in the recommendation that the president and cabinet should be removable in the event of a motion of no confidence passed by a simple majority in the legislature, a valid petition signed by a majority of registered electors, or in the event of the president being convicted of offences involving the abuse of office. The same consideration lay behind the recommendation that the term of office of the chief executive would be subject to an absolute limit of three terms. Attention was also given to limiting the president's opportunity to control or interfere in the election process, to undermine the independence of the public service, exercise undue influence over the police, or avoid financial investigation and audit. With relevant provisions expressed in the law of the constitution, there was concern that the rule of law should be upheld by safeguarding the independence of the courts. Otherwise the Convention placed less faith in checks and balances among institutions working in south Tarawa than on conferring responsibility on the public as a whole – particularly the public in the outer islands – through elected representatives subject to recall, and through electors having the right to petition for the removal of the president.

How representatives in the elected legislature should be selected, what they should represent, and how those elected should be held accountable were a further range of issues that gained much careful attention. In the outcome there were recommendations for each island other than Tarawa to be a single constituency, with single or multiple members depending on the size of the electorate; for the right of electors to recall their representatives; and for a legislative process designed to allow bills to be discussed between elected representatives and electors. Distrust of political parties prompted recommendations on the detailed process for electing members, and also on the procedure for selecting candidates to stand in the election for president. The aim was to institute processes which did not depend on the work of parties and which indeed discouraged their formation.

The terms in which these questions were discussed and recommendations agreed reflected the experience and cultural values of those present. Those from the outer islands were senior figures in island society. Periodically they expressed appreciation of the knowledge and direct experience of colony-wide government among what they described as the 'young men of south Tarawa', and they explicitly recognized that it was for these 'young men' to fill the offices in government and to have authority in the state of Kiribati. But it was for the old to speak for the public and in so doing to act as counsel to the 'young men' and as a check on them. In the Bairiki maneaba, they spoke for their islands as they would speak for their kin group in an island maneaba, but characteristically they did not speak in a particularistic manner for Butaritari or Aranuka, for example, but expressed their contributions as applying to the public as a whole. The older men and women had an inherent authority and expected, and commanded, respect. Ministers, politicians and officials deferred to the old men and women, whom they described as understanding Gilbertese ways and as rightly speaking for the Gilbertese people.

One thread running through the discussions was how ideas associated with the government of the country should be expressed and understood in terms of the Gilbertese language and experience. Historical experience was explicitly drawn on, or allusions made to it. Reference to Tem Baiteke and Tem Binoko coloured the discussion of whether there should be a head of state, not least because the term used, after discussion, to describe the office (translated into English as 'king') was the title associated with Tem Binoko and, indeed, other royal families in certain of the northern Gilbert Islands.[15] Similarly, the distrust of parties was a direct reflection of concern that tension between Catholics and Protestants – open conflict being part of the direct experience of some of those present[16] – would emerge in politics unless steps were taken to discourage or prevent it. In the three weeks of the Convention, more disapproving noises were directed at conflict arising from denominational rivalry than at any other topic. Finally, a theme throughout the discussion was the unity of the Gilbertese people, and the imperative of having a constitution and government which would be – in a recurring expression – for all from Makin to Arorae (from the most northerly to the most southerly island).

Yet in going back to the detailed notes on the discussions in the Convention, what is striking is the extent to which those taking part drew on contemporary experience, some of which came from beyond the Gilbert Islands. Debate over whether to have a largely ceremonial head of state with reserve powers was illustrated with reference to the Kerr–Whitlam episode in Australia in 1975, and the more recent constitutional crisis in Fiji in March and April

1977.[17] There was recurring reference to Hammer de Roburt as president of Nauru, about whose doings much was known. Many episodes were referred to with amused disapproval as examples of how those with power could abuse their positions. Among recent direct experiences in the Gilbert Islands, reference was made to the unsatisfactoriness of elections on a first-past-the-post basis when the result could be the election of someone with as little as 20 per cent of the vote representing the largest kin group. Although not directly discussed, as it had been in earlier seminars on the constitution, there were sufficient allusions to suggest that a critical experience in colouring contributions in the Convention was the policy of the then chief minister and government to establish a defence force. Having large army lorries pass along the narrow strip of land from Bairiki to Bonriki on south Tarawa was a visible expression of a government's anxiety to have a strengthened instrument for dealing with, among other things, strikes and disorder. It was a policy to which there was strong opposition. The action of establishing a defence force, which the government had taken as it moved towards internal self-government, gave added urgency and point to discussion in the Convention about the power and accountability of elected governments.

Regarded more detachedly, the discussion in the Constitutional Convention was conducted in terms that were a reminder of classic statements of a protective model of liberal democracy. Few in the Convention would have heard of Locke or Madison, let alone been influenced by *Two Treatises of Government* or *The Federalist Papers*, yet their concerns were with guarding against the abuse of power, protecting citizens from those in government, and ensuring that there were means for seeing that the government acted in the interests of the Gilbertese people as a whole. At the same time there was a concern that government should continue to achieve for the Gilbertese people the level of peace and order that delegates described as having been a feature of colonial rule. There was belief in the efficacy of representative government. Importance was attached to the rule of law and to safeguarding individual rights against the state. There was anxiety over what Madison termed 'faction' – which the Gilbertese recognized in kin groups, the churches and the self-interest of public servants. Throughout, the tenor of discussion, conducted in Gilbertese and expressing concerns and aspirations on behalf of the people from

Makin to Arorae, was recognizable in terms of the core ideas of liberal democracy.

And yet, did the work of the Constitutional Convention suggest that a Gilbertese culture moulded what had hitherto been dominated by a British cultural tradition? There are four prongs to the argument that the Convention did not, in reality, introduce a dimension to the constitution of Kiribati that reflected Gilbertese culture. First, the agenda for the Convention was set by the governor; second, the constitution as introduced was only partly a reflection of the work of the Convention; third, the experience of Gilbertese taking part in the Convention was itself structured by British culture; finally, because the constitution did not build in traditional Gilbertese institutions it was not characteristic of Pacific culture.

The first point has been made by Naboua Ratieta, chief minister of the Gilbert Islands when the colony became internally self-governing. He emphasized the significance of the questions forming the basis of discussion, and pointed to the impact the governor had through the list.

> All those questions, with the exception of a very few insignificant ones, which were put to the Convention to answer, were all, I think, leading questions which one can sort of anticipate what unsophisticated outer islanders' reactions were to them when they try to answer them.[18]

The argument is a valid one. Questions that the Convention used were those set out by the governor in a list of fifty-two. But the argument can be overstated. First, the list of questions was itself formulated after a series of seminars held with leading Gilbertese the year before the Convention. Second, the list was distributed in Gilbertese to all islands, along with other publicity briefing, as one basis for discussion by the public and their representatives. It had not been the governor's intention that the questions would constitute an agenda. On the first day of the Convention, on the governor's instructions, the chairman of the Convention sought a more open-ended discussion with the aim of delegates deciding on what to focus attention. The delegates from the outer islands rejected this approach, on the grounds that they had gathered opinions on the questions posed in the list and had a responsibility to report to the Convention, and, furthermore, that as persons less experienced in such matters, if the list was not used they would be outmanoeuvred by the young men of south Tarawa. Third, while the Convention did consider most of the questions on the governor's list, however cursorily, matters were discussed that did not relate directly to the questions posed. In particular the extended discussion of how the office of chief executive should be constituted, and the limits and checks on the office, ranged well beyond what was immediately suggested by the questions. Inevitably, on occasion, contributions were taken to be a little pointed.

The second reservation was that the independence constitution only partially reflected the work of the Convention and was significantly influenced by other sources. This is certainly correct. In the Gilbert Islands, the House of Assembly largely endorsed the recommendations, with minor changes. (The Committee of the House had made one major change – concerning the number of terms the president could serve – but this was subsequently reversed.[19]) On the other hand, the UK government had a substantial impact on the constitutional instrument. Independence constitutions for former dependencies had come to be used by the UK government as substitutes for bilateral agreements. By incorporating provisions into the constitution, British requirements became a part of domestic law in the former colony. However shortsighted the approach, this had become common practice. Certain provisions in the Kiribati constitution can be explained in this way. Most significantly, the British government – acting under pressure from domestic British opinion, from the prime minister of Fiji, and from the Banaban community on Rabi Island in Fiji – in effect made certain provisions a condition of granting independence to the Gilbert Islands, at least within its existing boundaries. As a result, a chapter was introduced into the constitution that granted rights to the Banaban community and to Banaba (Ocean Island), and imposed obligations on the government of Kiribati.

In addition to specific provisions, the constitutional instrument also retained the character of a law in the British tradition. It did not emerge as the brief, largely non-technical document, along the lines of the Nauru constitution, that the Convention had sought. It was drafted in terms consistent with British practice, with the chief responsibility belonging to the Foreign and Commonwealth Office in London. It was enacted as part of a British Order in Council. The draft had the prior agreement of the House of Assembly in the Gilbert Islands, but it required only a single resolution rather than consideration at each stage of the full legislative process.

There are two final reservations about the Gilbertese impact on the constitution. The Gilbertese taking part in the Convention drew on experience structured, at least in part, by the culture of the United Kingdom. The direct experience with colony-wide government was with the government established by the British. This was consistent with British law and practice. More tenuously, the substantial contributions made in the Convention by pastors and other church representatives may be regarded as reflecting alien cultural influences. This only points to the problem of differentiating what constitutes British and what Pacific or, more to the point, Gilbertese culture. By 1970, there was a Gilbertese political culture, which, like any political culture, had absorbed ideas and relationships from difference sources and mediated them through a changing national and local experience.

Finally, in the academic literature it has been suggested that the incorporation of traditional local institutions in a constitution should be taken as indicating whether traditional political thinking has been absorbed into the constitution. An example given of such incorporation was that of the House of Arikis in the Cook Islands.[20] Such an approach appears not only simplistic but misconceived. The fact that the Convention rejected, rather than recommended, having a second chamber comprising unimane and similar figures is an unconvincing indication of what impact Gilbertese culture had on the Kiribati constitution. Equally unconvincing is the suggestion that the failure to create at national level an institution imitating one existing in one or more islands is a test of whether Gilbertese culture had moulded the constitutional instrument. More relevant questions are who determined the form of the constitutional instrument, and whether it was designed by Gilbertese to reflect Gilbertese values, culture and experience.

The Convention was a Gilbertese gathering. Its size and membership gave it authority as a body that spoke for the Gilbertese public. The Convention decided in reality the central features of the independence constitution. It devised arrangements that did not replicate what was to be found in other former British colonies. These were Gilbertese solutions to problems understood and interpreted in the light of Gilbertese experience and culture. It was no part of the aim of the Convention to create a constitution somehow distinctively Gilbertese or Pacific. Nor was devising a constitution treated as a technical exercise for experts in constitutional design. The approach was that delegates could, and should, fashion solutions that were intelligible and sensible in the light of their perception and definition of problems, their past experience, their guesses and worries about how office-holders and others might behave in the future, and the values they saw as important. In the event, the distinctive Gilbertese character is partly disguised in the final instrument by the way it was elaborated and transformed before emerging as an Order in Council, but the constitution represents – in contrast to the Tuvalu constitution – a meeting between British and Gilbertese conceptions of problems and solutions in constitutional design.[21]

## Notes

1. P. Sack, 'Constitutionalism and 'Homegrown' Constitutions', in P. Sack (ed.), *Pacific Constitutions*, Law Department, ANU, Canberra, 1982, p. 1.

2. An account of these developments appears in B. Macdonald, *Cinderellas of Empire*, ANU Press, Canberra, 1982, pp. 221–43.

3. S.A. de Smith, *The New Commonwealth and its Constitutions*, Stevens, London, 1964, p. 68.

4. D.J. Murray, 'Constitution-making in Tuvalu and Kiribati', in Sack (ed.), *Pacific Constitutions*, p. 132.

5. Council of ministers, Constitutional convention, Memorandum No. 120/76, 21 September 1976.

6. Gilbert Islands, *Report of the Constitutional Convention 1977*, Government Printing Division, Bairiki, 1977.

7. Gilbert Islands, *Report of the Select Committee on the recommendations of the Constitutional Convention*, Government Printing Division, Bairiki, 1977.

8. *Report of the Gilbert Islands Constitutional Conference, London, November/December 1978*, HMSO, London, Cmnd 7445, 1979.

9. Council of ministers, Constitutional convention, Memorandum No. 120/76, 21 September 1976, paragraph 2.

10. See Y. Ghai, 'The Independence Constitution', in P. Larmour (ed.), *Politics in the Solomon Islands*, USP, Suva, 1983; and Y. Ghai, 'Constitutional Issues in the Transition to Independence', in R. Crocombe (ed.), *Foreign Forces in Pacific Politics*, Institute of Pacific Studies, USP, Suva, 1983, p. 35.

11. Naboua Ratieta, 'The First Gilbert Islands Government', in Kiribati Extension Centre, *Politics in Kiribati*, Kiribati Extension Centre, Tarawa, 1980, p. 19.

12. This is evident in the proceedings of the Select Committee in the

House of Assembly, Gilbert Islands, *Report of the Select Committee on the recommendations of the Constitutional Convention*, Government Printing Division, Bairiki, 1977. See also the comments of a minister at the time, Roniti Teiwaki, 'Inside the election', in Kiribati Extension Centre, *Politics in Kiribati*, Kiribati Extension Centre, Tarawa, 1980, p. 29. Inevitably those who have regarded the processes from the standpoint of British law and British colonial practice understate the importance of the Convention and of decisions in the Gilbert Islands. The assertion by Ghai that 'the procedure employed was essentially as laid down by Britain' can be reconciled with the facts only if this metropolitan-centred perspective is adopted. See Ghai, 'Constitutional Issues in the Transition to Independence', p. 28.

13. R. Lawrence, *Tamana Report: Victoria University of Wellington Rural Socio-economic Survey of the Gilbert and Ellice Islands*, Ministry of Local Government and Rural Development, Bairiki, 1977, p. 29.

14. The effect of this is seen in various provisions in accordance with which the president has to consult, or take the advice of, the cabinet. See, for example, the requirement on the president to act in accordance with the advice of the cabinet in declaring a state of emergency (s.16[2]).

15. For Tem Baiteke and Tem Binoko, see B. Macdonald, *Cinderellas of Empire*, ANU Press, Canberra, 1982, p. 28.

16. See for example W.H. Geddes, *North Tabiteuea Report: Victoria University of Wellington Rural Socio-economic survey of the Gilbert and Ellice Islands*, Ministry of Local Government and Rural Development, Bairiki, 1975, p. 21.

17. See for example D.A. Low, 'The Dismissal of a Prime Minister: Australia, 11 November 1975', and D.J. Murray, 'The Governor-General's Part in a Constitutional Crisis: Fiji 1977', both in D.A. Low (ed.), *Constitutional Heads and Political Crises*, Macmillan, London, 1988, pp. 90–125.

18. Naboua Ratieta, 'The First Gilbert Islands Government', p. 20.

19. Gilbert Islands, *Report of the Select Committee on the Recommendations of the Constitutional Convention*, Government Printing Division, Bairiki, 1977. The one important change made initially was to remove the recommendation that the president could serve for a maximum of three terms.

20. C.G. Powles, 'Law, Decision-making and Legal Services in Pacific Island States', in R.T. Shand (ed.), *The Island States of the Pacific and Indian Oceans: Anatomy of Development*, Development Studies Centre Monograph No. 23, ANU, Canberra, 1980, pp. 408–9.

21. For Ghai to describe the Kiribati constitution as having 'many "Westminster" characteristics' underplays the unique features in the Kiribati constitutional instrument and gives to his undefined Westminster model an unusually loose, and probably unhelpful, meaning. Y. Ghai and J. Cottrell, 'The Pacific Island States', in D. Butler and D.A. Low (eds.), *Surrogates for the Sovereign*, Macmillan, London, 1991.

# PART IV

# Traditional and European Behaviour: Sexuality as a Special Case of Pacific–European Interaction

## JOHN M. MACKENZIE

### Sex and Empire in the Pacific

Pacific islands have been associated with a relaxed attitude towards sex since the first appearance of French and British voyagers in the South Seas in the eighteenth century. Such a liberal approach to sexuality has, however, been viewed in widely differing ways by commentators over the past two hundred years. Inaccurate stereotypes developed which did little justice to the diversity of sexual custom and practice in the various groups of Pacific islands. Sexual openness and 'hospitality' have been viewed both as representing a guiltless Arcadian simplicity and as demonstrating a climatically determined depravity, or at the very least amorality, which required the reforming hand of Europe. Missionaries were to be the prime instrument for the introduction of a new morality, the extension of the sexual guilt of the Judaeo-Christian moral cosmos to the Pacific. In more recent times, sexual relations between Europeans and Pacific Islanders have been studied primarily in the context of the spread of venereal diseases to islands where they were previously unknown, leading to devastating effects upon health, fertility and the demographic integrity of the many different peoples of the region.

The three articles in this section demonstrate anew the dangers of the stereotype on both sides of human sexual contact in the

Pacific. As Niel Gunson argues in Chapter 16, missionaries (in this case mainly British) should not be essentialized as repressive and prudish any more than Pacific islanders should be seen as representing the ultimate in sexual liberation. Missionaries not only have to be understood in terms of their class and educational origins, but their sexual attitudes also need to be located in time and in particular predilections of specific denominations. They themselves, particularly in the early nineteenth and in the twentieth century, once they had been influenced by anthropological studies, were quite capable of a certain amount of tolerance of child marriage, some of the ritual male acts of certain traditions, even of polygamy. They also contracted local relationships, both heterosexual and homosexual, and sometimes discovered their own sexuality in the guise of a tolerant understanding of local mores. But equally, some of them also produced shocked reactions to the sexuality of their own children or saw liberated approaches to sex as evidence of moral destabilization, or even madness, in the climate – moral and natural – of the Pacific.

Hermann Hiery examines some of the same forces at work in the secular society of trade, settlement and government employment among the Germans (Chapter 17). Whereas the British took steps in the early twentieth century to regulate the sexual contacts between imperial officials and indigenous women in their African empire, no such measures were initially adopted by the Germans. And the Pacific record indicates that sexual contact could promote a variety of objectives and relationships in this imperial setting. Some were consciously seeking an escape from European restraints. Some were furthering economic ends by integrating into local society, sometimes becoming polygamous in the process. By adopting local liaisons, officials often made their jobs easier by facilitating connections with and knowledge of local society. Strikingly, Hiery argues that stricter Germans, who maintained their social and sexual distance from indigenous society, were probably more easily manipulated by local people.

But cross-cultural relationships also had striking effects on the social status and the sexual traditions of Pacific islanders. Women secured prestige for themselves and their families through European connections. Within the multifarious histories of indigenous sexual institutions, it is possible to discover instances of men expanding and inventing traditions and women struggling to assert their own freedoms. Complex systems of status and prestige were indeed transformed by European social and economic intervention. But such interventions were particularly disruptive when large numbers of male labour migrants were brought together on Melanesian plantations, leaving villages bereft of their menfolk. Moreover, as happened throughout the world, polygamous practices developed and changed as men earned money and were able to escape from the marriage controls of kin. And in this area legislative intervention by the Germans could produce controversial results and legal retreat.

Thus, the social and sexual relations between Germans and Pacific islanders cannot be satisfactorily analysed either as pure exploitation or as beneficial race contact. The parties to such relationships pursued their own objectives, and modified customs and attitudes in the process. Indigenous sexual codes were themselves caught up in a dynamic process which varied according to the relative strength or weakness of the economic impact and its accompanying social disruption. Even small numbers of imperial administrators, settlers and missionaries could be highly fractured, as evidenced by the hierarchies of snobbery and the anti-clericalism of many officials. It often seems to be the case that the smaller the scale of imperial society, the less monolithic it actually is. Even the powerful realities of economic exploitation could produce efforts on the part of both women and men to escape from some of the social and marital constrictions of traditional society.

As Amirah Inglis demonstrates in Chapter 18, no one should seek comfort in a supposedly progressive twentieth century. The Australian administration in Papua in the years between the two World Wars produced the most repressive sexual legislation to be found outside white-ruled southern Africa. At a time when fear of miscegenation and obsessions with racial purity were reaching their peak, white women were protected by legislation which laid down the most severe penalties, including capital punishment itself, for any form of touching or attempted rape by indigenous men. Sexual contacts, forced or otherwise, that took place in the other direction across the race line, were subjected to no such penalties. Inglis analyses the White Women's Protection Ordinance not only in terms of the neuroses of racial and sexual fear in Port Moresby, but also in the context of feminist histories that have not always taken account of extreme forms of repression of the indigenous male. In the social and economic hierarchy of colonial society, white women may often have found themselves in a position of strict subordination, but they were always superior to native men and were able, whether from their own fears or through the jealous terrors of their white menfolk, to secure 'black peril' legislation that had otherwise marked only the racist statute books of South Africa and Southern Rhodesia. The notion that the sub-imperialism of the Australians was any more liberal than that of Europe dies on the gibbet with the victims of such legislative ferocity.

# 16

# British Missionaries and Sexuality: The Polynesian Legacy and its Aftermath

## NIEL GUNSON

The history of missionaries and sexuality shows a great diversity of patterns within both missionary and missionized cultures. For all the repressive tendencies usually portrayed by missionary stereotypes, there is an equal degree of realistic awareness, enlightenment and even appreciation of traditional sexuality. Gender roles were certainly changed by missionary influence, both for the worse and for the better. Despite the general trend in the case studies of such theorists as Sigmund Freud, Alfred Kinsey, Margaret Mead and Michel Foucault, concepts of sexuality differed widely within the various societies, largely along functional or class lines, and permissive and restrictive behaviour tended to be cyclic and dependent on the politics of class.[1]

Just as sex is determined by nature, so sexuality is determined by culture. Pacific island societies differed from the invading cultures in possessing primal cultures that were closer to nature. Even so, there was a corresponding similarity between the classes or functional groups. Thus in most island societies men and women had clearly defined roles. Men were usually warriors or fishermen and were expected to be aggressive. Women were the child-bearers and were generally expected to be submissive and to engage in food-gathering, food-cultivation and on-shore or reef fishing.[2]

There were, however, men and women who did not conform to this norm. Priests, prophets and sorcerers were usually persons who found themselves different from the others by birth, such as epileptics, homosexuals, schizophrenics, and persons seen as having natural defects. Such individuals were often feared, tolerated and even highly revered, especially as they generally became the custodians of special knowledge.[3] In the more hierarchical societies, roles were often reversed or modified. High-chiefly women in Polynesia sometimes became warriors and behaved aggressively,[4] while high-chiefly men occasionally developed or acquired homosexual tastes.[5] In a few places, women separated themselves from the rest of society and formed amazon bands.[6] Children often displayed overt sexuality. Indeed, there was a great range of sexual diversity and standards of behaviour.

Sexuality in island societies was frequently restricted by social and political conventions, particularly in central Polynesia, for instance, where chiefly families of Samoan origin required public defloration of the wives of chiefs and where the strict brother–sister relationship, in which the brother guarded his sister's honour, operated as a moral force. In other societies, such as eastern Polynesia, experimental mating was permissible until the first child was born, after which there was often strict monogamy, though in families of rank, secondary wives (the wife's sister or classificatory sisters) were permitted, and bond friends had access rights. On some islands women, particularly high-chiefly women, took secondary husbands. In some societies adultery was severely punished.

In Britain the pattern of sexuality was similar, though further removed from nature.[7] Roles for men and women were still moulded on the spear–distaff pattern. Men of religion often saw themselves as different from other men. While some clergy, particularly Anglicans, had homosexual leanings, most Protestant ministers were conventionally heterosexual. In Europe, upper-class women, like their island sisters, had much more freedom to develop their sexuality and lifestyles as they wished,[8] becoming lady travellers or lesbian partners on their own terms, and upper-class men were able to adopt homosexual life styles, provided they restricted their affairs to their own class or their servants.[9] Even when charged by the law, the penalties were weighted against the common man, as when the Bishop of Clogher was let off lightly for being found in a compromising position with a soldier, while the soldier was transported to Botany Bay.[10] Children were frequently exposed to abuse, and throughout even the Victorian reign there was a great range of sexual diversity and standards of behaviour.

British missionaries mostly came from the lower middle and middle classes, those classes held responsible for the repression of sexuality and the strict imposition of gender roles in their own society. Certainly from the eighteenth century onwards, Evangelicals took a prominent role in moral reform movements, which greatly restricted sexuality.[11] Yet it would be a mistake to think that missionaries held the same attitudes to sexuality throughout the two centuries of contact.

The very early missionaries, used to a much laxer moral environment in Britain than their Victorian successors,[12] were surprisingly tolerant of indigenous sexual customs except for certain homosexual practices. In the first three decades of the London Missionary Society (LMS) mission in Tahiti, several missionaries took heathen wives or argued in favour of the idea;[13] one married a reformed prostitute from London;[14] the daughter of another became a prostitute in London;[15] and others consented to marry high-chiefly men and women to teenagers and children under ten.[16] One missionary, J.M. Orsmond, was quite prepared to discuss his erotic dreams (as symptoms of unregenerate nature) with his Tahitian converts though, at another time, he destroyed the pulpit he had made because he found a couple copulating in it.[17]

For the early missionaries, 'sodomy' – a term they used to include fellatio – was the most heinous sin, yet the missionary Henry Nott was prepared to sit with the Tahitian King Pomare II, working on the translation of the Bible, while the king caressed his favourite male attendant.[18] The missionaries were shocked to find gender roles reversed in the institution of transsexual behaviour, and supposed all *mahu* to be homosexual, whereas this was not the case.[19] Certainly many *mahu* did engage in fellatio, but others had normal sexual relations with women, and others appear to have been quite asexual.[20] The strength of missionary distaste is illustrated by their making it a condition that they would stay only if 'sodomy' was outlawed,[21] and their refusal to employ a converted *mahu* as a religious teacher.[22]

Missionary concepts of marriage tell us much about their attitudes to sexuality. While the early directors of the LMS took great pains to interview and examine the wives and prospective wives of candidates, they were mainly interested in their spiritual state. Missionaries in training were encouraged to keep their minds off young women and to avoid special friendships;[23] courtships sometimes lasted only a matter of weeks, introductions and formalities being arranged by pious friends or clergy. Widows in the mission fold were instructed to marry single missionaries and not return to Britain; and when four pious women were sent out as prospective wives in 1810, they were supposedly chosen by straw, no doubt with suitable prayers.[24] Little wonder, then, that some partners were incompatible and did not prove good role models for the people at large. Not only did Henry Nott draw the short straw, a woman with a fierce temper, but many of the other unions were equally unsuccessful.

Mrs Elder of Tahiti fell in love with a sea captain who shot himself, attempted suicide herself, and had to be tied to her bed, the missionaries commenting on her 'base and ungrateful behaviour' to her husband.[25] Elder himself came under fire for trying to persuade a shipboard 'prostitute from Port Jackson' to stop in Tahiti and become his wife.[26] Mrs Armitage had a reputation for beating her husband, and on one occasion on shipboard struck him so hard that the crockery fell down in the steward's pantry adjoining their cabin.[27] Nor was she the only husband-beater. The Reverend John Eyre at least got a loving mother figure for a wife since she was almost twice his age.[28] Some wives were regarded as being too fastidious throughout the mission era, and many could not stand the strain of living in a hostile and savage-seeming environment.[29] Some were seen as flighty and improper role models, the otherwise dutiful Mrs Bourne of Tahaa being censured for 'skipping along the beach in a skipping rope'.[30] I witnessed, 130 years later, a deputation waiting on the LMS missionary at Beru, Gilbert Islands, asking him to forbid his wife to knit on the Sabbath.

The main cause for the failure of the first mission to Tahiti appears to have been the predicament of the single brethren. As Davies informed the directors in 1806:

> It may not be improper to mention a thing which is known to several of you, that the natives highly disapprove of our living in a single life, and seem at a loss to know how to account for our so doing, one conjecture is, that it is owing to our being Priests, another is, that we either have to do with Taheitian Women, Mrs. Henry, or Mrs. Shelley, or do something worse – for they have no notion of any one's having the gift of continency, and so far as I know there is no such thing among them.[31]

The only missionaries to take Tahitian or Tongan wives formerly had been ostracized or excommunicated. By 1806 even the steady ones were beginning to waver. At the same time a number of women attempted to interest them sexually by playing ball, stripping and making venereous gestures in front of the mission house.[32] Elder believed that heathen Tahitian women were much more faithful than the other missionaries claimed, but the others argued that servants and friends had access to wives during their husbands' absence.[33] Henry Bicknell actually believed that the 'Natives in some respects would make better Wives than European women, as they can travel thro. the Rivers & live on the productions of the Island better' and said he would not object to such marriages.[34] In August 1808 Charles Wilson wrote of his intention to take a Tahitian wife but was talked out of it.[35] At length, in 1809, Henry Nott succumbed and went through a form of marriage with a chiefly woman from Raiatea.[36] The marriage lasted until Nott returned to live in Tahiti, and as it was not a Christian marriage Nott was free to unite with his short straw.

Although some of the early LMS missionaries in South Africa took local wives, these women were Christian, so there were supposedly no problems. In the Pacific, however, later generations of missionaries looked askance at interracial marriage. In fact, the few missionaries who had indigenous wives were former beach-combers who had been converted in the field and were already 'married', such as Matthew Hunkin in Samoa or William Miller in Tonga.[37] On the other hand, when widower Karl Schmidt began to court his house servant Salaneta, the relationship was declared scandalous even though they married, and he was dismissed from the mission.[38] This seemed to set the pattern for the future. Missionaries who appeared to find companionship with island women were thought to have sexual interests only.

Many missionaries believed they had found domestic bliss with the wives they had married before coming to the field, and there were many happy partnerships. The love poems of the Wesleyan John Hunt to his wife testify to a grand passion linked with their common task of saving souls.[39] Even the first missionary wives were expected to participate in the work of the mission, but it took an admonitory letter from one of the directors in 1818, which 'made them very angry for a while', before some of them began to work among the indigenous women. Davies commented: 'The female part of the mission have always been the loudest as to the claim of their share of property, but hitherto have shewn little disposition to forward the work of the mission in anyway.'[40] The changes made by the women fully participating were far-reaching, and soon the female mission became as important as the male. Even so, as late as September 1849, the Wesleyan Peter Turner felt that the missionary wives spent too much time supervising their households and the affairs of the family. 'This is wrong indeed. I am quite persuaded that our wives should do more in the work connected with the mission', he wrote, and he suggested that they should be expected to give an annual account of themselves, and that they should be noted more in the literature.[41]

In regard to the people, the greatest marriage problem facing the missionaries was polygamy, though in Polynesia at least it ceased to be a problem fairly soon after nominal national conversion. Evangelical missionaries could probably have justified polygamy by referring to Martin Madan's treatise *Thelyphthora* (London, 1780), which justified Christian polygamy, but the only missionary voice to defend taking another woman was the errant Church Missionary Society missionary, Thomas Kendall, who told the Wesleyan Samuel Leigh that he loved his Maori companion better than his wife, and 'pleaded in justification of his practice the case of David'.[42]

For the missionaries, the real worry was how to treat the surplus wives. Fortunately the LMS came up with rules based on the African experience. Unlike Madan, the directors felt that although polygamy was permitted in the Scriptures, 'it was never authorized, any more than lying, blasphemy and murder'. They believed a converted heathen should 'part with every woman with Whom he had cohabited as a wife, except the first whom he had taken', but they also recommended that if the women refused to go they should not be obliged to leave their husband. After the death of the first wife they should marry the next in order. They also recommended that the so-called concubines had a claim for support while they lived single. Anyone retaining more than one wife was not permitted to hold any church office.[43] Whether this last was observed everywhere is uncertain as Peter Turner heard that the LMS missionaries in Samoa were allowing persons to preach 'who have 2 or 3 wives, and that some have been baptized who live in Polygamy...'[44] The Tahiti-born Reverend Samuel Wilson of Samoa had two Samoan wives, no doubt in response to custom, and was soon dismissed by his brethren.[45]

The Methodists appear to have had greater difficulties than the LMS in dealing with polygamy, probably because of the long-drawn-out conversion process in Fiji and Tonga, and the political importance of marriage alliances. James Watkin reported that there were very few polygamists left in Tonga in 1833, that it ended in Lifuka in August 1834 with the marriage of the Governor to his chief wife, and at Utulau in 1836 with the marriage of the chief to one of his six wives.[46] Hunt found many irregularities among the Tongans in Fiji in the 1840s. 'Many of the Tonga people have got the idea that if they have but one wife, it is right to throw her away when they embrace Christianity and seek a new one...'[47]

Although Hunt had a paternalist view of indigenous sexuality, arguing that a chief had 'humbled' or 'ruined' the women who were formerly his wives, he had great respect for traditional morality and upheld the legitimacy of pagan marriage. He believed it was the duty of a man who had more than one wife 'to keep one as his wife and to provide for the rest and for their families in the best way he is able'.[48]

Polygamy was, of course, widespread in Melanesia and persisted longer. A.W. Murray reported in 1841 that a chief from the Isle of Pines had fifty wives while his son had twelve and common people had two, three or four. He believed that 'unlike almost every country', adultery was little thought of. Also, father and son had access to each other's wives.[49] In 1853 he claimed that most of the women on Aneiteum above the age of 30 had had more than one husband.[50] Similar claims could be made for all the islands.

Missionaries of the Victorian era have been condemned for repressing sexuality, for putting women in Mother Hubbards, and for introducing strict penal codes, which imposed their values on the people at large. Certainly there is evidence for repressive behaviour, but much of the severity was due to the way in which converted chiefs used the law to bolster their own power. The Broom Road around Tahiti got its name from being maintained and swept by women found guilty of fornication. Women could often be seen working on the road in the flimsy finery they were arrested in.[51] In Borabora, adulterous women were actually branded with the letter A, but most of the missionaries regarded this punishment and many of the floggings as severe.[52] Howe even thought the Tahitian prostitution and adultery laws too severe in 1848.[53] Missionaries found many flaws in the judicial systems that they had helped to introduce, and much magisterial abuse. In Tonga, for instance, Whewell complained in 1860 that the law stating that a person guilty of adultery could not remarry during the life of the innocent party condemned 'persons who have done wrong once in the married state to a life of celibacy or a life of sin', and a life of sin was the general rule.[54]

Many persons, particularly chiefly women, were accused of adultery because they displeased their husbands or fathers.[55] The Queen of Huahine had her husband judged for adultery so that she could divorce him and take a man she fancied.[56] The Chief Judge of Tahiti, described as a huge man, was married by a missionary to a little girl in 1827,[57] while in 1833 the missionary Charles Pitman complained that the chief magistrate of Avarua, Rarotonga, was in the 'habit of illicit intercourse with those who were committed to prison for adultery and other crimes, and the next morning would pass sentence upon them'.[58] Queen Pomare IV was married to a very young cousin in 1832, although not properly separated or divorced from her first husband, an event which led to the Chief Judge of Tahiti being 'judged' by some of his chiefly peers for allowing the marriage, and to the outbreak of a provincial war or insurrection.[59] Tati, another Tahitian judge, was married to a woman who had two other husbands living.[60]

Notwithstanding the apparent repression of sexuality, the missionaries lived in a climate where they were constantly exposed to overt sexuality and in some ways became inured to it. Throughout the nineteenth century, missionaries in eastern Polynesia complained of island children playing sexual games in the school yard.[61] They might be seen on the beach naked, wrote school teacher Buchanan, 'playing with their own and others privates for want of other toys'.[62] According to George Charter, in 1848 nearly every Society Islands girl had lost her virginity by the age of 12. Gyles in 1820 said by the age of eight, and Orsmond in 1827 by the age of seven.[63] Erotic games were also widespread especially at the courts of the Society Islands' rulers. In 1828, Orsmond recorded how the Queen's courtiers were organized into five male groups, who took turns to play games with the Queen's women which involved smoking and blowing smoke, violent gymnastics, and mounting the women.[64] Night creeping, or *mafera vahine*, as it was known in the Society Islands, was widespread throughout the islands.[65]

Of more concern were various forms of condoned rape. John Hunt complained how errant wives were punished in Fiji. An offending woman was taken into the young men's house and 'all the men of the place are ordered to go to her'. In another instance two women were raped by a large party of warriors before being killed and eaten. In a similar case in New Zealand (though not involving cannibalism), it seems clear that the offending woman had made some sort of breach of *tapu*, and the *war* party was required to have intercourse with her in order to make things *noa*, or free from divine prescription, a restoration of the balance of nature, which would be beyond the comprehension of most missionaries.[66] In Samoa, the missionaries reported that a young woman was held down by her father and brothers for the benefit of an English beachcomber.[67] Considering the sanctity of the brother–sister relationship, one supposes this was regarded as a forced marriage for which correct exchanges had been made. At a personal level, missionaries were particularly hurt when, after rising from prayers, senior churchmen, particularly in some parts of eastern Polynesia, continued to offer their foreign visitors female companions for the night.[68]

Constant exposure to overt sexuality meant that missionaries found it difficult to control their own children. Their own male children experimented in the bush and were expelled from school, and many of their daughters were housebound or constantly chaperoned.[69] On one occasion a missionary's wife heard a noise in the bedroom occupied by three of her daughters, and fainted on finding them with three young Tahitian men.[70] Another fainted on finding men under the beds of her two daughters.[71] Missionaries themselves fell victim to permissive standards of pre-marital behaviour.[72] Not only had several of the *Duff* missionaries taken partners, but also missionary Davies was rebuked for closeted petting; and numerous charges, not necessarily correct, were levelled at some of the more influential missionaries. Even in staid Tonga, one Wesleyan missionary was found in a compromising situation during the absence of his wife.[73]

In the main, missionaries accepted a doctrine of apartness for Christian converts, even within their own families. Sexual expression was a symptom of an essentially depraved nature, and confessing Christians must develop their sexuality within marriage or adopt chastity. There was thus a strong tolerance for natural sexuality, balanced by the hope that conversion would be effective.[74] Instead of casting out their offspring, many of the missionaries attempted to make the best of the situation, sometimes silently adopting their children's natural issue into their own families. They also fostered beachcombers' children who had lived with their fathers.

In several areas of sexuality, later missionaries differed dramatically in their attitudes from earlier ones. Although the marriage of minors was not encouraged, several of the missionaries were prepared to bless the unions with Christian ceremonies. Orsmond complained in 1827 that little girls were married 'for the sake of property', and some had had from three to six husbands in three or four years. Henry Nott married the Queen Mother of Tahiti to 'a little boy between 7 and 9 years' on the grounds that such marriages were customary.[75] In later times, particularly in Melanesia, missionaries became crusaders against child marriage. In the 1960s, for instance, missionaries in Papua were making stronger efforts to prevent the marriage of girls as young as 12, and to end the practice of bride price, originally thought to be good, but which had become mercenary, particularly around towns such as Port Moresby.[76]

Another area of sexuality where there were significant changes of attitude by the end of the nineteenth century was male initiation. In Tahiti the early missionaries had been horrified by the ritual homosexuality practised by the Arioi society, similar to the corn rituals of American Indians.[77] It was this ritual sodomy, rather than fellatio, that was apparently outlawed by the mother of Pomare II at the behest of the missionaries. By the time ritual sodomy was encountered by missionaries in Melanesia, many missionaries had acquired some anthropological training or knowledge, and were more prepared to understand what was taking place.[78] Although they deplored the 'sexual abuse' of boys, the attitudes of missionaries such as James Chalmers and J.H. Holmes were relatively enlightened; at least they did not condemn the initiation ceremonies without investigation, or suggest punishment, and they probably lamented that western society had not found good substitutes for turning boys into men.

Twentieth-century missionaries also deplored the fact that many of the old rites of passage had been removed.[79] Strangely enough, in the Cook Islands, a new rite of passage affecting sexuality was introduced, the *pakotianga rauru*, in which boys passed into puberty or young manhood by means of a hair-cutting ceremony. In traditional Polynesia, long hair was the mark of a warrior, and women often kept their hair short. The cutting of hair was often an arbitrary requirement made by the missionaries to distinguish their new converts from those who followed traditional custom.[80] While on the surface this looked like emasculation, the hair-cutting ceremony simply reversed the image of masculinity. Similarly, the introduction of new games such as cricket helped to re-create a masculine image, although, almost perversely, cricket became a woman's game in some areas.[81]

By a strange twist of fortune, the missionaries who penetrated Polynesia, where homosexuality was tolerated and partially institutionalized, were almost exclusively heterosexual, while a comparatively large number of missionaries with homosexual inclinations served in areas where homosexual behaviour was comparatively absent or confined to ritual initiation. The only examples in the Evangelical missions were an ex-convict agriculturalist and teacher in Tonga, a land praised by the missionaries for its traditional moral rectitude,[82] and the celebrated missionary William Yate, alleged to have seduced young men in both Tonga and New Zealand.[83] The ex-convict had probably acquired prison tastes, while Yate, a bachelor with a spinster sister, was probably more self-aware.

It was, however, in the Anglican missions in Vanuatu, the Solomons and Papua New Guinea that homosexual behaviour was much more common and even tolerated. Probably the proportion of homosexuals was more representative of the entire community than among Protestants, and certainly homosexuality was fostered by both the English public-school system and the Anglo-Catholic ethos.[84] Those who found an outlet for their sexuality and those who idealized Melanesian youth often stayed for long periods in the mission.[85] Scandals involved at least two bishops and a succession of clergy in both the Melanesian Mission and the Anglican Mission in Papua New Guinea, though some affairs were successfully concealed from public knowledge at the time.[86]

Perhaps the most sensational affair occurred almost forty years ago, when a young Anglican lay missionary in the Solomons hacked a young Solomon Islander to death, the pretext being that the Island youth was deliberately provoking and tempting him.[87] There are probably only two questions to ask. Did the Anglican youth have problems because of his own sexuality, or did the Solomon Islanders identify the ethos of the mission as being partially homosexual and therefore something to be cultivated in return for favours and property? Was the murderer a maladjusted homosexual or the victim of a *milieu* partially created by his own mission?

Female missionaries have also manifested unusual behaviour, though it would be difficult to discover whether those who were mentally disturbed became so because of problems of sexuality. Most 'madness' in the mission field seems to have been pathological, aggravated by uncongenial surroundings. Apart from a male missionary possibly suffering from schizophrenia and lycanthropy,[88] and Mrs Barff, who had religious dementia,[89] most cases of madness seem to have been severe nervous breakdowns.[90] At least one female missionary's behaviour in more recent times seems related to her sexuality, though the case is not well documented, and the agent for the Mission attributed her behaviour to the inherently evil nature of the particular Papuan village location.[91] The missionary lady in question apparently divested herself of her clothing and danced naked in the moonlight in the village. Whether or not she was dancing with the villagers, as Chalmers might have done, or whether it was a solo act in the manner of Stephen Tennant's 'troppo' missionary lady, as suggested by the biased male mission informant, is unclear.[92]

Any discussion of missionaries and sexuality should take into account the current Mead–Freeman debate, as it revolves around the testimony of a woman who was both *taupo* (village virgin) and church member.[93] We know from missionary records that although virginity was essential for the partners of high chiefs, a great deal of promiscuity took place amongst those of lower rank. According to Samuel Ella, despite missionary opposition, temporary arrangements were made for the village beau or *mānaia* to cohabit with 'the belle', and property was exchanged as for a lawful marriage.[94] Night-creeping was also commonplace. Theoretically, of course, as in western society, virginity was highly prized by the male hierarchy.

The missing factor in the Mead–Freeman debate is the perceived nature of reality in fulfilling sexuality. Unlike the West, it would seem that in cultures such as the Japanese and the Samoan

– Ruth Benedict's shame cultures[95] – it is possible to fulfil sexuality on a dream level, so to speak, so that those involved temporarily shut out reality and then resume normal life as if nothing has happened. At all costs face must be saved. While secrecy is difficult in an island society, those involved are virtually within the same dream space. It is doubtless significant that those who most openly supported the Freeman interpretation were women prominent in the Congregational Church, one of whom was the sister of the Head of State and whose 'professional virginity', like that of the female Tu'i Manu'a,[96] was a guarantee of the prosperity of the land.

In regard to female sexuality, missionaries from the Victorian era onwards believed that they were elevating the role of women by shaping their domestic independence as wives and mothers. They seemed blind to the fact that these roles were restricting to chiefly women, who had acted as administrators and leaders in traditional society. For women at large, however, the changes were significant. From their own experience over many decades, male missionaries appreciated the need to have educated partners. Although some of the first missionary wives were a great liability to their husbands, the majority were equal yoke-fellows, sharing translation work, medical and educational duties and presenting an image of more or less sexual equality.[97] Most women also taught their own domestic specialities. For the male missionaries, it was essential that indigenous male teachers and missionaries should have consorts with similar advantages.

The standard of female missionary education varied markedly, but as it was usually in the hands of missionary wives or single female teachers, such education almost certainly conformed to what they believed was in the best interest of the island women. As Mrs Ellis, wife of a former missionary to the islands, insinuated, it was important for a woman to know that she could be, or was, more intelligent than her husband, but it was also important for her not to show it.[98] Some missionary wives were much more intellectual than their husbands, but this enabled them to help their husbands rather than compete with them.[99]

The emphasis on the training of pastors' wives and island women in general was probably developed most thoroughly at Kwato, for many years an LMS station and afterwards an independent mission. Here, under Charles and Beatrice Abel, young

Papuan women were taught teaching and nursing skills and were regarded as highly as the young men.[100] In many earlier missions, the ministerial candidates and their prospective wives could have been mistaken for domestic servants, never becoming socially acceptable. Kwato was more like a finishing school for young ladies. Elite sexuality in Papua New Guinea owes much to the Kwato tradition. Other missions certainly promoted the education of women, though with less emphasis on leadership and separate careers. What it means to be a woman and what it means to be a man in the modern Pacific depends very much on how the people responded to missionary attitudes to sexuality in pre-colonial and colonial times.

Despite changing social attitudes to sexuality in Britain, involving both the emergence of a dominant middle-class morality and a more detached scientific or clinical view of sexual behaviour, the missionary situation always remained a highly heterogeneous one. Monolithic theorization does not seem to work, and as far as British missionaries are concerned, it would appear unwise to draw a sharp distinction between the 'sexual liberalism' in the late eighteenth and early nineteenth centuries, and Victorian prudery.

## Notes

1. The literature on the history of sexuality is vast and controversial. See particularly text and bibliographical notes to the first two chapers of Richard A. Posner, *Sex and Reason*, Cambridge, Mass. and London, 1992; and the introduction and notes to Ronald Hyam, *Empire and Sexuality: The British Experience*, Manchester and New York 1990. Although Hyam is correct in questioning the categories and labels of sexuality, his own categories, 'asexual' and 'bisexual', seem equally flawed. He also ignores the long-standing religious tradition that maintains that highly sexed persons are capable of sublimation. Robert I. Levy's *Tahitians: Mind and Experience in the Society Islands* (Chicago and London, 1973) is probably still the best introduction to Polynesian sexuality. See also Margaret Mead, *Coming of Age in Samoa*, London, 1929; Bengt Danielson, *Love in the South Seas*, London, 1956; and Robert C. Suggs, *Marquesan Sexual Behaviour*, New York, 1966. Works on Melanesian sexuality include H.I. Hogbin, *The Island of Menstruating Men*, San Francisco, 1970; Gilbert H. Herdt, *Guardians of the Flutes: Ideas of Masculinity*, New York, 1981; and Gilbert H. Herdt (ed.), *Ritualized Homosexuality in Melanesia*, Berkeley, 1984.

2. For gender roles and related matters for the Pacific, see Margaret

Jolly and Martha Macintyre (eds.), *Family and Gender in the Pacific: Domestic Contradictions and the Colonial Impact*, Cambridge, 1989; Caroline Ralston and Nicholas Thomas (eds.), 'Sanctity and Power: Gender in Polynesian History', *Journal of Pacific History*, vol. 22, no. 3 (1987), pp. 115–227; Penelope Schoeffel, 'Daughters of Sina: A Study of Gender Status and Power in Western Samoa', Ph.D. thesis, Australian National University, Canberra, 1979.

3. For accounts of how men and women became shamans, see Mircea Eliade, *Shamanism: Archaic Techniques of Ecstasy*, London, 1964, pp. 3–32, 125. For the connection with sexuality, see Walter L. Williams, *The Spirit and the Flesh: Sexual Diversity in American Indian Culture*, Boston, 1986, *passim*. The connection between homosexuality, shamanism and the religious temperament was first explored by Edward Carpenter in essays written in 1911 which appeared in his *Intermediate Types among Primitive Folk: A Study in Social Evolution*, London, 1914.

4. See particularly Niel Gunson, 'Great Women and Friendship Contract Rites in pre-Christian Tahiti', *JPS*, vol. 73, no. 1 (1964), pp. 53–69; Niel Gunson, 'Sacred Women Chiefs and Female "Headmen" in Polynesian History', in Ralston and Thomas, 'Sanctity and Power', pp. 139–71; and Jocelyn Linnekin, *Sacred Queens and Women of Consequence: Rank, Gender and Colonialism in the Hawaiian Islands*, Michigan, 1990.

5. The following Polynesian kings have been described as homosexual: Liloa of Hawaii, I'amafana of Samoa, and Pomare II of Tahiti.

6. Most notably the Vehine Hae in the Marquesas, but female 'tribes' were also reported in Samoa. John Williams learnt of dead Rarotongan women who hunted men at night, reminiscent of these bands.

7. There are now many studies of the history of European sexuality, and sexuality and religion, most notably Michel Foucault, *The History of Sexuality: An Introduction*, London, 1990 (first pub. 1976); Uta Ranke-Heinemann, *Eunuchs for Heaven: The Catholic Church and Sexuality*, London, 1990; Jeffrey Weeks, *Sex, Politics and Society: The Regulation of Sexuality since 1800*, London, 1981; Vern Bullough, *Sexual Variance in Society and History*, Chicago and London, 1976; *Homosexuality: A History*, New York, 1979; and John Boswell, *Christianity, Social Tolerance and Homosexuality*, Chicago, 1980. See also Martin Bauml Duberman et al., *Hidden from History: Reclaiming the Gay and Lesbian Past*, New York, 1989. Much work in this field emanates from the gay movement and reflects current preconceptions and theories of sexuality, which are open to debate.

8. A lady of rank had no difficulty in broadening her education and becoming a 'bluestocking', but as Lord Hastings recommended to his sister Lady Betty, she should learn as much as she could but not affect learning.

9. One has only to read the poems of Lord Rochester or the novels of Tobias Smollett to understand what took place.

10.  See A Gentleman connected with the Public Press, *The Bishop!! Particulars of the Charge against the Hon. Percy Jocelyn, Bishop of Clogher, for an Abominable Offence, with John Movelley, a Soldier of the First Regiment of Foot Guards, including the Evidence before the Magistrate at Marlborough-Street, and a Variety of Information and Remarks Which has never before appeared in Print*, London, 1822; H. Montgomery Hyde, *The Other Love*, London, 1972, pp. 99–101.

11.  The reports of many of these societies appeared regularly in the pages of such religious periodicals as *The Evangelical Magazine*. See also Ford K. Brown, *Fathers of the Victorians: The Age of Wilberforce*, Cambridge, 1961.

12.  In the Regency period it was quite common for fashionable women to appear at social functions with uncovered breasts. For a denunciation of 'decadent fashion', see an article 'On Modern Apparel', in *The Evangelical Magazine* for August 1804.

13.  These examples are discussed below.

14.  The first Mrs Hayward was the subject of a pamphlet allegedly called 'The Crooked Rib' by the polemicist Joseph Fox.

15.  For Sarah Henry (sometime Mrs Bland) see Niel Gunson, 'The Deviations of a Missionary Family: The Henrys of Tahiti', in J.W. Davidson and Deryck Scarr (eds.), *Pacific Islands Portraits*, Canberra, 1970, pp. 31–54.

16.  Examples are given below.

17.  J.M. Orsmond, Journal, 17 December 1824, LMS archives, South Sea Journals (SSJ) no. 77; J.M. Orsmond, Journal, 7 June 1838, SSJ no. 118, Council for World Mission Collection, School of Oriental and African Studies Library, University of London. See Niel Gunson, 'Missionaries and the Unmentionable: Christian Propriety and the Expanded Tahitian Dictionary', in Tom Dutton et al., *The Language Game: Papers in Memory of Donald C. Laycock*, Canberra, 1992, pp. 599–606.

18.  W.P. Crook, Journal, 6 February 1821, SSJ no. 54.

19.  J. Jefferson, Journal, 22 August 1800, SSJ no. 7.

20.  For a well-informed account of the *mahu*, see Levy, *Tahitians*, pp. 130–41.

21.  R. Hassall, Journal, 11 November 1797, SSJ no. 2.

22.  J. Davies, Journal, 9 January 1818, SSJ no. 50.

23.  See Niel Gunson, *Messengers of Grace: Evangelical Missionaries in the South Seas 1797–1860*, Melbourne and New York, 1978, p. 69n.

24.  The missionaries decided most things by lot. The story of the straws may be apocryphal, but Nott certainly went to marry Ann Turner in Sydney sight unseen.

25.  J. Davies, Journal, 27 October 1807, SSJ no. 31; 19 January 1809, SSJ no. 33.

26.  J. Davies, Journal, 30 September 1809, SSJ no. 33.

27.  D. Tyerman and G. Bennet, 22 August, 3 December 1821, LMS, South Sea Letters (SSL).

28. 'Old Mrs Eyre' was in fact aged 64 when she joined the mission, thirty-six years older than her husband.

29. The second Mrs Hayward disliked island food. Mrs Mary Polglase was 'exceedingly disgusted' by all she saw in Fiji, while Peter Turner reported that some wives 'cannot bear the natives to sit with them on the same form'. Peter Turner, Journal, 26 May 1853, MS B310, Mitchell Library. J.M. Orsmond complained of missionaries (both sexes) playing marbles, swinging, leapfrog, boating and horse-riding, 22 November 1840, 16 January 1841, SSL.

30. Orsmond, 13 January 1830, SSL.

31. Davies, Youl et al, Journal, 24 March 1806, SSJ no. 27, p. 12.

32. Ibid., p. 43.

33. Ibid., pp. 19, 22.

34. H. Bicknell to Dr Haweis, 25 December 1806, SSL.

35. J. Davies, Journal, 24 August 1808, SSJ no. 33.

36. Ibid., 22 July 1809.

37. See Gunson, *Messengers*, pp. 347, 353; A.W. Murray, 11 May 1842, SSL.

38. G. Turner, 20 March 1857; Pratt, 18 August 1857; Schmidt, 28 Decmber 1859, SSL.

39. The originals of Hunt's poems are contained in the Hunt Papers, Methodist Missionary Society Collection, School of Oriental and African Studies Library, University of London. For a published valentine, see Allen Birtwhistle, *In His Armour: The Life of John Hunt of Fiji*, London, 1854, p. 121.

40. J. Davies, Journal, 9 January 1818, SSJ no. 50.

41. P. Turner, Journal, 26 September 1849, MS B309, Mitchell Library.

42. S. Leigh, 6 April 1822, Letters from Leigh 1819–1824, Uncat. MS Set 197, Mitchell Library.

43. Report by Dr Waugh and Rev. Mr Rayson on the subject of marriages in Africa, 26 January 1818 in LMS, Examination Committee Minutes.

44. P. Turner, Journal, 14 September 1837, MS B303, Mitchell Library.

45. R. Ross, 20 November 1841, LMS, Australia Letters; Mills, 7 January 1839 (Minutes 6 February 1840); Pratt, 1 April 1840, SSL.

46. J. Watkin, Journal, 2 April 1833, 13 August 1834, 17 August 1836, MS A834, Mitchell Library.

47. J. Hunt, Private Journal, Methodist Overseas Missions (MOM), item 133, Mitchell Library, vol. 2, p. 84.

48. Ibid., pp. 87–8.

49. A.W. Murray, Journal, 13 April 1841, SSJ no. 130.

50. A.W. Murray and J.P. Sunderland, Journal, 22 October 1853, SSJ no. 147.

51. See J.M. Orsmond, Journal, 4 September 1832, SSJ no. 100; Howe, 30 October 1854, SSL. Apparently the Broom Road punishment was

replaced by prison in 1854.

52. P. Lesson, *Voyage autour du Monde ... sur la Corvette la Coquille*, 2 vols., Paris, 1839.

53. Howe, 13 March 1848, SSL.

54. J. Whewell, 20 December 1860, Tonga: Missionaries Letters 1852–1879, MOM item 170, Mitchell Library.

55. For cases of this kind, see J.M. Orsmond, Journal, 28 December 1822, SSJ no. 64; 9 September 1823, SSJ no. 68; 15 January 1824, SSJ no. 74.

56. Annual Report, Matavai and Papara, May 1827, SSL.

57. J.M. Orsmond, Journal, 9 March 1827, SSJ no. 87.

58. C. Pitman, Journal, 12 June 1833, SSJ no. 99.

59. J.M. Orsmond, Journal, 3 December 1832, 13 January 1833, SSJ no. 100; and Tahitian letters 1832–1833 in SSL.

60. J.M. Orsmond, 8 May 1839, SSL.

61. E.g. L.E. Threlkeld, 29 September 1818, SSL; J.M. Orsmond, Journal, 9 March 1827, SSJ no. 87; 24 October 1827, SSJ no. 91; 13 January 1833, SSJ no. 100.

62. E. Buchanan, 25 November 1842, SSL.

63. G. Charter, 21 April 1848, SSL; Answers to questions by Gyles, July 1820, SSL; J.M. Orsmond, Journal, 9 March 1827, SSJ no. 87; 24 October 1827, SSJ no. 91.

64. J.M. Orsmond, Journal, 1 November 1828, SSJ no. 92.

65. J.M. Orsmond, Journal, 23 September 1822, SSJ no. 64.

66. J. Hunt, Private Journal, 19 February 1844, Vol. 2, p. 200. The New Zealand case was reported by John White. Pers. comm. Dr Michael P.J. Reilly, Department of Maori Studies, University of Otago.

67. T. Powell, 17 November 1852, SSL.

68. E.g. G. Charter, 21 April 1848, SSL.

69. For more detailed discussion, see Gunson, 'Deviations'.

70. Lucy Thurston to American Board of Commissioners for Foreign Missions, 23 October 1834, quoted in personal communication from Catherine Stauder, The Kauai Museum, Lihue, Kauai, Hawaii, 3 March 1970.

71. Mrs Simpson, 23 July 1843; A. Simpson, 26 November 1844, SSL.

72. See Gunson, *Messengers*, pp. 153–7.

73. Ibid., pp. 157–8.

74. See Gunson, 'Deviations'.

75. J.M. Orsmond, Journal, 9 March 1827, SSJ no. 87.

76. *Sydney Morning Herald*, 11 July 1964; *Canberra Times*, 5 August 1964.

77. Although the missionary accounts in Latin do not appear to have survived, J.L. Young obtained particulars from sources known to derive from them.

78. Diane Langmore, *Tamate – a King: James Chalmers in New Guinea 1877–1901*, Melbourne, 1974, pp. 93–4. Recent research has suggested

that the *moguru* which Chalmers investigated was not 'homosexual', but it should be observed that there are three different levels of experience to consider: simulated sex (theatrical symbolism), orgiastic display (group rite), and pederastic dominance by mature males in which boys take on the role of women (sexual bondage). According to the late Irene M. Fletcher, LMS librarian who had access to restricted information, Chalmers exceeded moral bounds in identifying with the indigenous people (pers. comm.)

79. 'The old "heathen" sanctities and tabus governing the practices which so shocked our Victorian puritanism were infinitely preferable to the uncurbed free-licence of today.' Rev. W.G. Murphy of Rarotonga, LMS *Chronicle*, July 1952, p. 125.

80. Bourne and Williams required hair to be cut at Aitutaki (Journal, 9 July 1823, SSJ no. 67). Cutting off glossy hair up to three feet in length was a sign of Christian profession in early Mangaia (see SSL for 1853). For a 'Samoan with long hair as worn by dissipated characters', see Gunson, *Messengers*, p. 87, fig. 12.

81. Notably New Caledonia.

82. See J. Thomas, Private Journal, vol. 6, 28 November 1840, Methodist Missionary Society Collection (FBN Spec.Ser.40), School of Oriental and African Studies Library, University of London, Box 10 (655).

83. See Judith Binney, 'Whatever Happened to Poor Mr Yate?', *New Zealand Journal of History* 9 (1975), pp. 111–25.

84. See David Hilliard, 'UnEnglish and Unmanly: Anglo-Catholicism and Homosexuality', *Victorian Studies*, vol. 25, no. 2 (1982), pp. 181–210.

85. Note Charles H. Brooke who idealized young Melanesians in his novel *Percy Pomo: or, the Autobiography of a South Sea Islander*, London, 1881.

86. See particularly David Hilliard, *God's Gentlemen: A History of the Melanesian Mission 1849–1942*, Brisbane, 1978, pp. 90, 251.

87. Information on the Poole case, 1955, comes largely from contemporary press cuttings covering the arrest and trial.

88. Amongst other eccentricities William Waters imagined he murdered a man in the *Royal Admiral* in the shape of a dog.

89. John Barff to William Ellis, 21 July 1853, SSL.

90. See Gunson, *Messengers*, p. 161.

91. Pers. comm., Rev. Norman Cocks, Lewisham, 4 October 1956.

92. Stephen Tennant, *Leaves from a Missionary's Notebook*, London, 1937. Or perhaps the better analogy is with Don Blanding's *Virgin of Waikiki*, New York, 1928.

93. There is now a sizeable literature on this debate. For further detail (which I would qualify), see Lowell D. Holmes, *Quest for the Real Samoa*, South Hadley, Mass, 1987.

94. S. Ella, 'Samoa, &c.', *Australasian Association for the Advancement of Science Report* 4 (1893), p. 626.

95. Ruth Benedict, *The Chrysanthemum and the Sword*, Tokyo, 1982, pp. 222–4.

96. See Gunson, 'Sacred Women', pp. 148–50, 157.

97. Recent work on missionary wives includes Patricia Grimshaw, *Paths of Duty: American Missionary Wives in Nineteenth-Century Hawaii*, Honolulu, 1989; and May Zwiep, *Pilgrim Path: The First Company of Women Missionaries of Hawaii*, Madison, 1991.

98. [S. Ellis,] 'How to please a husband...', *The Morning Call: A Table Book of Literature and Art* 1 (1850), pp. 421–4.

99. Mrs Lilias Mills of Samoa stands out in particular. For her attainments in metaphysics, languages and literature, see *Illustrated Words of Grace*, November 1879, p. 90. Her life, by A.W. Murray, was serialized in that periodical.

100. This theme has been developed by Laura Zimmer-Tamakoshi, 'Nationalism and Sexuality in Papua New Guinea', *Pacific Studies*, vol. 16, no. 4 (1993), pp. 61–97.

# 17

# Germans, Pacific Islanders and Sexuality: German Impact and Indigenous Influence in Melanesia and Micronesia

HERMANN J. HIERY

## Pacific Influence

To what extent did Germans adopt the sexual morality of their Pacific surroundings? Notions of sexuality in these regions varied greatly, but in most cases had little in common with the puritanical ideas current in Victorian England and Biedermeier Germany. There were areas (for example, in New Guinea) where young men and women were expected to abstain from sexual intercourse before marriage, and this rule was enforced under the threat of immediate execution. But restraint in sexual behaviour was the exception rather than the rule, even in Melanesia. And in Micronesian cultures in particular, the dominant mood was one of permissiveness. In these societies, free, unattached sex before marriage was regarded as natural, and while sex outside marriage was forbidden in theory, in reality it took place constantly – 'the main thing is not to be caught'.[1] Not even the puritanical American Protestant missions in Micronesia managed to change much in this respect.[2] While people conformed externally, especially in such matters as wearing modest European clothing, they saw no reason to give up their sexual behaviour. All that changed was its setting. In parts of Micronesia, it was the custom for every young man to sleep with every young woman, and vice versa, for a certain length of time. Older women instructed the young girls in various sexual practices. On Truk there was not even a word for virginity.[3] In the

Central Carolines it was traditional for a man to give his wife to his guest for a night.[4]

Obviously, this kind of sexual behaviour deviated widely from that which was current in western and central Europe: 'the names of different varieties of perversity are ... so well known ... [that there are common expressions among Pacific Islanders] ... which even our doctors are hardly aware of.'[5] We must ask to what extent this sexual behaviour influenced the Germans living within its sphere, although the nature of the subject makes it an extremely difficult question to answer. We know of a number of cases in which mission staff were unable to keep their vows of chastity in the Pacific environment. There is relatively early evidence for this even from regions where the women by no means conformed to the traditional European ideal of female beauty.[6] In many cases, we can only guess to what extent the sexual behaviour of German planters, and even officials, was influenced by Pacific attitudes. There is much to suggest, however, that their response was not as puritanical as the popular view of Wilhelmine Germany would lead us to expect. Already under Neu-Guinea-Compagnie rule (1884–98), planters and officials in the capital, Finschhafen, were leading a dissolute life centring on alcohol and indigenous women. When the local people began to hide their women from the Europeans, the Europeans blamed the Protestant mission. One planter seriously proposed introducing Islam in order to make polygamy official and legal.[7] One of the large planters, Wahlen, who wielded a great deal of political influence in the colony of New Guinea, copied local polygamous behaviour. Indeed, he out-did the indigenous chiefs and *bik men* at their own game. At his home on the island of Maron, he kept a harem of indigenous girls who had been offered to him according to Micronesian custom.[8] Admittedly, Maron was on the periphery of the periphery and, moreover, a Micronesian enclave within Melanesian territory. But Pacific notions of sexuality reached right into the heart of Germany's administrative presence. Queen Emma, a Samoan who was famous for her infidelities, lived only a few hundred metres from the German Government House. She was married, in European 'legal' terms, to a total of four (European) men. Her romances are still talked about in the Pacific.[9] Emma's behaviour seems to have 'infected' all of her surroundings. A provocative tone, and libertine attitudes and practices, were nothing unusual.[10]

European men in the German Pacific seemed to take for granted extra-marital sexual relations and regular sex with indigenous women outside their semi- or fully legalized relationships with indigenous women. Even the Governor of New Guinea, Albert Hahl, is said to have lived with a Caroline Islander on Ponape before his marriage to a German baroness. He definitely had an indigenous wife, and probably a child from this relationship, in New Guinea.[11] His successor had hardly arrived when he already had a girl from the Marshall Islands as a 'housekeeper'. In fact she proved to be the real lady of government house.[12] The *Stationsleiter* of Kieta, Morobe and Palau were all married to indigenous women. The vast majority of the traders in Melanesia had local wives; in Micronesia the number of European men who were married to European women was insignificant. Nor was the converse unknown, namely, white women having relationships with indigenous men.[13]

Those European men who lived with indigenous women improved their local standing. Their social, political and not least economic position became more secure. It was much easier for them to gain access to land. Above all, they had a head start in knowledge of traditional contexts and behaviours, which could be a crucial factor in their survival. Both of the greatest authorities on indigenous customs, Kubary and Parkinson, were married to indigenous women.[14] Parkinson, at least, openly admitted that he himself practised one of the traditional customs that he described.[15] Their use of indigenous customs and habits shows how deeply a number of Europeans had penetrated the inner life of people who were, at first, totally alien to them. It also shows how profoundly they themselves had been shaped by these new ways of behaving. It is, at the very least, doubtful that they adopted these customs only when it was advantageous for them as Europeans, which is what they tried to tell other Europeans. In fact, there is a great deal of evidence that they increasingly adopted the lifestyles of the Pacific. Few Europeans would have seen much advantage in wearing the *laplap* and chewing betel nut, for example, as Kubary apparently did. Even the imperial governor, Hahl, took part in traditional celebrations wearing a grass skirt, and permitted Ponapese women to massage his naked torso with coconut oil, according to local custom.[16]

Local women also profited from cross-cultural relationships. For them and their families, co-habitation with a white man, even more so in a marriage that was officially recognized in European legal terms, was prestigious. The prestige gained was noticeable in interaction between extended families, and in their social standing relative to others. It is therefore not surprising that in societies with hierarchical structures, such as Micronesia, women from high social classes in particular 'usurped' European men for themselves, thus stabilizing the position of their families within hotly contested oligarchic structures. Sexual behaviour in many areas of the Pacific facilitated this sort of liaison, because traditionally women often took the initiative.

In general, it seems that officially, as far as Europe was concerned, people made an effort to keep up appearances, while on the spot, the practice of co-habitation between European men and indigenous women was certainly the rule. Indeed, any attempt to influence these relationships was rejected, or prevented from arising in the first place. There is no record of disciplinary steps having been taken against any of the officials involved. If a superior ever attempted to approach one of his subordinates because of his behaviour, to 'advise' or to 'admonish' him, he was received icily and had to countenance reactions that might go as far as death threats.[17]

A court case about adultery reveals much about the contemporary attitude towards sexuality in German New Guinea. Here, the sexual freedom characteristic of the Pacific actually received a special blessing from the highest circles. There can be no doubt that the accused woman's (a half-Samoan) behaviour totally contravened the bourgeois moral expectations of Wilhelmine Germany.[18] Before she had 'officially' committed adultery, 'without showing any visible signs of remorse',[19] while her husband was away in Sydney, she had conducted 'affairs with consequences' with at least two European and one Melanesian men. Some, but not all, of the 'consequences' were subsequently legitimated. Convicting the woman for adultery, the judge gave her a suspended sentence. The Catholic bishop applied to the Kaiser for a pardon, arguing that Pacific people of mixed race were 'by nature extremely weak and easily led', which 'considerably reduces their guilt'. The Governor, who was in Germany at the time, supported the application, adding that a Pacific woman's sexual misdemeanours should be judged differently from a European woman's. (He, in turn, was supported by the German colonial office, which added the marginal comment 'quite right'.) Finally, the Kaiser saw sense.[20] It is interesting that the betrayed husband's first and main concern was to get financial compensation from his rival. When the two men had come to a private arrangement, the husband subsequently withdrew his demand for the penalty to be exacted, despite the judgement that had been pronounced. The husband took back his wife, although the divorce had already come through.[21] Thus the European husband's reactions followed exactly the indigenous, Melanesian patterns of behaviour in the case of divorce.

However powerfully Pacific attitudes towards sexual morality may have influenced the Germans living there, we can state one thing with absolute certainty. The Germans living in the Pacific were not at all the adamant figures that have been frequently portrayed. They were connoisseurs of the pleasures that the Pacific had to offer, and in this respect they did not differ from the indigenous people among whom they lived.[22] By contrast, those Europeans who steadfastly refused to adjust their sexual rigorism were particularly vulnerable to indigenous attempts at manipulation.[23]

The ease with which German–European value systems could be disregarded in the Pacific made the Pacific colonies particularly attractive for Europeans who were dissatisfied with social restraints at home. Few, however, could afford to live in the far distant tropics. Among those who could, the German Pacific held a special attraction for those who, as deliberate 'drop-outs', rejected the German–European value and morality system. A number of German artists and 'intellectuals' from a theosophical group settled on the small uninhabited island of Kapakon in the Neulauenburg group of the Bismarck Archipelago. Nudists and strict vegetarians, their aim was to lead a Pacific life *sui generis*. Women sun-worshippers, too, left Germany for New Guinea to follow the call of the Pacific sun. But the majority of these early hippies did not stay long. Germans soon became painfully aware that they could not live on goodwill, coconuts and bananas alone without damaging their health. Notions of free love were quickly wrecked when the sexual freedom to which they aspired turned into a nightmare of sexual jealousy, rivalry and aggression. The community broke up when one of its leaders died under strange circumstances, as a result of a bitter quarrel over a woman.[24]

## German Impact

Generally, the German administration was little concerned with indigenous patterns of sexual behaviour. Many of the numerous Micronesian islands had initially only little contact with German officials anyway. In the absence of any German, a resident black beachcomber of West Indian origin, James Gibbon, had been appointed the official respresentative of the German colonial administration for Palau by the *Bezirksamtmann* of Yap. Among other things, Gibbon issued a proclamation that declared polygamy to be permitted behaviour.[25] After Gibbon's death, his successor, Wilhelm Winkler, the first German station leader of Palau, did indeed intervene in traditional behaviour. On Palau it was customary for a number of women to live with the men in their club houses for a limited period of time. During this time the women provided moral support, took an active part in discussions, and offered the men sex. The fact that the women or their families were paid for their services in traditional money was, for many Europeans, something reprehensible that reminded them of prostitution. In local society, however, an *armongol* did not lose her reputation because of her actions, but gained respect and increased her family's prestige. An *armongol*'s chances of marriage were enhanced, not diminished. While the Catholic mission denounced the whole tradition as a thoroughly immoral heathen custom, the station leader judged it from a more utilitarian point of view. As a former medical assistant with some medical training, he was convinced that the sexual promiscuity practised in the *bais* (men's club houses) spread sexually transmitted diseases, and thus contributed to the decline of the local population. He therefore used all the administrative means at his disposal to wither the *mongol* system.[26]

But it would be wrong to assume that the decline of the *mongol* system must be attributed solely to a decision by some German official. Winkler was married to a local woman from Palau. The suspicion that his actions were not without support from local women is substantiated by German sources of the time and later observations by two careful anthropologists.[27] There can be no doubt that women were pressed into this service against their will by their families who were keen on receiving compensation for the service provided.[28] Jealousy (and, consequently, aggressiveness) was aroused by the *mongol* system, as other women (and men) were not particularly happy about what their partners were doing in the *bai*. Certainly more research needs to be done, but it seems to be clear that, if the broad majority of young women were not against it, there were at least two sides within Palau's female society, one of which was strongly opposed to the traditional behaviour in the *bai* and sought means to eradicate it.

A similar custom existed on Yap, where the girls who took part were called *mesipil*. As on Palau, they possessed special rights and privileges, among them the permission to be present during the men's dances.[29] And similarly, as on Palau, the parents of the girl received ample rewards for the services their daughter(s) delivered in the *bäwai* (men's houses).[30] If there had not been a previous agreement with the parents, the girls were abducted into the *bäwai*. But these were still pre-arranged affairs, as the girl involved wanted to avoid reproaches 'which cling to her if she is prostituting herself'.[31] There were about one to three *mesipil* per village shortly after the turn of the century. The highest number was in a village close to the European centre of the island. European eye-witnesses also observed a steady increase in the number of villages that had *bäwais*. Contact with Europeans and the economic wealth that was a result of this contact had made it possible for the local men considerably to expand the traditional way of life.[32]

Population decline on Yap was even more marked than on Palau. One of the reasons given was that the Yapese men had more intercourse with the *mesipil* than with their wives. The *mesipil* themselves were keen on not becoming pregnant. Once pregnant they were forced to leave the house where they led 'a privileged and light-hearted life in every respect ... anxiously protected and pampered by all men'.[33] Abortion was therefore frequently practised by the *mesipil*.

As on Palau, there were differing views within the German administration as to the status of the *mesipil*. The government doctor claimed that to become a *mesipil* was considered a great honour. She was free from physical work, but still held an important position in public life, as matters of state politics were discussed in front of her. The *mesipil* herself was asked for advice in important affairs. The doctor's political superior, however, was convinced that a stay in the *bäwai* was seen not as an honour but rather a disgrace.[34]

It might well be that both somehow got a glimpse of the truth. The key to public understanding of the status of the *mesipil* seems to be the fact that there were at least two different groups of women in the *bäwai*. One group was acquired with the consent of the girl's family, the other with the tacit approval of the girl alone; some girls seem to have been used by all men, others had sexual contact only with certain members of a specific club in the *bäwai*. In some cases, men had to be matched with girls of equal social rank only, in others not.

For the colonial administration it was a delicate and puzzling problem. The consensus was that 'it is impossible just to do away with an ancient custom'.[35] In its stance toward the *mesipil* and the *bäwai* the government chose what it thought would be a moderate line: as a general condition, only those girls were allowed to enter a *bäwai* who had the explicit consent of their parents and the chief of the village where they came from. Furthermore, the number of *mesipil* was strictly limited.[36] This fundamentally changed the character of the *mesipil*, and she increasingly turned into a real village prostitute. The *bäwai*, on the other hand, developed into an officially sanctioned brothel.

On Palau and on Yap, the measures taken by the administration profoundly changed relations between men and women. It has been suggested that in being deprived of their functions, indigenous women lost much of the respect that was traditionally theirs, and forfeited much of their position. As we have shown, there were already differing views among the colonial administration at the time. There was certainly no unilateral German approach to wipe out indigenous traditions. Instead, the measures taken were much debated. German ethnologists in particular were openly critical of what the administration was doing. They denied that there was any connection between population decline and the *mongol* system. On the contrary, they argued, any deliberate and systematic attack on traditional practices must have a deleterious effect on the people.[37]

It seems to be a worthwhile question to ask whether the system prevalent in Palau and Yap when the German administration commenced was really as deeply rooted in ancient tradition as has been claimed then and later. While the origins of the *mongol* and the *mesipil* may go back to a distant past, all the indications we have seem to point to a crucial change following European contact but *before* the actual start of colonial administration. Not only did the number of girls who were kept in the men's houses increase, but their character changed as well. What probably started as an exchange of gifts developed more and more materialistic tunes; what had originally been merely one of many considerations in the acquisition of women now became the paramount motive. How far these elements influenced each other is still open to further research. But in my eyes there can be no doubt that there were already sufficient frictions and tensions as a result of the system that was practised in the *bai* and *bäwai*, for a considerable section within the local communities to welcome anything or anyone that would alter it.

Whereas in Micronesia it was predominantly the women whose lifestyles changed under the impact of the German administration, in Melanesia German measures primarily affected men. There, the large European plantations acted as a catalyst for changes in sexual behaviour. The concentration of so many men in one place encouraged homosexuality, which, in ritualized form, was not unknown in Melanesia. There was also a decided impact on the sexual behaviour of the few women who lived either in or next to the labour compounds. The over-supply of men and their sexual frustration fostered an attitude in which women came to regard any man as a willing partner for sex even if he did not want it or did not want to have it with her. Similarly, prostitution was promoted, possibly even initiated. But the increase in homosexuality and prostitution was by no means specific to German New Guinea. The same thing can be seen wherever there were large plantations in the Pacific.[38]

As an El Dorado of intra-Melanesian contact, European plantations brought together the most diverse cultures of traditionally isolated Melanesian societies. Life on the plantations made possible and encouraged mixed marriages, which would otherwise have been unthinkable. Relationships in which one of the partners would inevitably have been killed in the other partner's home could exist only on the plantations. For the same reason, plantations offered a refuge to men and women who, in their local cultures, were forbidden, on pain of death, to live together because, although they were not blood relations, they belonged to the same totem. The absolute ban on marriage, to which they had been subjected earlier, started to become hollow.[39]

The Babylon of varied Melanesian and European ways of behaviour suddenly brought hitherto unknown attitudes and practices into the limelight. What became more known increasingly also became more acceptable. Liberal and tolerant mores – loose morals as others saw it – were quite widespread. Around a nucleus of large plantations, a sexually permissive society arose that was a blend of suppressed Melanesian and European–German taboos and desires. Moreover, this development had a kind of built-in impetus of its own. There was a drive that encouraged others with similar sexual tendencies, previously banned or outlawed, to become recruited into the sexual maelstrom of Rabaul or Herbertshöhe. It affected Melanesians and Europeans alike, primarily men but certainly also women.

Sources about this development are rare, but they do exist. In most cases they are just hints or suggestions. There are a number of court cases that have survived that focus on homosexuality. The general picture seems to be that Europeans with sexually deviant behaviour were in danger of being compromised only when other Europeans searched for means to get rid of them, or were keen on inheriting their positions. Missionaries, as born critics of this way of life, were either excluded from the life on those plantations or, wisely, chose to exclude themselves, preferring the setting of 'undisturbed' village life. What happened on their own plantations is open to speculation alone. Their literate disciples were the first to give us an account of what impression might have been gained by people who arrived unprepared and unaware of what was going on, besides working copra:

> It is really not easy to stay clean in the centre of smut. The men deride and ridicule us; the women bear down on us and want to seduce us.... Whether I can withstand in the long run, I do not know.
>
> So much depravity as here I have never seen in my life. Until recently we were pagans and did many bad things, but never as publicly and shamefully as they do it here. We were ashamed, but here people do not feel ashamed. That is why they turn to us as well and urge us: go along as well! Several times we performed dances. But when the local women became quite wild about us we decided to give up dancing. Hence we don't dance any more. With these people there is nothing innocent; filth is always in their mind. Really, there are very bad goings-on here. If we say to the people: do you think it is right and proper what you are doing? They answer: everyone does it this way, why shouldn't we do it then as well?[40]

There can be no doubt that the prevalent sexual behaviour in the milieu of the great plantations intensified after the Australian occupation of Rabaul:

> White men had intercourse with brown, Chinese and Malay women. I also observed them doing bad things with boys. I saw how the whites started affairs not only with one, but with several women. I saw them making obscene gestures when they met a woman or a boy; they shamelessly asked [them] while I was passing by: 'Do you want to do it in this way?' Then I saw how the person concerned went with the white. But it was not only the whites who practised these habits, but the yellow and brown ones as well. The highest among the whites, however, did not do these things. Yet, I frequently saw them going to white women – not to their own, but to others. Many whites did that, and not secretly but in such a way that you could observe them while doing the bad thing through a window. *Opopong* (literally: 'my goodness!'), of it and of all these things I saw so much that I can not tell everything.[41]

In the deserted villages the women were more or less left to themselves. There, the neglected women looked for sexual substitutes. If they could not find a male partner, plants were used as sexual stimulants, or relief was even sought in bestiality.[42]

An extreme example of the sexual problems that confronted many women, as a consequence of heavy recruiting of their men, comes from the Lower Sepik River. Where women had always been notoriously forward they now turned aggressive. After 1914, when Australian labour recruiting went far beyond the restrictions the German administration had imposed,[43] the Sepik area was particularly affected. A group of women intended to bring their *tultul* to court, because he had neglected his duties by refusing to have intercourse with them. Since the Government was behind the recruitment of the men, they argued, it was up to the Government-appointed village official to keep them sexually satisfied. The *tultul* remonstrated that he had done his best, but that he had now reached his limit: 'Mi lez long pushpush, baimbai sakin bilong mi i lus finis' ('I am tired of intercourse. Soon my skin will become completely loose').[44]

Only the old *bikmen* were able to look after the women who had been left behind. Conversely, socially upwardly mobile Melanesians, like returning plantation workers, were in a better position than before to pay the bride-price for more than one woman. And they were keen to live in a way that was appropriate to their rising status. Thus the plantation system not only increased the frequency of polygamy, but was also a factor in multiplying the number of women living in polygamous relationships. In the Pacific, polygamy was an economic, not a moral, problem. Outside Melanesia, the Christian missions had succeeded in giving monogamy a legal monopoly. In New Guinea, where in most areas traders long preceded missionaries, culture contact favoured polygamy. Increasing trade meant increasing prosperity, thus making polygamy more practicable. In 1911, 5 per cent of marriages were polygamous in the German administration's catchment area on the New Guinea mainland. In the more remote regions, the figure was less than 2 per cent.[45]

This situation was a thorn in the flesh of both Protestant and Catholic missions. These had been established late, but eventually settled in the centre of European contact, on the Gazelle peninsula, in Neupommern. At their express wish, the Governor promulgated a marriage ordinance on 5 February 1904 which, as the Catholic bishop saw it, would 'help the principles of Christian marriage law to triumph among the indigenous people ... and consequently also abolish immoral, heathen practices'.[46] Co-operation between the colonial administration and the missions was by no means as natural as it may seem at first glance. The average German colonial official in the Pacific was decidedly 'liberal' and anti-clerical in his attitudes. There were so many clashes between the missions and the administration in the Pacific that historians have likened the situation to that in the *Kulturkampf* in Germany, when church was pitted against state in the 1870s.[47] We must remember, however, that in Melanesia the church was almost always the aggressive party, rarely the state. The marriage ordinance in German New Guinea was therefore the exception, not the rule, in church–state interaction. Similarly, it is a moot point whether the interplay between administrative and religious interests can be reduced to shared moral disapproval of indigenous sexual practices. It is likely that as far as the state was concerned, the conviction that the local population would die out as a result of existing practices was the crucial factor in this case. Polygamy was a threat to the balance of the generations, and represented a danger to a healthy demographic development.[48]

The Governor's marriage ordinance made adultery a criminal offence. To this extent it directly adopted the provisions of the

Reich penal code. While this regulation was couched in general terms, the punishment for bigamy applied only to Christians. The scope of the ordinance was further limited by territorial factors. Both crimes could be punished by a prison sentence of up to six months, but the regulations applied only in the north of the Gazelle peninsula and in the off-shore Neulauenburg group – in other words, in the immediate vicinity of the European heartland of German New Guinea.

For Melanesians, it was nothing new for adultery to attract punishment. Adultery and its consequences were among the most common causes of conflict in the everyday life of Melanesia. As the ordinance explicitly allowed for fines to be paid in shell money, on paper the German initiative did not deviate from the strategy pursued so far, of cautiously establishing European norms on the basis of existing Melanesian traditions. But current practice was diametrically opposed to the general German policy of intervening in relations between indigenous people only if this was necessary to prevent blood from being spilt. The instructions issued on 28 May and 18 July 1903[49] explicitly stated that all other cases were to be referred to the *Luluai*, if there was one, and if not, to the chief, for mediation. Thus marital conflicts among indigenous people and the punishment of adulterers clearly fell under the jurisdiction of *Luluai* or chief. The prosecution of bigamy was a completely new departure for German policy. It may have been argued that this law applied only to Christian Melanesians in a strictly defined area. But it became apparent relatively quickly that even among this, as yet small, group of Melanesians, understanding of this measure was extremely limited.

Just three months after the ordinance came into effect, the gaols of the capital, Herbertshöhe, were full to overflowing. This had never been the case before, and was never to happen again. By 29 April 1904, 54 local men and women had been taken into custody; by 26 April seven people had been sentenced to between one and three months in prison with hard labour. The whole district was seething, against the missions and the government equally. Indigenous men in particular sought a way around the imminent loss of their traditional privileges. Universal non-compliance with the regulations completely crippled the administration. The Governor was horrified, and instructed the missions to tread carefully, but they were not prepared to co-operate. The Catholic missionaries in particular still considered it a sporting challenge to track down cases of real or alleged adultery, and to report them. Desperate attempts by the administration to regain control over the situation gave the Melanesian side a chance to win back lost influence. After some pretty impenetrable intriguing between the triumphant missions, angry and withdrawn Melanesian men, and a government looking for any straw to clutch, the local side regained the initiative late in May 1904. To Urabia, a Tolai man, had asked the governor if he could have two wives if he were to leave the Catholic Church without becoming a member of the (Protestant) Wesleyan mission. Hahl explained the marriage ordinance to him. Its ban on polygamy did indeed apply only to Christians. The news spread like wildfire among male Melanesians, whose security had been undermined by the ordinance. A horrified Catholic Vicar-General reported to his bishop that local men had insisted that the Governor had said that they could get their second wives back if they renounced the Catholic faith. And a self-confident Melanesian man named Tukal explained to the German *Eingeborenenvogt* (local officer for indigenous affairs), in response to the mission's accusations, that he was polygamous: 'I am a heathen, and can therefore have two wives.'[50]

Faced with the competing claims of European morality and indigenous traditions, the Governor had at first, carefully, as he thought, taken the side of the German missions. When the full extent of his dilemma became apparent, he tried to steer more in the direction of his traditional policy of showing understanding for the views of the indigenous people. His superiors in Berlin supported him in this. They protested against what they described as uncalled for intervention by the missions in the lives of the indigenous people, and criticized the Governor for introducing the marriage ordinance in the first place. Hahl tried to defuse the situation by introducing an implementation regulation. 'Christians' convicted of polygamy were, in the first instance, to be 'instructed' about the unlawfulness of their behaviour. If the polygamous relationship was not dissolved, the indigenous judge, not the German official, was to impose a punishment. In cases of adultery, the German official was first to establish whether adultery in the local understanding had taken place at all. The current practice among the indigenous people, of a man simply leaving his wife and moving in with another woman, was thus recognized by German officials as legal divorce.[51]

This did nothing to clarify the confused situation. The mission now complained that the government had backed down, and was not prepared to accept the barely disguised restoration of the *status quo ante*. When news of the Baining Hills massacre[52] burst into this extremely tense situation, the administration saw no reason to take any further responsibility, even externally, for the aggressive cultural egoism of the Christian missions. Many contemporaries saw the slaughter of the monks, nuns and priests at the Sacred Heart Mission as a local reaction to the inflexibility of the missions. Even where the original ordinance had remained in force, and there was no reason for any reinterpretation, the situation now turned around. But although the *Reich* colonial office suggested, on a number of occasions, that the marriage ordinance should be formally repealed, the Governor never took this step. This was less out of an arrogant desire not to lose face, by changing a measure that he had introduced, than out of the well-founded fear that it would place relations between the Church and the government in the *Schutzgebiet*, which were tense already, under an additional strain.[53] Thus, in a thoroughly Melanesian manner, appearances were kept up. Hahl had long been convinced that the marriage ordinance itself had been a mistake. But as it had been watered down, step by step, until it was almost unrecognizable, it had lost its explosive force.

What remained was the prosecution of those cases of adultery that caused serious conflict within Melanesian village society. As a result of the colonial government's monopoly on capital punishment, cases of adultery in the Bismarck Archipelago soared. The extreme Melanesian deterrent – execution – was no longer allowed.[54] This change in Melanesian behaviour was a direct response to the greater personal freedom made possible by European contact. On the other hand, the increase in adultery unsettled local society. The general prohibition on adultery, which was not limited to Christians, in the ordinance of 1904 was therefore welcomed by village elders, who saw the threat of European punishment as a chance to limit, to some extent, the quarrels and disturbances caused by unfaithful men and women in their areas. Now the administration intervened through its indigenous representatives, the *Luluai*. It imposed fines in shell money, or turned to the cure-all of temporary banishment with forced labour. In the Governor's view, morally condemning 'unChristian' co-habitation, and gradually educating people to 'understand' the criminal nature of their offence was the job of the missions, not of the government.[55]

From December 1904, the Governor decreed that polygamy as such was no longer a punishable offence, even if the husband was a Christian. None the less, by 31 November a total of 51 cases had come to trial on the basis of his marriage ordinance. It is highly likely that the government's change of policy checked the imminent decline in the number of indigenous Christians, and helped the missions to find a way out of a situation in which they had become hopelessly embroiled. Yet in February 1905, Tovariga, a Melanesian man, left the Catholic Church because he could see no other way of keeping his two wives in an already Christian-dominated environment.[56]

But included in Hahl's reversal of policy was a condition that was a specific German introduction, and although it was as firmly opposed by Melanesian men as the earlier ordinance, it was adhered to. In future, Melanesian women also would have a legal right to divorce. This ensured that a women could not be forced to stay in a polygamous relationship against her will.[57] The decision was downright revolutionary in Melanesian society. It was one of the most far-reaching measures introduced by the German administration, although it has hardly been noticed so far, and it placed gender relations on a completely new footing. Traditionally, divorce had been an option only for men. Women were not in principle, or legally, denied the right to a divorce, but in a society that administered its own justice, where institutionalized forms of justice independent of individuals were unknown, it was practically impossible for women to initiate a separation. The practice of paying a bride-price made it even more unlikely, because it meant that in the case of a divorce, the husband could ask for his bride-price to be returned.[58] Thus, if a woman simply ran away from her husband, her own relatives often sent her back under humiliating conditions, beaten and abused. In certain regions, men had the additional 'right' to cut the ligaments in their wife's feet if she had run away, in order to make it impossible for her to escape a second time. Only if a man was in arrears with his bride-price, or if another man was prepared to 'redeem' a woman from her husband by paying another bride-price, did a women have a chance to get out of a relationship. 'Objective' reasons for divorce, such as maltreatment, let alone physical or mental incompatibility, were not recognized for women.

News of the administration's new guidelines spread astonishingly quickly. Since their arrival, the Europeans had noticed that more and more often, indigenous women sought their protection against maltreatment and physical abuse. Initially the missions were the main refuges,[59] but women increasingly also sought out the agencies of the state administration. Obviously inhumane customs, such as the strangulation of widows, practised on some of the islands of the Bismarck Archipelago, for example, were suppressed. Applications for divorce were first filed by women in the direct vicinity of the German administration. A peripatetic German court also gave women in remote areas the chance to consult a German magistrate, and they made growing use of it. Dealing with charges of assault brought by women against their husbands soon became part of the general repertoire of the administration of German justice for the indigenous people.[60]

The German administration's original attempt to intervene in the traditional relationship between the sexes in Melanesia had been a complete failure. It emerged relatively quickly that the measures that had been resolved upon were not practicable. The hypothetical option of enforcing the decisions that had been taken, against the will of the people, was not even considered. The Pacific, after all, was not Africa. The experiment was not repeated elsewhere. On the contrary, its experience in this case strengthened the administration's conviction that the intimate sphere of the lives of the indigenous people should be left well alone. There is no evidence of a missionary fervour on the part of the colonial government to cast what was found locally into a German–European mould as quickly as possible, let alone to assimilate it. In fact, the general mood tended to swing in the opposite direction. In Eastern Micronesia, even before the arrival of the Germans, the 'ordinary class' Marshall Islanders had attempted to undermine the ban on polygamy imposed by the Mission of the American Board, which was extremely hostile to local traditions, by filing routine applications for divorce. When the Mission tried to reunite divorced couples by force, the German authorities issued a strict prohibition on any such action.[61] The legacy of the German marriage ordinance was twofold. First, it institutionalized the typically Melanesian solution of compensation for adultery. And secondly, it laid the basis for the introduction into the existing social system of the idea of equal rights for women. Something we cannot prove, however, is that a legal rarity found in the state of Papua New Guinea derives from an adaptation of Hahl's marriage ordinance. Papua New Guinea, independent since 1975, is one of the very few non-Islamic states in the world that recognize polygamy as legal in traditional, non-Christian marriages.

## Notes

1. A. Erdland, *Die Marshall-Insulaner. Leben und Sitte, Sinn und Religion eines Südsee-Volkes*, Münster, 1914, 119.

2. Erdland, *Die Marshall-Insulaner*, p. 113, writes about the Marshall Islands: 'Even chiefs who have joined the American mission and are considered to be keen church-goers would rather be "thrown out" of the community for a number of weeks than give up their "right" [*ius primae noctis*]'. In the end, the obstinate eastern Micronesian oligarchy arrived at a sort of *modus vivendi* with the American Board of Foreign Missions on sexual issues. Thereafter, polygamous chiefs were permitted to have Christian wives, but their subjects were not. The prohibition on smoking, by contrast, was enforced across the board: Erdland, *Die Marshall-Insulaner*, p. 372.

3. Permissiveness: H[ans] Damm and E[rnst] Sarfert, *Inseln um Truk*, 2 vols, Hamburg, 1935, p. 147; Erdland, *Die Marshall-Insulaner*, p. 132; Augustin Krämer and Hans Nevermann, *Ralik-Ratak*, Hamburg, 1938, p. 184. Sexual instruction (*bogge*): Erdland, *Die Marshall-Insulaner*, p. 336; and Krämer and Nevermann, *Ralik-Ratak*, p. 194. Truk: Laurentius Bollig, *Die Bewohner der Truk-Inseln. Religion, Leben und kurze Grammatik eines Mikronesiervolkes*, Münster, 1927, pp. 98–9.

4. Augustin Krämer, *Zentralkarolinen*, vol. 1, Hamburg, 1937, p. 267; Wilhelm Müller (Wismar), *Yap*, vol. 1, Hamburg, 1917, p. 233; and Bollig, *Die Bewohner der Truk-Inseln*, p. 98 (for Truk). Women were threatened with banishment for 'loose behaviour': Krämer, *Zentralkarolinen*. For the practice of giving one's wife to a 'friend of equal rank' in the Marshall Islands, see Krämer and Nevermann, *Ralik-Ratak*, pp. 183, 185.

5. Augustin Krämer, *Palau*, vol. 2, Hamburg, 1919, p. 308. Erdland, a priest, speaks of a 'disgusting multiplicity of words for it': Erdland, *Die Marshall-Insulaner*, p. 132. The love songs which Krämer collected on the Marshall Islands were never published because Europeans considered their contents obscene: Krämer and Nevermann, *Ralik-Ratak*, p. 185. The German government doctors on the Marshall Islands were 'constantly being asked for aphrodisiacs': ibid.

6. The prime example from German New Guinea is an Italian priest, Constantino. Thrown out of the Sacred Heart Mission for having a

Melanesian wife, he set himself up as a (now polygamous) planter and waged a constant feud with the mission: Norbert Jacques, *Südsee. Ein Reisebuch*, München 1922, pp. 32–39. For the 'great temptations' suffered by the Protestant missionaries, Albert Hoffmann, *Lebenserinnerungen eines rheinischen Missionars*, vol. 1, Wuppertal, 1948, p. 341. In neighbouring Papua, the Anglicans' Victorian sexual morality was equally placed on trial: Diane Langmore, *Missionary Lives. Papua, 1874–1914*, Honolulu 1989, pp. 245–6 (contemporary comment: 'Single missionaries in New Guinea are a dead failure', ibid.).

7. Hoffmann, *Lebenserinnerungen*, p. 154.

8. Hank Nelson, review of *Germany in the Pacific and Far East*, in *Journal of Pacific History* 14 (1979), p. 64; see also Jacques, *Südsee*, pp. 14–15. Open polygamy was nothing unusual among the beachcombers – European settlers of dubious background. Pieter Hansen, a Danish trader for the Neu-Guinea-Compagnie on the Witu Islands, had one Polynesian and eight Melanesian wives. Some of them had been given to him, as in Wahlen's case, by neighbouring tribes, as 'recompense' for his participation in local battles. Burkhard Vieweg, *Big Fellow Man. Muschelgeld und Südseegeister. Authentische Berichte aus Deutsch-Neuguinea 1906–1909*, Weikersheim, 1990, pp. 272–3; and the Hungarian anthropologist, Lajos Biro, an eye-witness of the time, in Gabor Vargyas, *Data on the Pictorial History of North-East Papua New Guinea*, Budapest, 1986, pp. 47–8. Another Scandinavian, the Swede Nielsen, once a cabin boy of the infamous Pacific pirate Bully Hayes, was notorious in the whole of the Bismarck Archipelago for his harem: Jacques, *Südsee*, p. 145. In Micronesia the American trader David Dean O'Keefe had indigenous wives on Yap, Palau and Sonsorol (the islands where he preferred to trade), in addition to his 'legal' wife back in America: *Bezirksamtmann* Senfft, 21 March 1900 from Yap to the Colonial Division of the German Foreign Office; Bundesarchiv Potsdam (henceforth BAP): Reichskolonialamt (henceforth RKolA) no. 4956.

9. R.W. Robson, *Queen Emma. The Samoan-American Girl Who Founded an Empire in 19th Century New Guinea*, Sydney, 3rd edition 1973.

10. In 1908 Queen Emma's son by her first marriage rudely interrupted a number of German employees and officials at a drinking session by turning to the *Regierungssekretär* Wilhelm Warnecke and dropping the remark: 'Master Meyer [Warnecke's local name], I have just been to look for you at your home, but you weren't there, so I quickly laid your wife!' Warnecke replied: 'Oh – never mind, never mind, I'll reciprocate with your wife soon'. Vieweg, *Big Fellow Man*, p. 89.

11. See the photographic evidence in Hermann Hiery, *Das Deutsche Reich in der Südsee (1900–1921). Eine Annäherung an die Erfahrungen verschiedener Kulturen*, Göttingen, 1995, p. 55. The hints made by Hahl's successor Berg are informative for the period in Ponape. His own 'personal relations with the indigenous people [are] less intense ... than were

those of Dr Hahl.... I believe that I may add that Dr Hahl would not maintain these relations in the same way today, and that this change of heart is part of the reason why Dr Hahl does not wish to see Ponape again.' Berg, 8 June 1902, from Ponape to the Colonial Division; AAC: G 1–8; cf. also Peter Biskup, 'Dr. Albert Hahl – Sketch of a German Colonial Official', in *The Australian Journal of Politics and History* 14 (1968), pp. 342–57. In many cases, a woman's husband accepted the children his wife bore as a result of extra-marital sex with a white man as 'legitimate' children in term of traditional law; Berghausen, Jaluit, 12 October 1910, to the German Colonial Office; BAP: RKolA no. 3077.

12. James Lyng, *Island Films. Reminiscences of 'German New Guinea'*, Sydney, 1925, pp. 54–5 and 58–9.

13. Divorce decree by the Bezirksgericht (district court) in Friedrich-Wilhelmshafen, 5 May 1911; AAC: AA 1963/83 Bun 227. The first known case of a European woman having children by a Melanesian man was in July 1913: BAP: RKolA no. 5429.

14. Parkinson was married to a Samoan, but lived in New Guinea; Kubary was married to a woman from Ponape, but worked, among other places, in New Guinea and on Palau.

15. This was the notorious practice of *kamara*; cf. Richard Parkinson, *Dreißig Jahre in der Südsee. Land und Leute, Sitten und Gebräuche im Bismarck-Archipel und auf den deutschen Salomoinseln*, Stuttgart, 1907, p. 60. It is striking that Parkinson reports only the positive sides of his use of indigenous survival strategies, thus further emphasizing his elevated position as a European, while suppressing any aspects that would be considered negative by Europeans.

16. Cf. Paul Ebert, *Südsee-Erinnerungen*, Leipzig, 1924, p. 100; and Helmut Christmann, Peter Hempenstall and Dirk Anthony Ballendorf, *Die Karolinen-Inseln in deutscher Zeit. Eine kolonialgeschichtliche Fallstudie*, Münster and Hamburg, 1991, p. 90.

17. The planter Kolbe, a former officer, who was married to the half-Samoan 'Queen Emma', challenged the *Landeshauptmann* of New Guinea, Schmiele, to a duel, but Schmiele died before it could take place. A Javenese woman was blamed for the *Landeshauptmann*'s death: Hoffmann, *Lebenserinnerungen*, pp. 156–7. The reaction, when Solf tried to give an official some advice, was 'indignation', and he received anonymous threatening letters: Solf memorandum, 18 September [1906], in BAP: RKolA no. 5432. For the indignation of the German Samoan community against attempts by a member of the German *Verein für Rassenhygiene* (Association for Racial Hygiene) to spread his racist views, see my *Das Deutsche Reich in der Südsee*, p. 47. (The colonial administration had to take him into protective custody to prevent the furious masses from tarring and feathering him in public.)

18. On the strongly 'politicized' sexual morality of Wilhelmine Germany, see Thomas Nipperdey, *Deutsche Geschichte 1866–1918*, vol. 1,

2nd edition, München, 1991, pp. 95–112.

19. District Judge Wolff, 23 October 1902, from Herbertshöhe to the colonial division of the German foreign office; BAP: RKolA no. 4949.

20. BAP: RKolA no. 4949. Letters by Bishop Couppé, Vunapope, 5 August 1902, Governor Hahl, Traunstein, 21 December 1902, Pardon by Wilhelm II, 5 July 1903.

21. Ibid.

22. Statement by Henriette Godinet-Taylor, Apia, 13 January 1989. 'Apparently they enjoy life to the full over here': first impression by Friedrich Hoffmann, newly appointed plantation employee of the Neu-Guinea-Compagnie, after his arrival in German New Guinea; diary by Friedrich Hoffmann, 19 March 1908, Hamburg.

23. In one especially striking case, the local people used their knowledge of European puritanism and then applied Melanesian and European strategies in defence of their interests. When a priest from the Sacred Heart Mission attempted to abduct a girl from a village and take her to the mission nuns to be educated, a scuffle ensued. The priest did not give up, however, whereupon the girl, Ja Kulara, 'pulled down her *lavalava* [loin cloth], and called to me: "Look, father, I have uncovered myself".' Ja Kulara instantly achieved her aim. The Catholic priest immediately turned around, left the village, and gave up his attempt. None the less, the villagers prosecuted him for assault. Father Eberlein, Takabur, 16 November 1911 to the district office, Rabaul and Eberlein's statement to the district judge, Weber, and *Assessor* D. Gebhardt, Rabaul, 11 March 1912; AAC: G 254/4–87.

24. Cf. Hoffmann, *Lebenserinnerungen*, pp. 321–6; Parkinson, *Dreißig Jahre in der Südsee*, p. 204; and B. Pullen Burry, *In a German Colony or Four Weeks in New Britain*, London, 1909, pp. 125–6.

25. Hiery, *Das Deutsche Reich*, p. 267.

26. *Denkschrift über die Entwickelung der Schutzgebiete in Afrika und der Südsee im Jahre 1907/08* (Reichtags-Drucksache Nr. 1106), Berlin, 1909, p. 7069. At the time, there were 19 women in the *bais* of Koror alone. *Bezirksamtmann* Senfft, Yap, 4 February 1904; AAC: CRS G1, 7.

27. *Bezirksamtmann* Arno Senfft, Yap, 21 December 1905 (Palau women support German administration against traditionalists), BAP: RKolA no. 3003, printed in *DKB* 17 (1906), p. 283. Roland W. Force/Maryanne Force, *Just One House: A Description and Analysis of Kinship in the Palau Islands*, Honolulu, 1972, p. 24. Roland and Maryanne Force distinguish between women who were paired with a particular club member (club mates, *blolobl*) and those women who were available to *all* men of a club (*klemat el mengol*), the last arrangement being regarded as 'less than proper': ibid., p. 34 n.19.

28. Observation by the German Government Doctor Born, BAP: RKolA Nr. 3004. *Bezirksamtmann* Senfft noted that the birth of baby boys produced disappointment, as parents would hope for girls because of the

ensuing financial benefits: 'Bericht des Kaiserlichen Bezirksamtmanns Senfft über seine Rundresie durch die Westkarolinen und Palau-Inseln', *DKB* 17 (1906), pp. 281–4, here 282.

29. Some of the girls became quite famous; the wailing of the men of Lebinau about the death of Rutinek of Riken ('To the people of the great chief over the stars: Why do you always take away the best and most beautiful girls from our houses?...') became one of the most treasured songs and dances in Yap. [W.] Born, 'Einige Bemerkungen über Musik, Dichtkunst und Tanz der Yapleute', *Zeitschrift für Ethnologie* 35 (1903), pp. 134–42, here 135–6.

30. English transcription also *pebaey*.

31. Arno Senfft, 'Ethnographische Beiträge über die Karolineninsel Yap', *Petermanns Mitteilungen* 49 (1903), pp. 49–60, 83–7, here p. 53.

32. Ballawat village, close to Kolonia had only 20 adult men but 12 *mesipil*. Annual medical report by government doctor Born; *Jahresbericht über die Entwickelung der deutschen Schutzgebiete in Afrika und der Südsee im Jahre 1901/02*, Berlin, 1903, Anlage H, p. 368. The partly differing views by the *Bezirksamtmann* in an annotation, ibid.

33. Ibid.

34. Ibid. Any reproach that *Bezirksamtmann* Arno Senfft was either ignorant of or negatively biased toward Yapese culture could not be substantiated by facts; Senfft's list of praise for the Yapese ('I know of no people beside the Nauruans who can compete with them') includes 543 words; Senfft, 'Ethnographische Beiträge', pp. 49–50.

35. *Bezirksamtmann* Senfft 1901/02, p. 368.

36. Ibid.

37. Report by Government Doctor Born, Wilhelmshaven, 19 June 1915, BAP: RKolA no. 2622. Cf. Krämer, *Palau*, 293; and Müller (Wismar), *Yap*, pp. 232–3. Feminist views suggesting that sexual relations in the *bais* had nothing in common with prostitution, because local money was not the same as European money (Brigitta Hauser-Schäublin, 'Prostitution: Der fatale Irrtum. Das Mißverstehen weiblicher Sexualität in der Südsee durch die ersten Europäer', in *Weltbilder Sexualität*, Basel, 1987, pp. 9–39) are not only splitting hairs, but also (probably because they are based on re-interpretations of existing literature rather than field work) underestimate the enormous value of money (including traditional money, *udoud*) in Palauan society and in interpersonal relations; cf. Patrick Tellei, 'Modekngei: What is it, can it survive? View of a non-Modekngei Palauan', University of Hawai'i, Manoa, 1988, pp. 3–4; and Francesca Remengesau, 'Udoud: The Traditional Palauan Money; Legends and Speculations on its Origins', in Helmut Christmann (ed.), *Kolonisation und Dekolonisation. Referate des internationalen Kolonialgeschichtlichen Symposiums '89 an der Pädagogischen Hochschule Schwäbisch Gmünd*, Schwäbisch Gmünd, 1989, pp. 104–8.

38. Cf. S. M. Lambert, *A Doctor in Paradise*, Melbourne, 1943, pp. 22–

3; Stephen Windsor Reed, *The Making of Modern New Guinea: With Special Reference to the Culture Contact in the Mandated Territory*, Philadelphia, 1943, pp. 220–21; and Vieweg, *Big Fellow Man*, p. 228. In 1916, the Australian Royal Commission examining the chances of extending Australia's Pacific trade consulted Malinowski on 'sexual needs' on the European plantations. He said: 'It is an abnormal state of things, and the sexual problem is important, because it is almost impossible to think that a young native would spend three years of his life without having sexual intercourse without degenerating into sexual abnormality': 'British and Australian Trade in the South Pacific', *Parliamentary Papers of the Parliament of the Commonwealth of Australia*, 1918, p. 108. On ritual homosexuality in Melanesia cf. Gisela Bleibtreu-Ehrenberg, *Zur institutionellen Päderastie bei Papuas und Melanesiern*, Frankfurt am Main, 1980; and Gilbert H. Herdt (ed.), *Ritualized Homosexuality in Melanesia*, Berkeley and Los Angeles, 1984. Sexually aggressive behaviour of women: Letters by Kāte labourers in: Archives of the Neuendettelsau Mission, Nachlaß Keyßer Bd. 41 (very inidicative are the letters by Lokicne and Kulia, labourers in Rabaul, 1910, 1912 and 1913, and Mocjuc from Herbertshöhe, 1914).

39. Burry, *In a German Colony*, p. 221.

40. Letters by Tilijuc, 1910 and 1911. Tilijuc was a labourer in Rabaul. A similar letter by Mocjuc, Herbertshöhe 1911, Archives of the Neuendettelsau Lutheran Mission, Nachlaß Keyßer Bd. 41.

41. Gengguec about his experience in Rabaul, 12 September 1929, Archives of the Neuendettelsau Lutheran Mission, Nachlaß Keyßer Bd. 41. For another quotation from this source, see James Griffin/Hank Nelson/Stewart Firth, *Papua New Guinea. A Political History*, Richmond, 1979, p. 67.

42. Letter by Ngezinu Kpombung, 15 June 1918, Archives of the Neuendettelsau Lutheran Mission, Nachlaß Keyßer Bd. 41.

43. Hermann Joseph Hiery, *The Neglected War: The German South Pacific and the Influence of World War I*, Honolulu, 1995.

44. Reed, *The Making of Modern New Guinea*, p. 261.

45. 201 out of 3,918; *Amtsblatt für das Schutzgebiet Deutsch-Neuguinea*, vol. 3, no. 22 (15 November 1911), p. 242. In March 1913, 33 cases of polygamy out of a total of 1,557 marriages on the coast of New Guinea as far as the Busi (Markham), *Amtsblatt für das Schutzgebiet Deutsch-Neuguinea*, vol. 5, no. 9 (1 May 1913), p. 81; 46 out of 2,194 cases on the Witu Islands in the Bismarck Archipelago, which had hardly been touched by the administration; ibid., no. 23 (1 December 1913), p. 274. On first contact, only monogomous relationships were found on the island of Manam (northeastern New Guinea); *Amtsblatt für das Schutzgebiet Deutsch-Neuguinea*, vol. 4, no. 3 (1 February 1912). On polygamy as a consequence of culture contact in general, cf. Richard Thurnwald, 'Papuanisches und melanesisches Gebiet südlich des Äquators einschließlich Neuguinea', in Erich

Schultz-Ewerth and Leonhard Adam (eds.), *Das Eingeborenenrecht. Sitten und Gewohnheitsrechte der Eingeborenen der ehemaligen deutschen Kolonien in Afrika und in der Südsee*, vol. 2, Berlin, 1930, p. 601.

46. Hahl, 19 September 1903, from Herbertshöhe, in the preliminary report to the German foreign office, BAP: RKolA no. 4784. Bishop Couppé, 17 June 1904, from Vuna Pope to the Government, ibid.

47. Horst Gründer, 'Kulturkampf in Übersee. Katholische Mission und deutscher Kolonialstaat in Togo und Samoa', in *Archiv für Kulturgeschichte* 69 (1987), pp. 453–72.

48. The average fertility of women in polygamous relationships is one-third lower than that of women in monogamous relationships: Remi Clignet, *Many Wives, Many Powers: Authority and Power in Polygynous Families*, Evanston, 1970, p. 29.

49. For the introduction of indirect rule in German New Guinea and the creation of the offices of *Luluai* and *Tultul*, cf. Hiery, *Das Deutsche Reich*, pp. 116–18.

50. Tukal to Sigwanz, AAC: AA 1963/83 Bun 58. Father Eberlein to Bishop Couppe, 28 May 1904, and statement by To Urabia, Herbertshöhe, 15 June 1904, to Sigwanz, ibid.

51. Hahl, Herbertshöhe, 29 April 1904 to the German Foreign Office; note by the colonial division, 14 June 1904, and letter from Berlin to the Governor, 23 September 1904; implementation regulation, 20 February 1904 (draft), came into force on 20 July 1904, § 1 and 2; BAP: RKolA no. 4784.

52. In 1904 eleven nuns, brothers and priests of the catholic Sacred Heart Mission were murdered in the Baining mountains by some of their converts. The reasons for this so-called 'Baining massacre' have been open to much speculation among historians. Cf. Reiner Jaspers, 'Historische Untersuchungen zu einem Mord an Missionaren auf New Britain (Papua New Guinea) 1904', in *Zeitschrift für Missionswissenschaft und Religionswissenschaft* 63 (1979), pp. 1–24.

53. 'The old heathens will gloat if we make a distinction, in their favour ... between Christians and pagans.' Thus Erzberger criticized the interpretation of the marriage ordinance in the Reichstag as late as 31 January 1910. In his view, it was 'more a paper regulation': *Stenographische Berichte über die Verhandlungen des Reichstags*, vol. 259, Berlin, 1910, pp. 928–9. For Matthias Erzberger, the colonial arch-critic of the Center Party, cf. Klaus Epstein, *Matthias Erzberger and the Dilemma of German Democracy*, Princeton, N.J., 1959.

54. Those caught in the act were taken into the bush and killed there. In some regions, the corpses were then put on display as a deterrent. Reminiscences of Louisa Miller, University of Papua New Guinea, Port Moresby, New Guinea Collection, Manuscript Section: AL-264/2. The adulteress was normally killed by her brother or her uncle (mother's brother); Parkinson, *Dreißig Jahre in der Südsee*, p. 61.

55. Memorandum Hahl, Herbertshöhe, 21 October 1905, for the District Office; Australian Archives Canberra (henceforth AAC): AA 1963/83 Bun 27. Hahl, 31 January 1910 from Rabaul to the Reich colonial office; comment by the Reich colonial office, Referat A 10, ibid., BAP: RKolA no. 4786.

56. Attempts by the Governor to mediate were unsuccessful. Tovariga's declaration, 23 February 1905, in Herbertshöhe, to the *Bezirksamtmann* Kornmajer, ibid.

57. Hahl, 21 December 1904, from Herbertshöhe, to the German foreign office, BAP: RKolA no. 4784.

58. Easy-looking solutions, like the abolition of the whole system of having a bride-price, which the Australian Methodists were attempting in their mission in the Bismarck Archipelago, only aggravated the problem. A young woman had to be 'redeemed' from having become an outcast by the German Governor, who personally organized a belated traditional exchange. Hiery, *Das Deutsche Reich*, p. 253.

59. The Missions were also a refuge for women who tried to escape arranged marriages; a characteristic letter by a Melanesian girl in Hiery, *Das Deutsche Reich*, p. 180 n.15.

60. Files of the District Court in Herbertshöhe and the Station Court in Kaewieng, AAC: AA 1963/83 Bun 27 and 203; files concerning the peripatetic court, ibid., Bun 66.

61. Station leader Merz, 6 September 1910, to Governor Hahl, BAP: RKolA no. 3077.

# 18

# Re-Reading the White Women's Protection Ordinance

## AMIRAH INGLIS

### I

At dusk on 10 August 1925, Gertrude Doherty, the relieving Matron of the European hospital, was walking along Port Road in Port Moresby, capital of Papua, when she was suddenly attacked. Other people walking by ran to her assistance and frightened off her assailant, but not before they had identified him. The same evening, Malasai, a houseboy from Suau in the Eastern Division of Papua, was arrested and charged with attempted rape. Committed for trial a month later, he was found guilty by the judge, who also sentenced him under the Criminal Code to five years with hard labour.

Though such an attack was unusual, the threat of it had pre-occupied the non-Papuan community for some years. A small town numbering 577 men, women and children in the 1921 Australian census, Port Moresby was whiter than the northern Australian frontier town of Darwin or the New Guinea capital, Rabaul. In 1925 it still housed, like all frontier towns, a preponderance of men, but had begun to change during the 1920s, when white women began to arrive in numbers. Its white inhabitants were united, much more than they would have been at home in Australian towns, simply by being whites in an alien and, they often felt, hostile world. They were divided almost solely by their attitude to the government, personified by the extraordinary Lieutenant-Governor,

Hubert Murray, lawyer, scholar and athlete. Murray had arrived in Port Moresby in 1904 as Chief Judicial Officer, was appointed Lieutenant-Governor in 1908, and his protective policies drew him into conflict with white settlers.

Native Regulations, regularly amended since the first Australian government accepted control of British New Guinea in 1906 and changed the colony's name to Papua, were protectionist, enshrined prevailing beliefs in the inferiority of the native people, and established practices to keep them in order and separated from Europeans in their town. Residential areas had been segregated since the Native Regulations of 1914; one white trader, long established in a nearby Papuan village, was moved inside the town boundaries, and Papuan labour compounds were built outside them. No native was allowed inside the town boundaries after 9 p.m., and at all times Europeans had to be treated with respect, inside and outside the town. White women were already protected by Regulations that prohibited natives from being photographed for any film 'if the scene suggested anything of a sexual nature', or showed a white woman in close contact with natives, 'though there may be no sexual suggestion'.[1] Censorship prevented anyone from seeing films that showed brown- and white-skinned men and women being affectionate together. No Rudolf Valentino for Port Moresby. By the end of 1925, it was made an offence to show films at which natives and Europeans were present at the same time; Rudolf Valentino was restored to the Europeans, while Papuans, at separate screenings, watched westerns.

Papuan sexual behaviour scandalized the earliest missionaries and government officials: open sexuality, polygamy, sodomy, sexual freedom among the young, dancing and the giving of wives confirmed their belief that these pagan people had stronger sexual instincts than their own, instincts they were less able to control. But Prospero's fear – that Caliban wanted to rape his daughter – was a later phenomenon. It came with towns, with the arrival in the 1920s of respectable wives and families trying to make a living in hard economic times, or to administer the colony with inadequate resources, and with the arrival of Papuans to work for them. The fear was most powerful, at least most articulate, among the commercial and planting interests in the community, who also used their 'womenfolk' as a weapon to attack the governor's lenient 'native policy'.

Matron Doherty's attacker triggered off hysteria among members of the Port Moresby Chamber of Commerce, who drew up a petition, signed by two-thirds of the adult white males of the town:

> We the undersigned Residents of Port Moresby desire to draw the most earnest attention of the Lieutenant-Governor-in-Council to the series of crimes and insults offered to the European population, and particularly to European women and children, by natives. The effect of the prevalence of these crimes has been to render our womenfolk virtually prisoners in their own homes...[2]

The facts were exaggerated, but before the year was out two more white women were indecently dealt with, one in Port Moresby and one in the Gulf District. Mrs Gladys Clay, wife of one of the town's merchants and a nurse at the European hospital, was asleep there when she was awakened by a man clutching her genitals; she screamed and he ran away. After this the Lieutenant-Governor, who had scornfully rejected the Residents' petition, acceded to their demands for more drastic and exemplary punishment. On 6 January 1926, he introduced a new law into the Legislative Council to dispense it. The three most extraordinary features of the White Women's Protection Ordinance appeared in Section 3, which read: 'Any person who commits or attempts to commit the crime of rape upon any European woman or girl shall be guilty of a crime and being convicted thereof shall be liable to the punishment of death.' Death was the mandatory sentence for rape; the victims were specified – European women and girls; and death was the penalty for *attempted* rape.[3] All three features were unheard of in the law of any Australian state, or in the laws of Papua or the Mandated Territory; nor could I find such an Ordinance in any other British colony.

Stark as they were, the words of the Ordinance obscured the fact that 'any person' meant any Papuan or New Guinean. The government printer's leaflet made that clear when it translated the effect of the Ordinance into several languages, to be distributed to all magistrates, who were instructed to acquaint natives with its provisions. In the Mekeo language, the leaflet read: 'The Government has made a new law which says that any New Guinean man who makes advances to a white woman or girl and causes her harm will be punished severely ... wrongdoers will be put in prison

for life and, if the Government wishes, he [sic] will be hanged.'
Stephen Ame, a Mekeo man, recalled its meaning to me forty
years later in his village: 'If a Papuan smiled at a white woman, he
was gaoled; if he looked at her, he was gaoled; if he touched her,
he was gaoled; if he touched her on the breast, he would be
hanged.'[4]

Malasai of Suau was a lucky man. Three months later and he
may have shared the fate of Semesi, another houseboy, from Motu
Motu in the Gulf of Papua. In 1929 Semesi crawled over the
sleeping Mrs Jessie Fitch, wife of the manager of Steamships
Trading Company, a man who had for years been a belligerent
opponent of the Lieutenant-Governor. Semesi was caught, tried
under the White Women's Protection Ordinance, convicted and
sentenced to death. When he was whisked away on the morning of
his execution, and the residents informed that his sentence had
been commuted to life imprisonment with hard labour by order of
an Australian Labor Government opposed to capital punishment,
the outcry against the Lieutenant-Governor was deafening. Writers
to the *Papuan Courier* urged lynch law, and the commercial men of
the town formed themselves into a 'General Committee interested
in the Protection of White Women from molestation by natives',
thereby expressing dissatisfaction with government actions. 'Residents are still busily engaged in frightening one another, and the
local newspaper is no less busily engaged in frightening them all',
Murray wrote to the Australian Prime Minister,[5] but he nevertheless brought in Regulations further restricting the behaviour of
'foreign natives' in the town, and it was clear that the next man to
be convicted under section 3 of the White Women's Protection
Ordinance was not going to be so lucky. When he turned out to be
a Sergeant of Police, and his victim the 3-year-old daughter of the
European Police Officer, his fate was sealed. What Stephen
Mamadeni, from Baniara in the North-Eastern Division, had done
was not made public, nor was it rape; but he was undefended, and
he confessed and apologized on the gallows before being publicly
hanged outside Badili gaol in Port Moresby on 29 January 1934.

My investigations into the White Women's Protection Ordinance
began after I went to live in Port Moresby in 1967 and found
sexual anxiety and fear powerfully present among white and black.
'What's all this about?' I asked an anthropologist who had lived
and worked for many years among the Motu, the first colonized

Papuans, and he advised me to look at the White Women's Protection Ordinance. I was puzzled, when I did, that the otherwise benign Hubert Murray should have passed such a harsh and discriminatory piece of legislation; puzzled that if the Ordinance was mentioned at all in biographies of Murray or in histories of Papua, blame was attributed to the white women. They, it was said, had provoked attacks upon themselves.

As so often, the most striking account of such women was found in fiction. The mythical white woman made a dramatic appearance in the first novel written by a Papua New Guinean. Vincent Eri, a Toaripi man from Moveave, a village in the Gulf of Papua, was one of the first graduates of the University of Papua New Guinea, and later Sir Seri Eri, the Governor-General. Eri gave his hero the same family name as Semesi, the first man sentenced to death under the White Women's Protection Ordinance.

In Eri's story, Aravape, a man of the Gulf, works as a cook in Port Moresby; Hoiri Sevese, his nephew, is an adolescent village boy who has accompanied his father from the Gulf on one of the annual traditional trading expeditions to Hanuabada, the Great Village of the Motu people just along the bay from Moresby. While there, Hoiri and his father live in their relative's 'boy house', with his employers' consent.

As Aravape is settling down to a session of betel nut chewing, his mistress calls and he asks Hoiri to respond.

> Hurriedly Hoiri scaled the flight of steps into the living room but there wasn't anyone about. The shower was running.
> 'Aravape!'
> 'No, it's me, Hoiri.'
> 'Go and get my towel in the bedroom and bring it to me,' Mrs Jones ordered. Hoiri felt excited and uneasy. It was a while before he found the right towel.
> 'Here is your towel, *Sinabada*,' Hoiri called out.[6]
> 'Open the door and bring it to me,' she ordered.

Hoiri is reluctant. What if her husband should return? But he does what he is told and hides his face behind the shower curtain as he hands her the towel.

> All of a sudden the curtain was drawn back and there stood before him the wet dripping, banana-white figure of the woman who wanted the towel. Hoiri did not know whether to shut his eyes or open them wide.

As this is a male fantasy, he opens them.[7]

Another persistent white-lady stereotype has very recently re-appeared in *Rascal Rain*, an account by a young Australian writer, Inez Baranay, of a year spent as a volunteer in Papua New Guinea. She writes:

> there were a lot of expats of the old colonialist persuasion. The wives were known to be mem-sahibs of the worst kind. They approached the local supermarket manager, also an expat. They asked him to close the shop to native women at a certain time each week so the white ladies could do their shopping without having to rub shoulders.[8]

This behaviour had long been alleged, sometimes experienced; but more often, as in this account, heard by the writer from 'another part of the country'.

The white woman has always been the villain of the colonial encounter; no-one in colonial or anti-colonial fact or fiction has had a good word to say for this mythical creature, who had, by harshness or seduction, deliberately or in ignorance, put an end to the excellent relations existing between black and white men and women before she arrived. Accounts of colonization in other parts of the world all share the same cast of characters and the same plot: the white woman could do nothing right. As I began to dig among the archives of the Commonwealth Government, the news-papers, journals, and the registers of the Papuan Criminal Court, and to investigate the attacks on white women in the period up to the passage of the White Women's Protection Ordinance, I found a more complex set of circumstances. Relations before the arrival of white women were not idyllic, and before the passage of the Ordinance no one had been raped; none of the women or the girls who was attacked, touched or peeped at could be said to have invited her attack, and it was the men, not the women of the town, who expressed fear and anger and who petitioned for new laws. Formed by Marxism-Leninism, I sought the explanation of the White Women's Protection Ordinance, of all the colonial laws and regulations, in the economic and social structure of the colonial society whose headquarters were Port Moresby. My analysis re-vealed the conflicts, the deep social and economic gulf between colonized and colonizers, and the power struggles between the men of the Chamber of Commerce and Residents' Association and the Lieutenant-Governor, whose wrong-headed, paternal policies, they were convinced, caused the new 'cheekiness' among the natives. These struggles were raised to new heights by fear for their wives and children.

In 1967, when I arrived in Port Moresby, a dependant wife and mother, like many a white woman before me, I arrived in a colony preparing for independence, and felt myself to be an agent of that preparation. By then, the question about independence was not if but when. In that year, the first, the most disturbing face of the colonial relationship obscured every other consideration for me, and the account I wrote of Port Moresby for a liberal Australian journal was called 'A Tale of Two Cities'. My description of the gulf between the white, expatriate, rich rulers and the black, indigenous and poor ruled was indignant; my reaction to the behaviour of earlier colonizers was shock. The complexities of gender and sexual relations in the colonial situation, when I encountered them, were formidable, but I judged them to be secondary. White women had the lowest white jobs, but they were better paid than almost all black men. Both white and black men found this hard to take; Papuan and New Guinean men, fiercely male in their pride, found it harder. Some expatriate women, revelling in their little bit of power, shouted in tones they would scarcely have used at home to their dogs. Many did not. Men had been shouting louder and longer since the first days, but shouting, like drunkenness, seemed worse in women. And even when they were not shouting, women were giving orders to men, which again seemed unnatural. In 1967, as in the 1920s and 1930s, no one had much sympathy for the white women.

The behaviour of Papuans and New Guineans also challenged and puzzled outsiders of sympathetic heart and ready-made explanations. In Port Moresby, Papuan men stepped aside to let me pass on the town's few footpaths, and dropped their eyes; few whites were seen on the town buses, and our daughters were especially cautioned against travelling in them, as they were prevented from sitting next to their Papuan class-mates, who had to sit in a separate section of the town's picture theatre. In 1967, the first piece of advice given by the Country Women's Association of Port Moresby to new arrivals was this: 'White women are in constant danger from black men; you must wear modest clothes – NEVER shorts – and behave yourselves in ways that will not provoke black men to rape.'

When a young university librarian was raped by a university labourer while walking in daylight to the nearest shops, the fact that she was white, wearing the briefest mini-skirt, and living openly with a New Guinean student was said to give encouraging signals. You couldn't really blame the rapist for misunderstanding her dress and her sexual mores. As in 1926, some benevolent colonizers, arguing from the culture of Papuans, blamed the white women rather than the men who were accused of attacking them; others, among them independent young women who had come to Port Moresby from employment in Australian cities in the Age of Aquarius, angrily rejected this explanation. Liberal-minded to revolutionary, educated and rational, expatriate women connected with the university were daily confronted with conflicts of principle. Should white women take jobs and build up the resentment of indigenous men? Should the wife of a university lecturer be employed under the same conditions as her husband? Of course! It was a matter of principle. But that would make the division between white and black at the university even deeper, and this to some seemed a worse evil than denying our feminist principle of equal pay for the job. The dilemmas of sexual relations between colonized and colonizers were not easy to resolve, then, with the certainties of Marxist ideology.

## II

The White Women's Protection Ordinance, passed by the all-white and wholly appointed Papuan Legislative Council in 1926, was repealed in 1958; the colonizers have gone and the tiny white colonial town of Port Moresby has been transformed, since 1975, into the capital of the nation of Papua New Guinea. Modernization has brought the nation-state an elected parliament and capitalism. The lines of division have moved, and some Papua New Guineans are rich and powerful. But some things have not changed. In 1977, I returned to Port Moresby, to research the life story of Karo Araua, a man from the Gulf of Papua publicly hanged in 1938 for murder; a man who had earlier been brought out of prison to give evidence against one of his fellow villagers accused under the White Women's Protection Ordinance. The local paper reported attacks on women university students, and the Motuan Vice Chancellor, Renagi Lohia, was quoted: 'it is the way the women dress that causes the trouble.' The fear of rape is still powerful in Port Moresby, and more rational than it was in the late 1920s or late 1960s; but, though her influence remains in fact and story, the 'white woman' as an expression of the colonizers' fears and guilt, and symbol of their power, has disappeared with colonial rule.

My book, published in Australia in 1974 (1975 in Britain and the USA) was the first to question the received wisdom about the white woman. I was committed to classes and forces, to 'the white woman' rather than white women; later students of colonial societies examined the lives of actual white women: wives of missionaries and government officers, independent working women. Claudia Knapman, a historian and sociologist, published in 1986 a splendidly researched, wide-ranging study, *White Women in Fiji 1835–1930; The Ruin of Empire?*, and disproved the assertion that it was the white women who so soured race relations by their memsahibism that they brought about the end of empire. Helen Callaway, in her 1987 book, *Gender, Culture and Empire: European Women in Colonial Nigeria*, another thorough study, came to the same conclusion about that country. In both works, 'the white woman' was revealed to be a theoretical construct: actual white women in Fiji and Nigeria were diverse and played a more central and more constructive role in the colonial encounter. James Boutilier, in Denise O'Brien and Sharon W. Tiffany's *Rethinking Women's Roles* (1984), writing of the British Solomon Islands, and Diane Langmore (1989), in *Missionary Lives: Papua 1874–1914*, made the same point, though Boutilier sounded an early warning against romanticizing frontier women. Since then the white woman herself, on the bath mat or at the tea table, in town or on the plantation, is sometimes hard to encounter in the jungle of theoretical disputation that has grown up around her.

Historical studies have been transformed by gender studies, feminisms and new styles of scholarship, a transformation evident in the two large studies of white women in Papua New Guinea written in the twenty years since my book. During 1984–85, Judy Davis researched a doctoral thesis in history at the Australian National University on the subject of white women in Papua and New Guinea from the beginning of colonization to the present day. She died before it was finished but left draft chapters to be mined by other scholars. A feminist, Davis rejected official documents, on the grounds that they excluded women, and based her study almost entirely on interviews conducted with wives in the Retired Officers' Association. Clearly a woman of strong sympathy for these colonial women, she was able to gather a rich and lively women's perspective on past events. Her new insight into the White Women's Protection Ordinance rests on an interview with Mrs Elsie Champion, a woman then in her seventies. As a girl in Port Moresby, Elsie Ross had boarded first with the family of H.C. Champion, the Papuan Government Secretary during the 1920s and 1930s (whose son Ivan she later married), and then with the family of E.A. James, editor of the *Papuan Courier*, chief stirrer of opposition to the government and agitator for the protection of white womenfolk. Elsie Ross had been stroked on the thigh by one of James' houseboys while she slept, and retained a vivid memory of the event. She had been asleep, she told Judy Davis, and was woken by 'a black hand on her thigh, screamed and the owner ran away'. Earlier that evening, she recalls, she had performed an Egyptian dance, wearing a gown with a tiny bare midriff. One of James' houseboys 'must have been, maybe he was' looking through the window. 'I'd never have done a dance like that in a costume like that if there'd been any natives in the house.'[9] This new evidence explains, says Davis, 'the virulence of Mr James, the decisive role of Mr Champion Snr and of many other residents who actually knew Elsie Ross'.

Conventional historical sources made Inglis miss 'some key elements in an important historical process' and distort the picture. How was my picture distorted and what key elements did I miss? I knew that Elsie Ross had been attacked in E.A. James' residence, as I knew of every woman and her attacker, because all names and circumstances were recorded in the Criminal Register, which I had found among the old records of the Court. I decided not to publish any real names, perhaps moved by the same protective response that had at the time prevented publication of the names of white women, believing that everyone would prefer anonymity. I was wrong about the Papuans and may also have been wrong about the white women. What I did not know, for no one told me, not even her husband Ivan when I interviewed him, was that Elsie Ross later became Elsie Champion. But could her experience have 'explained' James's virulence or Secretary H.W. Champion's decisiveness when it happened a year *after* the Residents'

Petition, and eight months after the passage of the White Women's Protection Ordinance?

I ignored the women's perspective and concentrated on the crimes, the sentences and the male responses – a distorted account, it is true, not because I used documentary historical sources but because of my ideology. The colonized houseboy from Goodenough Island in the Eastern District received five years' hard labour and 15 strokes of a leather strap for stroking Elsie's thigh, a punishment that seemed altogether too harsh for the crime. I sympathized with the colonized houseboy and was hostile to E.A. James, anti-Papuan rouser of the business community. Elsie was a statistic to me. Now I read her information and memories as adding rich personal detail to the complex tapestry of gender and race relations. But what key elements do they add? And have not actions been wrongly explained by relying on her recollections?

Chilla Bulbeck's big book, *Australian Women in Papua New Guinea: Colonial Passages, 1920–1960*,[10] inherits earlier narratives and is shaped by feminist understandings. Her aim is to write the 'new story', one that 'places the white woman as an actor within historical constraints'.[11] She makes use of the shelves of empirical and theoretical studies written in the last 20 years to rewrite the story of Australian colonization in Papua New Guinea, inserts white women into a picture from which they have been excluded in the 'official' histories, and shows that they played a larger and more complex role than had been thought. She asserts not only that they were not part of the colonial 'project', that their lives were lived in a different 'register' from colonizing men, but that males have asked the wrong questions of them.

To compose the 'new story' with its different questions and answers, Bulbeck establishes her analysis on the narratives of 19 white women who lived in Papua and New Guinea from 1920 to 1960, and supports these by empirical and theoretical studies of colonization from many times and places. Like Davis, she reads all her testimonies quite uncritically. Oral testimony is a tool essential for uncovering the history of people who are pre-literate or whose lives have gone unrecorded, but what it tells is what informants have in their memories, or what they choose to reveal. Unsupported by other evidence it is inadequate. I was given wonderfully different versions of what Karo Araua said from the gallows by people present at his public hanging in Port Moresby in 1938.

I used all these accounts, in their diversity precious texts for under-standing their authors' perceptions, and through them the colonial condition. But they cannot all have been accurate reports of what Karo actually said.[12]

Bulbeck is indifferent to the specifics of history, an indifference justified by a new theory of colonial discourse, and by the testimony of one of Davis's women, whose experiences are said to 'reveal an apparent timelessness'.[13] Nor, despite a nod to geography, is there in this analysis much more account of place than of time. 'Matters of Sex' lead us to wander through colonies and centuries; recent literary scholarship, feminist philosophy and history are deployed; Thomas Carlyle, Mannoni, Fanon, and the latest third-world post-colonial feminist are quoted; a formidable bibliography has been assembled of pieces that add to the patchwork of explanation and description. New theories are drawn on and new language used, but since we are not anchored in Papua New Guinea from 1920 to 1960 and the testimonies are rarely invoked to illuminate or test the theoretical models, new words often obscure an already com-plex state of affairs. The life stories and reminiscences of more white women pose no new questions. If new answers are given, they are simply and arbitrarily imposed by the author, by defini-tion or by metaphor. When colonization is seen as 'essentially a masculine act: to conquer, to penetrate, to possess, to inseminate',[14] females are obviously excluded. Bulbeck excludes them also from complicity in the prevailing racial ideology.

Other feminist scholars have taken issue with the Eurocentrism of the women-centred studies. Jane Haggis, in her article *Gendering Colonialism or Colonising Gender* (1990)[15] argues that Callaway and Knapman's rehabilitation of white women in Fiji and Africa turns them into new mythical figures, and produces as simplistic a picture of colonial societies and relationships as the one they replace. Margaret Jolly, who writes of Vanuatu, agrees in 'Coloniz-ing Women: The Maternal Body and Empire'.[16] Some feminist scholars from former colonies want to abolish the white woman from history books and concentrate on themselves. Pacific women writing in *Pacific Women: Roles and Status of Women in Pacific Societies*[17] take issue with feminism itself as a foreign and coloniz-ing concept, and invoke tradition. Margaret Jolly sets out their position well in her 1991 article, 'The Politics of Difference: Feminism, Colonialism and Decolonization in Vanuatu'. While this passionately expressed nationalism is understandable, the white woman should not retrospectively be denied her part of the colonial condition, nor waved away by theory.

### III

Twenty years ago, imbued with Marxist-Leninist materialism, I explained the passage of the White Women's Protection Ordinance by the class interests and power of the planters and commercial sections of the colonizers, who stampeded the liberal Lieutenant-Governor. I still believe that was part of the truth. I now also believe, helped by a generation of scholarship, some of it feminist, that the explanations have to be more complex. I would want to add notions of masculine power and Murray's deep misogyny. Today I would also examine the fear of the other, the black man, among even the most enlightened male colonizers. I would also want to discover more about the white women of Port Moresby, and I would try to understand what drove Papuan men to touch, stroke or attempt sexual relations with *Sinabadas*, though it could mean death. And since I no longer believe in one big explanation for human relations, I would search in many places and learn from many people, but not from scholars who find answers by constructing the colonial past from first principles, no matter how worthy, or who invent a new language with which to argue among themselves. Life is too short. I believe now that we need well-documented and well-told histories of the colonized and the colonizers, in all their complexities, to help us understand the past – humane histories that speak to a wide audience.

### Notes

1. Amirah Inglis, *Not a White Woman Safe*, ANU Press, 1974. p. 53.
2. *Papuan Courier*, 18 September 1925, quoted in Inglis, *Not a White Woman Safe*, p. 62.
3. Legislative Council Meeting, No. 1, Commonwealth of Australia Parliamentary Debates, 1926, pp. 6–13; quoted in Inglis, *Not a White Woman Safe*, p. 71.
4. Ordinance in Mekeo language illustrated in Inglis, *Not a White Woman Safe*, facing p. 80. Stephen Ame's words, ibid., p. 83.
5. 6 February 1930, Commonwealth Archives Office, CRS A518, Item D840/1/5, quoted in Inglis, *Not a White Woman Safe*, p. 101.

6. *Sinabada*, a Motu word meaning big mother, was the Papuan term of respect used for all white women.

7. Vincent Eri, *The Crocodile*, Jacaranda Press, 1970, p. 41.

8. Angus and Robertson, 1994, p. 122

9. Judy Davis, section 10d, draft Ph.D. thesis, History Programme, ANU.

10. Cambridge University Press, Cambridge, 1992.

11. Ibid., p. 240.

12. Amirah Inglis, *Karo: the Life and Fate of a Papuan*, Institute of PNG Studies and ANU Press, 1982, ch. 6.

13. Bulbeck, p. 3.

14. Ibid., p. 221.

15. Women's Studies International Forum 13 (1–2), pp. 105–15.

16. In Anna Yeatman and Sneja Gunew (eds.), *Feminism and the Politics of Difference*, Allen & Unwin, London, 1993.

17. Taimoni Tongamoa (ed.), University of the South Pacific, Institute of Pacific Studies, Suva, 1988.

# About the Contributors

**Thomas Bargatzky** is Professor of Ethnology at the University of Bayreuth. He has published *Einführung in die Ethnologie* (1985) and *Einführung in die Kulturökologie* (1986).

**James Belich** teaches at Victoria University of Wellington, New Zealand, in the areas of racial ideas and the expansion of Europe, as well as New Zealand history. His publications include *The New Zealand Wars and the Victorian Interpretation of Racial Conflict* (Auckland University Press, Auckland, 1986), *'I Shall Not Die': Titokowaru's War: New Zeland, 1868–1869* (Allen & Unwin, Wellington, 1989) and a general history of New Zealand, *Making Peoples* (Penguin, Harmondsworth, 1996).

**Geoffrey Bolton** is Professor of History at Edith Cowan University, Mount Lawley, Western Australia. He has published *A Fine Country to Starve in* (Perth, 1972) and *Spoils and Spoilers: Australians Make Their Environment 1788–1980* (Sydney, 1981).

**Alfred W. Crosby** is Professor of American Studies at the University of Texas in Austin. His publications include *The Columbian Exchange. Biological and Cultural Consequences of 1492* (Greenwood Press, Westport, Conn., 1972), *Ecological Imperialism: The Biological Expansion of Europe, 900–1900* (Cambridge University Press, Cambridge, 1989; with numerous translations into several languages), and *America's Forgotten Pandemic: The Influenza of 1918* (Cambridge University Press, Cambridge, 1989).

**Niel Gunson** is Senior Lecturer at the Australian National University, The Research School of Pacific and Asian Studies. He published *Messengers of Grace: Evangelical Missionaries in the South Seas 1797–1860* (Oxford University Press, Melbourne, 1978).

**Gerd Hardach** is Professor for Social and Economic History at the University of Marburg, Germany. He has published *König Kopra: Die Marianen unter deutscher Herrschaft 1899–1914* (Franz Steiner, Stuttgart, 1990).

**Allan M. Healy** was formerly Extra-Mural Tutor, Makerere University, Uganda, and Fourah Bay College, Sierra Leone; Research Fellow in Pacific History, The Australian National University, Canberra; and Senior Lecturer in Southeast Asian History, University of Wollongong, Australia. He has published 'Monocultural Administration in a Multicultural Environment: The Australians in Papua New Guinea', in J.J. Eddy and J.R. Nethercote (eds.), *From Colony to Coloniser: Studies in Australian Administrative History* (Sydney, 1987).

**Peter Hempenstall** teaches Pacific history and the history of biography at the University of Newcastle, Australia. He has written on various aspects of colonial history, including resistance to colonial rule, social change under missionaries, cargo cults and the historiography of the field. His major publications for the Pacific include *Pacific Islanders under German Rule: A Study in the Meaning of Colonial Resistance* (Australian National University Press, Canberra, 1978), and (with Noel Rutherford) *Protest and Dissent in the Colonial Pacific* (University of the South Pacific, Suva, 1984). He has also written an acclaimed biography of an Australian religious and political radical, *The Meddlesome Priest: A Life of Ernest Burgmann*.

**Hermann Joseph Hiery** holds the Chair of Modern History at the University of Bayreuth, Germany. From 1993 to 1994 he was visiting Professor of German History at the University of Bordeaux III, France. Until 1996 he was Permanent Research Fellow at the German Historical Institute in London. His publications include *Das Deutsche Reich in der Südsee* (Vandenhoeck & Ruprecht, Göttingen, 1995) and *The Neglected War: The German South Pacific and the Influence of World War I* (University of Hawai'i Press, Honolulu, 1995).

**Amirah Inglis** is a Canberra historian and writer. She has published a prize-winning autobiography and several books on Papua New Guinea and Australia, including *Not a White Woman Safe: Sexual Anxiety and Politics in Port Moresby 1920–1934* (Australian National University Press, Canberra, 1974).

**Arthur J. Knoll** is the David E. Underdown Professor of History at The University of the South in Sewanee, Tennessee, where he specializes in European imperialism, African and Middle Eastern history, and military history. He is the author of *Togo under Imperial Germany, 1884–1914: A Case Study in Colonial Rule* (Stanford University Press, Stanford, Cal., 1978) and co-editor of *Germans in the Tropics: Essays in German Colonial History* (Greenwood Press, Westport, Conn., 1987, together with Lewis H. Gann).

**Sione Lātūkefu** was Professor of History at the University of Papua New Guinea. He published *Church and State in Tonga* (Australian National University Press, Canberra, 1974) and *Papua New Guinea: A Century of Colonial Impact 1884–1984* (The National Research Institute, Port Moresby, 1989).

**John M. MacKenzie** is Professor of Imperial History at Lancaster University. His many publications include *Propaganda and Empire: The Manipulation of British Public Opinion, 1880–1960* (Manchester University Press, Manchester, 1984), *The Empire of Nature: Hunting, Conservation and British Imperialism* (Manchester University Press, Manchester, 1988), and *Orientalism: History, Theory and the Arts* (Manchester Unversity Press, Manchester, 1995).

**J.R. McNeill** is Professor of History at Georgetown University in Washington, DC. He is author of *The Atlantic Empires of France and Spain* (University of North Carolina Press, Chapel Hill, 1985) and *The Mountains of the Mediterranean World: An Environmental History* (Cambridge University Press, Cambridge, 1992).

**David J. Murray** is Professor of Law at the Open University in Milton Keynes. He was Foundation Professor of Public Administration at the University of the South Pacific (1975–78), and constitutional adviser to the governments of the Gilbert Islands (1976–79) and Tuvalu (1976–78). His publications include *The West Indies and the Development of Colonial Government* (Clarendon Press, Oxford, 1965) and *The Government System in Southern Rhodesia* (Clarendon Press, Oxford, 1970). He is Joint General Editor of the *British Documents on the End of Empire*.

**Peter Sack** is Senior Lecturer in Law at the Research School of Social Sciences, Australian National University, Canberra. He has published widely on German colonial rule in New Guinea, including *Land between Two Laws: Early European Land Acquisitions in New Guinea* (Australian National University Press, Canberra, 1973). He has also edited *German New Guinea: The Annual Reports* (Australian National University Press, Canberra, 1979) and *Albert Hahl: Governor of New Guinea* (Australian National University Press, Canberra, 1980).

**Markus Schindlbeck** is Curator in the Department of Oceania at the Museum für Völkerkunde in Berlin. He edited *Die ethnographische Linse* (Berlin, 1989) and *Von Kokos zu Plastik. Südseekulturen im Wandel* (Reimer, Berlin, 1993).

**Woodruff Smith** is Professor of History and Dean of the Faculty of Liberal Arts at the University of Massachusetts in Boston. He is the author of *The German Colonial Empire* (University of North Carolina Press, Chapel Hill, 1978), *European Imperialism in the Nineteenth and Twentieth Centuries* (1982), *The Ideological Origins of Nazi Imperialism* (New York: Oxford University Press, 1986), and *Politics and the Sciences of Culture in Germany, 1840–1920* (Oxford University Press, New York, 1991). He is currently working on a book about the sociocultural factors underlying change in European demand for overseas products between 1600 and 1800.

# Index